Latino Mayors

Latino Mayors

POLITICAL CHANGE
IN THE POSTINDUSTRIAL CITY

Edited by

Marion Orr and Domingo Morel

Foreword by Luis Ricardo Fraga

TEMPLE UNIVERSITY PRESS
Philadelphia • Rome • Tokyo

TEMPLE UNIVERSITY PRESS
Philadelphia, Pennsylvania 19122
www.temple.edu/tempress

Library of Congress Cataloging-in-Publication Data

Names: Orr, Marion, 1962– editor. | Morel, Domingo, editor.
Title: Latino mayors : political change in the postindustrial city / edited by
    Marion Orr and Domingo Morel ; foreword by Luis Ricardo Fraga.
Description: Philadelphia, Pennsylvania : Temple University Press, 2018. |
    Includes bibliographical references and index.
Identifiers: LCCN 2017035623 (print) | LCCN 2017059741 (ebook) |
    ISBN 9781439915448 (E-book) | ISBN 9781439915424 (hardback : alk. paper) |
    ISBN 9781439915431 (paper : alk. paper)
Subjects: LCSH: Hispanic American mayors—Case studies. | Municipal
    government—United States—Case studies. | BISAC: POLITICAL SCIENCE /
    Public Policy / General. | POLITICAL SCIENCE / Public Policy / City Planning &
    Urban Development. | SOCIAL SCIENCE / Ethnic Studies / Hispanic
    American Studies.
Classification: LCC JS356 (ebook) | LCC JS356 .L38 2018 (print) |
    DDC 973.93092/368—dc23
LC record available at https://lccn.loc.gov/2017035623

Printed in the United States of America

9 8 7 6 5 4 3 2 1

To Professor Wilbur C. Rich

Scholar, mentor, and friend,

to whom all students of big-city mayors

are deeply indebted.

Contents

Part III   Latino Mayors in the East and South

**Part IV   Latino Mayors, Urban Voters,
            and the American City**

Foreword

Notre Dame Professor of Transformative
Latino Leadership
Joseph and Elizabeth Robbie Professor
of Political Science
Director, Institute for Latino Studies
University of Notre Dame

Cities have often been described as among the most informative laboratories of democracy. It has been argued that they are the initial places where many citizens begin to understand their government and participate in its work, and, because of the smaller size of city government, they are the first level of government that residents tend to consistently assess. Although cities are nowhere mentioned in the U.S. Constitution, they have often served as the initial places where the contestation for public authority has grappled with some of the fundamental principles of governance that the Constitution of 1787 was designed to address. Ideas and realities of how to balance liberty with equality, justice with opportunity, and participation with exclusion have often been worked out in local governments before they were addressed in state and national governments. It is certainly the case that Alexis de Tocqueville (1972 [1835]) and later Lord James Bryce (1995 [1888]), in their respective insightful and comprehensive considerations of American government, helped all of us appreciate just how significant local governments were to the grand project of American democracy.

Less well appreciated, but perhaps even more important, is that larger central cities have also been the levels of government where the nation's most significant social divisions have manifested themselves for generations. Divisions by economic class, ethnicity, immigration, and race have been present in cities since their beginning. Because people have chosen to migrate to and live in cities in search of greater prosperity, cities have always contained the most socially and ideologically diverse groupings of the American population since the nation's founding. Although the origins of the United States in many ways undoubtedly lie in the expansion of the population in rural areas as well, it is in cities that Americans of many different backgrounds, educations, skills, and needs have tried to provide for themselves and their families.

Because of this concentration of diverse populations, cities have been the laboratories where the nation's local governments, however unevenly, have had to address the tasks of balancing prosperity and poverty, inclusion and exclusion, dominance and marginalization, and hope and reality that flow from the concentration of a diverse citizenry. The most complex and often perennial social divisions of American society have always been first manifested and addressed in cities. Perhaps it is best to think of city governments as the places where the nation first attempts to come to terms with the limits and inconsistencies of the ideals of American democracy as they are lived by its citizens. What works and what does not work in cities and what is resolved or is not resolved in cities have always set patterns for the nation on what is possible and what is worth trying to attain to serve the common good.

The essays in this volume demonstrate clearly how these fundamental challenges of governance continue to manifest themselves in our larger cities when yet another historically marginalized group, Latinos, begins to gain some political power by electing candidates of choice to the highest elective position of city government, the mayor. Each of these chapters helps us understand how the election of Latinos to the office of mayor is simultaneously a sign of progress and a sign of continuing urban challenge. These chapters show how cities continue to be the locations where the challenges of American democracy are overcome or not overcome.

Among the common insights that the accomplished authors of this volume help us appreciate is the importance of economic context. The cities where the Latino mayors discussed in this volume have governed are not the industrial or redevelopment cities of the past. They are more often postindustrial cities with distinct economies and populations. Their economies, on the whole, tend to be growing rather than contracting. Similarly, their populations tend to be growing more than declining. Their systems of governance, on the whole, tend to be more inclusive of diverse subsets of the population than those of the past.

Nonetheless, some of the most significant issues these mayors confront are very similar to the issues faced by mayors of both the industrial and the redevelopment city. The details of these issues in the postindustrial city are distinct, but they are not substantively different. Among the questions Latino mayors must address are the following:

- How does a city balance the need for continued economic growth with the growing need for policies of opportunity expansion for many of its residents?
- How does one build not only electoral coalitions but also governing coalitions?
- How do, and how should, institutions of representation and governance translate demographic shifts into inclusive political access and political power?

These are old questions that appear in the new economic and social contexts of the postindustrial city.

The authors of this volume help us more deeply understand both the change and the continuity that have always characterized the political development of local governments in the United States and, in the process, the political development of the nation as a whole. Few would agree that the country, at any of its levels of government, has answered the preceding questions in a way consistent with America's highest ideals. What these authors provide us is yet another opportunity to consider these questions in the contemporary American nation-state. Perhaps it is only in asking these questions repeatedly that we might work, however slowly and unevenly, to develop answers that better serve the common good than those of the past. Latino mayors, like all current mayors, have the responsibility to work to develop these answers in the unique contexts of their contemporary cities.

REFERENCES

Bryce, Lord James. 1995 [1888]. *The American Commonwealth*. Indianapolis, IN: Liberty Fund.
Tocqueville, Alexis de. 1972 [1835]. *Democracy in America*. New York: Alfred A. Knopf.

Preface and Acknowledgments

This book is the first collective study of Latino mayors in the United States. A mayor is the most visible city official and sits at the apex of formal political power in the city, especially in cities where mayors have strong administrative, appointive, and budgetary authority. But whether they have significant or little formal authority, mayors are seen as primarily responsible for local policy and local economic conditions. This book explores the entry of Latino mayors and provides a foundation for understanding their rise and place in the American city. We focus on the emergence of Latino mayors within the context of the changing American city. Latino mayors are coming to power during an era that is different from the period when Irish Americans were elected to the mayor's office for the first time or when African American political incorporation and the election of big-city black mayors got under way. In this volume, we emphasize the emergence of Latino mayors within the context of the postindustrial city.

The Latino mayors covered in this book came to power as U.S. cities were undergoing profound economic and social transformation. A major feature of the postindustrial era is the technological developments that have enabled companies to locate away from the central city. With advancements in computers and telecommunications, major business corporations became more mechanized and mobile. These advances have serious implications for cities and their residents. For instance, Latino mayors were emerging when the nature of employment in cities was shifting from well-paying factory positions to more and more service jobs. Technological advancements fundamentally altered the economy of cities so that an ever-larger portion of the labor force was finding work in the service sector of the economy. As a result, there is greater wage polarization in which there are well-paying managerial and professional jobs at the top and more low-paying service positions at the bottom. The postindustrial economy put a premium on education and training. Workers without a good education are likely to be stuck at the bottom in jobs that often pay little more than minimum wages; offer few, if any, benefits; involve little opportunity for advancement; and are often only part-time. This volume explores how the constraints and opportunities of the postindustrial city shape the scope and nature of Latino mayoral leadership.

Latino mayors typically come to power in cities that are undergoing demographic change and experiencing Latino population growth. One of the central features of Latino mayoral politics that this book introduces is the significant role locally rooted community-based organizations play in mobilizing Latino communities to elect Latino mayors. In addition, this book examines Latino mayors' political campaigns and how race, ethnicity, class, and economic issues shaped the formation of their winning electoral coalition. A major theme that runs through many of the chapters in this volume is that Latino mayoral candidates tend to tone down racial and ethnic appeals and instead stress managerial competence, economic development, police-community relations, and increased responsiveness to home owners' concerns—issues that cut across ethnic and racial lines. The case studies in this volume also illuminate how Latino mayors navigate the political tensions that arise when they must assemble a governing coalition composed of corporate elites after having been elected to office by an electoral coalition anchored in low-income minority communities. Finally, the volume also addresses dimensions of leadership, providing analysis of the backgrounds, motivations, skills, styles, and coalition-building abilities of the nation's pioneering Latino mayors.

These issues were discussed at a workshop meeting and at the annual Anton-Lippitt Urban Conference sponsored by the A. Alfred Taubman Center for Public Policy at Brown University. We wish to thank Stefanie Chambers, Carlos Cuéllar, Emily M. Farris, Dario Moreno, Robert Preuhs, and Ellen Shiau for participating in the workshop and for their work on the chapters contributed to this book. Before the workshop was convened, the contributors were provided a background paper focused on the election and governance of Latino mayors and shared a draft of their papers with one another. At the workshop, through a wide-ranging discussion, the contributors identified themes and central concepts that connected the draft papers. The contributors also participated in a public conference along with Latino leaders from across the country, including Latino mayors and other Latino elected officials. Shortly thereafter, the contributors reconvened in Chicago at the annual meeting of the Midwest Political Science Association to discuss, critique, and further develop the essays.

Several people helped us complete this book. Clarence N. Stone read parts of the manuscript and provided thoughtful feedback. Our views on urban politics have been substantially enriched by his scholarship, especially his influential book, *Regime Politics*. Few people know more about mayors and mayoral leadership than Wilbur C. Rich. Professor Rich is the nation's preeminent political scientist on big-city mayors. Wilbur not only provided insightful feedback on several chapters but also directed us to important works on mayors. This book also benefited from the extraordinarily helpful comments of external reviewers who evaluated the manuscript for Temple University Press. They provided insightful criticism and useful suggestions that enabled the contributors to improve the quality of the book.

We would also like to thank the staff at Temple University Press. Aaron Javsicas, the editor in chief of Temple University Press, has been the consummate professional, providing good advice and feedback on many aspects of the project and overseeing it through to final production. Nikki Miller, Gary Kramer, and other Temple University Press staff treated the manuscript with care and were a pleasure to work with.

We would be remiss if we did not thank those affiliated with Brown University for their support and assistance. Isabel Costa, Melissa Nicholaus, and the staff at the Taubman Center provided critical institutional support for this project. The Taubman Center's Anton-Lippitt Endowment provided financial assistance that allowed the editors to convene the workshop and public conference. Ruth Gourevitch, a former Brown University undergraduate student who is now at the Urban Institute, helped organize the workshop and conference.

Finally, we wish to thank our spouses, Ramona L. Burton and Lisa Abreu Morel, and our families. We owe debts to them that cannot be repaid. Without their encouragement, reassurance, and, most important, love, this book would not have been possible.

Latino Mayors

I Introduction

1

Latino Mayors and the Evolution of Urban Politics

MARION ORR AND DOMINGO MOREL

T he face of America is changing, and so is its city politics. As late as the early 1960s, Latinos were almost totally excluded from city politics.* By the early 1980s, as Browning, Marshall, and Tabb (2003, p. 4) documented, "Latinos rose from exclusion to positions of authority as mayors, council members, and top managers and administrators" in local governments. Today, the vast majority (67 percent) of Latino elected officials in the United States serve at the municipal level on school boards, city councils, and county commissions, as mayors, and in other local elected offices. The number of Latino mayors, for example, has increased steadily over the past thirty years; it climbed from 139 in 1984 to 247 in 2009, an increase of 78 percent (NALEO 2010). Although Latino mayors are concentrated in the West and the Southwest, cities around the country, in the Northeast, the Midwest, and the South, also have Latino mayors. Latinos have been elected mayor in large cities, including Albuquerque, New Mexico; Miami, Florida; El Paso, Texas; Denver and Colorado Springs, Colorado; and Los Angeles and San Jose, California, among others.

This book focuses on the rise of Latino mayors and on their governing styles and policies. Why focus on Latino mayors? Because Latinos were almost invisible in post–World War II municipal politics, few urban scholars

---

* This text uses the terms "Latino" and "Hispanic" to "describe all individuals, foreign, and U.S.-born, who have ancestry in any of the Spanish-speaking nations of Latin America" (Garcia Bedolla, 2014, p. 3).

predicted their ascendancy to the city's highest office. Although their numbers have increased over the past thirty years, we know little about the rise of Latino mayors, the paths they have taken to the mayoralty, their governance experience once they have been elected, and how their mayoralties have affected the communities they represent. Put simply, the rise of Latino mayors has been a remarkable American story, but it also tells us something about ethnic succession, changing urban demography and political contexts, and the future of cities.

Winning the mayor's office typically signals the political coming-of-age of the racial or ethnic group of the person who holds the position. Ethnic and racial transitions of the mayor's office have long been a feature of American urban politics. In the late nineteenth and early twentieth centuries, Irish and Italian political leaders began to capture the mayor's office for the first time in Boston, Chicago, Cleveland, Pittsburgh, Philadelphia, New Haven, and other cities (Eisinger 1980). In the late 1960s, the United States began to witness a process of racial transition in which African Americans were elected to urban executive positions for the first time (Colburn and Adler 2001; Nelson and Meranto 1977; Rich 1989, 2007; Thompson 2006). Today, another process of ethnic and racial transition is occurring as Latino politicians replace white and African American politicians in city halls, including election as mayors (Filandra and Orr 2013; Sonnenshein 1999; 2003).

This volume presents case studies of Latino mayors in five large U.S. cities and one large urban county: Federico Peña of Denver, Colorado; Henry Cisneros, Ed Garza, and Julián Castro of San Antonio, Texas; Carlos Giménez of Miami-Dade County, Florida; Antonio Villaraigosa of Los Angeles; Eddie Perez and Pedro Segarra of Hartford, Connecticut; and Angel Taveras of Providence, Rhode Island. We have attempted to strike a balance in putting together this volume, blending essays that examine some of the most important pioneers with essays that explore the range of conditions and experiences that Latino mayors have confronted. This volume includes essays on Latino mayors in Sun Belt cities, such as San Antonio, Miami, and Los Angeles, and on Latino mayors in Snow Belt cities, such as Hartford and Providence.

In the remainder of this chapter, we provide a context for the case studies. We emphasize that Latino political incorporation is occurring at a particular stage and era in the economic, social, and political history of American cities. We explore the rise of Latino mayors within the context of the changing American city. To understand Latino mayors as a leading force in Latino political incorporation, we take a look back. First, we provide an examination of mayors during the period of the industrial city (roughly the 1830s to the 1930s), when ethnic Europeans, especially the

Irish, gained the mayor's office and political incorporation. Mayors were especially attentive to the provision of services and public works projects. Factories sprang up with little help from city hall. It was a period of centralized manufacturing and civic vitality in many cities. During this period, the mayor's job was seldom especially complicated.

Next, we stress that Latino mayors are coming to power in a context different from that of African American mayors. Black mayors came to power during the period of the redevelopment city (roughly the 1940s to the 1980s). The redevelopment city got under way in the post–World War II years, when the city was adapting to the automobile, hemorrhaging from white flight, and responding to deindustrialization. The redevelopment city saw African American mayors working in close alliance with downtown investor interests to revitalize downtowns, restore historic buildings, and expand transit systems.

We focus on the emergence of Latino mayors as an important facet of politics in the postindustrial city (roughly the 1990s to the present). Latino mayors are coming of age politically at a time when the U.S. economy is concerned with providing services based on knowledge, information, and technology more than with producing goods. It is shifting from a manufacturing to a service-based economy. In the postindustrial city, Latino mayors are working in a changing urban context in which concerns about downtown economic revitalization have given way to a heightened focus on other issues, such as education, immigration, affordable housing, and gentrification.

After this sketch of the changing political and economic contexts within which mayors have had to operate, the remainder of the chapter focuses on the contemporary scene and the rise of Latino mayors. First, we examine demographic change. However, in order to understand the office of mayor as an instance of "Demography is destiny," it is important to appreciate that other variables come into play. We call attention particularly to (a) the infrastructure of organizations and the ecology of civic engagement they form and (b) the skills that key actors (often the mayor) display in building coalitions. We further argue that these community organizations and leadership skills are brought into play in an urban context of constraints and opportunities. The nature of these constraints and opportunities varies with the times.

Mayors and the Industrial City

Latino mayors face a dramatically different situation from that of the mayors who governed during the era of the industrial city. From roughly the

1830s to the 1930s, the city was the epicenter of American industry. This was the period of the industrial city. A key function of the industrial city was to provide the infrastructure necessary for industrial growth. Roads and bridges for transportation, massive sewers to carry off industrial waste, and large supplies of water to furnish the huge factories were among some of the public works projects required for large-scale industrial production. In other words, mayors of the industrial city were heavily involved in city building (Kantor 1995). City governments also maintained public infrastructure, provided routine public services, enforced regulations, and maintained public safety.

Industrialization brought an urban explosion as factories sprang up in waterfront cities and diverse populations flocked to work in them. Between 1820 and 1919, 33.5 million European immigrants, mainly from Ireland, Russia, Poland, and Italy, arrived on American shores (Judd and Swanstrom 2006, pp. 26–37). The cities bore the brunt of this immigration. By 1870, 44 percent of New York City's residents had been born outside the United States; 48 percent in Chicago were foreign born, as were 49 percent in San Francisco (Judd and Swanstrom 2006, pp. 27–32). Cities tended to serve as processing centers for wave after wave of poor, lesser-skilled immigrants beginning their way up the economic ladder of material success. For example, the Irish were the first European ethnic group to migrate in massive numbers directly into the American industrial city (Erie 1988). The Irish immigrants who crowded into the segregated ghettos faced tremendous challenges. According to one account, living conditions in the Irish ghettos were "brutish, oppressive, and surrounded by open hostility" (Harrigan and Vogel 2000, p. 62).

As the nation's urban population continued to grow, the industrial city became an increasingly complex economic, political, and social organization. By the 1820s, cities were well on their way to adopting governmental structures similar to the national model. Mayors (elected citywide) served as chief executives, and citizens chose city councils (elected from districts) to perform legislative functions. During this earlier period, however, city councils were typically the dominant players in formulating municipal policy. Americans' lingering desire to avoid anything that resembled the British monarchy kept the city's chief executive position comparatively weak. Urban historians Howard Chudacoff and Judith Smith (1988, p. 151) observed that "before 1850 most mayors could exert only limited control over municipal policy." It would take cities several decades to persuade state governments to begin to deliver more authority in piecemeal fashion to the mayor's office (Frug and Barron 2008). One of the first such grants was authority given to the mayor to appoint and remove city administrators.

This shift not only brought more centralization to political authority and made it more popularly responsive but also opened the door for the development of the patronage system and machine-style politics (Erie 1988). Although there was no universal pattern, control of the office of mayor took on great importance.

By the 1860s and 1870s, a new style of city politics emerged in most large U.S. cities. Before the huge waves of European immigrants, political power in many American cities was controlled by a very small group of economic elites consisting of white Anglo-Saxon Protestants or Yankees (Kantor 1995). As the industrial city developed, new kinds of political leaders emerged. These new leaders were less affluent career politicians whose base of support was lodged in the segregated ethnic wards. The decentralized structure of the urban political system, combined with mass suffrage and ethnic residential segregation, created a new political climate in which social and political relationships became highly interconnected. In order to organize voters within and across the ethnic-based wards and to ensure their support, the new career politicians depended on the city budget (i.e., patronage jobs and contracts) to provide for the needs of their constituents. Patronage became the mechanism that held the political organizations or machines together. It provided the incentives for voter mobilization and allowed machine-style mayors to command large electoral majorities (Erie 1988; Trounstine 2008).

Irish Political Incorporation and the Industrial City

No other group took greater advantage of machine politics than the Irish (Erie 1988). Irish immigrants had the advantage of speaking English. Although Roman Catholicism was looked on with suspicion by certain segments of the dominant society, it served as a common bond, drawing the Irish community closer together. The broad patchwork of Irish Catholic parishes that developed provided an additional institutional structure for organizing Irish voters in the ghetto neighborhoods. Activist Irish Catholic priests used the church as an agency for mobilizing Irish communities. All these variables and factors, combined with the huge demographic changes, opened the way for the Irish eventually to control the mayor's office in many cities.

The Irish not only had advantages in organizing capacity and ethnic-group consciousness but also were beneficiaries of timing. They came to power in urban politics during the era of the industrial city, in which mayors worked in an environment characterized by economic growth and expansion. For example, the construction activity that was characteristic of the industrial city brought city hall into a close working relationship with local business leaders. For large and established businesses that had acquired a fixed stake in the industrial city (especially utility and transit companies), an alliance with the mayor's office was mutually beneficial (Kantor 1995, pp. 41–75). Machine politics structured elections and provided some political stability to city hall. By aligning with the local machine, businesses could have the security of knowing whom they were dealing with in city government. Business leaders were also given a strong voice in shaping economic policy. As Kantor (1995, p. 60) explained, "The major struggles over economic policy could take place within the business community. Once a consensus was achieved there, the centralized system of bribe-giving and favor-trading would assure the implementation of developmental decisions." Alliances with machine politicians have always been valuable to city business leaders.

Governing the Industrial City

The Irish mayors who governed the industrial city had at their disposal opportunities offered through patronage and machine-style politics (Erie 1988). Consequently, in many U.S. cities, the Irish controlled the vast majority of public-sector jobs as city clerks, policemen, firemen, and laborers. The Irish were able to "move solidly into the mainstream of American society" largely because of their group's control of the city's public- and private-sector patronage jobs (Harrigan and Vogel 2000, p. 68). Irish political control of the city became an avenue for group advancement. Steven Erie (1988) has persuasively argued that the Irish crowded into the largely low-paying, blue-collar urban public sector jobs. As a consequence, in socioeconomic status, the Irish lagged behind other ethnic groups who focused on more group effort in business and the professions. Nevertheless, Erie (1988, p. 261) acknowledged, "The Irish experience demonstrates some potential for group economic uplift through the local political process."

Mayors could depend on businesses to make jobs available to their people in exchange for providing those businesses favorable action on construction and other contracts. For example, under Mayor James Michael Curley, Boston spent lavishly on public works projects, building new schools, hospitals, and courthouses (Beatty 1992). Private contracts were awarded to businesses after they had agreed to hire individuals sent by Curley's political operatives. By all accounts, Curley centralized the powers of patronage in his own hands and distributed public works jobs in a way that enabled him to retain the loyalty and support of his Irish working-class electoral base.

Douglas Rae (2003) contrasted the mayoralty of Frank Rice (1910–1917), who served as mayor of New Haven during the height of the industrial city, with the mayoralty of Richard Lee (1954–1970), who held the position during the 1950s and 1960s. Rae's cross-time comparison highlighted some of the distinctive features associated with being a mayor during the era of the industrial city. His analysis reminds us that the capacity of mayors to govern varies in different contexts (see also Flanagan 2004). Mayor Rice's administration was labeled the "sidewalk republic" as an acknowledgment of his regime's reputation for providing a high level of "routine" services like street cleaning and maintenance, garbage collection, public schools, parks, sewers, and sidewalks for the citizens and commercial interests of the city (Rae 2003, pp. 183–211). Rice focused his limited powers on executing routine municipal-government services and did not undertake any grand plans to transform New Haven.

The industrial city was a place of opportunity and social mobility for millions of European immigrants and their offspring. Rae helps us appreciate how mayors who led cities during the industrial era could rely "in overwhelming degree on market forces" to "sustain opportunity" and "to attract and retain taxpaying citizens" (Rae 2003, p. 203). Mayors of industrial cities were fortunate to occupy city hall during the era when cities had strong urban manufacturing economies capable of creating a "powerful stream of wages and investment capital to energize the city" (Rae 2003, p. 18). During this period, the interests of important sectors of the business community were inextricably interwoven with those of the city government. When European immigrants began to pursue political incorporation, control of the mayor's office ultimately led to the infiltration of Irish and Italians into the private economic sectors of the city. The bustling economy characteristic of the industrial-city era helped keep the city moving.

Mayors and the Redevelopment City

The period of the redevelopment city was a transition between that of the industrial city and that of the postindustrial city. From roughly 1940 through the end of the 1980s, cities were adapting to the decline of the industrial city. Concerted efforts were devoted to rebuilding and rescuing decaying downtowns of the old industrial city. During this period, the relationship between city politics and economics became ever more apparent, and mayors began to "actively" seek solutions to problems like traffic congestion and urban blight (Salisbury 1964, p. 790). During the period of the redevelopment city, civic and political elites led the effort to revitalize downtowns and waterfronts and expand transit and transportation choices.

The federal government was a strong partner in promoting urban renewal and trying to arrest urban distress.

Governing the Redevelopment City

The period of the redevelopment city was a time of economic and social transition for cities. Cities were adapting to the age of the automobile and deindustrialization (Bluestone and Harrison 1984; Teaford 1990). In the 1930s and 1940s, mayors became actively involved in plans to adapt their downtowns to address traffic congestion caused by the rising use of the automobile (Teaford 1990, pp. 19–21). The automobile also caused businesses and people to push out farther from downtown, away from the central core of the industrial city. Census figures for 1940 confirmed that many U.S. cities, including Boston, Philadelphia, and Cleveland, suffered a decline in population. During the 1930s and 1940s, property values in downtown business districts, including St. Louis, Pittsburgh, Chicago, and Detroit, dropped precipitously (Teaford 1990). In cities across the country, business and civic leaders grew increasingly concerned about the commercial decline of cities' central business districts. In May 1940, a national business magazine exclaimed that big cities were "economically speaking . . . rotting at the core" (quoted in Teaford 1990, p. 19).

Mayors of the postwar redevelopment era worked to revitalize their cities within the context of deindustrialization. During the period of the industrial city, goods were almost entirely produced in large factories in a single city and then shipped to consumers and producer markets. However, after World War II, and especially after the mid-1960s, the increased mobility of capital allowed corporations to locate and relocate with much more flexibility and led to the economic decline of many central cities. Technological developments fundamentally altered the manufacturing process so that an ever-larger portion of the labor force found work in the service sector of the economy. Soon the service sector of the city economy grew at such a rate that it quickly surpassed manufacturing employment, the key labor market during the era of the industrial city. Numerous communities that were dependent on manufacturing suffered a long-term decline. Central cities became impoverished relative both to their prior condition and to their surrounding suburban municipalities. Cities became poorer and blacker. Soon many cities were losing population, a significant reversal from the days of the industrial city.

Mayors of the redevelopment city had to do more than focus on routine service provision. The context had changed. The Housing Act of 1949 and later the urban-renewal programs of the 1960s heightened the federal government's involvement in urban economic development. Supported on the one side by the city's access to federal funding and on the other by the commitment of local businesses to invest in the downtown, mayors formed strong coalitions with downtown corporate interests. Mayors now were at the center of the effort to demolish and change the urban landscape in the hope of redeveloping the city's economically troubled downtown (Salisbury 1964). They were aided by a cadre of professional technicians and planners trained in understanding the complexity of redeveloping existing urban environments (Mollenkopf 1983). Blocks and blocks of slum housing were razed. Roads were rerouted, and miles and miles of interstate highways were laid. Large, transformational endeavors with heavy involvement from city hall became routine in the redevelopment city (Stone and Sanders 1987; Fainstein et al. 1986). Deindustrialization made the job of mayor much more challenging and complicated. In addition to providing routine public services, mayors were now involved in "solving or alleviating particular problems" (Salisbury 1964, p. 788).

Black Politics and the Redevelopment City

Black mayors came to power in a context of urban constraints and opportunities different from that in which European immigrants had begun to pursue political incorporation in the early twentieth century. Like the rise of Irish American mayors generations earlier, the rise of black mayors was connected to demographic change in the city. During the late 1890s and into the early twentieth century, millions of African Americans from the rural South migrated to the cities of the urban North and West. Historians began to call this the Great Black Migration (Lemann 1991; Wilkerson 2010). During the Great Depression, black in-migration to northern urban centers slowed, but it picked up again during the 1940s and did not begin to taper off until the 1970s. It is estimated that by the 1970s, five million to six million African Americans had left the rural small towns of the South and had made their residence in Washington, D.C., New York, Newark, Philadelphia, Chicago, Detroit, and newer cities in the West, such as Oakland and Los Angeles. Blacks also made their way out of rural southern towns and into southern cities like Atlanta, Birmingham, and Memphis. In the same years, central cities such as Detroit and Newark were changing from overwhelmingly white to predominantly African American.

As whites fled the cities, the percentage of the black population increased, giving African American voters electoral clout. However, as the case studies in this volume make clear, demographic change alone is not enough to capture electoral control. People must organize and be mobilized

(Dreier 2007; Orr 2007). A strong sense of racial-group consciousness and a desire for equality were central factors for the political mobilization of blacks during the first half of the twentieth century (Dawson 1994; Shingles 1981). The passage of the 1964 Civil Rights Act opened public accommodations to blacks, and the 1965 Voting Rights Act outlawed the legal tactics used to restrict black voter participation. But despite these historic achievements, the African American community was still in a crisis. This was especially the case for the growing percentages of blacks living in the nation's central cities. Throughout the 1960s, surveys showed that African Americans consistently judged government services—schools, parks, recreation, garbage collection, and, above all, the police—to be less adequate than whites, even those whites living in the same cities (Jones et al. 1978).

From the mid-1960s to the late 1970s, specially targeted voter-education and registration drives in southern and northern cities added millions of blacks to the rolls of eligible voters. Black voters formed the bases for a new black politics (Preston, Henderson, and Puryear 1987; Walton 1972). The symbol of the new black urban politics became the African American mayor (Persons 1993). The election of big-city African American mayors began first in Cleveland (Carl Stokes) and Gary, Indiana (Richard Hatcher) in 1967. In 1970, Newark elected Kenneth Gibson as its first black mayor. Black mayors were elected for the first time in Detroit, Atlanta, and Los Angeles in 1973 and in Washington, D.C., in 1974. Black mayors signaled the gradual institutionalization of black political power in urban America.

Black Mayors and the Redevelopment City

The redevelopment city created a particular set of constraints and opportunities for black mayors. Black mayors were faced with the task of trying to attract investment capital to their cities during an era when geographic place, transportation access, physical infrastructure, and other locational advantages no longer tied businesses to a specific locale. They formed alliances with big corporations to invest in urban development, especially in declining downtown central business districts, and, armed with federal urban-redevelopment grants, fully embraced corporate-centered strategies for urban revitalization. This was the approach of black mayors in Detroit, Los Angeles, Atlanta, Newark, Washington, D.C., and other cities. Detroit's Coleman Young became one of the chief proponents of urban redevelopment focused on corporate investment in downtown business districts (Rich 1989; Young and Wheeler 1994). Los Angeles mayor Tom Bradley is also credited with transforming the city's downtown with "gleaming skyscrapers" and leading "the grandest downtown building program of any

American city" (Sonenshein 2003, p. 60; 1999). Black mayors became key players working with business leaders in a tight coalition to boost investor confidence in downtowns and stimulate urban revitalization.

Forging a governing regime with white economic elites created a special challenge for black mayors. Scholars criticized black mayors for too enthusiastically pursuing the corporate-centered approach to urban redevelopment (Nelson 1990; Preston 1990; Reed 1988; Whelan, Young, and Lauria 1994). They argued that corporate-centered downtown policies created unbalanced urban growth. Black mayors had to reassure their largely African American electoral base that they had not "sold out" to the white economic elites (Reed 1988, p. 101). Coleman Young, for example, forcefully argued that his emphasis on downtown urban redevelopment was in the "interest of nourishing" Detroit's poor and black neighborhoods (Young and Wheeler 1994, p. 315). Young and other black mayors who led cities during the redevelopment era maintained that the best strategy for improving the black condition was to expand job opportunities in the private sector throughout the city. However, critics charged that black mayors were too deferential to white economic elites and failed to give sufficient attention to the needs of low-income neighborhoods.

One of the consistent themes across much of the literature on the politics of the redevelopment city is that African American mayors were able to win elections by gaining the overwhelming support of black voters. However, once they were in office, black mayors tended to forge governing coalitions with the city's corporate elite and investor interests. Urban scholars make a distinction between an electoral coalition and a governing coalition. As we will see in the coming chapters, Latino mayors win office with strong support from Latino voters. However, once they are in city hall, they find that their governing agenda is pulled in the direction of the city's business community. Latino mayors, like other big-city mayors, are sympathetic to facilitating the economic growth of the city. The result is that they are likely to be drawn into an alliance with the city's corporate community.

When black mayors came into office in the 1960s and 1970s, some analysts wondered whether the "reforms" (at-large elections, direct primary elections, nonpartisan elections, city-manager systems, and expanded civil service coverage) adopted in the early twentieth century in many cities to wrest political control from the Irish machines and rid the cities of corruption would limit the mayors' ability to translate political power into black social and economic advancement (Friesema 1969; Preston 1976; Welch 1990). For example, in an essay published in the early 1970s, Francis Fox Piven (1973, p. 380) observed that blacks were gaining political power in the city "at a time when public employment has been pre-empted by older groups and is held fast through civil service provisions and collective bargaining contracts." "Most public jobs," Piven (1973, p. 380) added, "are no longer allocated in exchange for political allegiance, but through a 'merit' system based on formal qualifications." Black mayors, however, used aggressive affirmative-action programs to increase representation of African Americans in municipal government, including police departments (Browning, Marshall, and Tabb 1984; Eisinger 1982; Karnig and Welch 1989; Keller 1978; Rich 1989; Saltzstein 1989). Today, a substantial proportion of the African American middle class is employed in the government sector, including municipal employment (Dawson 1994, pp. 29–33). In addition, black mayors used their public authority to expand minority participation in city contracting and purchasing (Holmes 2011; Rich 1989; Stone 1989). During Maynard Jackson's two terms as mayor of Atlanta, the percentage of city contracts awarded to African American business firms rose substantially, from 2 percent in 1974 to 30 percent in 1980 (Holmes 2011, p. 174). These accomplishments suggest that black mayors were able to make a difference in the public sector.

Mayors and the Postindustrial City

Latino mayors are emerging as significant players in the postindustrial city. The postindustrial city is different from the redevelopment city. One of the distinguishing features of the postindustrial city is the rise and dominance of large multilocational corporations in local economies (Kantor 1995, pp. 77–111; Sassen 2001; Savitch 1988). These huge multilocational corporations are much larger than the businesses that dominated the economy during the industrial city and "control the movement of most goods, services, and capital throughout the United States" (Kantor 1995, p. 90). Because of their large size, many of the postindustrial corporations have multiple administrative and operational units often scattered across several locations. Advancement in telecommunication technologies, such as computers and fiber-optic cable, provided for greater efficiency in production and distribution, allowing huge corporations to disperse their production activities in different locales. The dispersal of production activities has meant that cities increasingly compete economically among themselves to be the site for the large corporations' decentralized operations (Peterson 1981).

In the postindustrial city, heavy industry no longer dominates the economy. The economy of the postindustrial city is characterized by a shift to service industries. Ever-increasing proportions of jobs are found in professional and personal services, such as health care, finance, insurance, information technology, and retail sales. In the postindustrial city, job growth has shifted to service industries and highly educated workers. Richard Florida (2002, p. 8) wrote that the postindustrial city has also spawned a new "creative" class, "people in science and engineering, architecture and design, education, arts, music and entertainment, whose economic function is to create ideas, new technology and/or new creative content."

The restructuring of the urban economy transformed the city's labor market. In the postindustrial city, the polarization of city occupations is more apparent. Educated and skilled workers benefit from the service-oriented economy. For example, Florida (2002, p. 9) wrote that in the postindustrial city, the creative class is "dominant in terms of wealth and income." There are a number of high-end and high-skilled positions for managers and professionals at the top and more low-paying service jobs (cleaning, cooking, waiting tables, stocking shelves) at the bottom. The entire economic restructuring process has left unskilled and semiskilled inner-city workers with significantly fewer opportunities for gainful employment. This has posed a particular dilemma for blacks and Latinos, two of the last racial/ethnic groups to arrive in the cities in large numbers (Wilson 1996). Blacks and Latinos are also underrepresented among those with higher education. Cities that had once served as processing centers for lesser-skilled immigrants preparing themselves for economic advancement now have become large repositories for workers with lessened economic prospects.

The politics of the postindustrial city also differs from the politics of earlier eras, and governing the postindustrial city differs from governing the redevelopment city. Established patterns of decision making were altered when large multinational corporations took over locally based companies and businesses (Heying 1997). The tight coalition of downtown commercial interests of banks, railroads, department stores, and local newspapers that Salisbury (1964) found held great sway during the postwar redevelopment era pulled back its involvement in civic and political affairs. In the postindustrial city, universities, medical centers, metropolitan business associations, environmental groups, and cultural institutions are taking a leadership role in local affairs (Katz and Bradley 2013; Maurrasse 2001; Rodin 2007; Stoker, Stone, and Horak 2015). Nonprofit foundations are also playing critical roles in the postindustrial city. In Baltimore, Pittsburgh, Chicago, and other cities, program officers and staffers of large foundations like the Annie E. Casey Foundation and the Ford Foundation are seeding programs devoted to improving housing and addressing other needs in poor neighborhoods, providing research and data analysis on important policy matters, and helping empower low-income communities

struggling to survive amid the changes and challenges of the postindustrial city.

Issues that were not high on the action agenda during the period of the
redevelopment city have been elevated during that of the postindustrial
city. Stone and Stoker (2015), for example, showed that leaders of the
postindustrial city now view economic growth and neighborhood improvement as complementary goals. The postindustrial city is situated within
the context of a "back-to-the-city" movement, in which young professionals
are carving out urban space within the central city (Ehrenhalt 2013; Hyra
2008). Developers and real estate agents have been selling young hipsters
the idea that it is not necessary to move downtown to achieve a sense of
urbanity. The young professionals pulled to the city by the huge multilocational corporations want to stay in happening places in neighborhoods
that offer activities. During the postwar redevelopment period, the class
divide played out at the neighborhood level in many U.S. cities and featured
battles over downtown renewal and slum clearance. The class cleavage was
between a corporate elite determined to make the downtown attractive to
the middle class and businesses and poor, working-class people resisting
neighborhood displacement (Ferman 1996; Stone 1976;). Back then, the
class struggle over neighborhoods was symbolized by the bulldozer. Today,
in the postindustrial city, displacement remains an issue, but now the issue
is gentrification. More middle-class families (often whites), particularly
singles and young married couples priced out of more expensive areas, have
moved to formerly poor areas of the city, especially neighborhoods that are
close to the work and entertainment opportunities of downtown (Freeman
2006; Hyra 2008). As Myron Levine (2015, p. 60) explained:

> Gentrification brings a new sense of vitality and a number of
> more specific benefits to cities. New investment helps to stabilize
> declining neighborhoods, upgrade residential structures, and in-
> crease an area's attractiveness to future investment. Gentrified
> areas also help a city to attract workers with advanced techno-
> logical and specialized skills, the sort of talented workforce that
> a city needs in order to compete for high-tech, legal, and financial
> service firms. Neighborhood upgrading expands the municipal
> tax base, yielding higher property-tax revenues and local income-
> tax receipts.

However, researchers have found that gentrification in communities
can be a double-edged sword (Freeman 2006; Hyra 2008). As Lance Freeman (2006, p. 93), an urban planner, put it, "Gentrification brings both

cheer and grief." Critics argue that gentrification can have harmful impacts, especially on poor, working-class families who are pushed out of neighborhoods because of rising housing values (Hyra 2008). Freeman (2006, p. 162) showed that "displacement haunts residents of gentrifying neighborhoods." Levine (2015, p. 56) explained, "Globalization intensifies the pressures underlying neighborhood gentrification. . . . Gentrification, in turn, helps to make a city attractive to global corporations that seek a talented workforce."

Globalization has made innovation and human capital critical driving elements in the economic fortunes of postindustrial cities. Public education is of vital importance to the viability of postindustrial cities. Trying to make the city appealing to the "creative class" creates a different set of challenges and opportunities. As multinational and multilocational corporations recruit more college-educated professionals with school-age children to work in the postindustrial city, issues related to public education and school reform become more salient. Moreover, survey research shows that education has long been one of the most important policy issues confronting Latino communities (Fraga et al. 2012). In many cities, more and more immigrant parents are organizing and pressuring school districts and local officials to address the needs of the changing population (Clarke et al. 2006; Fraga and Frost 2011; Orr and Rogers 2011; Orr et al. 2016; Su 2009). Governors and other state officials are increasingly monitoring the performance of city schools and prodding school districts to turn around failing city schools (Morel 2018). It is not surprising that in the postindustrial city, mayors are paying much more attention to public education than mayors who governed during the era of the redevelopment city (Henig, Hula, Orr, Pedescleaux 1999; Henig and Rich 2004; Orr 1999; Rich 1996; Viteritti 2009; Wong et al. 2007). For example, despite the jurisdictional barriers and their limited formal authority in school affairs, several of the Latino mayors covered in this volume have developed ways to influence local public education.

The increase in the Latino population and the need for expanded public services occurred as cities grappled with economic challenges related to the transformation from an industrial to a postindustrial economy. The typical postindustrial city struggles with balancing revenues with expenditures. In other words, many Latino mayors are leading municipal governments that are suffering from fiscal stress (Filandra and Orr 2013; Ladd and Yinger 1989). Federal cutbacks in social services and welfare programs have placed a bigger burden on city-government budgets. State revenue is a decreasing share of city budgets. Mayors of postindustrial cities struggle to make ends meet.

Latinos and the Postindustrial City

Racial/ethnic succession in the mayor's office is driven significantly by demographic change. The next sections examine the profound and interre-
lated demographic shifts occurring in the United States, shifts fueled by
the growing Latino population. As we show, the Latino population not only
is growing substantially but also is becoming more diverse and much more
dispersed than it was thirty years ago. However, we emphasize that although
demography is very important, its impact is not spontaneous. Such things
as organization and leadership skills play a vital part. We remind readers
of the important role of community organizing in the process of Latino
political incorporation.

Immigration and Demographic Change
in the Postindustrial City

Without question, population change prepares the ground for political
change. One of the most significant changes in American politics over the
past thirty years has been the demographic transformation of the Latino
population, that is, the size and proportion of Latinos living in the United
States. The Latino population in the United States grew nearly 60 percent
between 1990 and 2000 and increased 43 percent between 2000 and 2010.
The 2010 census showed that Latinos are now the fastest-growing and
largest (16.3 percent of the population versus 12.6 percent for African
Americans) minority group in the country, and this increase is largely fuel-
ing the trend toward whites being less than 50 percent of the U.S. population around 2050. The demographic change is being felt across the
country. Over half the U.S. Latino population is concentrated in the southwestern states. Latinos, mostly of Mexican origin, have always had a significant presence in the Southwest, but over the past forty years, the number
of Latino immigrants from Mexico and other Latin American countries
has increased in states like Texas, New Mexico, Arizona, and California.
Latinos of Puerto Rican descent have been a significant presence in parts
of New York, Florida, and Illinois since the middle of the twentieth century.
Florida has been home to a large population of Cuban immigrants who
came to the United States after Fidel Castro's rise to power in 1959.

The most important observation about these population changes is that
Latinos are more dispersed than ever before. Who would have predicted
that Latinos would move in large numbers to places like Lawrence, Massachusetts; Durham, North Carolina; Cicero, Illinois; Manchester, New
Hampshire; and Providence, Rhode Island? Every year, all of the nation's

largest cities become more Latino than the year before. The current growth in the Latino population is driven not by immigration but by native population birth. Between 2000 and 2008, the increase in native births was almost double that of foreign-born immigrants. Of the nearly 47 million persons of Hispanic origin living in the United States, about 29 million were born in the United States. The native-born now represent approximately 62 percent of all Latinos (Fraga et al. 2012, pp. 4–11). As Fraga and his colleagues (2012, p. 8) observed, "Latinos are substantially younger than the overall population, and Latinos born in the United States are younger than those immigrating from abroad; as a result, Hispanics will disproportionately contribute future population growth in the United States for the foreseeable future."

The cities in this volume vary in the size of their Latino populations. However, over the past three decades, each city has experienced significant Latino population growth. The cities in this volume with the largest share of the Latino population, Los Angeles, California (49 percent), Miami, Florida (70 percent), and San Antonio, Texas (63 percent), had roughly an 8 percent increase in their Latino populations between 1990 and 2010. Denver, where Latinos constituted 23 percent of the city's population in 1990, saw similar growth. Its Latino population grew by 9 percent between 1990 and 2010. The cities in our volume with the largest growth in their Latino populations were in New England. Hartford's Latino population grew by nearly 12 percent, and the Latino population of Providence, Rhode Island, grew by nearly 23 percent between 1990 and 2010.

Another major transformation of the Latino population in the United States since the 1980s is its increasing diversity. Latinos of Mexican ancestry still represent the largest percentage (64 percent) of the U.S. Latino population. Puerto Ricans make up about 9 percent, and Cubans constitute 3.5 percent of the Latino population. However, demographic data reveal that between 1990 and 2010, immigrants from Central America and the Latin Caribbean reduced the percentage of Puerto Ricans (from 12 percent to 9 percent) and Cubans (from 4.7 percent to 3.5 percent) as a proportion of the U.S. Latino population. As a result of substantial immigration from South America, Central America, and the Latin Caribbean, Dominicans, Salvadorans, Guatemalans, Colombians, and those from unspecified countries now make up approximately 22 percent of the U.S. Latino population.

The mayors discussed in this volume are, in part, products of these demographic changes, but they have presided over cities that span the entire diversity of the U.S. Latino population. Three of the cities studied in this volume have populations where persons of Mexican origin constitute the majority of their city's Latino population (Denver, Los Angeles, and San Antonio). Puerto Ricans represent the largest share of the Latino population in one city, Hartford (78 percent), and the second-largest share of the Latino population in Providence, Rhode Island (22 percent). Following Latinos of Mexican and Puerto Rican origin is a cluster of Latino subgroups that represent between 3 and 4 percent of the overall Latino population in the United States. Within this cluster are Latinos of Cuban and Dominican origin. Latinos of Cuban origin, who constitute roughly 4 percent of the Latino population in the United States, are concentrated in southern Florida. In Miami-Dade County, one of the localities in this study, Latinos of Cuban origin make up nearly 50 percent of the county's Latino population. Finally, Dominicans, who represent 3 percent of the Latino population in the United States, are the largest Latino population in Providence, Rhode Island (37 percent). Although Dominicans are the smallest of the major subgroups covered in this study, the Dominican population in the United States has increased by 85 percent since 2000, and Dominicans are one of the fastest-growing Latino groups in the United States (Pew Research Center 2013).

Barreto and Segura (2014, p. 23) have cautioned us not to overstate the increased level of diversity and have noted that Mexican Americans "dominate the [national] conversation" concerning Latinos. Nevertheless, it is clear that the U.S. Latino population now includes diverse subgroups. Moreover, the historical experiences of each subgroup vary significantly, and these differences shape political opinions and policy preferences. Many Cubans who came to the United States as refugees when Castro took over (and the generation after them) are motivated by strong anticommunism and are much more Republican and conservative than other Latino groups (Garcia Bedolla 2014, pp. 131–165). Puerto Rico is part of the United States, and therefore, every Puerto Rican born on the island or the mainland is automatically a U.S. citizen. Given their legal status as Americans, it is not surprising that immigration is not an immediate policy concern of Puerto Ricans (García Bedolla 2014, pp. 104–130; Jennings and Rivera 1984). Immigrants from El Salvador arrived in the United States in the 1980s after fleeing a brutal civil war in which the United States aligned itself with that country's repressive leadership. The U.S. government denied many Salvadorans asylum status, and some observers have argued that among Latino immigrants, Salvadorans have had the most negative experience with the U.S. government (Garcia Bedolla 2014, pp. 205–211). Hence it is not surprising that Salvadorans hold the most "restrictive definitions" about what it means to be "American" (Silber Mohamed 2014, 2017, p.96). Salvadorans also constitute the second-largest undocumented population (after Mexicans) in the United States. Unlike Puerto Ricans and Cubans,

Salvadorans living in the United States have an immediate concern about U.S. immigration policy.

As was suggested earlier, Latinos have moved to small midwestern suburban America and into old New England towns. In general, there has been a more widespread and less selective distribution of the Latino population. The Latino population is no longer concentrated in the western and southwestern states. There are growing Latino populations across the country. According to a Pew Research study, "One of the most prominent features of the growth of Hispanics since 1990 has been the dispersal of Hispanics to new destinations. . . . There are now many Hispanics residing in counties that until 1990 had small Hispanic populations" (Fry 2008). In 2000, the Latino population exceeded 10 percent of the total population in ten states. As evidence of their growing national presence, the 2010 U.S. Census revealed that the Latino population exceeded 10 percent of the total population in seventeen states. The Latino population has seen its greatest growth in "new-destination" areas in southern states like Georgia, North Carolina, Tennessee, Mississippi, and Virginia (Fraga et. al. 2010). Between 1990 and 2000, for example, the number of Latinos living in Arkansas increased 337 percent; in Georgia, 300 percent; and in North Carolina, 394 percent. Fraga et al. (2010, p. 6) observed that Latino growth rates in the South are "substantial" and "have significant political implications" for the region.

Immigration and the growth of the Latino population are changing the racial and ethnic landscape of cities in New England, a region not known for racial diversity (Torres 2006; Hero 2007). From the mid-1940s through the 1960s, hundreds of thousands of Puerto Ricans came to Massachusetts, Connecticut (Barber 2017) and Rhode Island (Itzigsohn 2009) to work in the declining urban manufacturing industries. Although their overall numbers were small compared with the size of Mexican American populations in the Southwest, Puerto Ricans have long been the dominant Latino group throughout southern New England (Torres 2006). However, today, the Dominican population in the United States, once concentrated in New York City, has swelled New England's Latino population (Itzigsohn 2009). "About one-quarter of Latin American and Caribbean immigrants to New England during the 1990s came from the Dominican Republic. Spanish-speaking South Americans—Colombians, Peruvians, and Ecuadorians—represented 15 percent, while Central Americans—Guatemalans, Hondurans, and Salvadorans—were 9 percent of the region's Latin American and Caribbean immigrants" (A.A. Barreto 2006, p. 295). Dominicans have also taken up residence in Florida and New Jersey. Although the Latino population is expected to continue to grow in the southwestern states, demographic

trends suggest that Latinos will continue to increase their share of the population in states throughout the United States.

Latinos and Group Mobilization in the Postindustrial City

Demographic change is very important in shaping urban politics. However,
as we discussed in the case of the Irish of the industrial city and that of
African Americans in the era of the redevelopment city, capturing the may-
or's office requires more than population numbers. Group organization
and group leadership play vital roles. When Browning, Marshall, and Tabb
(1984) studied black and Latino politics in ten California cities during the
turbulent period from 1960 to 1980, they found that community organizing was important as Hispanics sought to achieve political incorporation.
A typical pattern was the development of community organizations that
would first mobilize Latino residents around community issues (e.g., policing, schools, housing) and then work toward Latino political incorporation
(Jones-Correa 1998; Burns 2006). In addition, community organizations
taught Latino citizens how to become active in local elections. In most of the
cases presented in this volume (Denver is the lone exception), the pioneering Latino mayor benefited from the mobilization of Hispanic voters by
Latino community-based organizations before his election. In short, demography is very important, but it must be understood alongside such
factors as organization and leadership.

Latino group consciousness is another variable that combined with
changing demography to bring about Latino political incorporation. In the
postindustrial city, the massive influx of Latino immigrants into cities created a critical mass of people who shared language, traditions, and social
circumstances. Despite the increasing diversity among them, Latinos now
see themselves as a group. In 2006, the Latino National Survey found that
a large majority of Latino respondents felt a sense of shared commonality
among Latinos and Latino subgroups (Fraga et al. 2012). In other words,
Latinos are increasingly exhibiting what Michael Dawson (1994) has called
"linked fate." The majority of individual Latinos in the United States now
believe that their own self-interest is associated with the interest of Latinos as a group. The growing sense of group consciousness and group identity among Latinos has important political implications for city politics
(Sanchez 2006). Latinos' youthfulness, the matter of nativity, low levels of
trust in government, alienation from political institutions, and lack of political knowledge all combine to reduce the potential political influence of
Latino communities (Abrajano and Alvarez 2010; DeSipio 1996; Fraga

et al. 2012; Garcia 2011; Garcia and Sanchez 2008; Hero 1992; Hero et al. 2000). However, research has shown that group consciousness or "linked fate" can influence political behavior and facilitate group political mobilization. The expectation is that as Latinos gain a sense of group consciousness, it will translate into united activism to advance Latino group interests.

Finally, within the context of this growing group consciousness among Latinos, another consistent theme that runs through the discussions of all the Latino mayors in this volume is that nearly all of them campaigned on themes that deemphasized their Latino ancestry (Barreto 2007). The successful electoral formula for the mayors covered in this volume included being able to mobilize a broad set of voters through a deracialized campaign. Henry Cisneros, for example, the first modern Mexican American mayor of a major U.S. city, toned down overt racial appeals and sought to build support across racial and ethnic lines. After his election in 2005, Los Angeles mayor Antonio Villaraigosa told reporters, "I don't want to be known as the Latino mayor. I want to be known as the mayor who happens to be Latino who made a difference" (National Public Radio 2005). In Chapter 6, Stefanie Chambers and Emily Farris quote Hartford mayor Eddie Perez as saying, "I wanted to run a campaign that would result in the election of a Latino mayor of a capital city—not a Latino mayor. . . . I wanted to represent everyone." In short, Latino mayors used a deracialized approach to leadership that deemphasized race and ethnicity (Hamilton 1977; McCormick and Jones 1993). They emphasized good government, efficiency, economic development, and other measures that promised benefits across racial and ethnic lines.

Overview of This Book

In Chapter 2, Carlos Cuéllar provides a descriptive overview of the cities where Latinos have served as mayors across states and geographic regions. His study is one of the first to systematically explore where and to what extent Latinos are represented in mayors' offices across the United States. Cuéllar shows that the large majority of Latino mayors have served in cities in the West and the Southwest. However, beginning in the mid-1990s, there was an increase in the number of cities with Latino mayors in the northeastern states of New Jersey, Connecticut, and Massachusetts. Cuéllar describes the institutional arrangements that Latino mayors typically face in city government. For example, his analysis shows that Latino mayors generally serve in cities that have mayor-council forms of government, at-large city-council-district elections, nonpartisan elections, relatively small council sizes, and no mayoral term limits. Cuéllar also describes the institutional arrangements in the cities governed by the Latino mayors covered in this volume and how they compare with those in other cities with Latino mayors.

In examining mayoral politics in San Antonio from 1950 through 2014 in Chapter 3, Heywood T. Sanders focuses on the political challenge Henry Cisneros and mayors who succeeded him faced as they governed in a system with limited authority. Henry Cisneros will long be remembered as a significant political figure. San Antonio has a manager-council form of government. Sanders concludes that Cisneros was "largely constrained" by the city manager and senior staffers. San Antonio's mayor and city council rely almost exclusively on the successful passage of voter-approved city bonds to generate public funds to support major economic development initiatives. The use of bond referenda allowed community organizations like Communities Organized for Public Service (COPS) to influence the outcome of the city government's economic development priorities. Cisneros was re-elected three times, but he declined to run for reelection in 1989. Sanders also discusses Ed Garza and Julián Castro, San Antonio's other Latino mayors, and shows how term limits further weakened the mayor's office and subsequently constrained Mayor Garza. However, Julián Castro was able to follow the pattern of Cisneros by translating a weak mayor's office into national publicity.

In Chapter 4, Robert R. Preuhs employs precinct-level voting data and exit polls to describe and compare Federico Peña's successful 1983 and 1987 elections as Denver's first Latino mayor. Preuhs shows that in 1983 and 1987, Peña was able to win election in a city where Latinos constituted less than 20 percent of the population because he built and sustained a strong electoral coalition consisting of Latinos, African Americans, liberal whites, labor, the gay community, environmentalists, and women. Preuhs explains that in both elections, Peña ran a deracialized campaign and worked to turn out black and Latino voters. Preuhs also provides an overview of Mayor Peña's approach to policy. Today, Latinos make up 32 percent of Denver's total population. Since Peña's two terms, Denver has not elected another Latino as mayor. Employing election returns, polling data, media accounts, and interviews with Peña and other Latino activists in Denver, Preuhs presents a potential model for success of Latino mayoral candidates in cities where Latinos are a minority of the population. Preuhs's election formula is based on the realities of mobilization and coalition building, as well as deracialized campaigns and policy advocacy.

In Chapter 5 on Mayor Antonio Villaraigosa of Los Angeles, Ellen Shiau demonstrates the strength of coalition politics and the potential of building a progressive urban movement. As Shiau explains, Los Angeles experienced a dramatic increase in the number of immigrants from Mexico and from Guatemala, El Salvador, and other Central American countries. Many of them worked in the city's growing service-sector industries and in the 1980s and 1990s became the target of extensive union organizing by the AFL-CIO and Hotel Employees and Restaurant Employees (HERE). Shiau situates Villaraigosa's 2005 election within the context of the growing mobilization in the 1990s of unions, civil rights groups, community organization, and faith organizations in support of immigrant rights, school funding, fair wages, public transportation, and affordable housing. Once he was in office, Mayor Villaraigosa worked to improve education, launched a major gang-reduction initiative, hired more police officers for crime-plagued communities, and led successful efforts to raise the sales tax to support the expansion of public transportation. Shiau describes Villaraigosa as a skillful politician who came into office with a strong track record for building coalitions. However, Shiau explains that the structural limitations of Los Angeles's mayoral position (the mayor's office is statutorily weak, and municipal governance is fragmented) limited Villaraigosa's ability to make substantial changes. Villaraigosa's shifting political alliances during his administration suggest that his governing coalition often collided with the policy demands of his electoral coalition.

In Chapter 6, Stefanie Chambers and Emily M. Farris explore the rise of the first two Latino mayors of Hartford, Eddie Perez and Pedro Segarra. These mayors led the city from 2001 through 2015, a period when Latinos made up over half of the city's population. Both Perez and Segarra were Puerto Rican leaders in a city where the majority of Latino residents are Puerto Rican. Because this community is relatively unexplored in the Latino politics literature, the examination of Latino mayors in Hartford affords important insights. Moreover, this chapter sheds light on the important role played by Latino community groups in urban politics and the way deracialized mayoral campaigns operate in Hartford. Chambers and Farris show that neither Perez nor Segarra was able to significantly alter the socioeconomic status of Hartford's Latinos during their administrations. Even with very different leadership styles and policy priorities, neither leader could transcend the larger obstacles the city faced.

In Chapter 7, Dario Moreno and Maria Ilcheva present a discussion of Latino mayoral politics in Miami-Dade County, the largest county in the United States with a majority Latino population. Miami has a unique two-tier structure of local government that assigns many of the functions usually reserved for municipal government to county government. Miami-Dade County is ruled by a county charter that establishes a federated form of government led by an elected executive, the mayor. Since 1996, both the city of Miami and Miami-Dade County have elected Cuban mayors. The prominent role played by Cuban Americans, who are considerably more conservative and more Republican than other Latinos, gives Miami politics some unique characteristics.

Miami's exceptionalism manifested itself in the 2011 mayoral race when Carlos Giménez was elected county mayor by riding the wave of a taxpayer revolt. Giménez's path to the mayoralty was significantly different from those of other Latino mayors. Miami-Dade County's previous two mayors, Alex Pinellas and Carlos Alvarez, were part of growth-machine coalitions, supported by the county's major economic interests. Giménez took advantage of one of the most tumultuous years in Miami politics and was elected after voters overwhelmingly voted to recall Mayor Alvarez. Moreno and Ilcheva argue that the recall was an indication that voters had grown tired of Miami-Dade County's traditional growth-machine policies. By focusing on the Latino mayor of a large urban county, this chapter illustrates the diversity of communities that Latino mayors govern in the United States.

In Chapter 8, we are joined by Emily M. Farris in an examination of Angel Taveras, who was elected in 2010 as the first Latino mayor of Providence, the capital of Rhode Island. Providence is the third-largest city in New England and one of the fastest-growing "new-destination" cities for Latino immigrants. Providence has sizable populations of Dominicans, Puerto Ricans, Guatemalans, Mexicans, and Salvadorans and is racially and ethnically diverse. Although Latino electoral participation has been hampered by large numbers of recent immigrants who have not yet become citizens, demographic trends make Latino dominance in city politics all but inevitable. The authors examine Taveras's election within the context of the city's political history. They also look at the governance issues Mayor Taveras confronted. Throughout his term as mayor, Taveras concentrated on eliminating a huge structural deficit in the city's budget. He had to close several public schools, many of which were located in predominantly Latino neighborhoods. Although Taveras was criticized for closing the schools, his willingness to tackle the city's budget crisis earned him broad citywide approval. Indeed, throughout his term as mayor, public opinion surveys consistently showed that he held the highest job approval rating among all the state's top elected officials. The examination of Mayor Taveras presents an interesting case of a Latino mayor struggling to address the challenges of municipal fiscal stress.

In the concluding Chapter 9, we synthesize and assess the issues and observations made in prior chapters and dig deeper into some of the central themes of the volume. For example, we discuss the relationship among demographic change, the election of Latino mayors, and community organizing. We emphasize that community organization and leadership within the Latino community play a vital role in mobilizing the growing number of Latino voters. The mayors covered in this volume, for the most part, used a deracialized electoral strategy to win their city's highest elected office. We discuss how a deracialized campaign strategy might position Latino mayors to build broad-based electoral coalitions. We also explore and discuss the context in which Latino mayors have emerged, paying special attention to the changing opportunity structure in the postindustrial city. Compared with mayors of the industrial era, Latino mayors' capacity to meet the expectations of their constituents is constrained by changes in the economy and by institutional limitations of the mayor's office. Finally, we speculate about the future role Latino mayors might play in forging a progressive national urban agenda around issues related to inequality.

REFERENCES

Abrajano, Marisa A., and R. Michael Alvarez. 2010. *New Faces, New Voices: The Hispanic Electorate in America*. Princeton, NJ: Princeton University Press.

Barber, Llana. 2017. *Latino City: Immigration and Urban Crisis in Lawrence, Massachusetts, 1945–2000*. Chapel Hill, North Carolina: University of North Carolina Press.

Barreto, Amilcar Antonio. 2006. "The Evolving State of Latino Politics in New England." In *Latinos in New England*, edited by Andrés Torres, 291–309. Philadelphia: Temple University Press.

Barreto, Matt. 2007. "¡*Sí Se Puede!* Latino Candidates and the Mobilization of Latino Voters." *American Political Science Review* 101, no. 3 (August): 425–441.

Barreto, Matt, and Gary Segura. 2014. *Latino America: How America's Most Dynamic Population Is Poised to Transform the Politics of the Nation*. New York: Public Affairs Books.

Beatty, Jack. 1992. *The Rascal King: The Life and Times of James Michael Curley, 1874–1958*. New York: Addison-Wesley Publishing.

Bluestone, Barry, and Bennett Harrison. 1984. *The Deindustrialization of America*. New York: Basic Books, 1984.

Browning, P. Rufus, Dale Rogers Marshall, and David H. Tabb. 1984. *Protest Is Not Enough: The Struggle of Blacks and Hispanics for Equality in Urban Politics*. Berkeley: University of California Press.

———. 2003. "Can People of Color Achieve Equality in City Government? The Setting and the Issues." In *Racial Politics in American Cities*, edited by Rufus P. Browning, Dale Rogers Marshall and David H. Tabb, 3–16, New York: Longman Press.

Burns, Peter F. 2006. *Electoral Politics Is Not Enough: Racial and Ethnic Minorities and Urban Politics*. Albany: State University of New York Press.

Chudacoff, Howard P., and Judith E. Smith. 1988. *The Evolution of American Urban Society*. 3rd ed. Englewood Cliffs, NJ: Prentice Hall.

Clarke, Susan E., Rodney E. Hero, Mara S. Sidney, Luis R. Fraga, and Bari A. Erlichson. 2006. *Multiethnic Moments: The Politics of Urban Education Reform*. Philadelphia: Temple University Press.

Colburn, David R., and Jeffrey S. Adler, eds. 2001. *African-American Mayors: Race, Politics, and the American City*. Urbana: University of Illinois Press.

Dawson, Michael. 1994. *Behind the Mule: Race and Class in African-American Politics*. Princeton. NJ: Princeton University Press.

de la Garza, Rudolfo O., Louis DeSipio, F. Chris Garcia, John Garcia, and Angelo Falcon. 1992. *Latino Voices: Mexican, Puerto Rican, and Cuban Perspectives*. Boulder, CO: Westview Press.

DeSipio, Louis. 1996. *Counting on the Latino Vote: Latinos as the New Electorate*. Charlottesville: University Press of Virginia.

Dreier, Peter. 2007. "Community Organizing for What? Progressive Politics and Movement Building in America." In *Transforming the City: Community Organizing and the Challenge of Political Change*, edited by Marion Orr, 218–251. Lawrence: University Press of Kansas.

Ehrenhalt, Alan. 2013. *The Great Inversion and the Future of the American City*. New York: Vintage Books.

Eisinger, Peter K. 1980. *The Politics of Displacement: Racial and Ethnic Transition in Three American Cities*. New York: Academic Press.

———. 1982. "Black Employment in Municipal Jobs: The Impact of Black Political Power." *American Political Science Review* 76:380–392.

Erie, Steven P. 1988. *Rainbow's End: Irish Americans and the Dilemmas of Urban Machine Politics, 1840–1985*. Berkeley: University of California Press.

Fainstein, Susan S., Norman I. Fainstein, Richard C. Hill, Dennis Judd, and Michael Smith. 1986. *Restructuring the City: The Political Economy of Urban Redevelopment*. New York: Longman.

Filandra, Alexandra, and Marion Orr. 2013. "Anxieties of an Ethnic Transition: The Election of the First Latino Mayor in Providence, Rhode Island." *Urban Affairs Review* 49 (January): 3–31.

Flanagan, Richard. M. 2004. *Mayors and the Challenge of Urban Leadership*. New York: University Press of America.

Florida, Richard. 2002. *The Rise of the Creative Class: And How It's Transforming Work, Leisure, Community and Everyday Life*. New York: Basic Books.

Fraga, Luis Ricardo, and Ann Frost. 2011. "Democratic Institutions, Public Engagement, and Latinos in American Public Schools." In *Public Engagement for Public Education*, edited by Marion Orr and John Rogers, 117–138. Stanford, CA: Stanford University Press.

Fraga, Luis Ricardo, John A. Garcia, Rodney E. Hero, Michael Jones-Correa, Valerie Martinez-Ebers, and Gary M. Segura. 2010. *Latino Lives in America: Making It Home*. Philadelphia: Temple University Press.

———. 2012. *Latinos in the New Millennium*. New York: Cambridge University Press.

Freeman, Lance. 2006. *There Goes the 'Hood: Views on Gentrification from the Ground Up*. Philadelphia: Temple University Press.

Friesema, H. Paul. 1969. "Black Control of Central Cities: The Hollow Prize." *American Institute of Planners Journal* 35 (March): 75–79.

Frug, Gerald F., and David J. Barron. 2008. *City Bound: How States Stifle Urban Innovation*. Ithaca, NY: Cornell University Press.

Fry, Richard. 2008. *Latino Settlement in the New Century*. Washington, DC: Pew Hispanic Center.

Garcia, F. Chris, and Gabriel R. Sanchez. 2008. *Hispanics and the U.S. Political System: Moving into the Mainstream.* Upper Saddle River, NJ: Prentice Hall.

Garcia, John A. 2011. *Latino Politics in America: Community, Culture, and Interests.* Lanham, MD: Rowman and Littlefield.

García Bedolla, Lisa. 2014. *Latino Politics.* Malden, MA: Polity Press.

Hamilton, Charles V. 1977. "Deracialization: Examination of a Political Strategy." *First World* 1, no. 2:3–5.

Harrigan, John J., and Ronald K. Vogel. 2000. *Political Change in the Metropolis.* 6th ed. New York: Longman.

Henig, Jeffrey R., Richard C. Hula, Marion Orr, and Desiree Pedescleaux. 1999. *The Color of School Reform: Race, Politics, and the Challenge of Urban Education.* Princeton, NJ: Princeton University Press.

Henig, Jeffrey R., and Wilbur C. Rich, eds. 2004. *Mayors in the Middle: Politics, Race, and Mayoral Control of Urban Schools.* Princeton, NJ: Princeton University Press.

Hero, Rodney E. 1992. *Latinos and the U.S. Political System: Two-Tiered Pluralism.* Philadelphia: Temple University Press.

———. 2007. *Racial Diversity and Social Capital: Equality and Community in America.* New York: Cambridge University Press.

Hero, Rodney E., F. Chris Garcia, John Garcia, and Harry Pachon. 2000. "Latino Participation, Partisanship, and Office Holding." *PS: Political Science and Politics* 33, no. 3 (September): 529–534.

Heying, Charles H. 1997. "Civic Elites and Corporate Delocalization." *American Behavioral Scientist* 40:657–688.

Holmes, Robert A. 2011. *Maynard Jackson: A Biography.* Miami: Barnhardt and Ashe.

Horak, Martin, Juliet Musso, Ellen Shiau, Robert P. Stoker, and Clarence N. Stone. 2015. "Change Afoot." In *Urban Neighborhoods in a New Era: Revitalization Politics in the Postindustrial City,* edited by Clarence N. Stone and Robert P. Stoker, 1–32. Chicago: University of Chicago Press.

Hyra, Derek S. 2008. *The New Urban Renewal: The Economic Transformation of Harlem and Bronzeville.* Chicago: University of Chicago Press.

Itzigsohn, José. 2009. *Encountering American Faultlines: Race, Class, and the Dominican Experience in Providence.* New York: Russell Sage Foundation.

Jennings, James, and Monte Rivera, eds. 1984. *Puerto Rican Politics in the United States.* Westport, CT: Greenwood Press.

Jones, Bryan D., Saadia R. Greenberg, Clifford Kaufman, and Joseph Drew Source. 1978. "Service Delivery Rules and the Distribution of Local Government Services: Three Detroit Bureaucracies." *Journal of Politics* 40, no. 2 (May): 332–368.

Jones-Correa, Michael. 1998. *Between Two Nations: The Political Predicament of Latinos in New York City.* Ithaca, NY: Cornell University Press.

Judd, Dennis R., and Todd Swanstrom. 2006. *City Politics: The Political Economy of Urban America.* New York: Pearson-Longman.

Kantor, Paul. 1995. *The Dependent City Revisited: The Political Economy of Urban Development and Social Policy.* Boulder, CO: Westview Press.

Karnig, Albert, and Susan Welch. 1989. *Black Representation and Urban Policy.* Chicago: University of Chicago Press.

Katz, Bruce, and Jennifer Bradley. 2013. *Metropolitan Revolution.* Washington, DC: Brookings Institution.

Keller, Edmond J. 1978. "The Impact of Black Mayors on Urban Policy." *Annals of the American Academy of Political and Social Science* 439 (September): 40–52.

Ladd, Helen, and John Yinger. 1989. *America's Ailing Cities: Fiscal Health and the Design of Urban Policy*. Baltimore: Johns Hopkins University Press.

Lemann, Nicholas. 1991. *The Promised Land: The Great Migration and How It Changed America*. New York: Alfred A. Knopf.

Levine, Myron A. 2015. *Urban Politics: Cities and Suburbs in a Global Age*. New York: Routledge Publishers.

Maurrasse, David J. 2001. *Beyond the Campus: How Colleges and Universities Form Partnerships with Their Communities*. New York: Routledge.

McCormick, Joseph P., II, and Charles E. Jones. 1993. "The Conceptualization of Deracialization." In *Dilemmas of Black Politics: Issues of Leadership and Strategy*, edited by Georgia A. Persons, 66–84. New York: HarperCollins.

Mollenkopf, John H. 1983. *The Contested City*. Princeton, NJ: Princeton University Press.

Morel, Domingo. 2018. *Takeover: Race, Education, and Democracy*. New York: Oxford University Press.

National Association of Latino Elected Officials. 2010. "Roster of Latino Elected Officials." http://www.naleo.org/.

National Public Radio. 2005. "L.A. Mayor-Elect Antonio Villaraigosa." May 19, 2005. http://www.npr.org/templates/story. Accessed January 31, 2017.

Nelson, William E. 1990. "Black Mayoral Leadership: A Twenty-Year Perspective." *National Political Science Review* 2:188–195

Nelson, William E., and Phillip Meranto. 1977. *Electing Black Mayors: Political Action in the Black Community*. Columbus: Ohio State University Press.

Orr, Marion. 1999. *Black Social Capital: The Politics of School Reform in Baltimore, 1986–1999*. Lawrence: University Press of Kansas.

———, ed. 2007. *Transforming the City: Community Organizing and Challenge of Political Change*. Lawrence: University Press of Kansas.

Orr, Marion, and John Rogers, eds. 2011. *Public Engagement for Public Education: Joining Forces to Revitalize Democracy and Equalize Schools*. Stanford, CA: Stanford University Press.

Orr, Marion, Kenneth K. Wong, Emily Farris, and Domingo Morel. 2016. "Latino Public School Engagement and Political Socialization." In *Urban Citizenship and American Democracy*, edited by Amy Bridges and Michael Javen Fortner, 93–123. Albany: State University of New York Press.

Persons, Georgia A. 1993. "Black Mayoralties and the New Black Politics: From Insurgency to Racial Reconciliation." In *Dilemmas of Black Politics: Issues of Leadership and Strategy*, edited by Georgia A. Persons, 38–65. New York: HarperCollins.

Peterson, Paul. 1981. *City Limits*. Chicago: University of Chicago Press.

Pew Research Center. 2013. "Hispanics of Dominican Origin in the United States, 2011." http://www.pewhispanic.org/files/2013/06/DominicanFactsheet.pdf.

Preston, Michael B. 1976. "Limitations of Black Urban Power: The Case of Black Mayors." In *The New Urban Politics*, edited by Louis H. Masotti and Robert L. Lineberry, 111–131. Cambridge, MA: Ballinger.

———. 1990. "Big-City Black Mayors: An Overview." *National Political Science Review* 2:131–137.

Preston, Michael B., Lenneal J. Henderson Jr., and Paul L. Puryear. 1987. *The New Black Politics: The Search for Political Power*. New York: Longman.

Rae, Douglas W. 2003. *City: Urbanism and Its End*. New Haven, CT: Yale University Press.

Reed, Adolph, Jr. 1988. "The Black Urban Regime: Structural Origins and Constraints." In *Stirrings in the Jug: Black Politics in the Post-segregation Era*, edited by Adolph Reed Jr., 79–115. Minneapolis: University of Minnesota Press.

Rich, Wilbur C. 1989. *Coleman Young and Detroit Politics*. Detroit: Wayne State University Press.

———. 1996. *Black Mayors and School Politics: The Failure of Reform in Detroit, Gary, and Newark*. New York: Garland Press.

———. 2007. *David Dinkins and New York City Politics: Race, Images, and the Media*. Albany: State University of New York Press.

Rodin, Judith. 2007. *The University and Urban Revival*. Philadelphia: University of Pennsylvania Press.

Salisbury, Robert. 1964. "Urban Politics: The New Convergence of Power." *Journal of Politics* 26, no. 4 (November): 775–797.

Saltzstein, Grace Hall. 1989. "Black Mayors and Police Policies." *Journal of Politics* 51, no. 3 (August): 525–544.

Sanchez, Gabriel R. 2006. "The Role of Group Consciousness in Political Participation among Latinos in the United States." *American Politics Research* 34, no. 4:427–451.

Sassen, Saskia. 2001. *The Global City: New York, London, Tokyo*. Princeton, NJ: Princeton University Press.

Savitch, H. V. 1988. *Post-industrial Cities: Politics and Planning in New York, Paris, and London*. Princeton, NJ: Princeton University Press.

Shingles, Richard. 1981. "Black Consciousness and Political Participation: The Missing Link." *American Political Science Review* 75:76–91.

Silber Mohamed, Heather. 2014. "Can Protests Make Latinos 'American'? Identity, Immigration Politics, and the 2006 Marches." *American Politics Research* 41, no. 2:298–327.

———. 2017. *The New Americans? Immigration, Protest, and the Politics of Latino Identity*. Lawrence: University Press of Kansas.

Sonenshein, Raphael J. 1993. *Politics in Black and White: Race and Power in Los Angeles*. Princeton, NJ: Princeton University Press.

———. 2003. "Post-incorporation Politics in Los Angeles." In *Racial Politics in American Cities*, edited by Rufus P. Browning, Dale Rogers Marshall, and David H. Tabb, 52–76. New York: Longman.

Stoker, Robert P., Clarence N. Stone, and Martin Horak. 2015. "Contending with Structural Inequality in a New Era." In *Urban Neighborhoods in a New Era: Revitalization Politics in the Postindustrial City*, edited by Clarence N. Stone and Robert P. Stoker, 209–249. Chicago: University of Chicago Press.

Stone, Clarence N. 1976. Economic Growth and Neighborhood Discontent: System Bias in the Urban Renewal Program of Atlanta. Chapel Hill, N.C.: University of North Carolina Press.

———. 1989. *Regime Politics: Governing Atlanta, 1946–1988*. Lawrence: University Press of Kansas.

Stone, Clarence N., and Heywood T. Sanders, eds. 1987. *The Politics of Urban Development*. Lawrence: University Press of Kansas.

Stone, Clarence N., and Robert P. Stoker, eds. 2015. *Urban Neighborhoods in a New Era: Revitalization Politics in the Postindustrial City*. Chicago: University of Chicago Press.

Su, Celina. 2009. *Streetwise for Book Smarts: Grassroots Organizing and Education Reform in the Bronx*. Ithaca, NY: Cornell University Press.

Teaford, Jon C. 1990. *The Rough Road to Renaissance: Urban Revitalization in America, 1940–1985*. Baltimore: Johns Hopkins University Press.

Thompson, J. Phillip, III. 2006. *Double Trouble: Black Mayors, Black Communities, and the Call for a Deep Democracy*. New York: Oxford University Press.

Torres, Andrés, ed. 2006. *Latinos in New England*. Philadelphia: Temple University Press.

Trounstine, Jessica. 2008. *Political Monopolies in American Cities: The Rise and Fall of Bosses and Reformers*. Chicago: University of Chicago Press.

Viteritti, Joseph P., ed. 2009. *When Mayors Take Charge: School Governance in the City*. Washington, DC: Brookings Institution.

Walton, Hanes, Jr. 1971. *Black Politics: A Theoretical and Structural Analysis*. Philadelphia: J. B. Lippincott.

Welch, Susan. 1990. The Impact of At-Large Elections on the Representation of Blacks and Hispanics." *Journal of Politics* 52, no. 4 (November): 1050–1076.

Whelan, Robert K., Alma H. Young, and Mickey Lauria. 1994. "Urban Regimes and Racial Politics in New Orleans." *Journal of Urban Affairs* 16, no. 1:1–21.

Wilkerson, Isabel. 2010. *The Warmth of Other Suns: The Epic Story of America's Great Migration*. New York: Vintage Books.

Wilson, William J. 1996. *When Work Disappears: The World of the New Urban Poor*. New York: Vintage Books.

Wong, Kenneth K., Francis X. Shen, Dorothea Anagnostopoulos, and Stacey Rutledge. 2007. *The Education Mayor: Improving America's Schools*. Washington, DC: Georgetown University Press.

Young, Coleman, and Lonnie Wheeler. 1994. *Hard Stuff: The Autobiography of Mayor Coleman Young*. New York: Viking Press.

2

Patterns of Representation

A Descriptive Analysis of Latino-Mayor Cities in the United States

CARLOS E. CUÉLLAR

EDITORS' NOTE

The descriptive analysis provided in this chapter delineates key patterns in the demographic and political context of Latino-mayor cities in the United States, such as how Latino mayoral representation has changed over time, where Latino mayors currently serve, and under what conditions they govern. Patterns of Latino mayoral representation from 1984 to 2016 show an 81 percent increase in the number of Latino mayors overall. The largest growth in Latino representation, particularly during the decade from 2006 to 2016, occurred in the South and the Northeast of the United States, including the states of Florida, New Jersey, and Rhode Island. Although Latinos' numerical strength is a key characteristic of cities with Latino mayors, the data in this chapter reveal that several Latino mayors govern in varying demographic contexts. That is, a substantial number of Latino mayors govern in cities where Latinos are not dominant or where no racial or ethnic group is dominant.

Mayors do not operate in a vacuum. There are structural dynamics that affect and shape the scope and nature of mayoral leadership. For example, Carlos Cuéllar shows that Latino mayors typically govern in cities with a council-manager form of government (57 percent of Latino mayors), at-large city councils (78 percent), no term limits for elected city leaders (only 14 percent have term limits), and nonpartisan elections (only 3 percent have partisan elections). As several of the authors in this volume explain, in a council-manager system, mayors are not especially powerful. These institutional arrangements have implications

not only for why Latinos are represented in the mayoralty but also for how La-
tino mayors govern to address problems in their city.

Since Browning, Marshall, and Tabb's (1984) innovative study of minority political incorporation, scholars have sought to explain how
and why racial and ethnic minorities have gained influence in the
American federal system. A major focus of subsequent work has been the
causes and consequences of minority descriptive representation in Congress,
state legislatures, city councils, school boards, and bureaucracies. Although the collective scholarship on representation has made substantial
contributions to the discipline, one major limitation is that no systematic
study of Latino mayors exists to date. This is a key limitation given how
important representation at this level of government can be for Latinos,
a large and expanding ethnic group seeking to become further politically
incorporated. For example, the research suggests not only that mayors are
central to the policy-making process, but also that minority mayors (African Americans) can have a positive influence on minority (African
American) communities and their incorporation into the political sphere
(Eisinger 1982; Marschall and Shah 2005; Stein 2003; Trounstine 2009).

The existing research on Latino mayors has primarily focused on explaining electoral outcomes (e.g., racial/ethnic voting patterns, turnout, and
vote choice) in races with one notable Latino candidate in a select number
of cities, including San Antonio, Denver, Los Angeles, New York, and Miami
(Barreto, Villarreal, and Woods 2005; Hero 1987; Kaufmann 2003; Muñoz
and Henry 1990; Sonenshein and Pinkus 2002). Typically, these case studies center on notable "first" Latino mayors (Barreto 2007; Geron 2005; Rosales 2000). What is needed, however, is an extensive study of the general
patterns of Latino mayoral representation on a national scale. That the data
needed to examine the state of Latino representation in U.S. mayoralties
are vast and disaggregated could explain the lack of systematic analysis. However, the absence of such studies has also prevented key questions about
Latino descriptive representation from being empirically examined, such
as the following: Who are the most notable Latino mayors? How many Latino mayors are there? How many have ever served? Where have they
served? Under what conditions do they govern? Examining Latino descriptive representation is one of the essential topics of Latino politics because
the "who," "what," and "where" questions about descriptive representation
provide a basis for evaluating the extent to which it matters in addressing
Latinos' symbolic and substantive interests. Answering these questions will
also help determine how healthy American democracy is. That is, knowing
the extent to which Latinos are represented in the mayoralty will show what

progress has been made since language minorities were protected under the Voting Rights Act and how much work remains to be done.

The research in this chapter provides an empirical description of the landscape of Latino mayoralties. It begins by describing the extent to which Latinos have gained representation in the mayoralty from 1984 to 2016, using data provided by the National Association of Latino Elected and Appointed Officials (NALEO). The findings show steady but incremental growth of Latino mayoralties over thirty-three years, but the most interesting trend is that most of the growth is taking place in regions outside the Southwest. After the time-series analysis, an overview is presented of the contemporary geographic distribution of Latino-mayor cities. This will help readers visualize where Latino mayors served across the nation in 2016. Data from the U.S. Census Bureau are also presented to highlight the various racial and ethnic demographic attributes of contemporary Latino-mayor cities. The data reveal that Latinos are considerably influential or outright dominant in population size in contemporary Latino-mayor cities. However, not all Latino mayors serve in Latino-majority demographic contexts. The chapter illustrates where these multiethnic or nonmajority contexts are located.

Given the emphasis in the previous research on the influence of institutional governing arrangements, data from the International City/County Management Association (ICMA) and other sources are used to empirically describe the typical institutional context under which contemporary Latino mayors govern. The results show that Latino-mayor cities' institutional structures and governing arrangements are not very different from those of a typical American city. It is worth noting, however, that in Latino-mayor cities, on average, 45 percent of city council seats are filled by Latinos. The implications of these findings are explored further in this chapter. Finally, special attention is paid to highlighting the demographic and institutional context of the case studies in this volume to provide some guidance to readers on the chapters ahead. These case studies not only highlight the politics and policies of postindustrial cities in America but also provide key insights about the future of American politics at different stages of demographic and political diversity. For example, Latinos are only approximately 19 percent of the voting eligible population in Denver. In Providence and Los Angeles, Latinos are slightly more populous; these cities' voting eligible Latinos make up approximately 30 percent of the population. Latinos are considerably more populous in Hartford, San Antonio, and Miami-Dade County. Thus the politics and policies of these distinct cases surrounding the success of Latino mayors can highlight where the United States is heading politically.

Patterns of Latino Mayoral
Representation Over Time

To empirically describe patterns of Latino mayoral representation over time, this section relies on directories of Latino elected officials published yearly from 1984 to 2016 by the National Association of Latino Elected and Appointed Officials (NALEO). In particular, these sources are used to generate a yearly count of the total number of Latino mayors serving in office. The data in Figure 2.1 show the incremental change in the number of Latino mayors spanning three decades. During the first decade, from 1984 to 1994, the average number of Latino mayors was 166. During the second decade, from 1995 to 2005, the average number of Latino mayors increased by 30 percent, to 214. From 2006 to 2016, the average number of Latino mayors increased by 11.2 percent, to 237. Although the growth of Latino mayors during the most recent decade (2006–2016) was not as large as during the decade before (1995–2005), Latino mayoral representation has steadily increased over time. However, if we compare the number of Latino mayors from 1984, the earliest year with available NALEO data, to 2016, the latest year with available NALEO data, the change is quite stark. During this thirty-three-year period, there was an 81.3 percent increase in the number of Latino mayors. This evidences that Latinos' political strength in municipal government has increased over time, at least by one measure: descriptive representation in the city's top executive office.

When the yearly count of Latino mayors in key southwestern states, including Arizona, California, Colorado, New Mexico, and Texas, is isolated, the data in Figure 2.1 reveal not only that a vast majority (83.3 percent) of Latino mayors are consistently located in these states, but also that the growth in the average number of Latino mayors between the first decade (1984–1994) and the second (1995–2005) is quite similar to the national trend. The data in Figure 2.1 further show that from 1984 to 1994, the average number of Latino mayors in southwestern states was 153. From 1995 to 2005, the average number of Latino mayors in the Southwest increased by 29.2 percent, to 197. From 2006 to 2016, the average number of Latino mayors in the Southwest increased by 5.2 percent, to 207. This is a point of departure from the 11.2 percent increase in the same decade at the national level, suggesting that much of the growth in Latino mayoralties during this period occurred outside the Southwest.

The data in Figure 2.2 show the average number of Latino mayors from 1984 to 2016 in the western,[1] midwestern,[2] southern,[3] and northeastern[4] states. In the West and the Midwest, the average number of Latino may-

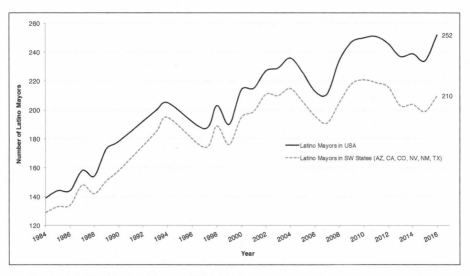

Figure 2.1 Total Latino Mayors, 1984–2016
Source: National Association of Latino Elected and Appointed Officials (NALEO).

ors was 3.1 and 3.3, respectively. Although these regions have a modest count of Latino mayors over the thirty-three years, a statistic worth noting is that the western region quadrupled the number of Latino mayors from 2006 to 2016. The most interesting patterns of Latino mayoral representation according to Figure 2.2 are in the northeastern and southern states.

Over a thirty-three-year period, the Northeast saw the number of Latino mayors increase from zero in 1984 to fourteen in 2016, an average increase of 4.35 Latino mayors for three consecutive decades. The South (not including the state of Texas) has experienced the largest increase in the number of Latino mayors of any of the four regions outside the Southwest, tripling its number of Latino mayors from 1984 to 2016. It is important to note that the South experienced an 83 percent increase in the average number of Latino mayors from one decade (1995–2005) to the next (2006–2016). Thus the strongest growth of Latino mayoral representation in the South occurred in the past ten years. Although the South and the Northeast have a modest number of Latino mayors compared with the Southwest, these regions have seen substantial gains in Latino mayoral representation and should not be dismissed from further study.

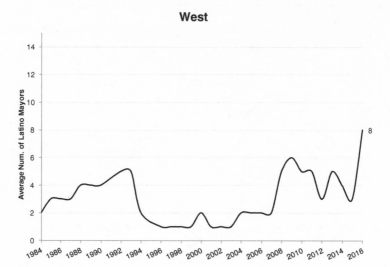

West

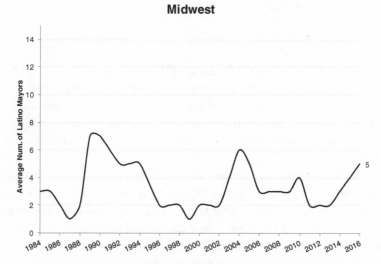

Midwest

West: ID, MT, OR, WA, WY, UT, HI, AK
Midwest: ND, SD, NE, KS, MN, IA, MO, WI, IL, IN, MI, OH, OK
Northeast: PA, NY, NJ, CT, RI, MA, VT, NH, ME
South: AR, LA, MS, AL, TN, KY, WV, VA, MD, DE, NC, SC, GA, FL, Washington, DC

Figure 2.2 Latino Mayors by U.S. Region, 1984–2016 (Excluding Southwestern States)
Source: National Association of Latino Elected and Appointed Officials (NALEO).

Northeast

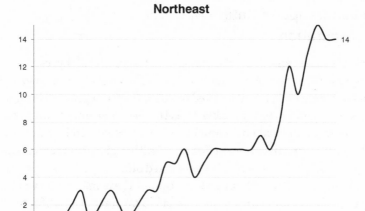

South

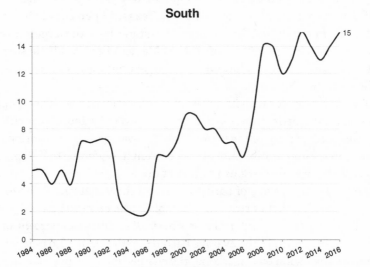

The Landscape of Latino Mayoral Representation

To provide some context on the status of Latino mayoral representation in the United States, the data in Table 2.1 show the level of government where 6,176 Latino elected officials served in 2016, from Congress to local school boards. A notable pattern in Table 2.1 is that 94.4 percent of Latino elected officials served in local government, 5.1 percent served in state government, and 0.5 percent served in Congress. Although Latino representation clearly has a local tilt, only 252 Latino elected officials, or 4.1 percent, served as city mayors in 2016. About 76.2 percent of these mayors served in municipalities located in three states: Texas (37.7 percent), California (24.6 percent), and New Mexico (13.9 percent). Texas and California are the states with the largest sheer number of Latinos in the country. The 2010 decennial census statistics indicate that approximately 14 million Latinos live in California and 9.5 million Latinos live in Texas, 47 percent of the Latino population in the United States. These two states have the largest proportion of Latinos in their states after New Mexico. Thus it is little surprise that Texas and California produce the largest number of Latino mayors in the country.

Table 2.2 provides insight on the characteristics of the Latino population in Latino-mayor cities. On average, Latinos in Latino-mayor cities in 2016 were 69.2 percent of the population. The average city-level Latino population ranges from a minimum of 10.2 percent in Wyoming to 79.7 percent in Texas. Besides the obvious point that on average, Latino-mayor cities have high concentrations of Latinos, the data show that variability exists. Table 2.2 also highlights two other notable patterns in the data. First, in Latino-mayor cities located in the Southwest (i.e., where 83 percent of Latino mayors are found), the average Latino population is 68.6 percent, the highest of any region by far. Second, the change in Latino population from 2000 to 2010 was much higher in Latino-mayor cities located in regions outside the Southwest, particularly in the South and Northeast. In these regions, the average change in the Latino population from 2000 to 2010 was 15.1 and 10.2 percentage points, respectively. Compared with an increase of only 1.2 percentage points in the Latino population in the Southwest from 2000 to 2010, this is quite remarkable and indicates that Latinos' numerical strength has increased in southern and northeastern municipalities that had Latino mayors in 2016.

Mayoralties are like state gubernatorial offices in that only one person serves in the post for a predefined term length; therefore, there can be only as many mayors as there are cities in the United States at a specific time.

TABLE 2.1 LATINO ELECTED OFFICIALS BY LEVEL OF GOVERNMENT, 2016

State	Total Latino elected officials (LEOs) Num.	%	Congress Num.	State gov't Num.	County gov't Num.	School board Num.	Other local office Num.	Muni gov't (except mayor) Num.	Total Latino mayors Num.	%	Latino (male) mayors Num.	%	Latina (female) mayors Num.	%
Arizona	349	5.7	2	20	21	145	53	97	11	4.4	9	82	2	18
California	*1,426*	*23.1*	*10*	*24*	*33*	*752*	*198*	*347*	*62*	*24.6*	*49*	*79*	*13*	*21*
Colorado	163	2.6	0	11	24	39	24	58	7	2.8	4	57	3	43
Florida	172	2.8	4	22	13	0	53	66	14	5.6	11	79	3	21
Idaho	14	0.2	1	0	0	7	1	4	1	0.4	0	0	1	100
Illinois	115	1.9	1	14	10	14	20	52	4	1.6	4	100	0	0
Massachusetts	51	0.8	0	6	0	18	1	25	1	0.4	1	100	0	0
Maryland	18	0.3	0	6	2	2	0	7	1	0.4	0	0	1	100
New Jersey	145	2.3	2	10	9	46	1	69	8	3.2	7	88	1	13
New Mexico	*683*	*11.1*	*2*	*50*	*103*	*147*	*157*	*189*	*35*	*13.9*	*27*	*77*	*8*	*23*
New York	170	2.8	2	23	8	40	46	50	1	0.4	1	100	0	0
Ohio	14	0.2	0	2	3	3	0	5	1	0.4	0	0	1	100
Pennsylvania	21	0.3	0	2	0	6	5	6	2	0.8	2	100	0	0
Rhode Island	18	0.3	0	6	0	1	0	9	2	0.8	2	100	0	0
Texas	*2,498*	*40.4*	*6*	*43*	*287*	*1,050*	*501*	*516*	*95*	*37.7*	*69*	*73*	*26*	*27*
Utah	10	0.2	0	5	0	1	0	3	1	0.4	1	100	0	0
Washington	46	0.7	1	3	0	14	0	24	4	1.6	2	50	2	50
Wyoming	10	0.2	0	2	1	1	0	4	2	0.8	2	100	0	0
Other states	253	4.1	1	66	16	58	37	75	0	0.0	0	0	0	0
United States	6,176		32	315	530	2,344	1,097	1,606	252		191		61	
Percentage of LEOs			0.5%	5.1%	8.6%	38.0%	17.8%	26.0%	4.1%		76%		24%	

Source: NALEO (2016).

TABLE 2.2 LATINO POPULATION CHARACTERISTICS IN LATINO-MAYOR CITIES BY STATE, 2016

	Latino-mayor cities, 2016	Avg. city-level Latino pop., 2000 (%)	Avg. city-level Latino pop., 2010 (%)	Avg. Latino pop. change, 2000–2010 (%)	Min. Latino pop. change, 2000–2010 (%)	Max. Latino pop. change, 2000–2010 (%)
Arizona	11	70.9	69.5	−1.4	−16.4	9.6
California	62	63.3	67.2	3.9	−15.7	16.0
Colorado	7	59.1	61.1	2.0	−4.5	6.4
New Mexico	35	65.9	65.4	−0.4	−11.2	12.2
Texas	95	77.5	79.7	2.1	−22.0	17.1
Southwest	*210*	*67.3*	*68.6*	*1.2*	*−14.0*	*12.2*
Illinois	4	37.1	47.8	10.8	2.5	21.4
Ohio	1	9.8	14.2	4.4	4.4	4.4
Midwest	*5*	*23.4*	*31.0*	*7.6*	*3.4*	*12.9*
Florida	14	53.6	64.5	8.5	4.2	19.7
Maryland	1	23.6	45.3	21.6	21.6	21.6
South	*15*	*38.6*	*54.9*	*15.1*	*12.9*	*20.7*
Massachusetts	1	59.7	73.8	14.1	14.1	14.1
New Jersey	8	44.1	52.8	8.7	−0.7	17.7
New York	1	19.9	26.4	6.6	6.6	6.6
Pennsylvania	2	9.3	20.4	11.1	10.5	11.7
Rhode Island	2	38.9	49.2	10.3	8.1	12.5
Northeast	*14*	*34.4*	*44.5*	*10.2*	*7.7*	*12.5*
Utah	1	11.3	13.4	2.1	2.1	2.1
Washington	4	68.7	75.0	6.3	2.9	8.0
Wyoming	2	6.7	10.2	3.5	2.0	5.0
Idaho	1	76.4	75.9	−0.5	−0.5	−0.5
West	*8*	*40.8*	*43.6*	*2.9*	*1.6*	*3.6*
Total	252	66.0	69.2	3.1	−22.0	21.6

Sources: NALEO (2016); 2010 U.S. Census.

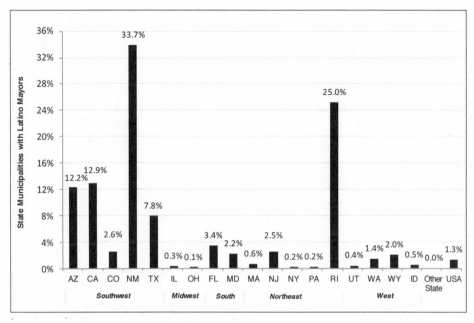

Figure 2.3 State Municipalities with Latino Mayors, 2016
Source: NALEO (2016); U.S. Census Bureau's 2014 American Community Survey.

To assess the extent to which each state has Latino mayoral representation, Figure 2.3 shows the percentage of incorporated cities that had a Latino mayor in 2016. Overall, a mere 1.3 percent of 19,411 incorporated cities in the United States had a Latino mayor.[5] By this metric, the election of Latino mayors is a rare occurrence. New Mexico has the highest share of municipalities—33.7 percent—represented by a Latino mayor ($N=104$). In Rhode Island, 25 percent of municipalities had a Latino mayor in 2016. Although Rhode Island has few incorporated cities ($N=8$) compared with other states, no other state (except New Mexico) comes close to the share of the state's cities represented by Latinos. All other states seem to have a trivial level of Latino mayoral representation. For example, in California, only 12.9 percent ($N=480$) of its municipalities have Latino mayors; in Arizona, 12.2 percent ($N=90$); and in Texas, 7.8 percent ($N=1,211$).

Figure 2.4 provides a visual illustration of the distinct patterns of Latino mayoral representation within and across U.S. states. In Texas, most of the Latino mayors serve in the southern half of the state, with a distinct concentration in the Rio Grande valley. In addition, Texas has Latino mayors serving along the Texas–New Mexico border, from El Paso to the Panhandle. In New Mexico, Latino mayors cover virtually the entire state. Arizona's Latino mayors are concentrated in the southern part of the state, from the

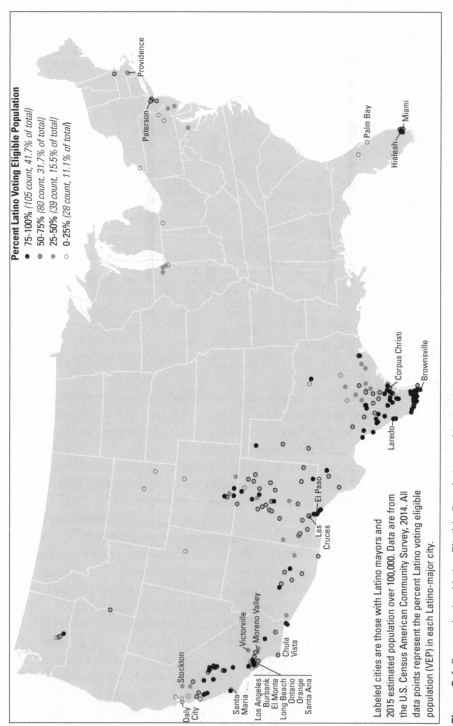

Percent Latino Voting Eligible Population

- ● 75-100% *(105 count, 41.7% of total)*
- ◕ 50-75% *(80 count, 31.7% of total)*
- ◔ 25-50% *(39 count, 15.5% of total)*
- ○ 0-25% *(28 count, 11.1% of total)*

Providence

Paterson

Palm Bay

Hialeah — Miami

Corpus Christi

Brownsville

Laredo

Las Cruces

El Paso

Victorville

Moreno Valley

Chula Vista

Stockton

Santa Maria

Los Angeles
Burbank
El Monte
Long Beach
Ontario
Orange
Santa Ana

Daly City

Labeled cities are those with Latino mayors and 2015 estimated population over 100,000. Data are from the U.S. Census American Community Survey, 2014. All data points represent the percent Latino voting eligible population (VEP) in each Latino-major city.

Figure 2.4 Percent Latino Voting Eligible Population and Latino Mayors

Sources: NALEO (2016); voting eligible population (VEP) compiled from the U.S. Census Bureau's 2014 American Community Survey.

Phoenix metro area to the U.S.-Mexico border. California has Latino mayors covering a large swath of the state. Latino mayors serve in California cities as far north as Daly City and as far south as Chula Vista, which is located near the U.S.-Mexico border. In Colorado, nearly all Latino mayors are concentrated in the southern part of the state, near the border with New Mexico. There are pockets of Latino mayors outside the Southwest, primarily in New Jersey and Florida. The 2016 Latino-mayor cities in New Jersey included Passaic, Paterson, Perth Amboy, and West New York. The Latino-mayor cities in southern Florida are clustered around the Miami metro area.

To further illustrate the political context in which Latino mayors govern, Figure 2.4 describes the percent Latino eligible voter population in each Latino-mayor city in 2016. The U.S. Census Bureau's 2014 American Community Survey five-year estimates were used to differentiate the political strength of Latinos into four categories: "minimally" influential (0–25 percent Latino VEP), "moderately" influential (25.1–50 percent Latino VEP), "considerably" influential (50.1–75 percent Latino VEP), and "dominant" (75.1–100 percent Latino VEP). The data in Figure 2.4 show that 73.4 percent of Latino-mayor cities have considerably influential (31.7 percent) or dominant (41.7 percent) Latino populations. Only 15.5 percent of Latino-mayor cities have moderately influential Latino populations, and 11.1 percent of Latino-mayor cities have minimally influential populations. Thus a notable trait among Latino-mayor cities is that they have considerably influential Latino populations. According to previous research, a foundational explanation of the descriptive representation of racial or ethnic minorities in any political office is largely tied to the influence of the group, typically measured in terms of sheer population size (Browning, Marshall, and Tabb 1984; Casellas 2009; Hero 1992; Karnig and Welch 1980; Lublin 1997; Marschall and Ruhil 2006). This factor can influence participation rates, the strength of the voting bloc, and the depth of the minority candidate pool. Given that a large majority of Latino-mayor cities have sizable Latino populations, there is some evidence to suggest that they not only would have a steady stream of Latino candidates to compete for the mayoralty but also the capacity to supply the coethnic votes to support Latino candidates.[6]

In the Southwest, it is also worth highlighting that some variability exists in the degree of Latino influence in Latino-mayor cities. For example, 64.2 percent of Texas's Latino-mayor cities are Latino dominant, while in California and New Mexico, only 37 and 20 percent, respectively, of their Latino-mayor cities fit in this category. California is unique in that Latino influence as a percentage of the Latino voting eligible population (VEP) is more evenly distributed across all categories of Latino influence outlined above. The percentage of the Latino VEP is considerably influential in approximately 27.4 percent of California's Latino-mayor cities, moderately influential in 19 percent, and minimally influential in 16 percent. Latino eligible voters are substantially less populous in Latino-mayor cities located outside the Southwest, except in the southern state of Florida. For example, the Latino VEP in the West is 33.3 percent, 37.1 percent in the Northeast, and 23.1 percent in the Midwest. These statistics point to a need for further exploration of the distribution of non-Latino populations in Latino-mayor cities.

Racial and Ethnic Demographic Characteristics of Latino-Mayor Cities

Table 2.3 shows that on average, cities with Latino mayors have a 26.5 percent Anglo (non-Latino white) voting eligible population (VEP), a 4.8 black VEP, a 3.5 percent Asian VEP, and a 1.3 percent Native American VEP. Thus the Latino-Anglo racial paradigm in Latino-mayor cities is clearly the most common, particularly in the Southwest. However, Texas's Latino-mayor cities stand out slightly more than those of any other state because Latinos are a large share of the population, with an average 76.2 percent of the VEP compared with the average 20.5 percent Anglo VEP. By contrast, the average Anglo voting eligible populations in New Mexico's and Colorado's Latino-mayor cities are 34 percent and 39.8 percent, respectively. According to the statistics in Table 2.3, California's Latino-mayor cities have, on average, more populous black and Asian eligible voting blocs.

Latino populations are dominant in the Southwest, where 83 percent of Latino-mayor cities are located. Anglos, on average, are more dominant in Latino-mayor cities in the West, Midwest, and Northeast, so the incidence of Latino-mayor cities does not depend solely on having a Latino majority. It is also worth noting that in states such as Illinois, Maryland, New Jersey, and Rhode Island, no racial or ethnic group has a definitive majority of the population in Latino-mayor cities. These results echo the notion that Latino-mayor cities are not entirely Latino dominant and suggest that because Latino mayors have served in multiracial or multiethnic contexts, they can continue to do so. The research in Browning, Marshall, and Tabb (2003) emphasizes how biracial or multiracial coalitions are often the key to political incorporation of racial and ethnic minorities. In particular, coalitions have formed to elect black mayors in big cities, including New York, New Orleans, and Los Angeles, and Latino mayors in Los Angeles, and Denver (Browning, Marshall, and Tabb 2003; Hero 1992; Marschall and Ruhil 2006). Although coalitions between Latinos and African Americans

TABLE 2.3 RACIAL AND ETHNIC MAKEUP OF VEP* IN LATINO-MAYOR CITIES BY STATE

	Latino-mayor cities, 2016	Avg. Latino VEP, 2014 (%)	Avg. black VEP 2014, (%)	Avg. white VEP, 2014 (%)	Avg. Asian VEP, 2014 (%)	Avg. Native American VEP, 2014 (%)
Arizona	11	65.3	3.9	24.7	0.5	6.6
California	62	59.3	5.6	21.6	11.3	0.9
Colorado	7	58.0	0.7	39.8	0.6	1.2
New Mexico	35	62.5	0.9	34.0	0.4	2.0
Texas	95	76.2	3.2	20.5	0.5	0.8
Southwest	*210*	*64.2*	*2.8*	*28.1*	*2.6*	*2.3*
Illinois	4	32.1	23.1	41.3	2.4	0.3
Ohio	1	14.2	0.2	84.5	0.0	0.5
Midwest	*5*	*23.1*	*11.6*	*62.9*	*1.2*	*0.4*
Florida	14	61.3	11.3	25.3	1.8	0.3
Maryland	1	34.9	45.6	16.1	0.9	0.0
South	*15*	*48.1*	*28.5*	*20.7*	*1.4*	*0.1*
Massachusetts	1	65.5	6.2	28.0	3.2	0.4
New Jersey	8	46.8	15.6	32.0	6.9	0.3
New York	1	20.7	4.6	74.1	0.0	0.3
Pennsylvania	2	16.2	8.1	74.0	0.4	0.0
Rhode Island	2	36.1	15.8	46.1	2.2	0.9
Northeast	*14*	*37.1*	*10.1*	*50.8*	*2.5*	*0.4*
Utah	1	10.1	0.0	88.2	0.3	0.3
Washington	4	62.3	0.9	29.5	0.7	6.3
Wyoming	2	8.2	0.6	89.2	0.7	0.8
Idaho	1	52.4	0.0	40.2	0.0	3.3
West	*8*	*33.3*	*0.4*	*61.7*	*0.4*	*2.7*
USA	252	64.1	4.8	26.5	3.5	1.3

Sources: NALEO (2016); U.S. Census Bureau's 2014 American Community Survey 5-year estimates.

*VEP=Voting eligible population

are expected to form because of their shared socioeconomic and political circumstances, some research has found that black-Latino coalitions face barriers because of perceptions of competition or social distance between blacks and Latinos (McClain and Karnig 1990; Meier et al. 2004). Given these barriers to coalition formation, coalitions among Latinos and Anglos and African Americans and Anglos are also likely to develop (McClain and Karnig 1990; Meier and Stewart 1991; Rocha 2007).

Regardless of how coalitions have formed or failed to form in large, notable cities, the implications of the findings in this section are many (Hill, Moreno, and Cue 2001; Kaufmann 2003; Sonenshein and Pinkus 2002). Since Latino mayors in 2016 served in a variety of demographic contexts (even in non-Latino-dominant ones), the electoral issues may or may not reflect the racial and ethnic divide; they may encompass the whole community or focus on specific communities; and they may or may not reflect national political debates. Future studies should focus on how racial and ethnic coalitions form to elect Latino mayors in distinct racial contexts to help peer into the future of American politics under increasing diversity.

The data described up to this point reveal that the typical Latino-mayor city has a considerably influential Latino population, meaning that the Latino voting eligible population (VEP) is at least 50 percent or above. But to what extent did Latino-influential cities have Latino mayors in 2016? In other words, are there other Latino-majority cities in the United States that could have had Latino mayors in 2016 but did not? If so, how many of these cities lack Latino representation in the mayor's office? To examine these questions, data were combined from the 2014 American Community Survey five-year estimates and the 2016 NALEO directory of Latino elected officials. There are 377 incorporated cities in the United States that had a majority of Latino eligible voters. The outlined circles in Figure 2.5 point to the 192 (51 percent) Latino-majority cities with no Latino mayor in 2016. The solid-filled squares in Figure 2.5 identify the 185 (49 percent) Latino-majority cities with a Latino mayor in 2016. This is a notable finding primarily because of the relatively high number of Latino-majority cities with Latino mayors. Although there were 192 Latino-influential cities that did not have Latino mayors in 2016, there is reason for optimism about the state of Latino mayoral representation in these contexts because nearly half of the cities that are expected to have Latino representation do have representation. Moreover, because these data are a snapshot of Latino mayoral representation in 2016, it is certainly possible that some of the Latino-influential cities without Latino mayors in Figure 2.5 could have had a Latino mayor at some point in the past.

A closer inspection of the current state of Latino mayoral representation in Latino-influential cities by state and region in Figure 2.5 shows that in the Southwest, representation is quite robust. For example, 63 percent of New Mexico's and 56 percent of Arizona's Latino-influential cities had Latino mayors in 2016. Texas, at 50.9 percent, was slightly less represented than New Mexico and Arizona. California and Colorado have the lowest rates of Latino-influential cities represented by Latino mayors, currently standing at 46.5 and 23.5 percent, respectively. The state of Florida, located in the South, also seems to have healthy levels of Latino mayoral representation. Approximately 63 percent of Florida's Latino-influential cities had Latino mayors in 2016. In the Northeast, Massachusetts's only Latino-influential city, Lawrence, had a Latino mayor. In New Jersey, four of the eight Latino-influential cities had Latino mayors. Thus Latino mayoral representation in the Northeast is quite healthy. The same is not true for Latino-influential cities in the Midwest. The states of Illinois, Iowa, North Dakota, and South Dakota combined have seven Latino-influential cities, none of which had a Latino mayor. In the state of Washington, Latino mayors in 2016 were scant; only 25 percent of its twelve Latino-influential cities had Latino mayors. The data in Figure 2.5 demonstrate that Latino mayoral representation, particularly in Latino-influential cities, is not equal across states and regions.

In contrast to the analysis of Latino mayoral representation in the preceding paragraphs, the following paragraphs explore the racial and ethnic demographic makeup of Latino-mayor cities that have minimally to moderately influential Latino populations (i.e., cities where the Latino VEP is less than 50 percent of the population). This will highlight where Latino mayors have been successful in the absence of a numerically dominant coethnic population.

Table 2.4 shows that the average Latino VEP in these sixty-seven Latino-mayor cities is 28.4 percent, while the average Anglo VEP is 50 percent. The Asian and African American VEPs are 8.2 and 11.3 percent, respectively. In the Southwest, the average Anglo VEP is slightly higher than the overall average at 55.8 percent, while the Latino VEP is 31.1 percent. The black VEP and the Asian VEP are a combined 10.5 percent in southwestern Latino-mayor cities with minimally influential Latino populations. Out of all southwestern states with Latino mayors, California has a unique pattern in that no racial/ethnic group has an average VEP that is more than 50 percent. In other words, California's Latino-mayor cities, with minimally influential Latino populations, are multiethnic. California is also unique in that these Latino-mayor cities have a substantial Asian VEP. In the South, for example, in the states of Florida and Maryland,

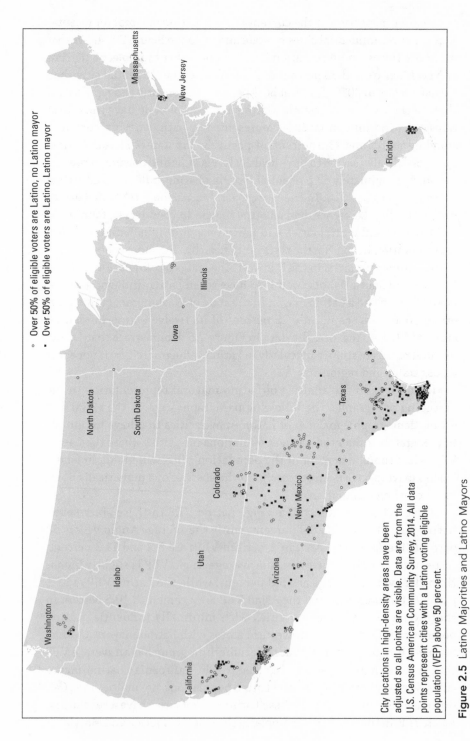

○ Over 50% of eligible voters are Latino, no Latino mayor

■ Over 50% of eligible voters are Latino, Latino mayor

City locations in high-density areas have been adjusted so all points are visible. Data are from the U.S. Census American Community Survey, 2014. All data points represent cities with a Latino voting eligible population (VEP) above 50 percent.

Figure 2.5 Latino Majorities and Latino Mayors

Sources: NALEO (2016); voting eligible population (VEP) compiled from the U.S. Census Bureau's 2014 American Community Survey.

TABLE 2.4 RACIAL/ETHNIC MAKEUP OF LATINO-MAYOR CITIES WITH A MODERATELY INFLUENTIAL LATINO POPULATION BY STATE

	Latino-mayor cities, 2016	Avg. Latino VEP, 2014 (%)	Avg. black VEP, 2014 (%)	Avg. white VEP, 2014 (%)	Avg. Asian VEP, 2014 (%)	Avg. Native American VEP, 2014 (%)	Avg. Latino change, 2000–2010 (%)
Arizona	2	26.0	3.7	66.6	0.5	1.4	-1.3
California	22	29.0	9.7	36.4	21.2	0.7	5.0
Colorado	3	33.1	1.3	63.4	0.8	1.7	3.8
New Mexico	5	36.4	0.4	58.8	0.5	3.2	0.4
Texas	12	30.8	13.6	53.7	0.7	0.2	5.3
Southwest	*44*	*31.1*	*5.7*	*55.8*	*4.8*	*1.5*	*2.6*
Florida	4	20.4	29.9	47.3	2.3	0.3	6.5
Maryland	1	34.9	45.6	16.1	0.9	0.0	21.6
South	*5*	*27.6*	*37.7*	*31.7*	*1.6*	*0.1*	*14.1*
Illinois	4	32.1	23.1	41.3	2.4	0.3	10.8
Ohio	1	14.2	0.2	84.5	0.0	0.5	4.4
Midwest	*5*	*23.1*	*11.6*	*62.9*	*1.2*	*0.4*	*7.6*
New Jersey	4	31.9	13.3	45.7	10.3	0.1	11.5
New York	1	20.7	4.6	74.1	0.0	0.3	6.6
Pennsylvania	2	16.2	8.1	74.0	0.4	0.0	11.1
Rhode Island	2	36.1	15.8	46.1	2.2	0.9	10.3
Northeast	*9*	*26.2*	*10.5*	*60.0*	*3.2*	*0.3*	*9.9*
Utah	1	10.1	0.0	88.2	0.3	0.3	2.1
Washington	1	24.6	1.6	68.7	1.0	2.1	7.6
Wyoming	2	8.2	0.6	89.2	0.7	0.8	3.5
West	*4*	*14.3*	*0.8*	*82.0*	*0.7*	*1.1*	*4.4*
USA	67	28.4	11.3	50.0	8.2	0.8	5.9

Sources: NALEO (2016); U.S. Census Bureau's 2014 American Community Survey 5-year estimates.

Note: Cities with a moderately influential Latino population are those where the Latino voting eligible population (VEP) is less than 50 percent.

Latino-mayor cities are also multiethnic, but, as Table 2.4 shows, the average African American VEP is 37.7 percent. In New Jersey and Rhode Island, Latino-mayor cities are also multiethnic. However, the Anglo and Latino populations are more evenly divided. In New York and Pennsylvania, Latino-mayor cities are predominantly Anglo. The same holds true for Latino-mayor cities in the West. All in all, Table 2.4 highlights the varying demographic contexts that make up Latino-mayor cities where the Latino VEP is less than 50 percent.

In addition to the racial/ethnic makeup of Latino-mayor cities, it is worth exploring the overall city population patterns. The data in Figure 2.6 show that 63.8 percent of 252 Latino-mayor cities in 2016 had fewer than 17,000 total inhabitants. Cities such as McFarland, California; Alamosa, Colorado; Las Vegas, New Mexico; Mercedes, Texas; and Wapato, Washington, fit this profile. According to Figure 2.6, Latino-mayor cities with a population between 17,000 and 35,000 make up only 11.5 percent of the cases. For example, these cities include Douglas, Arizona; Marina, California; Hialeah Gardens, Florida; Central Falls, Rhode Island; and San Benito, Texas. Only 26 (10.3 percent) of Latino-mayor cities have a population between 50,000 and 90,000, including Delano, California; Lawrence, Massachusetts; Perth Amboy, New Jersey; Santa Fe, New Mexico; and Edinburg, Texas. Among the most populous Latino-mayor cities in 2016, approximately 25 (9.9 percent) had more than 90,000 inhabitants. Approximately 56 percent of Latino-mayor cities with a population above 90,000 are located in California. The three most populous Latino-mayor cities in California are Los Angeles, Santa Ana, and Chula Vista. These cities are located in the southern part of the state. The most sizable Latino-mayor cities in Texas in 2016 included El Paso, Corpus Christi, Laredo, and Brownsville, all of which are on or near (Corpus Christi) the U.S.-Mexico border. Florida's most sizable Latino-mayor cities include Miami, Hialeah, and Palm Bay. Other notable Latino-mayor cities with large populations include Paterson, New Jersey; Las Cruces, New Mexico; Providence, Rhode Island; and Yakima, Washington. For further details on Latino-mayor cities' population statistics see the Appendix to this chapter.

Discussions of city population are relevant to politics because the size of the jurisdiction has governing implications for mayors. On the one hand, larger cities have more staff and personnel resources to provide services, from tree trimming to garbage collection to police protection. On the other hand, these contexts require that more services be delivered. These dynamics can affect not only the managerial responsibilities of mayors but also the political viability (or vulnerabilities) of sitting mayors and their potential challengers. Previous research has found that residents in smaller cit-

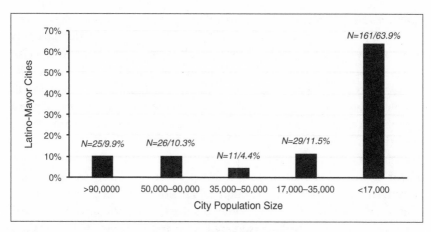

Figure 2.6 Latino-Mayor Cities by City Population Size, 2016
Sources: NALEO (2016); U.S. Census Bureau's 2014 American Community Survey.

ies are more politically active than residents in larger cities (Oliver 2000; but see Kelleher and Lowery 2004; Kelleher and Lowery 2009). The implication is that small-city politics and policies are less affected by special interests than those in big cities (Svorney 2002). As for elections, previous research also suggests that larger districts increase the costs for candidates to compete for the city's top executive office primarily because they require more resources to raise money, mobilize voters, and wage a competitive political campaign (Black 1972; Hogan 2004). As we have seen in this section, most Latino mayors govern in small cities with fewer than 17,000 inhabitants. Thus city size can influence not only how Latino mayors govern but also how Latino candidates form their electoral strategies.

Institutional Characteristics of Latino-Mayor Cities

To describe the contemporary governing structures of Latino-mayor cities, resources were pooled from the 2009 NALEO directory, the International City/County Management Association's (ICMA) Municipal Form of Government Surveys (1981, 1986, 1991, 1996, 2001, 2006), city websites, city charters, and personal contacts with city clerks.[7] Four major governing arrangements for Latino-mayor cities are examined here: (1) the form of government, (2) the structure of city council districts, (3) mayoral term limits, and (4) partisan elections.

Table 2.5 shows that among the three most common forms of government, the mayor-council system, the council-manager system, and the commission system, the most prevalent in Latino-mayor cities is the council-manager system. About 57 percent of Latino-mayor cities have this form of government. This system typically gives less power to the city mayor, and both the city council and the mayor are responsible for making policy together with the advice of the appointed city manager. The national sample of the 2006 ICMA Municipal Form of Government Survey indicates that 55 percent of U.S. cities have this form of government. The proportion of Latino-mayor cities with council-manager governments is therefore not very unusual. However, 40 percent of the Latino-mayor cities have mayor-council systems. These systems provide mayors with significant administrative authority. Although this is not the most prevalent form of government among Latino-mayor cities, it is not uncommon for Latino-mayor cities to be associated with institutions that provide a powerful platform to set the political agenda. According to the 2006 ICMA survey, about 34 percent of U.S. cities have this form of government, so Latino-mayor cities are slightly overrepresented in this category. The least common form of government both in the United States and in Latino-mayor cities is the commission system. In this system, members of a board of elected commissioners serve as heads of specific departments and collectively sit as the legislative body of the government. Of the seven Latino-

TABLE 2.5   INSTITUTIONAL CHARACTERISTICS OF LATINO-MAYOR CITIES, 2009

Variable	ICMA sample (%)	Latino-mayor cities (number)	Mean	Std. dev.	Min.	Max.
City population	—	247	44,331	247,590	18	3,796,840
Mayor-council government	0.34	228	0.4	0.49	0	1
Council-manager government	0.55	228	0.57	0.5	0	1
Commission government	0.009	228	0.03	0.18	0	1
Council size*	6	217	5.6	1.6	2	16
At-large districts	0.66	228	0.74	0.45	0	1
Single-member districts (SMDs)	0.17	228	0.13	0.33	0	1
Mixed (at-large, SMDs)	0.17	228	0.08	0.27	0	1
Partisan elections	0.2	227	0.03	0.17	0	1
Mayoral term limits	0.09	204	0.14	0.35	0	1
Number of Latino city councilors	—	247	2.33	1.87	0	8
Percent Latinos on city council	—	217	0.45	0.35	0	1

Sources: NALEO (2009); ICMA Municipal Form of Government Surveys (2001–2006); U.S. Census Bureau's 2009 American Community Survey 5-year estimates.
* Average size of all city councils.

mayor cities with commission governments, six are in Texas, and one is in New Jersey.

Table 2.6 further describes the patterns of governing arrangements in Latino-mayor cities by state. The data show that 121 Latino-mayor cities in 2009 (or 49 percent) in the Southwest had council-manager governments, as did 87 percent of the Latino-mayor cities in California. Half of Texas's Latino-mayor cities are council-manager, and the other half are mayor-council. Florida's Latino-mayor cities are also equally split between these two forms of government. In contrast, New Jersey's Latino-mayor cities are all mayor-council governments. New Mexico has twice as many Latino-mayor cities with mayor-council systems as Latino-mayor cities with council-manager systems. Previous research has found that cities that have council-manager or commission forms of government (a Progressive Era reform) are more likely to have black mayors than cities with mayor-council governments (Marschall and Ruhil 2006). Because council-manager governments emphasize the professionalization of service delivery via independently appointed bureaucrats, the political environment can be less competitive. This in turn may facilitate the inclusion of minorities in municipal government not only because minority candidates experience less resistance from other groups in the voting booth, but also because multiracial coalitions are more likely to form (Hero and Clarke 2003; Sonenshein 2003). Researchers also suggest that minority candidates can expect less resistance in cities with these Progressive Era–reform types of governing structures and therefore are more likely to be elected (Hero and Clarke 2003; Sonenshein 2003).

As for the rules governing the district structure for city council members, 78 percent of Latino-mayor cities with available institutional data elect their city council members at-large. That is, these city council members represent the entire city rather than a specific geographic area (or district) within the city. Only 29 of the 213 Latino-mayor cities with data elect their city council members in geographically designated districts. A few Latino-mayor cities combine these two methods by electing some council members at-large and some from districts.

Table 2.6 shows that very few cities with Latino mayors have partisan elections. Of the 227 Latino-mayor cities for which institutional data were available in 2009, only 7 (3 percent) have partisan elections. The previous literature also suggests that it is rare for cities, especially less populous ones, to have partisan municipal elections.[8] However, the 2016 NALEO directory identified 29 (11.5 percent) of Latino mayors as affiliated with the Democratic Party but only 7 Latino mayors (2.8 percent) as affiliated with the Republican Party. The NALEO was not able to determine the partisan

TABLE 2.6 LATINO-MAYOR CITIES AND THEIR INSTITUTIONS BY STATE, 2009

State	Latino-mayor cities, 2009	Latino-mayor cities with mayor-council gov't	Latino-mayor cities with council-manager gov't	Latino-mayor cities with commission gov't	Latino-mayor cities with only at-large (multimember) districts	Latino-mayor cities with only single member districts	Latino-mayor cities with mixed at-large and SMDs	Latino-mayor cities with partisan elections	Latino-mayor cities with term limits	Avg. council size in Latino-mayor cities	Latinos in city council in Latino-mayor cities, 2009 (avg, %)
Arizona	15	3	12	0	13	1	1	1	3	6.8	54
California	62	8	54	0	51	3	1	0	8	5.2	46
Colorado	6	0	4	0	2	0	2	0	2	6.75	38
New Mexico	39	21	10	0	19	9	2	2	2	5.4	55
Texas	96	40	41	6	62	12	8	0	10	5.4	44
Southwest	*218*	*72*	*121*	*6*	*147*	*25*	*14*	*3*	*25*	*5.91*	*47*
Florida	13	7	6	0	10	1	1	0	3	5.46	25
Maryland	1	0	1	0	1	0	0	0	0	4	0
South	*14*	*7*	*7*	*0*	*11*	*1*	*1*	*0*	*3*	*4.73*	*13*
Indiana	1	1	0	0	0	0	1	1	0	9	78
Wisconsin	1	1	0	0	0	1	0	0	0	16	0
Missouri	1	1	0	0	0	1	0	0	0	8	0
Midwest	*3*	*3*	*0*	*0*	*0*	*2*	*1*	*1*	*0*	*11*	*26*
New Jersey	5	4	0	1	3	0	2	0	0	6.2	24
Connecticut	1	1	0	0	1	0	0	1	0	9	33
Northeast	*6*	*5*	*0*	*1*	*4*	*0*	*2*	*1*	*0*	*7.6*	*29*
Washington	6	4	2	0	6	0	0	2	1	6	44
West	*6*	*4*	*2*	*0*	*6*	*0*	*0*	*2*	*1*	*6*	*44*
Total	247	91/228 (40%)	130/228 (57%)	7/227 (3%)	168/228 (74%)	28/228 (13%)	18/228 (8%)	7/227 (3%)	29/204 (14%)	5.6	45

Sources: NALEO (2009); ICMA Municipal Form of Government Surveys (2001–2006).

affiliation of the remaining 85.7 percent of Latino mayors in 2016. However, both elected officials and voters do have partisan preferences that reflect partisan politics at the national level. Research by Gerber and Hopkins (2011) revealed that under certain conditions, mayors act on their partisan preferences in shaping public policy. For example, their findings showed that when mayors affiliated with the Republican Party are elected, public spending on police and fire protection increases. It would be fascinating to study these political outcomes for Latino-mayor cities to determine whether the same patterns hold up.

Another governing arrangement worth studying for Latino-mayor cities is the use of term limits. This institutional structure limits the number of consecutive terms that incumbents can serve. In theory, it can facilitate the transfer of power from entrenched politicians (e.g., incumbents). It is clear from the literature that it is extremely difficult for a challenger to unseat an incumbent (members of Congress tend not only to win more often but also to win by larger margins) (Cox and Katz 1996; Cox and Morgenstern 1993; Ansolabehere and Snyder 2002). However, there is a debate in the literature about how term limits influence representation at the local level. For example, Trounstine and Valdini (2008) showed that term limits have no impact on the proportion of black and Latino representation in city councils, but that they have a positive and significant effect on the proportion of female city council members. The data in Table 2.6 show that only about 14 percent of Latino-mayor cities in 2009 had term limits. However, this is slightly higher than the national average; the ICMA surveys indicate that only 9 percent of municipalities surveyed had term limits for mayors.

In regard to representation in the highest office in municipal politics, the research highlights the concept of "political capacity" for racial/ethnic minority groups. In order for groups to have the capacity to successfully become part of a governing coalition, they need a pipeline of qualified candidates with previous political experience, name recognition, political networks, and financial resources. One reliable pipeline in municipal government—and a natural stepping-stone to the mayoralty—is the city legislative body. Marschall and Ruhil (2006) found that cities with more African American city council members are more likely to have black mayors than cities with fewer descriptive representatives in the city legislature. Smith, Reingold, and Owens (2012) also found that more female city legislators have a positive impact on the presence of female mayors.

There is ample anecdotal evidence that successful Latino mayoral candidates have previous experience serving in the city legislature. Thus election of Latinos to the city's top executive position may require sufficient levels of descriptive representation in the city council. To what extent do Latino-mayor cities have a critical mass of political capacity in the city legislature? To descriptively analyze Latino representation on city councils, data from the 2009 NALEO directory and the ICMA Municipal Form of Government Surveys were used to generate a frequency count of Latino city council members in each Latino-mayor city. The average share of Latinos in city councils in Latino-mayor cities is reported in Table 2.6. The empirical evidence shows that the average proportion of Latinos in city councils in all Latino-mayor cities is approximately 45 percent. There is, however, some variation on this measure. In particular, the proportion of Latinos in city councils ranges from 0 percent all the way to 100 percent. The data in Table 2.6 are disaggregated by state. The proportion of Latinos in city councils in Latino-mayor cities in Connecticut, Florida, and New Jersey, on average, is between 24 and 33 percent. In other states, the average Latino composition of the city council is much higher; Washington, Texas, California, Arizona, and New Mexico have an average council composition between 44 to 55 percent Latino. Thus, the Latino political capacity in these states is quite substantial.

Brief Overview of the Demographic and Institutional Context of This Volume's Case Studies

The research in this volume focuses on six cases in the United States where Latinos have secured the mayoralty: Los Angeles, California; Denver, Colorado; San Antonio, Texas; Providence, Rhode Island; Hartford, Connecticut; and Miami-Dade County, Florida. This section provides an overview of the demographic, political, and institutional characteristics of these cases. The data in Table 2.7 show that the cases have populations between 125,000 (Hartford) and 3.8 million (Los Angeles). The data on Latino mayors described in the preceding sections indicate that these cities are not typical of cities where Latino mayors serve. The mayors at the helm of these municipalities represent large numbers of residents. From 2000 to 2010, San Antonio, Denver, and Miami-Dade County experienced modest population growth, according to Table 2.7. Nonetheless, all cases had positive total population growth over the past decade.

The data in Table 2.7 also reveal the voting eligible population (VEP) for each racial/ethnic group. The average across all six cases is 39.8 percent Latino VEP, 37.8 percent white VEP, 17.1 percent black VEP, and 3.9 percent Asian VEP. In 2016 Latino-mayor cities in general, Latinos are substantially

TABLE 2.7   RACIAL/ETHNIC MAKEUP OF CASE STUDIES IN THIS VOLUME

City	Total population, 2010	Latino VEP,* 2014 (%)	Non-Latino white VEP, 2014 (%)	Asian VEP, 2014 (%)	Native American VEP, 2014 (%)	Black VEP, 2014 (%)	Change in total Latino pop., 2000–2010 (%)	Change in total pop., 2000–2010 (%)
Los Angeles, CA	3,792,621	33.1	40.2	11.8	0.5	12.3	2.0	2.6
Miami-Dade, FL	2,496,435	60.0	18.4	1.5	0.2	19.9	7.7	10.8
San Antonio, TX	1,327,407	57.2	32.5	1.8	0.7	7.4	4.5	16.0
Denver, CO	600,158	19.7	65.2	2.7	1.2	9.9	0.1	8.2
Providence, RI	178,042	27.0	51.2	4.2	1.2	15.4	8.1	2.6
Hartford, CT	124,775	41.7	19.0	1.3	0.3	37.6	2.9	2.6
Average	1,419,906	39.8	37.8	3.9	0.7	17.1	4.2	2.6

Sources: 2000 U.S. Census; 2010 U.S. Census; U.S. Census Bureau's 2014 American Community Survey 5-year estimates.
*VEP=Voting eligible population

more populous. Specifically, the average Latino VEP in the 252 Latino-mayor cities is 64.1 percent, nearly 25 percentage points higher than the average for the cases explored in this volume. The cases that most closely resemble the average Latino-mayor city are Miami-Dade County (60 percent Latino VEP) and San Antonio (57.2 percent Latino VEP). What is interesting, however, is the considerable variability in Latino population in the six case studies in this volume. Denver has the lowest Latino VEP at 19.7 percent and is considered to have a minimally influential Latino population. Providence, Los Angeles, and Hartford have moderately influential Latino populations, while San Antonio and Miami-Dade County have considerably influential Latino populations. Thus Latinos are neither trivial nor outright dominant in the volume cases.

Non-Latino whites are considerably influential in San Antonio, Los Angeles, Providence, and Denver. In both Miami-Dade County and Hartford, non-Latino whites are minimally influential, making up less than 20 percent of the VEP. African Americans are most influential in Hartford, making up nearly 38 percent of the VEP. It is evident from the data in Table 2.7 that African Americans are significant and are clearly part of the social fabric of these volume case studies. This is especially true in cases such as Los Angeles, where no racial/ethnic group has a majority of the population, or Miami-Dade County, which has equal parts of Anglos and blacks vis-à-vis the nearly dominant Latino population.

There are clear avenues for developing multiracial coalitions in Denver, Providence, and Hartford. For example, Denver's combined black and Latino VEP is nearly 30 percent. A winning coalition in Denver could include whites, blacks, and Latinos, as has occurred in the past to elect Wellington Webb (a black mayor) and Federico Peña (a Latino mayor). Providence has a combined black and Latino population of 42.4 percent, a rather sizable nonwhite population that could be pivotal in elections. In Los Angeles, the combined black and Latino population is 45 percent of the VEP. The other unique aspect of Los Angeles is the size of the Asian population, nearly 12 percent of the VEP. Regardless of the variation in the demographic profiles of the six case studies, all except Denver experienced a growth of the Latino population over the past decade. In fact, the average percentage change in these cities' Latino population is about 4 percentage points. The politics and policies of these cities will inevitably change as a result of demographic changes.

To describe the institutional context for most of the cases explored in this volume, data were gathered from city charters and city websites. In particular, Table 2.8 describes the form of government, district structure, council size, use of term limits, and partisan structure of elections. Four cases have mayor-council governments: Los Angeles, Denver, Providence, and Hartford. Although the formal political power of mayors varies among these cities, there is greater potential for mayors in these cities to influence the city's political agenda independent of the city's legislative body. San Antonio has a council-manager system. This does not mean that city mayors are not influential. However, mayors are required to work more closely with the city council and in conjunction with the appointed city manager to address any policy issues. The council-manager form of government is the most common among Latino-mayor cities (as described earlier), so most of the cases examined in this volume are not representative of the typical Latino-mayor city in this respect. Three cases examined in this volume have term limits for city-government officials: Los Angeles, San Antonio, and Providence. Table 2.8 also shows that only Providence has partisan elections for municipal offices. Approximately 20 percent of U.S. cities that responded to the ICMA Municipal Form of Government Survey in 2006 indicated that partisan labels were printed on the ballot.

In each case explored in this volume, a Latino has served in the office of the mayor. However, variability exists in the number of Latino mayors who have served and the length of time the city's top executive office has been occupied by a Latino. For example, Los Angeles did not have a Latino mayor until 2005 but has had Latino candidates vie for the mayoralty consistently since 2001. San Antonio experienced a dry spell of Latino representation in the city's top executive office after Henry Cisneros left office in 1989. Although Latino candidates ran for the mayoralty in San Antonio in 1991 and 1997, the next Latino to win the office was Ed Garza in 2001. Denver's Federico Peña made history as the city's first Latino to serve as mayor in 1983. Since then, Latino candidates have run for the office with no success, one in 2003 (Donald Mares) and another in 2007 (Danny Lopez). Providence presents an interesting case because another Latino (Jorge Elorza) won the keys to the mayor's office in 2014 after the historic candidacy of Angel Taveras in 2010. Table 2.8 also describes the recent Latino composition in the city councils. Latinos have a wide-ranging degree of representation in city legislatures, from a low of 23 percent of the council seats in Denver to a high of 60 percent of the seats in San Antonio. In five cases, city council members represent single-member districts. Hartford is the only case in this volume that elects its council members in at-large, multimember districts. This has not, however, impeded the political incorporation of Latinos into the city government.

TABLE 2.8   VOLUME CASE STUDIES

City	Population, 2010	Latino mayors and notable candidates	Terms in office	Form of government	At-large / district structure	Partisan elections	Term limits	Council size	Latinos on council, 2014
Los Angeles, CA	3,792,621	Eric Garcetti Antonio Villaraigosa Emanuel A. Pleitez Richard Alarcón Xavier Becerra	2013–present 2005–2013 Candidate, 2001 Candidate, 2013 Candidate, 2005 Candidate, 2001	Mayor-council	District	No	Yes	15	5 (33%)
Miami-Dade, FL	2,563,885	Carlos A. Giménez Carlos Alvarez Alex Penelas	2011–present 2004–2011 1996–2004	Mayor-council	District	No	Yes	13	7 (53%)
San Antonio, TX	1,327,407	Julián Castro Edward D. Garza Henry G. Cisneros Henry Ávila Maria A. Berriozábal	2009–2014 Candidate, 2005 2001–2005 1981–1989 Candidate, 1997 Candidate, 1991	Council-manager	District	No	Yes	10	6 (60%)
Denver, CO	600,158	Federico Peña Danny F. López Donald J. Mares	1983–1991 Candidate, 2007 Candidate, 2003	Mayor-council	Mixed*	No	No	13	3 (23%)†
Providence, RI	178,042	Jorge Elorza	2014–present	Mayor-council	District	Yes	Yes	15	4 (27%)
Hartford, CT	124,775	Angel Taveras Pedro E. Segarra Eddie A. Perez Edwin Vargas Jr.	2011–2014 2010–present 2001–2010 Candidate, 2011	Mayor-council	At-large	Yes	No	9	3 (33%)

Sources: ICMA Form of Government Surveys (2001–2006); city websites; city charters; NALEO Directories (1984–2016); election results gathered by author.

* The council has thirteen members; eleven are elected in equally populated single-member districts, and two are elected at-large.

† One member is elected at-large, and two are elected in single-member districts.

The city of Hartford has had a Latino mayor since 2001, when Eddie Perez was elected; he served from 2001 to 2010 and was succeeded by Pedro Segarra.

Conclusion

The descriptive analysis in this chapter delineates key patterns related to the demographic and political context of Latino-mayor cities. Among these patterns is the steady gain in the number of Latino mayors serving over time, particularly in the South and the Northeast of the United States. The growth of the Latino population from 2000 to 2010 was particularly high in Latino-mayor cities outside the Southwest. This finding hints at increased political representation in the future, particularly in cities that have experienced substantial Latino population growth. Another key finding is that a vast majority of Latino-mayor cities are located in the Southwest and have sizable Latino populations. The numerical strength of Latinos seems to be a key characteristic of Latino-mayor cities.

This is not to say, however, that Latinos are the most influential racial/ethnic group in all Latino-mayor cities. In approximately 26 percent of Latino-mayor cities in 2016, some other racial/ethnic group was dominant. In a handful of cases, no racial/ethnic group constituted a majority of the population. Thus Latino mayors serve in a variety of demographic contexts. However, representation does not occur in all contexts where Latinos are a considerable size of the population (above 50 percent of the VEP). The findings in this chapter reveal that there are hundreds of cities where Latinos could serve but do not. Granted, this is a snapshot of Latino mayoral representation in 2016. Future studies should further explore the cities where Latinos have ever served as mayor.

Appendix: Population Statistics for Latino-Mayor Cities, 2016

	Latino-mayor cities, 2016	Avg. city pop., 2010	Median city pop., 2010	City pop. std. deviation	Min. city pop., 2010	Max. city pop., 2010
Arizona	11	9,314	5,652	7,901	353	25,505
California	62	126,364	36,177	480,580	1,422	3,792,621
Colorado	7	13,206	4,444	23,925	404	66,859
Florida	14	64,704	13,733	113,398	838	399,457
Idaho	1	1,533	1,533	—	1,533	1,533
Illinois	4	34,431	28,681	15,058	23,706	56,657
Maryland	1	3,046	3,046	—	3,046	3,046
Massachusetts	1	76,377	76,377	—	76,377	76,377
New Jersey	8	53,990	50,261	43,835	2,978	146,199
New Mexico	35	8,784	1,655	19,457	193	97,618
New York	1	12,563	12,563	—	12,563	12,563
Ohio	1	7,332	7,332	—	7,332	7,332
Pennsylvania	2	4,405	4,405	272	4,212	4,597
Rhode Island	2	98,709	98,709	112,194	19,376	178,042
Texas	95	24,314	4,193	78,445	19	649,121
Utah	1	2,201	2,201	—	2,201	2,201
Washington	4	26,825	6,973	42,915	2,286	91,067
Wyoming	2	28,232	28,232	38,303	1,147	55,316
Total	252	49,981	9,613	247,883	19	3,792,621

Source: NALEO (2016); 2010 U.S. Census.

NOTES

1. The West region, as defined in this research, includes the states of Idaho, Montana, Oregon, Washington, Wyoming, Utah, Hawaii, and Alaska.

2. The Midwest region, as defined in this research, includes the states of North Dakota, South Dakota, Nebraska, Kansas, Minnesota, Iowa, Missouri, Wisconsin, Illinois, Indiana, Michigan, Ohio, and Oklahoma.

3. The South region, as defined in this research, includes the states of Arkansas, Louisiana, Mississippi, Alabama, Tennessee, Kentucky, West Virginia, Virginia, Maryland, Delaware, North Carolina, South Carolina, Georgia, and Florida.

4. The Northeast region, as defined in this research, includes the states of Pennsylvania, New York, New Jersey, Connecticut, Rhode Island, Massachusetts, Vermont, New Hampshire, and Maine.

5. These data were gathered from the U.S. Census Bureau's 2014 American Community Survey 5-year estimates.

6. For more on the causes and consequences of Latino mayoral representation, see the multivariate analysis in Cuéllar (2014).

7. The ICMA Municipal Form of Government Surveys are mailed to municipal clerks in municipalities with populations 2,500 and over and to municipalities with populations less than 2,500 in an ICMA database. The response rate for the 2006 ICMA

survey was 46.7 percent. Given this response rate and the ICMA target population, several measures were taken to account for as many institutional arrangements as possible of the 247 Latino-mayor cities in 2009. Each Municipal Form of Government Survey, starting with the latest survey wave (2006), was merged with the list of Latino-mayor cities to gather as much data as possible. Specifically, the 2006 ICMA survey provided institutional information for 74 Latino-mayor cities, the 2001 ICMA survey for 35 Latino mayor-cities, the 1996 ICMA for 31 Latino-mayor cities, and the 1986 ICMA for 7 Latino-mayor cities. This yielded institutional data for 163 (or 66 percent) of Latino-mayor cities in 2009. The remaining cities' websites and city charters were further investigated to increase the coverage of institutional data needed to analyze the 247 Latino-mayor cities. Given that many cities either provided limited information about their governing structures on their websites or had no websites at all, many city clerks were contacted by phone or e-mail. Ultimately, this multimethod approach helped secure the institutional characteristics of approximately 92 percent of the 247 Latino-mayor cities in 2009.

8. The one city in Arizona with a Latino mayor, South Tucson, eliminated partisan elections in 2008 via a local initiative. Tucson (not South Tucson) is the only city in Arizona that continues to designate municipal candidates' partisan affiliation on the electoral ballot. For more on this, see Hajnal, Lewis, and Louch (2002) and O'Dell (2008).

REFERENCES

Ansolabehere, Stephen, and James M. Snyder Jr. 2002. "The Incumbency Advantage in U.S. Elections: An Analysis of State and Federal Offices, 1942–2000." *Election Law Journal* 1:315–338.

Barreto, Matt A. 2007. "*¡Si Se Puede!* Latino Candidates and the Mobilization of Latino Voters." *American Political Science Review* 101, no. 3 (August):425–441.

Barreto, Matt A., Mario Villarreal, and Nathan D. Woods. 2005. "Metropolitan Latino political behavior: Voter turnout and candidate preference in Los Angeles." *Journal of Urban Affairs* 27: 71–91.

Black, Gordon S. 1972. "A Theory of Political Ambition: Career Choices and the Role of Structural Incentives." *American Political Science Review* 6:144–159.

Browning, Rufus P., Dale Rogers Marshall, and David H. Tabb. 1984. *Protest Is Not Enough: The Struggle of Blacks and Hispanics for Equality in Urban Politics.* Berkeley: University of California Press.

———. 2003. "Has Political Incorporation Been Achieved? Is It Enough?" In *Racial Politics in American Cities*, 3rd ed., edited by Rufus Browning, Dale Rogers Marshall, and David H. Tabb, 357–387. New York: Longman.

Casellas, Jason P. 2009. "The Institutional and Demographic Determinants of Latino Representation in U.S. Legislatures." *Legislative Studies Quarterly* 35:399–426.

Cox, Gary W., and Jonathan N. Katz. 1996. "Why Did the Incumbency Advantage in U.S. House Elections Grow?" *American Journal of Political Science* 40:478–497.

Cox, Gary W., and Scott Morgenstern. 1993. "The Increasing Advantage of Incumbency in the United States." *Legislative Studies Quarterly* 18:495–514.

Cuéllar, Carlos E. 2014. "Running and Winning: Patterns of Latino Candidate Emergence and Success in Mayoral Elections." In *The Keys to City Hall: Local Politics and*

Mayoral Elections in 21st Century America, edited by Sean D. Foreman and Marcia Godwin, 52–74. New York: Routledge.

Eisinger, Peter K. 1982. "Black Employment in Municipal Jobs: The Impact of Black Political Power." *American Political Science Review* 76:380–392.

Gerber, Elisabeth R., and Daniel J. Hopkins. 2011. "When Mayors Matter: Estimating the Impact of Mayoral Partisanship on City Policy." *American Journal of Political Science* 55, no. 2:326–339.

Geron, Kim. 2005. *Latino Political Power*. Boulder, CO: Lynne Rienner.

Hajnal, Zoltan L., Paul G. Lewis, and Hugh Louch. 2002. *Municipal Elections in California: Turnout, Timing, and Competition*. San Francisco: Public Policy Institute of California.

Hero, Rodney E. 1987. "The Election of Hispanics in City Government: An Examination of the Election of Federico Peña as Mayor of Denver." *Western Political Quarterly* 40, no. 1:93–105.

———. 1992. *Latinos and the U.S. Political System: Two-Tiered Pluralism*. Philadelphia: Temple University Press.

Hero, Rodney E., and Susan E. Clarke. 2003. "Latinos, Blacks, and Multiethnic Politics in Denver: Realigning Power and Influence in the Struggle for Equality." In *Racial Politics in American Cities*, 3rd ed., edited by Rufus P. Browning, Dale Rogers Marshall, and David H. Tabb, 309–330. New York: Longman.

Hogan, Robert E. 2004. "Challenger Emergence, Incumbent Success, and Electoral Accountability in State Legislative Elections." *Journal of Politics* 66:1283–1303.

Karnig, Albert K., and Susan Welch. 1980. *Black Representation and Urban Policy*. Chicago: University of Chicago Press.

Kaufmann, Karen M. 2003. "Black and Latino Voters in Denver: Responses to Each Other's Political Leadership." *Political Science Quarterly* 118:107–126.

Kelleher, Christine A., and David Lowery. 2004. "Political Participation and Metropolitan Institutional Contexts." *Urban Affairs Review* 39, no. 6:720–757.

———. 2009. "Central City Size, Metropolitan Institutions and Political Participation." *British Journal of Political Science* 39, no. 1:59–92.

Lublin, David. 1997. "The Election of African Americans and Latinos to the U.S. House of Representatives, 1972–1994." *American Politics Quarterly* 25, no. 3 (July):269–286.

Marschall, Melissa J., and Anirudh V. S. Ruhil. 2006. "The Pomp of Power: Black Mayoralties in Urban America." *Social Science Quarterly* 87:828–850.

Marschall, Melissa J., and Paru Shah. 2005. "Keeping policy churn off the agenda: Urban education and civic capacity." *Policy Studies Journal* 33:161–180.

McClain, Paula D., and Albert K. Karnig. 1990. "Black and Hispanic Socioeconomic and Political Competition." *American Political Science Review* 84:535–545.

Meier, Kenneth J., Paula D. McClain, Jerry L. Polinard, and Robert D. Wrinkle. 2004. "Divided or Together? Conflict and Cooperation between African Americans and Latinos." *Political Research Quarterly* 57:399–409.

Meier, Kenneth J., and Joseph Stewart Jr. 1991. "Cooperation and Conflict in Multiracial School Districts." *Journal of Politics* 53:1123–1133.

Muñoz, Carlos, Jr., and Charles P. Henry. 1990. "Coalition Politics in San Antonio and Denver: The Cisneros and Peña Mayoral Campaigns." In *Racial Politics in American Cities*, edited by Rufus P. Browning, Dale Rogers Marshall, and David H. Tabb, 179–190. White Plains, NY: Longman.

National Association of Latino Elected and Appointed Officials (NALEO). 2009. *National Directory of Latino Elected Officials*. Los Angeles, CA: NALEO Educational Fund.

———. 2016. *National Directory of Latino Elected Officials*. Los Angeles, CA: NALEO Educational Fund.

O'Dell, Rob. 2008. "Tucson's Election Process Is under Fire." *Arizona Daily Star*, December 15.

Oliver, J. Eric. 2000. "City Size and Civic Involvement in Metropolitan America." *American Political Science Review* 94, no. 2:361–373.

Rocha, Rene R. 2007. "Black-Brown Coalitions in Local School Board Elections." *Political Research Quarterly* 60:315–327.

Rosales, Rodolfo. 2000. *The Illusion of Inclusion: The Untold Story of San Antonio*. Austin: University of Texas Press.

Smith, Adrienne R., Beth Reingold, and Michael Leo Owens. 2012. "The Political Determinants of Women's Descriptive Representation in Cities." *Political Research Quarterly* 65:315–329.

Sonenshein, Raphael, J. 2003. "Post-incorporation Politics in Los Angeles." In *Racial Politics in American Cities*, 3rd ed., edited by Rufus P. Browning, Dale Rogers Marshall, and David H. Tabb, 51–76. New York: Longman.

Sonenshein, Raphael J., and Susan H. Pinkus. 2002. "The Dynamics of Latino Political Incorporation: The 2001 Los Angeles Mayoral Elections as Seen in *Los Angeles Times* Exit Polls." *PS: Political Science and Politics* 35, no. 1:67–74.

Stein, Lana. 2003. "Mayoral Politics." In *Cities, Politics, and Policy: A Comparative Analysis*, edited by John Pelissero, 148–168. New York: CQ Press.

Svorney, Shirley. 2002. "When It Comes to Cities, Smaller Is Better." *Los Angeles Times*, June 3. http://articles.latimes.com/2002/jun/03/opinion/oe-svorny03.

Trounstine, Jessica. 2009. "All Politics Is Local: The Reemergence of the Study of City Politics." *Perspectives on Politics* 7:611–618.

Trounstine, Jessica, and Melody E. Valdini. 2008. "The Context Matters: The Effects of Single-Member versus At-Large Districts on City Council Diversity." *American Journal of Political Science* 52:554–569.

II Latino Mayors in the West and Southwest

3

Mayoral Politics and Policies in a Divided City

Latino Mayors in San Antonio

HEYWOOD T. SANDERS

EDITORS' NOTE

Two of San Antonio's Latino mayors, Henry Cisneros and Julián Castro, achieved substantial national prominence, first as mayor and subsequently as secretary of the U.S. Department of Housing and Urban Development. Both, together with Ed Garza, elected mayor in 2001, also illustrate the limits faced by Latino mayors in winning election and then governing a large, multicultural city.

In San Antonio's council-manager governance system, the mayor serves as the presiding officer of an eleven-member city council and as the only citywide elected official. The two-year term and the lack of executive authority over the city budget and programs make it difficult for any mayor to plan and implement major policy initiatives. These factors also force mayors to build and sustain governing coalitions rather different from their electoral coalitions. Even with a Hispanic-majority population, mayoral candidates are obliged to build broad, cross-racial voting support. Cisneros, Castro, and, to a lesser extent, Garza promoted agendas focused on economic growth and job creation, including such things as a domed sports stadium, convention-center expansion, a major golf resort, and a downtown streetcar system.

Although the effort to boost high-wage jobs regularly won broad community support, expensive public development initiatives split the mayors from the city's principal community-based organization, Communities Organized for Public Service (COPS). As COPS pressed an agenda focused on inner-city improvement and living-wage jobs, it directly opposed the stadium proposal and the golf resort, but both were ultimately approved. Despite the election of Cisneros, Garza, and

Castro and continuing population growth, San Antonio remains a sharply divided community in both income segregation and economic opportunity, and no recent San Antonio mayor has succeeded in winning higher electoral office.

In April 1981, Henry Cisneros was elected as the first Mexican American mayor in San Antonio's modern history. For the city and the national media, Cisneros represented a new era in Mexican American political visibility and impact. The *New York Times* described his victory as an "impressive political feat" and quoted the new mayor as saying, "We have managed to transcend the ethnic factor" ("Mayor-Elect" 1981). Indeed, having garnered 62 percent of the vote, Cisneros appeared to have captured, according to the *Times*, a substantial portion of the vote on the city's largely non-Hispanic north side—"He actually came close to carrying those areas outright." The office Cisneros secured differs from that of many major cities. Under San Antonio's council-manager charter, the mayor is elected on a nonpartisan ballot, exercises no executive power, and simply serves as the presiding officer of the eleven-member city council. But as the only official elected citywide, Cisneros was in a position to gain a great deal of visibility and media attention, both locally and nationally.

Rather than heralding a new era in Latino control of the mayor's office, Cisneros's four two-year terms yielded a political backlash. His successor faced a serious budget deficit when she assumed office in 1989, and a petition drive resulted in a 1991 vote that overwhelmingly imposed some of the most restrictive term limits in the nation, constraining the mayor and city council members to two two-year terms followed by a lifetime ban from that particular city office.

San Antonio did not see another Latino mayor until 2001, when Ed Garza managed a successful campaign for the office. Rather than marking a sea change in electoral politics in San Antonio, Henry Cisneros's 1981 victory was merely one step in what has long been a contest over political control among the city's ethnic and racial groups and among local business and civic leaders.

History and Context

San Antonio adopted a council-manager charter in May 1951 after years of political struggle between machine organizations and reformers during the first half of the twentieth century. The successful adoption of the manager arrangement did not bring the triumph local business leaders and reformers had long sought. In the wake of a massive annexation of outlying areas in 1952, a small group of property owners elected a new slate of council members, who promptly fired the city manager. The chaos that ensued at city hall led to yet another reformist effort, the creation of a nonpartisan local political organization in December 1954 committed to "stability and integrity in city government," the Good Government League (GGL).

The GGL was formally a membership organization open to all. In reality, it was designed and managed by a small board of the city's business elite, which selected candidates for city offices, put together a complete slate of prospective council members, and financed and dominated city elections. From 1955 through 1971, "GGL candidates held 77 of 81, or 95.1%, of the total council seats available" (Fraga 1988, p. 539). The GGL's electoral success was largely based on the mobilization of the city's middle- and upper-income Anglo population. Fraga (1988) noted that the highest levels of GGL electoral support came from predominantly white rather than Hispanic or black precincts, and that there were consistently significant positive correlations between GGL voting support and median home value throughout this period.

Through its control of city council seats and the selection of the city manager, the GGL could effectively determine city policy and priorities. Foremost among them was public support for new urban growth. With its economy long tied to the military, the city saw its population boom during World War II, from about 254,000 in 1940 to over 408,000 by 1950. That growth effectively overwhelmed the city's public infrastructure and created a constant demand for new public investment. Before the GGL's ascendancy, the city's efforts to pass bond issues for major capital improvements had been decidedly uneven. Even with the electoral victory of the council-manager plan, a package of bond proposals covering new expressways, flood control, and sewage improvements met defeat in January 1954 (Sanders 1990).

In growing San Antonio, the successful passage of city bond issues for new streets, sewers, and flood control was a vital necessity for a group of business leaders focused on urban expansion and development of outlying land. The creation of the GGL's electoral coalition provided the vehicle for finally securing consistent passage of those infrastructure bond issues.

The commitment of the GGL city councils to growth, fueled by public infrastructure and urban-renewal investment, did not necessarily extend to all parts of the city. The west side, once dubbed "Little Mexico" by the local daily newspapers, long managed without paved streets, curbs, and gutters or storm drainage. As late as 1951, *Look* magazine could portray a city where "oddly neglected by the authorities were San Antonio's 9000 pit privies—mostly in the Mexican section—each one shared by as many as

seven families" (Gillenson 1951). Although city voters regularly approved
bond issues for flood control and storm drainage during the GGL years,
the promises that west-side flooding would be alleviated somehow were
never met.

Collapse of the GGL; Enter COPS

The GGL managed a total victory at the polls in April 1971, winning eight
of nine seats outright in the general election and one more victory in a runoff election two weeks later. But the political environment of the city was
very different from that when the council-manager system had been approved two decades earlier. The federal antipoverty and Model Cities programs had begun to change political participation and involvement on the
west side, as had the emergence of an activist Chicano political movement.
The city's fiscal environment was also different. In the wake of the GGL's
policies, the city's net debt had grown from $41.5 million in 1960 to $63.8
million in 1972. The solution to generating new city revenue was annexation of outlying areas, and the city manager in 1972 recommended the addition of 63.4 square miles to the city, the largest single annexation since
1952.

The 1972 proposal split the business community and generated a wave
of popular opposition. The conflict over annexation and the city's development policies led to a sharp division among the city's business leaders that
fractured the GGL. At the same time the GGL was in eclipse, a new political force was developing in the city's Hispanic neighborhoods, Communities Organized for Public Service (COPS).

Communities Organized for Public Service had begun with the efforts
of Ernesto Cortes, trained as an organizer at the Saul Alinsky–founded Industrial Areas Foundation in Chicago. With the support of local churches
and the Catholic archdiocese, Cortes began a series of "house meetings" with
residents of the city's west and south sides, seeking out their problems and
needs. In these largely Hispanic neighborhoods, even the most basic public facilities and services were deficient or absent. Using individual Catholic
parishes as its organizing base, COPS developed community leaders and
built an organization capable of pressuring both the city's business leaders and elected officials to redress the imbalances in public priorities and
spending. The COPS organization would continue to play a central role on
an array of major policy and public investment issues, pressing for city
funds for storm drainage and opposing efforts to promote the city as a place
for low-wage employment.

Voting Rights and Federal Intervention

In April 1976, the U.S. Department of Justice delivered the message that the city's recent annexations of outlying territory violated the federal Voting Rights Act. The Justice Department offered the city a stark choice: either void the annexations or "adopt a system of fairly drawn single member wards" (Cotrell and Stevens 1977, p. 86).

Despite some anger over the federal government's intervention, the only real local debate was over how the new single-member-district plan would look. Two years earlier, city voters had turned down a scheme for an eleven-member council with seven district seats and four at-large seats. A charter commission appointed by the council finally presented a plan with ten single-member council districts and a mayor elected at-large.

Backers of the district plan argued that districts "will mean elections where the votes of people—not money—count heavily," and that "ten districts will mean even, uniform growth for all of San Antonio" ("Ten Reasons Why" 1977). The January 15, 1977, vote was remarkably close; the district plan won with a 51.4 percent majority. The "ethnic" dimension of the vote was clear—in predominantly Spanish-speaking voting precincts, the district scheme won 89.1 percent of the vote. In precincts with less than 30 percent Spanish-speaking voters, the vote was just 32.5 percent in favor (Brischetto, Cotrell, and Stevens 1983, p. 92).

The April 1977 city election, the first under the new plan, represented both a sharp change and a certain continuity. Mayor Lila Cockrell placed first in the general election, beating John Monfrey as she had two years earlier, with council member Jose San Martin finishing a distant third. Cockrell ultimately won the runoff race with 59 percent of the vote. The voting results neatly followed the city's ethnic and racial divide. In the general election, San Martin captured 51.2 percent of the vote in Council District 5 on the city's west side. Cockrell managed only 18.3 percent. Council District 10, a predominantly white area in the northeastern part of the city, gave San Martin just 9.4 percent, while Cockrell garnered 55.6 percent.

The new district-elected council looked very different from its GGL-dominated predecessors. The previous council had included "six Anglo-Americans, two Mexican-Americans, and one black," while the new body was "made up of five Anglo-Americans, five Mexican-Americans (one with a dash of Chinese) and one black" and included Henry Cisneros representing the downtown and inner-city District 1 (McCrory 1977). The ethnic and racial split on the council quickly emerged on the issue of north- versus south-side development with a battle over the development of a massive new suburban shopping mall.

The divisions emerged again in early 1978 as the members sought to craft a package of bond projects to put before the voters. Downtown business interests pressed for construction of a new downtown street loop. COPS protested that using federal Community Development Block Grant dollars for the loop would shift money from badly needed improvements in the inner city, and it gained the support of the new "minority majority" on the council. The response by Mayor Cockrell and north-side council members was first to call for postponement of the scheduled March 1978 bond vote and then oppose it. The opposition of the Anglo council members led to the defeat of the entire bond program. It was now obvious that council division and the antagonism of Anglo voters and north-side development interests could stymie major policy initiatives and large-scale capital investment.

After Cockrell's reelection in April 1979, the new council developed a new approach to distributing bond projects and dollars. Each of the ten council members was allotted the same dollar amount of bond funding. The equal-division approach neatly assured that every member benefited and could claim that his or her district would receive its fair share. With no overt division or opposition, the 1980 bond program sailed to an easy victory at the polls. That success, along with the equal division by district, set the pattern for bond programs for the next twenty years.

Electing Mayor Cisneros

Well before the April 1981 city election, it was clear to observers of local politics that Henry Cisneros was poised to run for mayor. Cisneros had grown up on the west side, son of a retired army officer and a politically active mother. Cisneros's uncle, printer Ruben Mungia, had long been an unofficial godfather to the city's Hispanic politicos. Cisneros attended Texas A&M University, graduating with a B.A. in 1967. He gained a master's degree in urban planning at Texas A&M, worked for a time in San Antonio's Model Cities program, earned a second master's in public administration from Harvard University in 1970, followed by a stint as a White House fellow, and then a doctorate in public administration from George Washington University in 1976. He returned to San Antonio to join the faculty of the University of Texas at San Antonio.

First elected to the council on a GGL ticket in 1975, Cisneros had distinguished himself as quite different from his more activist Hispanic colleagues. By 1980, he had found a number of allies within the local business leadership. In 1981, incumbent mayor Lila Cockrell chose not to run, leaving the mayoral race open.

The April 1981 race pitted Cisneros against longtime GGL council member John Steen and some lesser candidates. Cisneros saw the possibility of gaining a reasonable share of the white vote "because you can get twenty-eight percent as a progressive who's standing up for the city as a whole—jobs, economic development, from labor unions, from white liberals, from neighborhood activists, and other people who represented some of the newer interests in town" (Cisneros 1997). The race saw a substantial surge in voter turnout; more than 156,000 votes were cast, fully 37 percent more than in 1977. Many of those new votes were in west- and south-side precincts. Cisneros beat Steen with 61.6 percent of the vote. In his home district, District 1, which included the downtown and inner city, he polled 87.5 percent, and on the west side, in District 5, he garnered 93.3 percent of the vote. But in predominantly Anglo northwest-side District 8, he managed just 42.4 percent, and in the more conservative northeast-side District 10, his vote was just 37.2 percent. He also received significant support from the city's predominantly African American east side, with 76.6 percent of the vote in District 2.

Henry Cisneros's electoral victory was saluted by the national media; the *New York Times* headlined "Mayor-Elect of San Antonio Hails Vote as a Victory over the 'Ethnic Factor'" ("Mayor-Elect" 1981). The message of economic growth was central to Cisneros's appeal for business leaders. Cisneros told the *Washington Post*, "If I can show both sides we're in this together for the long run and the developers get into the atmosphere of unity and the city gets in support of some new programs and bond issues, then we may be able to make it" (Balz 1981).

Mayor Cisneros and Changing City Politics

San Antonio's council-manager system provided both obvious limitations and some potential opportunities for the new mayor. Without any executive authority or responsibility, Cisneros was largely constrained by the attitude and intent of the appointed city manager and the senior city staff. At the same time, as the mayor of a large city, with national visibility and no need to be involved in day-to-day managerial issues, Cisneros was free to use the position as a bully pulpit for shaping public opinion, sustaining a council majority, and promoting his own ambitions. Among his earliest initiatives was finding a new city manager. In October 1981, incumbent manager Tom Huebner resigned under pressure and was replaced by former assistant city manager Lou Fox.

On the financial side, continuing growth provided some real opportunity for boosting city revenues and debt. San Antonio's population had increased by 20 percent from 1970 to 1980. There had been significant new housing and commercial development. And the split over spending that had blocked the 1978 bond program appeared mended—an April 1980 proposal to restore the fire-damaged Municipal Auditorium had passed with a 63 percent yes vote.

Cisneros could also take political advantage of the federal programs still available at the end of the redevelopment era. An Urban Development Action Grant provided support for the Vista Verde South project, which cleared land for a new festival marketplace shopping mall and new high-tech plants on the near west side. In early 1988, the new Rivercenter shopping mall opened downtown, aided by yet another action grant.

Two broad policy efforts effectively defined the first few years of the Cisneros mayoralty. The mayor regularly flew to California in an effort to lure aerospace and high-tech companies to the city and promoted San Antonio as a locus for new bioscience and biomedical research and high-wage employment. The high-tech quest took overt form with Cisneros's release of his "Orange Book," "San Antonio's Place in the Technology Economy: A Review of Opportunities and a Blueprint for Action," in September 1982.

The city garnered an early spate of publicity when mainframe-computer manufacturer Control Data Corporation (CDC) announced that it would build a new plant on the near west side as part of Vista Verde South. Cisneros could describe his vision of west-side welfare mothers employed in technology manufacturing, with the promise that the 250 CDC employees in early 1983 would soon grow to 1,000 or even 2,000 (King 1983). Control Data soon added a hard-drive manufacturing facility and a small-business incubator, the Business and Technology Center. New plants were also under way or planned by Advanced Micro Devices, Sprague Electric, and Farinon Electric.

As the high-tech strategy was gaining national visibility, Cisneros was also engineering a consensus on long-term capital needs. A drainage task force drafted a ten-year program of major bond programs every second year, with the first to be voted on in early 1983. A companion streets task force planned a similar ten-year bond program for new and expanded streets, primarily to serve the growing north side. Thus, as Cisneros faced reelection in early 1983, he had managed to craft an image of a vigorous, consensus-building city leader dedicated to aiding the city's lower-income neighbor-hoods (and COPS) even as he pursued new business investment from around the world.

The April 1983 election results were an overwhelming triumph for Henry Cisneros against only token opposition. He received 92 percent of the vote, and the first installment of the ten-year drainage bond program for $60 million garnered an 83 percent yes vote. The city's voters also returned all ten district council members to office.

As the mayor's high-tech strategy developed, he continued to back plans for new bond issues. The first of the planned five-part streets bond issues was on the ballot in April 1984 and won a 73 percent majority. Cisneros had at that point assembled a substantial electoral coalition across the city that was seemingly capable both of assuring his own reelection and providing a strong majority for new spending and policy initiatives.

The mayor also gained a substantial measure of national visibility, flying to Minnesota in mid-1984 to be interviewed for the vice presidential slot on the Democratic ticket by prospective presidential nominee Walter Mondale. He also delivered an address at the Democratic National Convention.

Cisneros's electoral strategy perhaps hit its high-water mark in the April 1985 city election. For the first time since 1981, he faced a serious opponent in former council member Phil Pyndus, but he managed a victory with 73 percent of the vote. At the same time, the voters also approved a $100 million bond package that combined the streets and drainage bonds promised earlier with issues for parks and libraries. But there were also some portents of political problems. The 1985 mayoral vote drew a total of almost 129,000 votes, a turnout under the more than 156,000 votes cast in the 1981 mayoral race. And the top issue in the $100 million bond package managed just a 64 percent yes vote, a significant drop from the 1983 and 1984 bond results.

The 1985 electoral results were somewhat balanced by a series of job-creation and economic development victories. In late 1984, Control Data Corporation opened its Business and Technology Center incubator on the near west side. The plans for a new downtown enclosed shopping mall were progressing with the announcement by the Marriott Corporation that it would build a 1,000-room hotel as part of the project. And in what was perhaps the most spectacular announcement, William Jovanovich of the Harcourt Brace Jovanovich Corporation committed to building a new Sea World theme park in San Antonio. For many local observers, the development of Sea World heralded the prospect that the city could emerge as the "next Orlando," combining national tourist-destination appeal and high-tech employment. San Antonio and its mayor appeared to be on a roll.

The first major issue on which Henry Cisneros faced real public opposition and ultimately lost began with the decision by the city council in May 1985 to add fluoride to the city's water supply. San Antonio voters had turned down fluoridation at the polls in April 1966, and a second attempt by the city council in 1977 had been stopped even before a public vote. A group of citizens, led by the city's Homeowner-Taxpayer Association, began a petition drive shortly after the council's action, seeking to place the fluoridation question on the ballot for a public vote.

The antifluoridation forces succeeded in getting more than 40,000 signatures in just eight weeks and forced the council to schedule a vote in November. Despite the editorial backing of the city's two daily newspapers and a series of television ads featuring Surgeon General C. Everett Koop and Mayor Cisneros, the antifluoridation forces managed a victory, 52 percent to 48 percent. Perhaps more striking than the vote outcome was the electoral pattern—the fluoride issue carried in north-side Anglo voting precincts but failed in Hispanic-majority precincts, where 73 percent of voters voted against fluoridation (Scudder and Spitzer 1987).

The fluoride vote was a striking failure for a mayor who had long capitalized on his ability to sustain a strong electoral coalition. The Homeowner-Taxpayer Association and its head, C. A. Stubbs, followed up with another petition drive, designed to force a vote on a spending-cap proposal that would limit the growth in the city's revenues. By May 1986, Stubbs announced that the group had gained enough voter signatures to put the spending-cap restriction on an August ballot.

The Greater San Antonio Chamber of Commerce, fearing that the spending limit would impair local growth, spent some $250,000 in campaigning against the cap. The business leadership was joined by COPS, whose founder, Ernie Cortes, argued, "If we don't beat this spending cap in San Antonio, it will reverberate in every city in Texas" (Maraniss 1986). The mayor's efforts and the unity of business and the COPS organization combined to defeat the cap proposal, with a 66.5 percent no vote.

After the defeat of the spending-cap proposal in August 1986, Cisneros sailed to an easy victory with 73 percent of the vote in April 1987, along with a modest $23.6 million public safety bond issue. Cisneros's electoral coalition appeared to stabilize, leaving the mayor free to concentrate on his own growth and development and focus on perhaps the grandest public project of his mayoralty—development of a domed stadium.

Economic Development in Postindustrial San Antonio

A new stadium that could be the lure for a future National Football League (NFL) team had long been a dream of the city's leading businessmen. Cisneros had been quietly promoting and working on the prospects for a domed stadium from about 1983, only to face a series of roadblocks over financing. Paying for the dome with a bond issue and general revenues polled poorly and brought objections from COPS, which wanted the city to keep its commitment to drainage and neighborhood improvements.

In the aftermath of the spending-cap defeat, Cisneros proposed an entirely new financing scheme in December 1986. The plan would use a portion of the state sales tax allocated to local transit agencies, but not then levied in San Antonio, for five years. The sales tax neatly avoided the pitfalls of the earlier schemes, but it required an elaborate set of political deals and arrangements. The VIA Transit agency board had to approve it first, and then Cisneros had to sell the state legislature on the notion of making a "regional economic generator" eligible for the sales tax. Cisneros finally managed to get the bill passed in the very last minutes of the legislative session in June 1987.

In September, the Chamber of Commerce announced its backing for the dome proposal, and the Homeowner-Taxpayer Association announced its opposition. In a sharp change from previous spending initiatives, COPS came out against the dome, arguing that the stadium would support only low-wage tourism jobs. Faced with COPS's position and the possible loss of Hispanic votes, Cisneros tried to shift financing to a public-private partnership based on capturing increased revenues from development around the dome. As the partnership scheme was being worked on, the city council set a formal public vote on the dome for January 1989.

With the vote and the sides set, Henry Cisneros made a dramatic announcement in October 1988—he would not be a candidate for mayor in May 1989. Rumors of the mayor's affair with a fund-raiser had circulated widely through the city during 1988. By the fall, the city was treated to Cisneros's announcement of his love for Linda Medlar, along with widespread speculation in the local media about the mayor's political future.

During the campaign, the dome was termed a "multipurpose convention and sports facility," and local tourism officials promised that it would bring a large number of major new conventions to San Antonio. The Chamber of Commerce also commissioned an economic impact analysis that forecast that the new stadium would generate some 6,000 new jobs. But COPS had earlier clashed with the chamber's leadership over the pursuit of low-wage jobs and chose to actively campaign against Cisneros and the business community on the dome, bringing in its own economics experts to contest the chamber's study and arguing that the city should pursue a broader economic development strategy.

The final verdict of local voters was 53 percent in favor to 47 percent opposed, with substantial electoral support in largely Hispanic precincts on the west and south sides. Cisneros briefly flirted with the idea of entering the May 1989 mayoral race but found little backing. He did push for one final bond project in his final months in office, a proposal for a new downtown central library paired with neighborhood literacy centers that passed in May.

Assessing San Antonio's First Latino Mayor

Henry Cisneros was a remarkably charismatic personality and a very skilled politician, using a part-time, largely powerless office to forge a coalition that reelected him three times and supported an array of bond proposals and ultimately the sales tax for the Alamodome. In marked contrast to his predecessor, Lila Cockrell, Cisneros managed an outward-looking political style, promoting the city and its job prospects across the United States and internationally while gaining substantial national visibility for himself. At the same time, through a tight rein on the city council, he was able to sustain fairly consistent support from district council members.

In many ways, his efforts exemplified the character of the redevelopment-era city. An emphasis on job creation and economic growth served the interests of local business leaders while at the same time promising the kinds of high-wage, high-tech jobs that brought support from COPS. He promoted downtown development efforts, often employing federal grant funds, including the Rivercenter Mall, the Tri-Party transit improvements, and the Alamodome, even as he embraced projects like the Texas Research Park and Sea World that supported growth in outlying areas.

Cisneros's tenure also took advantage of some unusual circumstances in both the city and the nation. Private construction boomed through the early and mid-1980s, much of it financed by savings and loan institutions under relaxed federal rules. From 1984 to 1988, the assessed value of property in the city grew by over 58 percent. That property-value growth allowed the city to issue new debt for capital projects without raising the property-tax rate. Henry Cisneros could sell new bond programs to the voters with the promise that they would not have to bear the cost.

That fiscal dynamic changed dramatically after 1988. The oil bust brought a dramatic slowdown to the economies of Texas cities, including San Antonio. Many area savings and loan institutions failed, including the city's largest, and home foreclosures rose dramatically as well.

For San Antonio's city government, property-tax values began to fall in fiscal 1989 and continued to drop even as the need to pay off the growing debt rose. That problem would become fully visible only after Henry Cisneros left the mayor's office. Some of the projects that Cisneros had embraced and promoted during the boom years also began to turn sour. The promise of high-tech jobs on the west side had begun to stall in the summer of 1985, when Control Data sold its Magnetic Peripherals plant. After brief use by a local firm, the vacant building was sold at a foreclosure action in 1994 and was finally bought by the city for use as a police substation. Two years earlier, the Control Data plant building was repurposed as the city's municipal court. The retail centerpiece of the larger Vista Verde South project, a "festival marketplace" named Fiesta Plaza, was described by the Los Angeles Times in late 1992: "The broken windows of the great pink building are boarded up and most of the copper wiring has been stripped out by vandals" (Kennedy and Tumulty 1992). The building was subsequently demolished to provide the site for a new downtown campus of the University of Texas at San Antonio.

Rivercenter Mall, the cornerstone of the city's downtown revitalization efforts, opened in 1988, but rather than boasting the high-end retailers such as Neiman-Marcus the city and developer had planned, it was anchored by the local Joske's (later Dillard's) department store and a Lord & Taylor store. The Lord & Taylor store closed within a year and was turned into a Texas store, Foley's (now Macy's). The 500-acre, $140 million Sea World of Texas theme park opened in April 1988 with a substantial marketing blitz and the promise of three million annual visitors amid talk of San Antonio as the new Orlando. The park hit attendance of 2.87 million in 1988, but that number dropped to 1.68 million in 1990, at which time it was largely closed during the winter months.

Henry Cisneros's capstone public project, the Alamodome stadium, opened in April 1993 in time to host the annual U.S. Olympic Festival, but the dome never attracted the NFL team that Cisneros and local business leaders had hoped to see. It was used as an arena by the NBA Spurs for a time but never lured a major-league team to San Antonio. And athough it has seen occasional use by convention groups, even before it opened, the city began to pursue yet another expansion of the Henry B. Gonzalez Convention Center.

Mayors and Mayoral Politics after Henry Cisneros

After Henry Cisneros decided not to run for reelection in 1989, the city's business leaders coalesced behind Lila Cockrell. In a mayoral race marked by an unusually low turnout (just under 79,000 total votes cast out of over 436,000 registered voters), Cockrell managed an easy victory over a set of unknown opponents. The ease of her election win was not matched by the issues she faced. The council adopted a 12.1 percent tax increase for the coming fiscal year, an increase that could be rolled back under state law to a maximum of 8 percent. Veteran spending opponent C. A. Stubbs launched a petition drive that gained 51,000 signatures to force a tax-rollback election in February 1990.

The tax rollback proved a sizable victory for Stubbs and the Homeowner-Taxpayer Association, winning with 64.1 percent of the vote in an election with 40,000 more votes cast than in the May mayoral race. It marked a sharp vote against the city's previous fiscal policies, carrying nine of the city's ten council districts. Even before the rollback vote, Cisneros's longtime city manager, Lou Fox, resigned in October 1989 in the wake of criticism of the city's management.

The outcome of the tax-rollback vote and continuing issues from the Cisneros years—a generous police contract, environmental issues at the site of the Alamodome, the budget shortfall, and the city's purchase of downtown buildings—combined to weaken Lila Cockrell as a candidate for reelection. The May 1991 mayoral race attracted a total of eleven candidates—some "unknowns," four incumbent council members, a leader in the antifluoridation and rollback fights (Kay Turner), and Cockrell.

The leading Hispanic candidate was Maria Berriozábal, who had succeeded Henry Cisneros in representing District 1, the downtown and inner-city district. Opposing her were council members Nelson Wolff, who represented District 8, a predominantly Anglo area on the city's northwest side; Jimmy Hasslocher, who represented District 10 on the northeast side; and Van Henry Archer, who had represented District 9 covering the growing north central part of the city.

The results put Maria Berriozábal in the lead with just over 30 percent of the vote. Nelson Wolff finished second with 26 percent, putting the two into a runoff election. Lila Cockrell finished third with about 22 percent of the vote. It was a stunning defeat for the incumbent mayor and set up a runoff neatly divided between Hispanic and Anglo candidates. The most striking electoral outcome involved two propositions that had been put on the May ballot via a petition effort again led by C. A. Stubbs, Kay Turner, and their allies in the Homeowner-Taxpayer Association.

One proposition called for the abandonment of the city's first surface-water-supply project, the Applewhite Dam and Reservoir. A parallel petition effort also placed a proposal for term limits on the May ballot. The term-limit initiative called for a limit of two two-year terms for the mayor and city council members, followed by a lifetime ban. For local observers, the term-limit proposal was an outgrowth of the earlier tax-rollback election, a "vote of no-confidence in Cisneros' dream for San Antonio and a return to the days when the city defined itself in narrow, insular ways" (Jarboe 1990). The term-limit initiative proved widely popular, succeeding with over 65 percent of the vote. The proposal won a majority in 248 of the city's 252 precincts, with support from areas both primarily Anglo and primarily Hispanic. Term limits would prove to dramatically reshape both the character of city elections and the behavior of elected officials.

In the runoff election, Wolff beat Berriozábal with 52.6 percent of the vote citywide. The runoff voting hewed to the city's historic pattern. Sylvia Manzano and Arturo Vega (2013, p. 106) reported that the correlation between the percentage of the vote for Berriozábal and the percentage of Spanish-surnamed registrants at the precinct level was +0.87. The problem for Berriozábal was that the primarily Hispanic precincts on the west and south sides simply did not produce the level of voting support for her that they had provided for Henry Cisneros.

In policy terms, the Wolff mayoralty bore a strong resemblance to Henry Cisneros's efforts. Wolff promoted efforts to boost growth and economic development and supported a massive expansion of the city's Henry B. Gonzalez Convention Center through a dedicated addition of 2 percent to the city's hotel occupancy tax.

Wolff faced only token opposition in his reelection bid in 1993 but immediately became a lame duck. The (small) electorate at a May mayoral election could succeed in choosing one candidate over another and electing a mayor, but that mayor began a two-year term with the possibility of only one additional term before the lifetime ban. It was difficult to build a coalition around any major project or policy issue in that time. And merely winning the mayor's race was absolutely no guarantee that a mayor could mobilize the electorate behind a particular project.

Term limits had a parallel impact on council members. The Hispanic council members who had worked to change city policies in the 1980s were now term-limited out of office and were replaced by younger, less experienced members. The constant turnover of council members also shifted the balance of institutional knowledge and information to the city manager and the professional city staff. The city would not see a serious, credible Hispanic candidate for mayor until 2001.

The Election of Ed Garza

As Mayor Howard Peak's second term neared its term-limited end in late 2000, incumbent council members, also facing term limits, began to maneuver for the May 2001 mayoral election. Tim Bannwolf, representing District 9, announced in late November. His principal opponent soon emerged, District 7 council member Ed Garza. As Bruce Davidson of the *Express-News* saw his candidacy, "To become the city's second Hispanic mayor in modern times, Garza must energize the West Side while attracting a healthy percentage to the North Side's mother lode of votes" (Davidson 2000).

Ed Garza had grown up in the city's Jefferson neighborhood, then a mixed Anglo and Mexican American middle-class area. He became active in the local neighborhood association as a teenager and then went on to graduate from Texas A&M University with an undergraduate degree in landscape architecture and a master's in urban planning. He worked as an aide for one San Antonio council member and subsequently worked for state representative Pete Gallego. In 1997, at age thirty, he won a seat on the San Antonio City Council representing District 7.

The race between Garza and Bannwolf came to involve more questions of personality and style than of policy substance. Garza stressed neighborhood services and infrastructure, while Bannwolf stressed his commitment to job growth and education. Each was aided by the backing of one or another segment of the city's business leadership. The outcome of the voting saw Ed Garza capture the mayor's office with 59.2 percent of the vote, compared with Bannwolf's 29 percent. San Antonio would thus have its first Hispanic mayor since Henry Cisneros's win twenty years before.

Garza's electoral success very much paralleled Cisneros's win in 1981. Garza pulled in 74 percent of the vote in his home district, District 7. In heavily Hispanic west-side District 5, Garza managed to win 87 percent support, and in north-side District 10, he edged out Bannwolf by 44 votes.

Immediately after assuming office, Garza set out a detailed policy agenda including city-charter change and revision of term limits, a revamping of city contract procedures, and a revival of his predecessor's Better Jobs effort. Garza pressed ahead first on charter change, backing a vote in November to create an independent city auditor's position and revising some civil service requirements. But the city council backed off a vote to change council term limits, fearing a voter backlash.

Like other San Antonio mayors before him, Ed Garza was faced early in his term with a divisive issue well outside his agenda. In the spring of 2001, Lumbermen's Investment Corporation announced plans to develop a 2,800-acre golf resort on the north side over the aquifer recharge zone, just beyond the city limits, using special state legislation to create a "conservation and improvement district" that would capture all the property, sales, and hotel taxes in the district to pay for the cost of public improvements. Lumbermen's said that the cost of the full resort could reach $1 billion. The city council initially supported the special district, but over the fall, the proposed "PGA Village" resort turned into a heated controversy over the loss of tax revenue, the potential threat to the city's water supply, and the appeal of gaining the national visibility of a Professional Golfers' Association (PGA) golf resort.

Garza sought to find a compromise that included greater environmental protections, together with a commitment to a living-wage agreement to satisfy COPS. But after the council approved the development agreement by a 9–2 vote, local environmentalists who organized as the Smart Growth Coalition joined COPS in a petition campaign to put the resort-project agreement on the ballot.

By June 2002, the coalition had collected over 77,000 signatures, enough to force a November vote. Lumbermen's was unwilling to see a vote and withdrew the project from city review, effectively killing it. The vote on the project was never held. But even as the Lumbermen's project was evaporating, county officials and local business leaders were attempting to lure another professional golf group to the project.

An effort led by former mayor Nelson Wolff, now Bexar County judge, sought to revive the Lumbermen's resort project, this time with the organization of professional golfers, the PGA Tour. With some of the central elements of the previous deal retained, including restricting the scale of development, assuring a living wage for hotel employees, and promising not to annex the area for twenty-nine years, the city council adopted the development plan in early January 2005 on a 10–1 vote.

The PGA saga exemplified some realities of the post-Cisneros era. Although the mayor continued to often play the role of chief job promoter, he or she was seriously hampered by the four-year maximum imposed by term limits. Major deals, particularly if they provoked the long-standing divide between the north and south sides in the city, could not be readily managed even in two mayoral or council terms. And as before, success in winning a mayoral election did not necessarily translate into a capacity to win public approval for a project or a proposal at the polls.

Garza also faced a very serious problem with his city council colleagues—outright corruption. In early October 2002, two council members, John Sanders and Kike Martin, were arrested by the FBI together with a local lawyer/lobbyist and an attorney with the Heard, Linebarger law firm. The Heard firm had long handled back tax collections for the city. The federal indictment charged that one lawyer had systematically bribed the council members in order to assure a continuation of the city's tax-collection business.

The arrests were a deep embarrassment to the mayor and the city. The *Express-News* editorialized, "The mayor, who has been in no way personally tainted by the scandal that hit City Hall like a bomb on Wednesday, has the task of restoring shaken public confidence in local government," and it pressed Garza to follow through on his promise to appoint a commission on integrity in government and persuade the indicted council members to resign ("Mayor Must Outrun" 2002). By the end of the month, Raul Prado, a former council member, was accused in a separate bribery case involving construction contracts with the local community-college district. Then, even as the integrity panel was doing its work, a third sitting council member, David Garcia, representing west-side District 5, pleaded guilty to misusing campaign funds for personal purposes.

Ed Garza managed an easy reelection victory in May 2003 with 68.3 percent of the vote, boosted in part by the February 2003 announcement that Toyota would build a major truck-manufacturing plant to employ some 2,000 on the city's south side. The most telling commentary, however, was the turnout—just 5.5 percent. The scandals of the previous months had simply turned many voters off the local process. Garza was thus wary of how far to go in supporting the integrity panel's proposal for extending term limits. He finally chose in early 2004 to back a modest change—a limit of two three-year terms and allowing the opportunity to run again after sitting out a term. The full council finally embraced a limit of three three-year terms, allowing service for up to nine years, as well as eliminating the lifetime ban. The city's business leaders endorsed the term-limits extension, and the *Express-News* provided editorial support.

The voters proved decidedly less enthusiastic. Proposition One, the term-limit extension, was voted down overwhelmingly, with only 34 percent of the voters approving. Three other charter-change proposals fared no better. Perhaps most striking in the charter-change results was the consistency across the city's council districts. The best performance of the term-limit-change proposal came in west-side District 5, with a vote of 42 percent in favor. In every other council district, the opposition topped 60 percent. Even in Garza's former council district, District 7, the vote was 64 percent against extending term limits. It was a stunning defeat for Garza and the council and a measure of how low public regard for the council and city government had fallen.

The public's assessment of city hall was not aided just three months later when overt conflict broke out between a majority of council members and the city manager, Terry Brechtel, ultimately ending in her firing. One local columnist summed up Garza's mayoral tenure: "Garza was not a bad mayor. What he was, was an extremely bad leader and communicator" (Castillo 2005). It was a remarkably modest legacy for an individual once touted as the "next Henry Cisneros."

The Rise of Julián Castro

The May 2001 election that brought Ed Garza the mayor's office also saw the election of his replacement representing District 7. From a field of six, Julián Castro won the seat with 61 percent of the vote. Castro, at age twenty-six, was the youngest council member in the city's history.

Julián Castro and his twin brother, Joaquin, had been raised in an intensely political home environment. Their mother, Rosie, had worked for the Mexican-American Unity Council, had run for city council as part of the Committee for Barrio Betterment in 1971, and had later chaired the Bexar County Raza Unida Party. Growing up in the tumult of west-side politics, the twins were clearly primed for public service careers. At Stanford University, Julián wrote his senior honors thesis on the mayoralty of Henry Cisneros before completing a law degree at Harvard and beginning a legal career in San Antonio.

Over a year before Garza's second term ended, incumbent council members began to position themselves for the mayoral contest in May 2005. Among the clear early contenders were Julián Castro, from Council District 7, and Carroll Schubert, from District 9. Schubert was aided by early support from development interests who viewed him as a progrowth, low-tax conservative. Castro, in contrast, had won the opposition of many in the business community for his vote against the PGA project.

A small group of local businesspeople, including *Express-News* publisher Larry Walker, sought an alternative candidate to Castro and Schubert, someone with both experience and no attachment to the city council and its recent performance. They chose to back sixty-nine-year-old retired judge Phil Hardberger, who announced his candidacy in April 2004. As the campaign progressed in early 2005, Castro and Hardberger appeared to be leading in polls. Hardberger touted himself as an outsider and criticized Castro as an insider who had supported the firing of City Manager Brechtel. Castro in turn chastised Hardberger as the candidate of the "big-money" crowd. Schubert's role was that of a fiscal conservative also supportive of continuing north-side development.

The May 2005 results put Castro in first place with 42 percent of the vote, followed by Hardberger at 30 percent. Schubert, with just over 26 percent, could manage only third place and thus was out of runoff contention. The general-election results followed the predictable San Antonio pattern. Castro garnered strong support in largely Hispanic precincts, gaining 79.1 percent of the vote in Council District 5. Hardberger performed poorly in Hispanic precincts and made the runoff largely with Anglo votes on the north side, winning 38 percent in District 10 to Castro's 20 percent. Castro's performance among Anglo voters was strikingly poor.

The runoff race thus pitted Castro against Hardberger on June 7. The result was remarkably tight: Hardberger won the mayor's office with 51.5 percent of the vote, a lead of about 3,800 votes out of 130,000 cast. Hardberger's win was widely interpreted both as an assertion of the role of the city's business community and development interests and as a mandate to bring a different kind of mayoral leadership than Ed Garza had provided.

Phil Hardberger quickly succeeded in placing his personal stamp on the mayor's office. One accomplishment was the hiring of a new city manager, Sheryl Sculley, from Phoenix in September 2005. From 1981 to 2005, San Antonio's city managers had been locals who had previously served the city either as assistant city managers or senior staff. Perhaps her most striking innovation came in restructuring the city's regular general-obligation bond program.

Since 1980, a succession of managers and councils had divided up proposed bond dollars effectively evenly across the ten council districts. That changed in 2007. The city manager and finance staff pegged the total amount at $550 million, the sum that could be managed with the current property-tax rate. Each council member would be allotted $5 million for district projects. The balance of $500 million would be allocated to citywide efforts to be chosen by a citizen committee largely from lists prepared by city staff.

The May 2007 ballot included the mayoral and council races, as well as four individual bond proposals. With no substantial opposition, Mayor Hardberger was reelected with 77 percent of the vote, although the turnout amounted to only 10.2 percent. The bond projects also won overwhelming majorities, with the street bonds getting a 76 percent yes vote.

With a new two-year term assured and the passage of the biggest bond program in the city's history, Hardberger turned to what had been one of the most difficult and controversial issues in the city's recent political history—term limits. He chose to defer tackling term limits for a time because of polling that suggested that it would be a tough fight.

In his January 2008 State of the City speech, Hardberger proposed to continue the two-year terms set in the 1951 charter but to set a limit of four consecutive terms. He also made a point of keeping the current term limits in effect for himself and the city council then in office. Hardberger began fund-raising for the charter-revision effort in June and made it a personal issue, very much a test of his personal integrity.

The November 4 results surprised a number of veteran city hall observers because the term-limits extension passed with 51.6 percent of the vote. Hardberger's success in overturning the 1991 term limits was in many ways the high point of his mayoralty, but it also stood as a testament to the limits on the mayor's office and the realities of San Antonio politics. It had taken an experienced public official, albeit one quite different from other contemporary mayors and council members, to achieve a goal that the business leadership and the local newspaper had been demanding for years.

The Election of Mayor Julián Castro

Julián Castro had made no secret of continuing to seek the mayor's job after his loss to Phil Hardberger in 2005. When Hardberger was reelected in 2007, Castro sought to position himself as the leading candidate for the open seat in 2009. He told *Express-News* columnist Bruce Davidson in June 2007, "We came close in 2005. I have spent the last two years building bridges with folks who did not support my campaign in 2005" (Davidson 2007).

With Castro's mayoral bid nearly certain, the more relevant question was who would oppose him. One alternative emerged in the fall of 2008— local public relations executive Trish DeBerry. DeBerry was then managing the campaign to change term limits. She had previously managed Ed Garza's mayoral campaigns and had represented Lumbermen's on the proposed PGA Village. DeBerry was obviously a political insider, but she had no previous electoral experience and little name recognition citywide.

In the end, the race proved not much of a contest. With a turnout of just 11.6 percent of registered voters, Castro won with 56.2 percent, thus avoiding a runoff. DeBerry managed only 29 percent. Castro's victory reflected the voting patterns that dated back at least to the advent of district elections in 1977. Castro swept predominantly Hispanic District 5 with 82.6 percent, but in north-side District 9 he managed just 35.1 percent and a similar 39.1 percent in District 10.

Castro's success can be contrasted with that of Henry Cisneros in 1981. Cisneros had won with 61.6 percent of the vote in a city election where more than 156,000 votes were cast. Castro's 56.2 percent victory over a leading opponent with no political experience was decidedly more modest. Even more striking was the size of the electorate. In 2009, despite a substantial increase in San Antonio's population, only 89,835 votes were cast, down from the 115,194 total votes cast in the 2005 race between Hardberger and Castro. Indeed, in winning in 2009, Castro garnered fewer total votes than he had received in the 2005 race. Castro's 2009 performance was also weaker than Ed Garza's victory in 2001, at 59.2 percent, with a total vote of 101,095.

The policy questions Castro faced in his first few weeks in office were somewhat different from his personal agenda. The city-owned utility, CPS Energy, proposed expanding the South Texas Nuclear Plant to serve growing energy needs. The cost for more nuclear energy would be some $5 billion, likely forcing an increase in electricity rates.

Castro sought a middle ground, but CPS management provided him with an unusual opportunity. A leak from CPS staff in late October revealed that cost estimates for the nuclear plant had gone up dramatically, by some $4 billion. In the face of clear evidence that management had misled both the CPS board and the city council, two senior managers were suspended, and the interim general manager was forced to resign.

With public confidence in the utility's management and the city's oversight shaken, Castro forced out the CPS board chair and promised a new board of directors and new leadership at the city-owned utility. The nuclear plant expansion was shelved, and CPS began to increase its focus on and investment in renewable energy. Castro was able to use his limited authority but high public visibility both to shape a policy and to appear to be a strong leader. In that role, Castro was very much emulating Henry Cisneros.

The parallels between Castro and Cisneros in style and public relations were not happenstance. Castro had written his senior thesis at Stanford University on the Cisneros mayoralty, and he had long reached out to an earlier generation of San Antonio's Hispanic leaders. In one of his early initiatives, he announced a community-wide "self-examination and planning process" dubbed SA2020, consciously modeled after Cisneros's Target '90 effort. The SA2020 effort sought to involve a broad cross section of the San Antonio community in setting a decade-long vision for the city. It was tied to specific goals in a host of areas: arts and culture, downtown development, education, government accountability, and transportation, to be monitored and reported.

Castro similarly proclaimed a "Decade of Downtown," with city commitments to rebuilding Hemisfair Park with new streets and housing, undertaking yet another expansion of the Henry B. Gonzalez Convention Center, and financing part of a downtown streetcar system. The city also supported the December 2011 "Strategic Framework Plan for the Center City," which led to a set of public incentives for new development of market-rate housing around the downtown core. Those incentives provided a boon to both developers and central-area property owners, promoting both new construction and adaptive residential reuse in former industrial zones and gentrification in some older neighborhoods.

In late 2010, Castro unveiled plans for a "brainpower initiative," using a city sales-tax increase to aid some facets of local education, in common with other mayoral efforts in the postindustrial era. With SA2020 and the start of his education initiative, Castro positioned himself as a candidate for reelection in May 2011.

The 2011 mayoral race was effectively no race at all. Castro drew no substantive opposition and won with 81.4 percent of the vote. Still, the voter turnout sank well below the roughly 90,000 votes cast two years earlier, to just 52,606, a tiny turnout of 7.1 percent of registered voters.

Where Castro's first term had largely been defined by symbolic issues—the conflict over CPS and nuclear power, the SA2020 planning effort—his second was marked by two major policy efforts. The first, a bond package on the ballot in 2012, was a continuation of the city's capital investment policy of a general-obligation bond program on the ballot every five years. The package was again put together by a citizen committee and city staff, rather than allocated by council district, and totaled $596 million, heavily weighted toward downtown projects and outlying street improvements.

The May 2012 bond vote proved an easy electoral victory; the top-polling streets bond passed with 72 percent of the votes. But the pattern of low turnout continued, with a total of just 40,569 votes cast, substantially fewer than the over 52,000 in the previous May's mayoral race.

The mayor's Brainpower Task Force, likely at the instigation of the mayor and his staff, chose to focus solely on early childhood education with a program dubbed "Pre-K for SA." The prekindergarten program was designed to offer full-day pre-K classes for eligible four-year-olds. It was also targeted at economically disadvantaged students, although a special lottery system would allow limited participation by tuition-paying families. In short, it was designed to appeal to a local electorate (particularly more affluent north siders) that might be reluctant to embrace another sales-tax increase.

The vote on the Pre-K tax in November 2012 proved a victory for Castro and his policy vision, albeit a somewhat close one. In a very large turnout race coincident with the presidential contest (over 364,000 votes cast), Pre-K won with 53.6 percent. Even before the successful Pre-K vote, Castro had emerged on the national political scene in highly visible fashion. As the keynote speaker at the September 2012 Democratic National Convention, he had the opportunity to tell his personal story and place himself as an up-and-coming Democratic politico. As one local columnist put it, "Sometimes it feels like Mayor Julián Castro is everywhere but here, running for every office but the one he has" (Brodesky 2013).

Castro easily won the May 2013 mayoral contest and his third term, albeit with a vote of 66.5 percent, down from the 81 percent of two years before. But once again turnout was down, to a mere 6.9 percent of registered voters. And as he became more visible in national Democratic politics during 2013, some local issues began to emerge as overtly conflictual.

One centerpiece of Castro's SA2020 initiative and the Decade of Downtown was the development of a downtown streetcar system. Local voters had turned down a citywide light-rail system in 2000, and rail transit remained a divisive issue in a city largely dependent on the car. The city government had initially joined VIA Transit and the county government in a three-way financing scheme that was also premised on significant federal grant assistance. The city's share was to be provided through a special assessment district along the streetcar route so that adjacent property owners would pay. But those owners balked, obliging the city to finance its $32 million share with bonds—bonds that were intentionally not subject to a public vote.

The council vote on the streetcar financing was 9–2, with two northside members dissenting. That was one indication of the developing conflict over the streetcar plan. A group of conservative political activists began to actively campaign against the proposal and in early 2014 launched a petition drive to force a public vote. The effort was joined by the city firefighters' union, then engaged in a dispute over a new contract.

News broke in mid-May 2014 that Mayor Castro would be nominated by President Obama as the next secretary of housing and urban development. Once again, Castro was following the path of Henry Cisneros in taking the cabinet position at HUD. The new job offered him greater executive experience and opportunity for national visibility. It also allowed him to sidestep the growing controversy over the streetcar system and other local issues.

With Castro's resignation as mayor in 2014, the council was obliged to appoint one of its own as interim mayor to fill out a term until June 2015. Promising not to run for a full term, District 2 council member Ivy Taylor was selected as interim mayor, the city's first African American in the post. Just days after her selection in late July, Taylor announced that the street-car plan was dead.

Coda

The departure of Julián Castro for Washington provided an opening for the May 2015 mayoral election that was soon filled by an array of candidates. In early August 2014, state representative Mike Villarreal was first to announce. Leticia Van de Putte, former state senator and Democratic candidate for lieutenant governor in 2014, joined the race in November, followed by County Commissioner Tommy Adkisson, who represented the southeast part of the county, in December. The roster was filled out by Interim Mayor Taylor, who announced in late February, arguing that some of her colleagues had encouraged her to run despite her earlier promise.

The May 9 general election proved quite close among the leading candidates. Leticia Van de Putte polled almost 26,000 votes and a margin of 30.4 percent. Ivy Taylor finished second, with 28.4 percent, putting her into a runoff race with Van de Putte. Villarreal finished in third place with 26.1 percent, and Adkisson polled just 9.8 percent. Taylor polled strongly in her home council district, District 2, with 48.9 percent. She also did well in north-side, largely Anglo District 10, garnering 35.8 percent to Van de Putte's 22.9 percent. In the historic pattern, Van de Putte polled best in predominantly Hispanic areas, such as the west-side District 5, which she won with 53.1 percent.

The June 9 runoff between Van de Putte and Taylor thus pitted a well-known Latina Democratic state politico against an incumbent African American mayor. The results followed the now-typical pattern. Van de Putte polled most strongly among Hispanics, with a vote of 77.2 percent in District 5. Taylor was aided by substantial north-side Anglo voting support (65.3 percent in District 10) and by a strong vote in the city's substantially black district, District 2 (62.3 percent). Taylor secured the office with 51.7 percent of the total vote.

Mayors, Politics, and Governance in San Antonio

Henry Cisneros's election in 1981 was widely hailed as the harbinger of a new era in city politics: a charismatic young Hispanic professional following a long line of Anglo business-leader mayors. Cisneros achieved a great deal for the city and national prominence for himself, but he never sought or gained elective office beyond the city's mayoralty.

The reality of mayoral politics in San Antonio is that despite a significant Hispanic majority, it has been difficult to translate population numbers into electoral control. May city elections have long seen a significantly lower turnout in Hispanic than in Anglo precincts, and so the Anglo vote—alone or in combination with African American votes—effectively decides the mayoral race. Henry Cisneros succeeded because he could pair a turnout surge in Hispanic areas with a sufficient Anglo vote—although far from a majority—to win.

That combination would prove difficult and elusive for his successors. Maria Berriozábal failed to generate sufficient Hispanic votes to beat Nelson Wolff. Ed Garza succeeded against a weak Anglo opponent. And Julián Castro's victory in 2009 came only after his defeat in 2005 and against a major opponent with little citywide name recognition.

The prize of the mayor's office is also rather modest. In a city-manager city, the mayor has little actual authority and is simply one vote among eleven in a nonpartisan post. Ambitious San Antonio politicos generally seek partisan office, from state legislative positions to county commissioner seats, for political advancement. And the partisan route has substantial limits for Democratic politicians, given the Republican domination of statewide offices. Both Henry Cisneros and Julián Castro were able to use the mayor's office as a bully pulpit, garnering national attention while avoiding many of the day-to-day political issues faced by mayors who are chief executives and achieving the cabinet position of secretary of housing and urban development. Yet among San Antonio mayors elected since 1977, only Nelson Wolff subsequently gained major elective office. What Marilyn Gittell said in 1963—"Metropolitan Mayor: Dead End"—appears fully apropos in San Antonio (Gittell 1963).

REFERENCES

Balz, Dan. 1981. "Candidate Preaching Economic Growth Wins Big in San Antonio." *Washington Post*, April 6.

Brischetto, Robert, Charles Cotrell, and R. Michael Stevens. 1983. "Conflict and Change in the Political Culture of San Antonio in the 1970s." In *The Politics of San Antonio*, edited by David Johnson, John Booth, and Richard Harris, 75–94. Lincoln: University of Nebraska Press.

Brodesky, Josh. 2013. "Castro Stardust Overshadows Substance." *San Antonio Express-News*, September 20.

Castillo, Jaime. 2005. "Garza Has Made Few Friends, but He Hasn't Been a Bad Mayor." *San Antonio Express-News*, January 29.

Cisneros, Henry. 1997. Oral history interview with Sterlin Holmesly, Institute of Texan Cultures, University of Texas at San Antonio.

Cotrell, Charles, and R. Michael Stevens. 1977. "The 1975 Voting Rights Act and San Antonio, Texas." *Publius* 8, no. 1:79–99.

Davidson, Bruce. 2000. "Mayoral Race Ready for Lift Off." *San Antonio Express-News*, November 23.

———. 2007. "A Conversation with Julián Castro." *San Antonio Express-News*, June 24.

Fraga, Luis. 1988. "Domination through Democratic Means: Nonpartisan Slating Groups in City Electoral Politics." *Urban Affairs Review* 23, no. 4:528–555.

Gillenson, Lewis. 1951. "Forgotten People." *Look*, March 27, 29–36.

Gittell, Marilyn. 1963. "Metropolitan Mayor: Dead End." *Public Administration Review* 23, no. 1:20–24.

Jarboe, Jan. 1990. "Back to the Past." *Texas Monthly*, April, 130–132.

Kennedy, J. Michael, and Karen Tumulty. 1992. "A 'Pink Elephant' Cisneros Can't Forget." *Los Angeles Times*, December 19.

King, Wayne. 1983. "San Antonio Steps out of Texas Shadows and Leaps for a High-Tech Future." *New York Times*, March 18.

Manzano, Sylvia, and Arturo Vega. 2013. "I Don't See Color, I Just Vote for the Best Candidate." In *The Roots of Latino Urban Agency*, edited by Sharon Navarro and Rodolfo Rosales, 97–119. Denton: University of North Texas Press.

Maraniss, David. 1986. "The Eyes of Texas Are on San Antonio's Spending Cap." *Washington Post*, August 5.

"Mayor-Elect of San Antonio Hails Vote as a Victory over the 'Ethnic Factor.'" 1981. *New York Times*, April 6.

"Mayor Must Outrun This Speeding Train." 2002. *San Antonio Express-News*, October 12.

McCrory, James. 1977. "Cockrell Sails Past Monfrey." *San Antonio Express-News*, April 17.

Sanders, Heywood. 1990. "Building a New Urban Infrastructure: The Creation of Postwar San Antonio." In *Urban Texas: Politics and Development*, edited by Char Miller and Heywood Sanders, 154–173. College Station: Texas A & M Press.

———1997. "Communities Organized for Public Service and Neighborhood Revitalization in San Antonio." In *Public Policy and Community*, edited by Robert Wilson, 36–68. Austin: University of Texas Press.

Scudder, Jack, and Neil Spitzer. 1987. "San Antonio's Battle over Fluoridation." *Wilson Quarterly* 11 (Summer): 162–171.

"Ten Reasons Why San Antonio Needs Ten Districts." 1977. Campaign flyer.

4

The Election of Federico Peña of Denver

The Challenge of Succession

Robert R. Preuhs

EDITORS' NOTE

In 1983, two years after Henry Cisneros became the first Latino mayor of San Antonio, Federico Peña became another pioneer as the first Latino mayor of Denver. His two terms as mayor, from 1983 to 1991, fell at the end of the redevelopment era and the beginning of the postindustrial era. These were the only years during which Denver, a city with a long history of Latino presence, albeit a Latino minority, was served by an elected Latino mayor. Peña's election and subsequent administration provide a unique perspective from which to explore the rise and influence of Latino mayors in the United States. Employing an array of data, including interviews with Mayor Peña and other Latino activists in Denver, Robert Preuhs presents a potential model for success of Latino candidates in Latino-minority cities based on the realities of mobilization and coalition building, as well as deracialized campaigns and policy advocacy. Preuhs uses Peña's elections to explore the conditions for electoral success for Latino mayors.

In 1983, the political context was right for a Peña victory. For example, Peña, then a state representative, capitalized on voters' concern about corruption in the incumbent administration. Voters, Preuhs argues, were looking for new city leadership. In addition, Peña campaigned on themes that avoided overt racial/ethnic appeals. Peña adopted deracialized campaign themes (accountability, sound management, transparency, and economic growth) that appealed to Denver's white liberals and the city's business leadership. Peña's campaign projected him as the candidate of all the people. However, just as in elections of Latino mayors in San Antonio, Hartford, Providence, and Los Angeles, Preuhs shows that Latino vot-

ers nevertheless turned out in large numbers to vote for Peña. Racial/ethnic vot-
ing patterns remained despite Peña's deracialized campaign.

Preuhs also explores Mayor Peña's approach to policy. He notes that the de-
gree to which Peña's policy agenda affected the Latino community is unclear.
Denver's Latino community is not as well organized as Latino communities in San
Antonio, Los Angeles, and Hartford. Preuhs further speculates about the
scope and nature of Latino community organizing and mobilization in Denver
and provides a forward-looking discussion of the prospects for Latino mayoral
candidates.

In 1983, Federico Peña became the first Latino mayor of Denver, Colorado. He was reelected to a second term in 1987 but declined to run for
a third term in 1991. Mayor Peña is unique among the Latino mayors in
this volume in that his tenure spanned the end of the redevelopment era
and the early beginning of the postindustrial era. The eight years from 1983
and 1991 represent the only period during which Denver, a city with a significant, albeit minority, Latino community was served by an elected Latino mayor. Peña's election and subsequent administration therefore
provide a unique perspective from which to explore the rise and influence
of Latino mayors in the United States and the prospects for future electoral success. Based on evidence from a person-to-person interview with
Federico Peña, media accounts at the time, and quantitative election and
survey data, this chapter presents an analysis of Peña's electoral campaigns, his approach to policy and coalitional politics, and finally, a forward-
looking discussion of the prospects for Latino mayoral candidates and a
second elected Latino mayor of Denver. What emerges is a deracialized
electoral and governing approach based on the realities of voter mobilization and coalition building.

As a candidate, Peña downplayed his Mexican ancestry. This approach
helped him win office in a city where non-Hispanic whites constitute a clear
majority of the voters. As Muñoz and Henry (1990, p. 185) observed, "Peña's
campaign strategy was to stress broad-based issues and project himself as
the candidate of all the people." As mayor, Peña emphasized economic development and growth (Hero 1992; Muñoz and Henry 1990). In Chapter 1, Marion Orr and Domingo Morel argue that during the redevelopment
era (when Peña was first elected), big-city mayors were preoccupied with
rebuilding downtowns. For Peña, a policy focused on economic growth had
an additional attraction in that it promised benefits across racial and ethnic lines. Peña, like other big-city mayors of the redevelopment era, maintained that all residents of the city benefited from economic growth. At the
same time, Peña's case also suggests that for a Latino mayor, a deracialized

approach is a two-edged sword that has both benefits and drawbacks. Peña's case also highlights the role of Latino community organizations. As discussed later, unlike many of the mayors covered in this volume, Peña did not have strong relationships with Latino advocacy groups and Latino community-based organizations. This chapter suggests that the lack of strong and cohesive community-based organizations in Denver's Latino community makes it difficult to build and sustain minority intergroup relationships. This in turn lessens the likelihood of electing another Latino mayor in Denver.

Electing Latino Mayors: Potential Conditions for Victory

As Carlos Cuéllar explains in Chapter 2, the number of Latino mayors has grown dramatically over the past several decades, and Latino mayors have often been elected in cities with relatively large, generally majority, Latino populations. Demographics undoubtedly matter, particularly when coupled with mobilization of minority voters. But in minority-Latino cities such as Denver, the Latino vote fails to be a sufficient condition for election to city-wide office.

Browning, Marshall, and Tabb's (1984) work on minority political incorporation points to several additional conditions that aid the election of minority mayors and their influence once in office. First, coalitional support is necessary when numerical minorities seek office, specifically, support by other minority groups and liberal or progressive whites. Second, system openness allows minority candidates to run as viable alternatives because of both access to political organizational support and the more basic condition of de jure and de facto voting rights for minority voters.

Muñoz and Henry (1986) expanded on these conditions by suggesting that openness in Peña's case was also due to a widespread discontent with a current city administration that did not seem up to the task of managing the city efficiently and promoting economic growth. In other words, openness can also refer to the willingness of the electorate to seek alternatives to established political regimes.

Although coalitional support and a political system open to minority incorporation are fundamental, research on statewide electoral politics points to nonracialized campaigns as another key factor in the election of Latinos in constituencies lacking a majority-Latino population (see Juenke and Sampaio 2010). The risk of losing some coethnic electoral support by deemphasizing a candidate's ethnic background accompanies the larger benefit of not cuing other racial- and ethnic-group voters to vote against the candidate. Although racial/ethnic-bloc voting is likely to occur regardless of candidate efforts when voters are aware of surnames and physical traits, the degree to which it occurs among non-Latinos can be mitigated by framing the campaign broadly rather than appealing directly to one or more members of a potential rainbow coalition (Muñoz and Henry 1986).

Each of these conditions—a sizable Latino population, voter mobilization, diverse coalitional support, system openness, and nonracialized campaigns—played an important role in the election of Federico Peña and likely will continue to influence the prospects for the election of another Latino mayor of Denver. However, as Peña's case and many of the other cases in this volume suggest, the active participation of Latino community-based organizations is another important condition scholars must consider when they examine the election of Latino mayors.

The conditions for electoral success and the political context also affect the ability of Latino mayors to govern. As elected officials, mayors need to please their electoral base, and thus the sometimes conflicting desires of significant electoral-coalition partners constrain the degree to which mayors can change policy and produce benefits. Moreover, if a mayor has run a nonracialized campaign, the potential for specific benefits may be reduced if policy promises made during the electoral cycle fall short of actual policy adoption and implementation. In addition, the institutional and structural context in which the mayor presides affects her or his ability to influence wide-ranging policy decisions. For instance, although all mayors may play a symbolic role as the focal point of city government, mayors in reformed, or council-manager, forms of government hold limited powers and thus rely primarily on support from a city council. In Chapter 3 of this volume, Heywood Sanders shows how the authority of San Antonio's first Latino mayor was limited by that city's council-manager system. Mayors in strong-mayor systems, where mayors wield substantial budgetary and appointment powers, are less constrained and thus are more likely to influence policy direction and its implementation.

Structurally, city governments are motivated in many ways to privilege economic growth and development over social services and redistributive policies when they face a mobile citizenry able to relocate to another jurisdiction if tax and benefit mixtures fail to satisfy their preferences (Peterson 1981). This structural impediment is linked to what scholars have termed the "hollow prize"—the mayor's office in a city with few resources when white flight to the suburbs has resulted in the hollowing out of the core city's population, wealth, and resources (Friesma 1969; Kraus and Swanstrom 2001). Hollow prizes limit the ability of Latino mayors to provide resources and benefits to Latino communities. To overcome this

limitation, minority mayors may face additional pressure to focus on re-
source (and revenue) building through economic growth and development
strategies that in turn could provide spillover benefits to minority communities. In short, institutional and political contexts, as well as structural
constraints, potentially affect the ability of minority mayors to deliver significant tangible benefits to minority communities.

Denver's Political and Demographic Contexts

The basic elements of Denver city government and the city's demographics serve as important contextual factors in examining the degree to which
the conditions described in the preceding section help in understanding the
Peña campaign's success and his administration's impact on the city and
minority communities. As Carlos Cuéllar noted in Chapter 2, most Latino
mayors serve in city governments where the mayor has weak statutory
powers. Denver's Federico Peña, however, was an exception. Since 1904,
Denver has had a strong-mayor form of government, with the brief exception of a three-year experiment with a commission starting in 1913. In
1916, voters returned all executive power to the mayor and thus made
Denver's mayor one of the most powerful mayors in the United States
(City and County of Denver 2014). The mayor is elected every four years
and is limited to three terms (twelve years) following the 1994 passage of
statewide term limits. The strength of the mayor's office lies in its power
to draft city budget proposals, as well as appoint heads of the ten major
departments and over fifty additional personnel who serve in the administration or as agency heads. The mayor also holds veto power over council
decisions. The council consists of thirteen members elected every four
years, with two at-large members and eleven from geographic districts.
Both city council and mayoral elections are nonpartisan. The council can
override a mayoral veto with nine votes. In short, the mayor's office in
Denver offers institutional power, with the potential to direct appointees
and resources impactfully. In this sense, it is no hollow prize.

Demographically, Denver is a diverse city, but the majority of the population is non-Latino white. As Table 4.1 shows, the demographic context
in Denver evolved over the four and a half decades from 1970 to 2013. The
Latino population as a percentage of residents increased from approximately 15 percent in 1970 to over 30 percent in 2013. The African American population remained relatively stable, while non-Latino whites left the
city for the suburbs between 1970 and 2000. Only between 2000 and 2013
did the white population modestly increase in relative size from its low of

TABLE 4.1   ETHNIC AND RACIAL CHARACTERISTICS OF DENVER, 1970–2013

	1970	1980	1990	2000	2010	2013
Percent Latino	15.2	18.8	23.0	31.7	31.8	30.9
Percent black	9.1	12.0	12.4	10.8	10.2	10.2
Percent non-Latino white	74.5	66.3	61.4	51.9	52.2	53.4
Total population	514,678	492,365	467,610	554,636	600,158	649,495

Sources: U.S. Census, various years; 1970 estimates for Latino and non-Latino whites based on 15% sample.

51.9 percent in 2000 to 53.4 percent in 2013. The rise of the Latino population largely reflects new immigration. Gains in the white population reflect both young families following the urbanist trend and large infill redevelopments, as well as the emergence of Denver as a destination for young, skilled workers with lifestyle choices that reflect Denver's proximity to the mountains and a growing creative class (Florida 2002). The population overall has resurged after a significant downturn during the 1980s and 1990s. The demographic context raises two important considerations. First, when Federico Peña was elected mayor, he faced a rather high demographic hurdle. Even a rainbow coalition of black and Latino voters would require significant support from white voters. Second, the demographic context has changed such that Latino candidates, while still requiring white support for a victory, are in a much better position numerically to win if Latino voters rally around their candidacy.

The demographic breakdown presented in Table 4.1 also highlights the historic nexus of demographic and institutional contexts. Until 1975, no Latinos sat on the thirteen-member city council. After court-ordered redistricting in 1971, one Latino served until the 1987 election, which resulted in the election of two Latinos to the Third and Ninth Districts, which had originally been created to foster greater descriptive representation. Latinos have held two district-based seats since. A Latino candidate won the at-large election in 1991 but lost in 1995. In 2003, three Latinos won seats on the council (Districts 1, 3, and 9), and in 2011, one at-large and two district-based seats were held by Latino council members. The rise of Latino representation has been real, but given that Latinos constitute 30 percent of the population, it is important to note that Latinos still hold only 23 percent of the council seats and approached parity in earlier periods only because of smaller Latino populations and smaller percentages of ineligible Latino voters.

In the case studies presented in this volume, all but one of the mayors who were the first Latinos to win election to their city's highest office did so after years of grassroots coalition building by influential Latino community-based organizations. Denver's Federico Peña is that lone exception. Although Denver has been home to a relatively small but longtime activist Latino and Chicano community, including civil rights figure Rodolfo "Corky" Gonzalez, the political clout of Latino community organizations has been muted and politically fractured (Muñoz and Henry 1986). "There has not been a strong Mexican American organization in the Denver area since the late 1960s and early 1970s. Mexican American political leadership in Denver has been historically fragmented" (Muñoz and Henry 1990, p. 184). More recently, Clarke and Hero (2003, p. 320) argued that Latinos in "Denver continue to be saddled with historical divisions within their community. These cleavages can be traced back for generations." In Denver, bloc voting and Latino organizational clout, investigated later, have not attained the level in, say, San Antonio that resulted in Henry Cisneros's election or that in Hartford that led to Eddie Perez's election (Muñoz and Henry 1986). Instead, efforts in the 1980s to strengthen the Hispanic League and the Southwest Voter Registration Education Project in Colorado tended to experience organizational issues, while in the 2010s the Latino Forum, Padres Unidos, and NEWSED Community Development Corporation have remained active mostly in smaller-scale social and economic justice activities or specific issues, and thus their electoral clout has been relatively low. For instance, Peña's victories came despite the lack of any endorsement from a Latino organization (Muñoz and Henry 1986), and local press accounts of mobilization in the 1983 and 1987 campaigns cited Democratic Party and campaign efforts but failed to mention a Latino organization as a significant element of the process (Enda 1987, p. 8; "Strategies Differ among Mayoral Candidates," 1983, p. 8). In short, although Latino organizations are present in Denver, they have not maintained the high profile in citywide elections that minority advocacy organizations in San Antonio, Los Angeles, Providence, and other cities have experienced in electoral influence (Muñoz and Henry 1986).

Denver and the Peña Elections

The political and demographic contexts outlined in the preceding section are key elements in understanding how Latino mayors come to hold office in general. In what follows, the focus turns to applying these conditions to the specific case of Federico Peña's elections, his administrative success, and the potential for Denver to elect another Latino mayor.

In 1983, Denver's demographics and electoral context were far from an ideal backdrop for Latino success in a citywide election. Denver had never elected a Latino mayor in its over one-hundred-year history as both the territorial capital and, after Colorado statehood in 1876, the state capital. As depicted in Table 4.1, the Latino population in the 1980s was about 18 percent of the city's population; African Americans represented an additional 12 percent of the population, and non-Latino whites accounted for the bulk of the remaining 65 to 70 percent of the city's population. Moreover, voting rates among Latinos and blacks in city elections remained relatively low; insiders estimated that only about 6 to 7 percent of the electorate was Latino, and that blacks represented a proportion of the electorate well below their 12 percent share of the city's 1980 population (Hero 1987, p. 101; Peña 2013). White voters thus dominated citywide elections, even with a strong Latino–African American coalition. Latino or African American candidates could not win elections by relying simply on racial/ethnic-bloc voting (Muñoz and Henry 1986). Winning elections required electoral coalitions with other groups, and in 1983 many doubted that a Latino candidate would be able to unseat three-term incumbent mayor William (Bill) H. McNichols Jr. (Hero 1987).

Federico Peña's candidacy for mayor fit both the traditional model of an ambitious politician and the untraditional model of success based on a deracialized campaign message and a strategic voter-mobilization effort ("Strategies Differ among Mayoral Candidates" 1983, p. 8). On paper, Peña seemed well suited for higher office because of his background. He held a law degree from the University of Texas. Like many of the Latino mayors discussed in this volume, he became politicized through his involvement and activism in Latino-focused advocacy groups. After moving to Denver in 1973, Peña worked with a variety of community organizations, including the Mexican American Legal Defense Fund. He was involved in neighborhood associations and worked as a private attorney specializing in civil rights and voting rights cases (Straayer 2011). At the relatively young age of thirty-one, Peña ran a successful campaign for a seat in the Colorado House of Representatives in 1978, serving a district in a historically Latino area of Denver. He rose quickly to power within the legislative party and was chosen minority leader of the Democratic caucus in 1980 (his second term). Given his community involvement, a legal background, and a high-profile role in the state House's Democratic caucus, a run for citywide office perhaps seemed like a natural trajectory for Peña.

However, a run for mayor was far from an obvious step from Peña's seat in the Colorado House of Representatives (Peña 2013). The context of the mayoral election in 1983 presented serious obstacles. First, the incumbent was the three-term mayor Bill McNichols, who was initially backed by the Latino community as the most viable candidate to face what was seen as a worse outcome in the potential election of the district attorney, Dale Tooley. Nevertheless, it was clear to many observers that McNichols was vulnerable because of accusations of cronyism and stagnation in public policy vision ("For Mayor of Denver" 1983, p. 82; "William McNichols" 1983, p. 6). Second, as noted earlier, precedent was not on Peña's side, and a run based strictly on racial/ethnic-bloc voting would not provide a satisfactory margin even to gain entry into the runoff election that would follow the general election if a candidate failed to gain more than 50 percent of the vote (Muñoz and Henry 1986). Third, mayoral candidates competed in an odd-year election with consistently low voter turnout, giving the incumbent a marginal advantage that had served McNichols well during the previous two elections. Finally, the list of potential candidates was long, including prominent representatives from the African American community, who could split votes among a minority coalition.

According to Peña (2013), his recruitment into the mayoral race occurred at a meeting with four friends and political insiders in Denver. Peña had not considered a run for the office, in part because of the expectation of the incumbent's or the district attorney's win. The conditions for the incumbent's victories, moreover, arose in the low-turnout odd-year elections; more liberal representatives won in even-year elections, when turnout exceeded that in mayoral elections by many percentage points. The electoral victories of Democratic U.S. representative Patricia Schroeder (who served from 1973 to 1997) indicated that a more liberal coalition, with increased turnout from both Latino and African American districts, in particular, but also generally elevated turnout, could defeat the more moderate coalition that would presumably back Mayor McNichols or Dale Tooley. The fledgling campaign's plan was to register new voters and mobilize those who historically had skipped the mayoral election but had participated in the state and federal elections (Hero 1987). Peña became convinced that the numbers would be in his favor in a higher-turnout election (Peña 2013). Moreover, he was backed by a variety of Democratic Party insiders, including staffers from Governor Richard Lamm's and Senator Gary Hart's organizations ("Strategies Differ among Mayoral Candidates" 1983, p. 8). His campaign manager, Tom Nussbaum, later to become chief of staff, had been part of Lamm's gubernatorial campaign, and Peña's years in the state legislature provided links to statewide support within the Democratic Party's organization and a high profile within the Latino community.

During this recruitment period, Peña became aware of the potential electoral power of a diverse coalition of supporters. He also became convinced that Denver's mayor had the institutional power to make fundamental changes (Peña 2013). For example, racial/ethnic and income disparities were evident in urban service delivery and city hiring in both civil service and appointed offices. Peña believed that a mayor could address issues like minority public employment and perhaps energize minority voters to participate. Denver's air quality, exemplified by the notorious "Brown Cloud" of particulates that visibly engulfed the city, and a toxic-waste site in the former Lowery Air Force Base ("Denver Mayoral Candidates" 1983, p. 7) were targeted by the growing environmental movement energized statewide by Democratic governor Richard Lamm, who spearheaded the voters' rejection of Colorado's bid to host the Winter Olympics in part because of environmental concerns. Peña hoped that he could mobilize the city's growing environmental movement.

Although Colorado's legislative delegation reflected relatively high levels of female elected officials, and Denver's congressional district had elected Patricia Schroeder for five terms by 1983, Denver mayoral candidates and administrations historically did not appeal to women, who could be strong supporters of Peña's candidacy. The economic troubles of the city also led to a desire from labor for a change. Labor unions lined up to support Peña. The gay community, still underground in many ways in Denver in the early 1980s, was never brought into the political discussions and thus provided an untapped base of voters and contributors for Peña's electoral coalition. Finally, although Denver is often characterized in the scholarly literature as being "neighborhood-oriented" (see Judd 1986), the reality is that only a handful of affluent neighborhoods tend to attract the attention of city planners (Clarke 2015). As a candidate, Peña talked frequently about "building up of the neighborhoods" and providing "access to city government" to all neighborhood groups (Muñoz and Henry 1990, p. 185). In all, a variety of groups constituting a fairly traditional liberal coalition were concerned about the status quo and ripe for mobilization (Hero 1987; Muñoz and Henry 1986; Peña 2013).

As a mayor who would serve at the end of the redevelopment era and the beginning of the postindustrial era, Peña would have to contend with the imperative of economic growth. Denver's corporate community increasingly voiced an eagerness to prepare Denver for the twenty-first-century postindustrial economy and was starting to feel that the city was adrift in terms of master planning and economic development projects. The oil bust and collateral private-sector failures led to an economic context ripe for renewed development efforts. A convention center was needed, the airport required expansion, and downtown erosion was a topic the current mayor had not adequately addressed and could be incorporated into a campaign that would also appeal to the business community. These were all themes noted in the endorsement of Peña by Denver's more conservative paper, the

Rocky Mountain News ("For Mayor of Denver" 1983, p. 82). In all, an electoral coalition of Latinos, blacks, labor, environmentalists, women, the gay community, and even some in the business community could serve as a potent force to win the mayoral election. Peña would be less a Latino candidate and more a coalition leader and energizer of what had been a latent winning coalition.

Peña ran his 1983 campaign on the slogan "Imagine a Great City." The breadth of the slogan allowed all potential coalition partners to read into it what they wanted (Peña 2013). Under this big-tent approach to policy, the campaign relied on what Peña (2013) recalled as "thousands of volunteers" in an unprecedented voter-registration and mobilization drive that targeted racial- and ethnic-minority and poor neighborhoods in an attempt to bolster the traditionally low turnout of these key members of the liberal coalition ("Strategies Differ among Mayoral Candidates" 1983, p. 8). Indeed, in many of the poorest districts and districts with the most highly concentrated populations of Latinos and African Americans, voter turnout increased dramatically (Hero 1987; Hero and Beatty 1989).

Denver holds mayoral elections in a spring general election; multiple candidates compete in what is technically a nonpartisan election, with a runoff between the top two candidates in June if no candidate receives more than 50 percent of the vote in the general election. All the candidates in 1983 were Democrats. Peña entered the race early and felt confident of winning throughout the campaign (Peña 2013). To galvanize the electoral coalition, the campaign relied on several key themes and detailed position papers to communicate a policy agenda, unprecedented in its concreteness, intended to mobilize his coalition ("For Mayor of Denver" 1983, p. 82). The key themes that emerged in the campaign avoided overt racial/ethnic appeals and instead focused on good government and accountability ("Strategies Differ among Mayoral Candidates" 1983, p. 8). Rodney Hero (1987, pp. 95–96) noted three major themes from Peña's literature detailing the goals and concerns to be addressed in the first hundred days in office:

1. "Denver is unprepared for the future. We have not planned or prepared adequately for the city's physical, economic, or social development." Peña claimed that he would: consolidate city agencies responsible for planning and development; restore planning and staff resources; review current zoning citywide; put forth an agenda for developing the city's major undeveloped parcels of land; evaluate Denver's economic base and future revenue sources through a blue ribbon panel.

2. "Denver's government lacks accountability and sound management." Peña claimed that he would: recruit qualified replacements for all cabinet positions; review all existing city leases and contracts; begin management and efficiency studies of each department; institute an open, performance-based budget process; conduct town meetings throughout the city.

3. "Denver must pursue cooperative relationships with suburban jurisdictions and the state." Peña specified a number of intergovernmental efforts he would undertake to address several intergovernmental issues facing the city, including air pollution.

Peña's own recollection of these themes is consistent with this analysis (Peña 2013), as was local press coverage. Transparency, inclusion, and accountability were key points, along with providing vision and leadership in moving Denver toward economic and social prosperity. It was a deracialized campaign that appealed to the liberal coalitional partners and the business community that felt underserved by the current mayor and lacked enthusiasm for the prominent alternatives.

Peña's main opponents in the general election included the current mayor, District Attorney Dale Tooley, and Wellington Webb, an African American who had served in the state legislature and several federal appointments (and would become mayor in 1991). Most political observers viewed Tooley as the favorite to oust McNichols, but negative views of the district attorney from the Latino and African American communities provided some opening for Peña. These views were primarily driven by the ongoing tension with the police, which Peña seemed to recognize in a response to questions of police action in one press-covered campaign stop by saying, "We have some problems on the police force. We all know what they are" (Krieger 1983, p. 7). Two implications arose from the discontent with the city and current city elected officials. First, many in the Latino community were early supporters of McNichols because he was viewed as the most viable opposition to the district attorney. Second, the discontent signaled that McNichols could be defeated by whoever would be his opponent in the runoff election if one was held.

As the general-election campaign progressed, key endorsements helped propel Peña's campaign. Manager of Safety Dan Hoffman endorsed Peña and alleviated some concerns raised about Peña being soft on crime. Businessman Lee Ambrose, a well-known Republican and developer, endorsed Peña because of his vision and development goals and helped broaden support among the business community (Ambrose, however, supported

Peña's opponent in 1987's reelection bid [Johnson 1987, p. 52]). The key high-profile endorsement emerged from the more conservative of the two major newspapers in Denver, the *Rocky Mountain News*. In its endorsement, the paper stated, "On all of these issues [from economic growth and a new airport to social services], Peña has firm and usually valuable ideas about what to do. And he has the temperament and style to stay out in front on problems. Denver no longer will be a city that just reacts" ("For Mayor of Denver" 1983, p. 82). The newspaper's endorsement helped pique interest in Peña's campaign and added support among more traditional Denver voters. In addition, Peña received endorsements from prominent labor groups and the Sierra Club, which underscored the basis for his electoral coalition (Hero 1987).

Because of the appeal to his liberal coalition and his mobilization efforts, Peña led candidates in the general election with 36.4 percent of the vote and would face Dale Tooley, the district attorney, who received 30.8 percent of the vote, in the runoff. The incumbent, Bill McNichols, received only 19.1 percent, and Webb, the African American candidate, received 7.1 percent of the vote and would later endorse Peña in the runoff election (Hero 1987). Table 4.2 presents the mayoral election results for prominent candidates for this election and subsequent elections in which a major Latino candidate ran. The runoff election between Peña and Tooley featured several points of contention, varying from the degree to which Peña was "soft on crime" to a difference in philosophy regarding collective bargaining rights, which Peña supported (Hero 1987). Overall, however, Peña attempted to downplay philosophical differences and ran on both the need for change and a vision that would help a broad set of constituencies, including his electoral coalition.

In the June runoff, Peña won with 51.4 percent of the vote to Tooley's 48.6 percent. Peña attributed his election victory to increased voter mobilization and appeals to a broad coalition of voters seeking change from the incumbency and policies that might address more progressive approaches to local governing (Peña 2013). The increase in voter mobilization seems to be supported by postelection analyses of precinct-level data that stated that Peña "benefitted from new registration" (Hero 1987, p. 100), as well as efforts by many of the campaigns to increase voter participation ("Strategies Differ among Mayoral Candidates" 1983, p. 8). Turnout was approximately 72 percent of the voting-age population. Moreover, the percentage of new voters was found to be highly correlated with support for Peña in both the general and runoff elections (Hero 1987, p. 100). Clearly, the campaign's ability to address low-voter-turnout bias toward the more moderate and establishment candidates in previous mayoral races through voter-

TABLE 4.2   OUTCOMES OF DENVER MAYORAL ELECTIONS
WITH MAJOR LATINO CANDIDATES, TOTAL VOTES AND
PERCENTAGE OF VOTE

	General election	Runoff election
1983		
Peña	48,320 (36.01%)	79,542 (51.44%)
Tooley	41,126 (30.65%)	75,097 (48.56%)
McNichols	25,638 (19.11%)	
1987		
Peña	51,650 (36.82%)	79,645 (50.97%)
Bain	58,003 (41.35%)	76,648 (49.03%)
2003		
Mares	25,308 (22.29%)	38,126 (35.42%)
Hickenlooper	49,185 (43.33%)	69,526 (64.58%)
Zavaras	14,145 (12.46%)	
2011		
Mejia	29,310 (25.51%)	
Hancock	30,974 (26.96%)	71,265 (58.14%)
Romer	32,328 (28.14%)	51,318 (41.86%)

Note: Sources for general and runoff election data for 1983, 2003, 2011 and the
1987 runoff election are based on "Official Election Results" from the City and
County of Denver, various years, https://www.denvergov.org/content/denvergov/en
/denver-elections-divison/records-data-maps/elections-data-and-maps.html. The
1987 general election results are not available from the City and County of Denver,
and thus were calculated based on candidate totals from "Denver Mayor Facing a
Runoff after Finishing Second in Election," *New York Times,* May 20, 1987, http://www
.nytimes.com/1987/05/20/us/denver-mayor-facing-a-runoff-after-finishing-second
-in-election.html. Total votes cast were used to calculate percentage of votes cast in
the 1987 General Election and were reported by the City and County of Denver,
"Historical voter registration and turnouts by year," https://www.denvergov.org
/content/denvergov/en/denver-elections-divison/records-data-maps.html.

registration and mobilization efforts helped Peña. Nevertheless, voter
turnout was still lower in precincts that supported Peña, which reflects
the structural barriers to relying on support from this type of coalition.

Support in the general election, nonetheless, did reflect the campaign's
broader liberal coalition (Hero 1987, p. 101). Precincts with higher percentages of Spanish speakers, African Americans, the unemployed, and Democrats were associated with higher aggregate support for Peña. Precincts
with more whites and higher income were less likely to support Peña than
precincts that had fewer whites and lower incomes. Thus the story of Peña's victory in 1983 was partially one of mobilization of key precincts reflective of the traditional liberal coalition.

Racial/ethnic-bloc voting, while downplayed to the extent possible by
a candidate with a Spanish surname and clear ties to the Latino community,

also played a role in the general election ("Strategies Differ among Mayoral Candidates" 1983, p. 8). Figure 4.1 presents exit-poll data by racial/ethnic group drawn from a variety of sources for both the 1983 runoff and subsequent elections that included prominent Latino candidates, where available. Kaufman (2003, p. 115) reported exit-poll results that reflected wide disparities in support for Peña in the 1983 runoff election. Ninety-six percent of Latinos and 86 percent of blacks supported Peña in the election, compared with only 42 percent of whites. These individual-level data support the precinct-level results reported by Hero in his 1987 study. Thus, although the general themes of the campaign were deracialized, a point stressed by Peña (2013) and supported by press accounts ("Strategies Differ among Mayoral Candidates" 1983, p. 8), the racialized and ethnic voting patterns in Denver remained during this campaign. As other authors in this volume note, Latino mayors elected in Los Angeles, San Antonio, Hartford, and Providence also ran campaigns that deemphasized race and ethnicity.

During his first term, Peña was criticized on a number of dimensions, including his inability to quickly appoint a full cabinet and the failure of a push for a new convention center (Straayer 2011). Economic development continued to be slow, and the 1983 election win occurred amid a continuing decline in the population of the core city. Peña nevertheless generally maintained his previous coalitional support (see Figure 4.1 and Table 4.2), but he did lose some of his previous high-profile supporters (Johnson 1987, p. 52). Peña came in second in the 1987 general election; his opponent Don

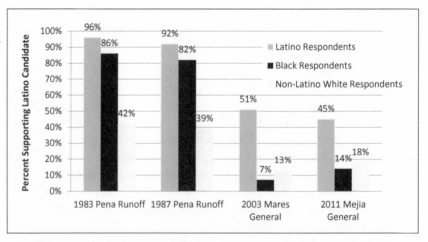

Figure 4.1 Support for Latino Mayoral Candidates by Racial and Ethnic Groups
Sources: For 1983 and 1987, Kaufman (2003); for 2003 and 2011, Survey USA (2003, 2011).

Bain, a Republican, came in first with 41percent. In the 1987 runoff election, Peña won with 51 percent to Bain's 49 percent. The Chamber of Commerce endorsed Peña, reflecting his continued support among the business community. As noted in Figure 4.1, racial/ethnic-bloc voting also remained; the general election's exit polls suggested continued support from both the Latino community (92 percent supported Peña) and the black community (82 percent supported Peña), while whites supported Bain (only 39 percent of whites supported Peña) (Kaufman 2003, p. 115). The election did not reach the voter-turnout highs of 1983, but the victory was credited to last-minute Democratic Party mobilization efforts to curtail a Republican victory and some high-profile campaign support to target Latino voters (San Antonio Mayor Henry Cisneros made a campaign stop, for instance) (Enda 1987; Weiss 1987a). Thus, with continued support from his initial campaign's liberal coalition and his ability to maintain some business-community support, Peña was narrowly reelected to a second term in 1987. This would be the last time a Latino candidate would win an election for the office of mayor of Denver.

Overall, then, the electoral victories of Federico Peña can be attributed to what scholars call a traditional liberal coalition (Browning, Marshall and Tabb 1984) set within the progrowth constraints faced by local governing institutions (Peterson 1981). The promises of diversifying decision-making institutions, increasing accountability, addressing local concerns such as air pollution, and renewing efforts to promote economic development all acted within a context of real economic stagnation felt across major cities in the early 1980s, as well as perceived administrative and policy stagnation in the municipal government in Denver. In terms of the openness of the system, the campaign in 1983 benefited from a popular desire to seek a candidate from outside the current administration, which was called "slow-moving and beset with cronyism" ("For Mayor of Denver" 1983, p. 82). This campaign and context led to Peña's initial victory. As one prominent pollster noted, in 1983, it was simply time for a change (Ciruli 2003). Peña's reelection can be attributed to a status quo in electoral-coalition membership and likely his incumbency advantage over a Republican opponent in a Democratic city.

All of this, of course, occurred within the context of racial and ethnic coalitions that were reflected in relatively cohesive voting for Peña among blacks and Latinos in both elections despite a deracialized campaign. Latino support never fell below 92 percent for Peña, while African Americans voted for Peña at rates above 80 percent in both elections (see Figure 4.1). When his reelection campaign seemed to lack the mobilization of minority voters it had had in 1983, Peña questioned his opponent's openness and responsiveness to minority concerns in what seemed an attempt to rally support (Hero and Beatty 1989) and brought in high-profile Latino politicians, such as Mayor Henry Cisneros of San Antonio, to address Latino neighborhoods. Peña also forced the resignation of the police chief in May 1987 in what could be conceived as a move to placate ongoing concerns regarding police action ("Police Chief Resigned" 1987, p. 1). Although the issues were generally deracialized, and Latinos and African Americans did not have the votes to dictate elections, their cohesive support for Peña certainly contributed to his victories. For instance, at an estimated 20 percent of the electorate, the combined Latino and African American vote accounted for about 16 to 18 percent of the margin of victory according to exit polls.

Mayor Federico Peña: Governing during the Redevelopment and Postindustrial Eras

When Peña took office in 1983, he faced the reality of a city budget deficit amid the Denver area's economic doldrums. According to Peña, his general theme of imagining a great Denver was accomplished over his two terms as mayor (Peña 2013). He increased citizen input, made the city government more transparent, added to the diversity in city administrators and commissions, and generally promoted new ideas. His State of the City Addresses in 1985 and 1988 (the two available for researchers to examine) pointed to a variety of successes, such as a new economic development agency; new sidewalks, parks, and community gardens, including three hundred additional blocks in the neighborhood watch program; and aid to first-time home buyers (Peña 1985). Nevertheless, his opponents in 1987 pointed to several shortcomings and what Hero and Beatty (1989) described as a general level of dissatisfaction with an administration that was seen to have accomplished very little in Peña's first term. One of the most significant failures was the 1985 defeat of a convention-center bond issue to which Peña provided high-profile backing. Peña's second term was viewed as more successful, albeit not devoid of controversy. After a snowstorm crippled the city in late 1987, and with opponents looking for an advantageous opportunity, one group began the process of a recall, which ultimately never came to fruition ("Recall Movement Launched" 1988).

Peña himself viewed his administration as largely accomplishing the broad range of goals he set out to achieve in 1983 (Peña 2013). Early in his first term, he faced a budget crisis as Denver was entering a recession. The process of prioritizing policy expenditures limited the breadth of policy initiatives pursued. For instance, the Denver Regional Council of Governments was in the process of finalizing its report on upgrading or relocating Denver's Stapleton Airport, which required significant expansion and faced lawsuits over aircraft noise in Denver's racially bifurcated Park Hill neighborhood. Peña was instrumental in the deal brokered by the Colorado General Assembly that eventually annexed land in parts of neighboring Adams County. Voters in Denver approved the plan in 1989 after Adams County voters approved the annexation in 1988. The airport was one of the primary concerns cited by the *RMN*'s endorsement in 1983.

Although the time frame spanned two terms, Peña (2013) pointed out that the airport relocation and expansion illustrated several elements of his campaigns' themes and their successful accomplishment. First, they highlighted the constraints on mayoral behavior. Budget constraints, as well as intergovernmental relations, leave less room for policy initiatives than many might expect, and the elimination of general revenue sharing during his first full term left a significant budget shortfall (Peña 1985). Second, pursuing economic development does not preclude serving minority interests. Stapleton Airport was located next to a poor, historically black neighborhood. Noise and air pollution attributed to the airport were subjects of contention and lawsuits. Peña viewed the airport relocation as both a boon to the economy of Denver and a mechanism leading to increased property values in the Park Hill neighborhood. Moreover, since the relocation, the former Stapleton Airport has become one of the most successful urban residential infill developments in the country (DURA 2015). In short, Peña's support for the airport relocation seems to serve as an example of his approach to governing and minority advocacy—redistribution via development, or development with redistributive benefits.

Peña also pointed to several other aspects of his success as mayor and his impact on a variety of constituencies (Peña 2013). He noted progress toward achieving overall economic development goals through efforts to expand or revitalize wealthier neighborhoods (such as the Cherry Creek Shopping Center, which has become a high-end residential and retail area in the city) and attempts to help the historically black Five Points neighborhood and the historically Latino West 38th Avenue developments (Peña 1985). His focus on retail, driven by the reality that retail sales taxes constitute 50 percent of the city's budget, highlights the balancing of the necessity of economic development with the provision of city services. Other accomplishments Peña pointed to included encouraging a strong downtown partnership, seeking new development opportunities, such as attracting a major amusement park to downtown Denver, and laying the groundwork for a major-league baseball team and, after the failed first attempt, a new convention center. Each of these activities reflects what might be considered the general developmental orientation of local governments (Peterson 1981) or the reality of regime politics with a developmental component (Stone 1989).

The degree to which the Peña administration objectively served the Latino community or members of his liberal coalition is less clear. Peña (2013) argued that significant progress was made, and that he was the first mayor to pay attention to his coalition partners' concerns (aside from the business community's) and to rebalance priorities. Just as black mayors of the redevelopment era worked to open contract opportunities to black-owned firms, Peña sought to do the same for Latino-owned firms. Peña's policy challenge was to reduce the overall size of city contracts put out to bid or provide multiple parcels for goods and services that were traditionally allotted only to very large businesses capable of providing the size and breadth of services specified by large contracts (Peña 2013). The reduction of the size of contracts allowed minority-owned businesses to compete for governmental business to a much greater degree than under previous contracting rules and resulted in an increase from 22 percent to 34 percent of construction contracting going to minority- or women-owned businesses in his first two years in office (Peña 1985).

Other efforts were more in line with the interpretation that minority groups were given renewed attention in the prioritization of city economic development efforts and city services. Peña pointed to revitalization of Latino, African American, and Asian business corridors, as well as bond programs to improve infrastructure. Moreover, inclusion of minority representatives on appointed boards and commissions not only served as a practical mechanism for policy influence and symbolic recognition but also helped develop what Peña called a "deep bench" of future leaders with governmental experience (Peña 2013). New parks, initiatives to clean up graffiti, and paving alleys in minority neighborhoods were all initiatives that Peña viewed as unprecedented policy attention to minority constituencies. In short, the Peña administration, while focusing on economic development, was perhaps the first to pay attention to minority interests in a meaningful way (Hero 1987).

Voters' Perceptions and Impact of Denver's Latino Mayor

The degree to which Peña's efforts and recollections coincided with the views of Latino and African American constituents is an important consideration. Kaufman's (2003) study of the impact of Peña's (and subsequently Webb's) administrations seems to indicate that overall, Latino and African American public opinion about the state of the city reflected some gains for these groups under the Peña administration. For instance, "Under Peña in 1987, 69 percent of Latinos felt the city was on the right track compared to only 56 percent of blacks and 36 percent of whites. Similarly in 1991, before Peña left office, 79 percent of Latinos thought the city was on the right track compared to 57 percent of blacks and 66 percent of whites" (Kaufman 2003, p. 118). Although black approval seemed stagnant, it was still above that of whites in 1987, while Latinos felt most confident, and confidence improved during Peña's second term. Part of the stagnation of black satisfaction may have been due to a perceived lack of incorporation into the Peña administration, as evidenced by strong calls by black community groups to increase black appointees after his second election (Weiss 1987b, p. 6). Thus, although there are undoubtedly biases due to coethnic representation, Latinos, while still underperforming whites in objective economic status (Kaufman 2003, p. 118), were more satisfied under the Peña administration than whites in general. At the least, a preliminary conclusion seems to be that Peña indeed served the Latino component of his electoral coalition.

Beyond satisfaction with the direction of the city, Hero's (1990) study of the impact of Hispanics in local government provides some evidence of the effect of Peña's first term on several indicators of Latino empowerment. In 1983, Latinos for the first time were overrepresented on the city council (Hero 1990, p. 408). Although this was likely due to the unprecedented Latino turnout in that election year (Kaufman 2003), Latinos also maintained more than parity between population and city council seats in 1987. Hero also measured political incorporation following Browning, Marshall and Tabb's (1984) scale that accounts for the degree to which minorities held the position of mayor and seats on the city council, as well as membership in the dominant coalition. Employing this scale, Hero (1990) found that political incorporation jumped threefold, from a score of 2 to 6.5, in Denver after Peña's election. As late as 1972, in contrast, Latinos' incorporation measured zero. Denver city government's Latino employees also increased under Peña, albeit modestly. From 1982 to 1986, the percentage of city workers who were Latino increased from 25.6 to 27.6, and the percentage of city administrators and officials rose from 10.4 percent to 11.6 percent (Hero 1990, p. 410). The increase in overall employment numbers likely reflects a general trend toward more Latino city workers that is apparent from 1973 onward. However, the increase in officials and administrators is a reversal of a decrease in both overall rates and parity ratios experienced from 1977 to 1982.

Another view of the Peña administration's effect on the diversification of city government is presented in Figure 4.2, which reports the percentage of Latino and black city employees by high- and low-wage categories, along with overall percentages of Latinos and blacks within the population. Peña's administration clearly coincided with both a growing Latino population and growing proportions of Latinos within the ranks of low-wage city employees. It is unclear, however, how much of the rise in Latino employment can be attributed to the mayor's office being held by a Latino and how much to demographic growth. The evidence also suggests that Latinos failed to gain footholds at the same rate as their population in high-wage city employment during Peña's administration and subsequent years. Thus, while opening up government employment to Latinos might reasonably be claimed as a benefit to Latinos, policy and administrative influence (with high-wage employment as a proxy) remained stagnant during and after the Peña administration.

It appears that Latino citizens realized some objective gains in employment, albeit limited in scope, but fewer gains in empowerment during the Peña administration; their ratings of the perceived direction of the city also rose. Overall, however, Peña's policy priorities and impact seem in line with general expectations from both the urban policy literature in general and the literature on descriptive representation (Browning, Marshall, and Tabb 1984; Sonenshein and Pinkus 2002). From the former, Peña's emphasis on economic development, from advocacy of the airport expansion and the convention center to development-oriented approaches to neighborhood revitalization, is well in line with the expectation that mayors, and city governments in general, are constrained to an economic development focus (Peña 1985, 1988; Peterson 1981) and face the reality of teaming up with

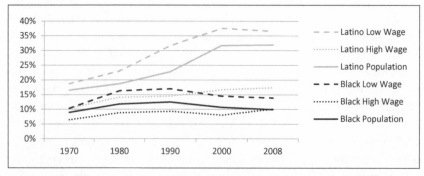

Figure 4.2 Latino and Black Denver City Employees as a Percentage of Wage-Level Employment, 1970–2008
Source: Urban Institute (2012).

business interests to accomplish goals (Stone 1989). Both of the State of the City Addresses available from the Peña administration emphasize economic development accomplishments that seem to underscore at least the requirement of framing success in economic terms (Peña 1985, 1988).

Nevertheless, Peña's contention that he helped rebalance priorities, address long-neglected concerns of minority and poor neighborhoods, and diversify city government is supported by some specific policy initiatives and the approval of at least the Latino community, if not by real gains in employment and long-term empowerment. Moreover, a major theme of his State of the City Address in 1988 was the focus on helping children and families through economic justice and opportunity issues, such as better schools, welfare reform, and job training that fell in line with national trends in Democratic Party models for improving the lives of lower-class and, concurrently, minority urban residents. In short, descriptive representation, as manifested in the Peña administration, resulted in attention to issues and frames that were not addressed by the dominant (economically) oriented dimensions of local governments, although objective success was more limited (Hero and Preuhs 2013; Mansbridge 1999; Marschall and Shah 2007). This attention certainly could have been anticipated by reflecting on his winning campaign strategy.

Prospects for a Future Latino Mayor of Denver

Federico Peña won reelection in 1987 and served as mayor until 1991, at the cusp of the beginning of the postindustrial era. Peña's 1987 victory in the Denver mayoral election marked the last time a Latino won the office. Peña, however, was not the only Latino mayor of Denver. After Peña, Wellington Webb, the city's first African American mayor, served three terms, at which point he was term-limited due to Colorado's adoption of statewide term limits in 1994. Webb was succeeded by John Hickenlooper, who became governor of Colorado in January 2011. On January 12, 2011, Guillermo "Bill" Vidal, the deputy mayor under Hickenlooper, was sworn in as mayor and became the second Latino mayor of Denver. Vidal served until July 18, 2011, when Michael Hancock was sworn into office after winning the regularly scheduled runoff election. Although Vidal's six-month term as mayor of Denver technically places him in the category of Latino mayors, his early indication that he would not seek the seat vacated by his former boss, as well as his short tenure as mayor, led to a caretaker and nonpolitical role that limited his impact. Moreover, the deputy mayor is appointed and historically has had little or no institutional power or role. Nevertheless, Vidal's position as deputy mayor should be noted as a reflection of the long-term, but perhaps not decisive, influence of the Latino community in Denver politics. What might be the prospects for the election of another Latino mayor in Denver?

As noted earlier, Peña's electoral victory can be attributed to an electoral context of dissatisfaction with an incumbent mayor (the openness of the system), a strong message aimed at that general context (a deracialized campaign), and an unprecedented voter-mobilization drive combined with relatively high degrees of coethnic voting and support from the African American community, as well as a broad liberal coalition. The degree to which these conditions are required for a subsequent victory by a Latino mayoral candidate and the changing political and demographic landscape provide insight into the potential for Denver to elect another Latino mayor.

Demographically, Denver provides more fertile ground for the election of a Latino mayor than when Peña was first elected in 1983. The 2010 census figures indicate that non-Latino whites hold a slight majority, with 52.2 percent of the population, while Latinos represent 32 percent and African Americans just over 10 percent of the population (see table 4.1). Although voter participation rates are still depressed for Latinos due to immigration status and a younger population, the Latino population has grown roughly 50 percent since 1983, while whites have declined as a percentage of the population from about 70 percent to just over 50 percent. Moreover, the city has experienced growth during the past decade, much of which is attributed to a combination of Latinos and young white, well-educated professionals who seem both ripe for coalitional membership and are less racially/ethnically conscious. The potential for a winning liberal coalition backing a Latino candidate remains.

Nevertheless, the demographic trend has been apparent over the past two decades, but Latino candidates have been unsuccessful in winning the mayor's office. This may be due in part to the lack of an anti-incumbent context and the pairing of candidates across the elections, and thus a less open political system from a campaign-messaging standpoint. Few contests since 1983 (and perhaps 1987) seemed to reflect the same level of discontent with the direction of the city as when the three-term incumbent McNichols took third place in the 1983 general election. Since 1968, no mayor has held the seat for fewer than two terms. In 1991, Wellington Webb, a longtime Democratic officeholder and federal appointee (and general-election candidate during Peña's initial bid) won election as an underdog against Republican district attorney Norm Early, also an African American. The following two elections produced no competitive Latino candidates, and Webb secured his third-term victory in the general election by winning over 80 percent of the vote and avoiding a runoff election.

Term limited, Webb did not run in 2003, and the open seat produced the first legitimate Latino candidacy since Peña's 1987 victory. Don Mares, the two-term city auditor, ran an unsuccessful race against the eventual winner, John Hickenlooper. Hickenlooper secured 43.3 percent of the vote in the general election to Mares's 22.3 percent. Mares was successful primarily in Latino districts, but Hickenlooper's ability to capture a wide range of constituencies led to his eventual victory. In the runoff, with a 44.8 percent turnout of registered voters, Hickenlooper captured over 64 percent of the vote to Mares's 35 percent (see Table 4.2). The election again revealed the racial/ethnic-bloc voting reported in earlier analyses of the Peña victories, but in a context of relatively low voter turnout.

In fact, racial/ethnic voting in Denver seemed to reflect the general patterns that emerged during the Peña campaigns. Figure 4.3 presents the simple correlation coefficients (Pearson's r) between the vote for the Latino candidate and Latinos as a percentage of the population for precinct-level data for elections with a prominent Latino candidate given available data. Reported by Hero (1989), the correlations for Peña's 1983 general and runoff elections were .654 and .512; the correlation for Mares's 2003 runoff spiked to .868. Although one must be careful not to attribute these patterns to individual voters, Mares's base of support was clearly, and seemingly to a greater extent than Peña's, Latino communities. This provides a hint of the necessity of a broader coalition to win the mayor's office in Denver.

Individual-level data confirm this general pattern. In a general-election-eve poll conducted by Survey USA (see Figure 4.1), 51 percent of Latinos supported Mares, 54 percent of blacks supported Penfield Tate (a longtime African American legislator), and 50 percent of whites supported Hickenlooper (Survey USA 2003). Support for Mares among African Americans (7 percent) and whites (13 percent) was well below his support from Latinos, which in turn was quite split. Moreover, Mares failed to gain support from any of the broader liberal constituencies that led to Peña's victory. For instance, 44 percent of liberals supported Hickenlooper, compared with 16 percent who supported Mares. In fact, outside Latino support, Hickenlooper led every demographic group reported by Survey USA. The liberal coalition combined with the business community to support Hickenlooper in 2003. (Hickenlooper was a prominent owner of several local establishments and a pioneer in the brew-pub revival in downtown Denver.) That coalition, so fundamental to the Peña victory, was lacking in 2003 when Denver once again chose its next two-term mayor. In 2007, Hickenlooper

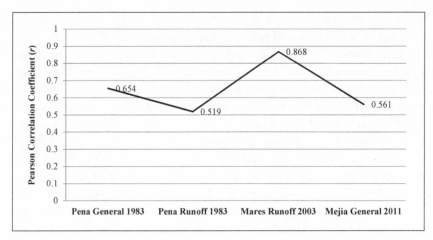

Figure 4.3 Precinct-Level Correlations between Latino Voting-Age Population and Percentage of Vote for Latino Candidate
Source: Peña data from Hero (1989); Mares data from Barreto (2007); Mejia data calculated by author.
Note: Mejia data reflect correlations for precincts with greater than 20 percent Latino citizen voting-age population.

secured his second term easily with 86 percent of the vote in the general election, thus avoiding a runoff. His sole opponent, Danny López, a Public Works Department employee who presented a liberal antiestablishment platform, never gained serious and widespread support from the traditional liberal coalition or the broader Latino community. (López ran again in 2011 but garnered less than 1 percent of the vote in the general election when faced with more prominent opponents.)

The 2011 open-seat election presented another opportunity for a Latino mayoral candidate. James Mejia, who had served in Wellington Webb's cabinet, as well as helping to establish the Denver Preschool Program, had garnered a citywide election victory for an at-large seat on the Denver Public Schools Board of Education. Mejia was the most viable Latino mayoral candidate since Mares in 2003 and, with ties to both the Webb administration and Hickenlooper's gubernatorial campaign, had the potential to gain the support of the liberal coalition that had eluded previous Latino candidates. His campaign ended when he placed third in the 2011 general election. Mejia's 25.51 percent of the vote fell 1,664 votes shy of the second-place candidate and eventual winner, Michael B. Hancock (see Table 4.2). Chris Romer, son of former governor Roy Romer, garnered the most votes with 28.14 percent. Voter turnout was low, around 38 percent of registered voters.

Precinct results once again indicated the strong presence of racial-bloc voting. Traditional Latino strongholds in Northwest and West Denver supported Mejia, Hancock secured Northeast Denver's traditional black neighborhoods, and Romer did well in predominantly white South Denver. As noted in Figure 4.3, the precinct-level correlation between Latino population and support for Mejia in the general election was around .564, not far from the correlation coefficient found for Peña almost thirty years before Mejia's loss, but lower than the correlation for Mares's runoff election. In both Mares's and Mejia's losses, precincts with larger Latino populations were by far the most supportive, as noted in Table 4.3. And, as with the Mares and Peña campaigns, precinct-level data reflected individual-level data from polls conducted before the election, as Figure 4.1 highlights (Survey USA 2011; see also Barreto 2007). Mejia and Hancock were supported by a plurality (over 40 percent) of Latino and African American respondents. Neither received more than 18 percent of white respondents' support.

Mejia's coalition, however, did approximate Peña's in many ways. He ran a deracialized campaign, emphasizing education, and contrasted his positions with Romer's, a tactical mistake Mejia himself lamented (2014), rather than focusing on Hancock and trying to increase support among the African American community (as well as diminishing Hancock's support among Latinos, which was at about 11 percent before the election, compared with 21 percent for Romer [Survey USA 2011]). Mejia's efforts to pull votes from the frontrunner may have cost him support among both the Latino and African American communities. In regard to other potential

TABLE 4.3   MEAN PRECINCT-LEVEL SUPPORT FOR LATINO CANDIDATES FOR DENVER MAYOR BY PRECINCT-LEVEL LATINO VAP, 2003 RUNOFF AND 2011 GENERAL ELECTIONS

	< 20% Latino VAP precincts	20%–40% Latino VAP* precincts	40%–60% Latino VAP precincts	> 60% Latino VAP precincts	Citywide election results
Mean percentage of vote for Mares, runoff (2003)	30.74% (264)	45.22% (70)	58.30% (42)	70.29% (41)	35.42%
Mean Percentage of vote for Mejia, general (2011)	23.25% (260)	23.72% (81)	33.33% (40)	39.00% (47)	25.51%

Sources: For 2003 data: Matt Barreto, http://faculty.washington.edu/mbarreto/data/index.html; for 2011 data: City and County of Denver Clerk and Recorder, "Returns and Voter Turnout by Precinct" and "Hispanic Voter Turnout by Precinct," http://www.denvergov.org/ClerkandRecorder/ElectionsVoting/ArchivesandRecords/20110503MunicipalGeneralElection/tabid/440258/Default.aspx.

Note: Cell entries indicate average percentage vote for Latino candidate for precinct-level returns. Citywide election results are based on all votes cast, not on an average of precincts.

*VAP=Voting-age population

coalition members who had added to Peña's victory in 1983, liberals and women, in particular, favored Mejia by slight margins (about 5 percent) over Hancock, but the percentages were roughly split. One factor that likely hurt Mejia was the lack of an establishment candidate perceived to be insensitive to liberal causes or at least stagnant in regard to economic and urban development policy, as had been the case with the McNichols administration or the Tooley candidacy. The choice was between ideologically matched opponents from different minority constituencies.

Mejia attributed his slim loss to strategic and tactical mistakes during the campaign, from an overly technical approach to policy discussions to a miscalculation in a campaign that paid too little attention to the eventual second-place winner (Mejia 2014). But Mejia also emphasized deracialized campaign messaging and gained reasonable support from a broad constituency. The presence of a strong African American candidate eventually split the minority-group coalition in the general election and resulted in a close election that might have gone the other way if a variety of minor circumstances had changed (such as an increase in Latino voter turnout). The racial/ethnic split between black and Latino support suggests an interesting paradox for Latino candidates. Although a deracialized campaign with broad coalitional appeals seems like a necessary condition for success, a contention supported by both Peña (2013) and Mejia (2014), failing to mobilize the Latino base (with voter turnout for Latinos in largely Latino districts rarely reaching more than about 35 percent [City and County of Denver Clerk and Recorder 2011]) likely cost Mejia a spot in the runoff. Faced with mobilizing Latino supporters at the cost of alienating potential coalition partners, Latino mayoral candidates in Denver must walk a tightrope between subtle ethnic appeals in the general election and deracialized appeals to gain broader support.

Conclusion

Previous research on Federico Peña's election as Denver's first Latino mayor emphasized several conditions that were necessary for success (Muñoz and Henry 1986): (1) the continued presence of a large Latino voting bloc, (2) high voter mobilization and turnout, (3) an unpopular incumbent administration or a view that the current system is ripe for change, (4) a charismatic Latino candidate who is able to mobilize a broad set of constituencies through a deracialized campaign, and (5) a condition overlooked in some of the previous literature—the absence of a strong African American candidate who can appeal to constituencies outside the African American community. In each of the elections since Peña's 1987 victory, one or more of these conditions did not exist. The 2011 mayoral election provided the best opportunity for a Latino mayoral victory, but the lack of a unified multiracial coalition at the general-election stage, low voter turnout, and small margins of support for the Latino candidate among coalition members led to a victory for the African American candidate. In many ways, the same liberal coalition that helped Peña secure office has been the basis for the election of two African American mayors since 1991 whose administrations span five four-year terms, in a major city with an African American population under 12 percent of the total population.

Federico Peña also sees the potential for another Latino mayor (Peña 2013). First, he correctly notes that it is statistically easier to win an election for Latinos now than in the past. Denver's Latinos account for just over 30 percent of the city's population, and as its high proportion of under-eighteen citizens attains voting age, Latino voter influence should increase (see Table 4.1). Second, there is broad community acceptance of the notion that Latinos can be good mayors—a perception that was not part of the political context in 1983. Third, as reflected by some scholarly analysis of Colorado statewide elections (Juenke and Sampaio 2010), the campaign needs to be deracialized. To Peña, this means that Latino candidates need to fundamentally believe and make it clear that one is not a racial/ethnic candidate. He gives the following advice to potential candidates: "Don't think of yourself as African American, Latino, Asian. Think of yourself as a person. You have great ideas, want to serve, can accomplish great things. You are willing to listen to people and want to serve, and sympathize. You just happen to be Latino" (Peña 2013). The *Rocky Mountain News*'s endorsement in 1983 echoed these sentiments in supporting Peña. Mejia seconds this approach and suggests that Denver's demographics, politics, and the need for a coalition to elect a Latino mayor in a Latino-minority city require framing the base as not simply coethnic groups (Mejia 2014). This sentiment reflects the necessity of the broader condition or deracialized campaigns and the need to establish a large, liberal, policy-oriented coalition for Latino mayors to win mayoral races in cities without a Latino majority in the electorate.

Given continued racial/ethnic-bloc voting and the reality that although Latinos constitute a large portion of Denver's electorate, Latino candidates still require support from a broader liberal coalition, the potential for another mayoral electoral victory by a Latino candidate remains strong but uncertain. At the same time, despite the conventional wisdom that suggests that Latino candidates must run a deracialized campaign for electoral success, the findings from this study also point to the limits of a deracialized strategy. As Mejia's experience illustrates, the success of Latino candidates is highly dependent on maximizing turnout of the Latino electorate, so a deracialized campaign may be counterproductive. Thus, success for Latino candidates may depend on creating the appearance of a deracialized campaign to appeal to the broader electorate while simultaneously embracing a coethnic strategy within the Latino community.

Denver's population has increased substantially as economic opportunity, as well as inequality, has grown, resulting in an electorate that remains typical of urban liberal sentiments (Denver's Democratic U.S. house member, Diana DeGette, won reelection to her eleventh term with 68 percent of the vote in 2014). Importantly, however, the condition of perceived cronyism and stagnation that led to Peña's success has not seemed evident as recent mayors have reached out to the broader liberal coalition while pursuing development and growth strategies that have made Denver one of the more attractive cities for business, young residents, and the creative/technology class. As a result, many of the underlying and widespread currents of economic discontent and sense of stagnation that led to Peña's victory will be absent for the foreseeable future. Nevertheless, minority candidates for mayor have succeeded, and thus the city's demonstrated ability to elect minority mayors (winning the office in six of the eight elections since 1983) provides evidence of the potential for future success.

Beyond a deracialized campaign, however, coordination across minority candidacies may be required under the rules of the general- and runoff-election system. The 2011 election indicated that the liberal coalition was split between the African American and Latino candidates in the general election. A small margin propelled the African American candidate to the runoff. Moreover, the pattern of racial and ethnic voting remained almost unchanged from the 1983 election. With highly qualified candidates from both the Latino and African American communities seeking support to build a winning coalition, there is little incentive to strategically withhold one group's candidate. Although the Latino and African American communities in Denver agree on most major ideological issues, some important issues regarding educational reform and development initiatives are apparent even today. In short, as Kaufman (2003) and others have noted (Sonenshein and Pinkus 2002; Sonenshein 2003; Sonenshein and Drayse 2006), there may be cracks in the rainbow that reflect Latino–African American conflict at the local level in Denver even though broader coalitions emerge over more ideological and national-level issues (Hero and Preuhs 2013).

Finally, viewed within the context of many of the other chapters in this volume, the case study of Federico Peña shows how important community-based organizations are in Latino mayoral politics. Latino community-based organizations are not strong in Denver. As Clarke (2015, p. 159) explained, "Latinos are not as well organized and not as influential as African Americans." Latino community-based organizations are important for several reasons. They provide a space for future Latino mayors to become politicized and gain political experience. They play a vital role in naturalizing immigrants, helping immigrants register to vote, informing them about policy issues, and mobilizing them on Election Day (Andersen 2010). Latino community-based organizations can also push Latino mayors to advance policies that are beneficial to the Latino community (Orr 2007b). Peña, for instance, "placed greater emphasis on economic development" than on social services and other redistributive policies (Hero 1992, p. 124). The presence of robust and active community-based organizations in the Latino community might have encouraged Mayor Peña to pursue broader policies. Because "community organizing is about engaging disadvantaged communities in order to achieve power," it also has the potential to bring Denver's Latino and African-American community closer together (Orr 2007a, p. 16).

REFERENCES

Andersen, Kristi. 2010. *New Immigrant Communities: Finding a Place in Local Politics*. Boulder, CO: Lynne Rienner.

Barreto, Matt A. 2007. "*¡Sí Se Puede!* Latino Candidates and the Mobilization of Latino Voters." *American Political Science Review* 101:425–441.

Browning, Rufus P., Dale Rogers Marshall, and David H. Tabb. 1984. *Protest Is Not Enough: The Struggle of Blacks and Hispanics in Urban Politics*. Berkeley: University of California Press.

Ciruli, Floyd. 2003. "Regime Change: Denver City Election, May 2003." http://www.ciruli.com/archives/denmayor/overview.htm#Anchor-Election-6575.

City and County of Denver Clerk and Recorder. 2011 "Hispanic Voter Turnout by Precinct." http://www.denvergov.org/ClerkandRecorder/ElectionsVoting/ArchivesandRecords/20110503MunicipalGeneralElection/tabid/440258/Default.aspx.

City and County of Denver. 2014 "History of Denver's Mayor-Council Government." http://www.denvergov.org/citycouncil/DenverCityCouncil/AboutUs/tabid/436356/Default.aspx.

Clarke, Susan E. 2015. "The New Politics in a Postindustrial City: Intersecting Policies in Denver." In *Urban Neighborhoods in a New Era: Revitalization Politics in the Postindustrial City*, edited by Clarence N. Stone and Robert Stoker, 155–181. Chicago: University of Chicago Press.

Clarke, Susan E., and Rodney E. Hero. 2003. "Latinos, Blacks, and Multiethnic Politics in Denver: Realigning Power and Influence in the Struggle for Equality." In *Racial Politics in American Cities*, edited by Rufus P. Browning, Dale Rogers Marshall, and David H. Tabb, 309–330. New York: Longman.

"Denver Mayoral Candidates Look at Issues of Hazardous Substance Disposal." 1983. *Rocky Mountain News*, April 25, 7.

DURA (Denver Urban Renewal Authority). 2015. "Stapleton." http://www.renewdenver
.org/redevelopment/dura-redevelopment-projects/denver-county/stapleton.html.

Enda, Jodi. 1987. "Last-Minute Drive to Get Out Vote Aided Peña." *Rocky Mountain
News*, June 17, 8.

Florida, Richard. 2002. *The Rise of the Creative Class: And How It's Transforming Work,
Leisure, Community and Everyday Life*. New York: Basic Books.

"For Mayor of Denver, Federico Peña." 1983. *Rocky Mountain News*, April 24, 82.

Friesema, H. Paul. 1969. "Black Control of Central Cities: The Hollow Prize." *Journal of
the American Planning Association* 35, no. 2:75–79

Hero, Rodney E. 1987. "The Election of Hispanics in City Government: An Examination
of the Election of Federico Peña as Mayor of Denver." *Western Political Quarterly* 40,
no. 1 (March): 93–105.

———. 1989. "Multiracial Coalitions in City Elections Involving Minority Candidates:
Some Evidence from Denver." *Urban Affairs Quarterly* 25, no. 2 (December): 342–351.

———. 1990. "Hispanics in Urban Government and Politics: Some Findings, Com-
parisons and Implications." *Western Political Quarterly* 43, no. 2 (June): 403–414.

———. 1992. *Latinos and the U.S. Political System: Two-Tiered Pluralism*. Philadelphia:
Temple University Press.

Hero, Rodney E., and Kathleen Beatty. 1989. "The Elections of Federico Peña as Mayor
of Denver: Analysis and Implications." *Social Science Quarterly* 70, no. 2 (June): 300–310.

Hero, Rodney E., and Robert R. Preuhs. 2013. *Black-Latino Relations in U.S. National
Politics: Beyond Conflict or Cooperation*. New York: Cambridge University Press.

Johnson, Constance. 1987. "Half of First-Term Backers Still behind Peña." *Rocky Mountain News*, May 17, 52.

Judd, Dennis R. 1986. "Electoral Coalitions, Minority Mayors, and the Contradictions
in the Municipal Policy Agenda." In *Cities In Stress: A New Look at the Urban Crisis*, vol.
30, edited by Mark Gottdiener, Urban Affairs Annual Reviews, 145–170. Thousand
Oaks, CA: Sage Publications.

Juenke, Eric Gonzalez, and Anna Christina Sampaio. 2010. "Deracialization and Latino
Politics: The Case of the Salazar Brothers in Colorado." *Political Research Quarterly* 63,
no. 1 (March): 43–54.

Kaufmann, Karen M. 2003. "Black and Latino Voters in Denver: Responses to Each
Other's Political Leadership." *Political Science Quarterly* 118, no. 1 (Spring): 107–112.

Kraus, Neil and Todd Swanstrom. 2001. "Minority Mayors and the Hollow-Prize Problem." *PS: Political Science and Politics* 34, no. 1:99–105.

Krieger, Dave. 1983. "Can Charisma Win for Federico Pena?: Mayoral Candidate Turn-
ing to 'the People' for Support." *Rocky Mountain News*, March 13, 7.

Mansbridge, Jane. 1999. "Should Blacks Represent Blacks and Women Represent
Women? A Contingent 'Yes.'" *Journal of Politics* 61, no. 3:627–657.

Marschall, Melissa, and Paru Shah. 2007. "The Attitudinal Effects of Minority Incorporation: Examining the Racial Dimensions of Trust in Urban America." *Urban Affairs Review* 42 (May): 629–658.

Mejia, James. 2014. In-person interview by the author, January 13.

Muñoz, Carlos, Jr., and Charles P. Henry. 1986. "Rainbow Coalitions in Four Big Cities:
San Antonio, Denver, Chicago and Philadelphia." *PS: Political Science and Politics* 61,
no. 3 (Summer): 598–609.

———. 1990. "Coalition Politics in San Antonio and Denver: The Cisneros and
Peña Mayoral Campaigns." In *Racial Politics in American Cities*, edited by Rufus P.

Browning, Dale Rogers Marshall, and David H. Tabb, 179–190. White Plains, NY: Longman.

Orr, Marion. 2007a. "Community Organizing and the Changing Ecology of Civic Engagement." In *Transforming the City: Community Organizing and the Challenge of Political Change*, edited by Marion Orr, 1–27. Lawrence: University Press of Kansas.

———, ed. 2007b. *Transforming the City: Community Organizing and the Challenge of Political Change*. Lawrence: University Press of Kansas.

Peña, Fedrico. 1985. *State of the City Address*. July 10.

———. 1988. *State of the City Address*. July 13.

———. 2013. Personal phone interview with Federico Peña by the author, October 3.

Peterson, Paul. 1981. *City Limits*. Chicago, IL: University of Chicago Press

"Police Chief Resigned under Pressure from Mayor Federico Peña." 1987. *Rocky Mountain News*, May 1, 1.

"Recall Movement Launced." 1988. *Rocky Mountain News*, January 21, 28.

Sonenshein, Raphael J. 2003. "Post-incorporation Politics in Los Angeles." In *Racial Politics in American Cities*, edited by Rufus P. Browning, Dale Rogers Marshall, and David H. Tabb, 3rd ed., 51–75. New York: Longman.

Sonenshein, Raphael, and Mark H. Drayse. 2006. "Urban Electoral Coalitions in an Age of Immigration: Time and Place in the 2001 and 2005 Los Angeles Mayoral Primaries." *Political Geography* 25:571–595.

Sonenshein, Raphael J., and Susan H. Pinkus. 2002. "The Dynamics of Latino Political Incorporation: The 2001 Los Angeles Mayoral Elections as Seen in *Los Angeles Times* Exit Polls." *PS: Political Science and Politics* 35:67–74.

Straayer, John D. 2011. "Pena, Federico (b.1947)." In *Encyclopedia of the Great Plain*, edited by David J. Wishart. Lincoln, NE: University of Nebraska Press. http://plainshumanities.unl.edu/encyclopedia/doc/egp.ha.032.

"Strategies Differ among Mayoral Candidates." 1983. *Rocky Mountain News*, April 25, p. 8.

Stone, Clarence N. 1989. *Regime Politics: Governing Atlanta 1946–1988*. Lawrence, KS: University of Kansas Press.

Survey USA. 2003. "Election Eve: Hickenlooper atop a Crowded Denver Mayoral Field." http://www.surveyusa.com/2003_Elections/CO030505Denver.pdf.

———. 2011. "Results of SurveyUSA Election Poll #18119." http://www.surveyusa.com/client/PollReport.aspx?g=0d97ba84-311b-4098-9b10-83c270014b86.

Urban Institute. 2012. "The Racial and Ethnic Composition of Local Government Employees in Large Metro Areas, 1960–2010." http://www.metrotrends.org/commentary/race-and-local-government.cfm.

Weiss, Suzanne. 1987a. "Peña Gets 2nd Term." *Rocky Mountain News*, June 17, 6.

———. 1987b. "Black Leaders Hand Peña a Deadline on Demands." *Rocky Mountain News*, October 15, 6.

"William McNichols May Trade Barbs with Challengers." 1983. *Rocky Mountain News*, April 25, 6.

5

Coalition Building in Los Angeles

The Administration of Mayor Antonio Villaraigosa

ELLEN SHIAU

EDITORS' NOTE

The election of Mayor Antonio Villaraigosa (2005–2013) of Los Angeles stands as a leading example of the process of political change in American urban politics. Villaraigosa became the first Latino mayor elected in the city since 1872. Villaraigosa's election signaled the growing political clout of Latinos in the city, as well as the ability of a Latino candidate to attract a multiethnic coalition of support.

In this chapter, Ellen Shiau describes Mayor Villaraigosa's election and governance. She traces changes in Los Angeles's population, especially the growth of the Latino population. Few U.S. cities exemplify the political economy of the postindustrial city more than Los Angeles. For example, Shiau argues that Latinos have become an increasingly important segment of Los Angeles's immigrant population. She explains how their growth is tied to the expansion of low-wage, service-sector jobs that dominate Los Angeles's postindustrial economy.

Like several of the other Latino mayors in this volume, Villaraigosa became politicized through his involvement in progressive Latino community-based organizations. Shiau describes and analyzes the coalition of progressive labor and community organizations that mobilized Latino immigrants to support Villaraigosa's election. Shiau also examines the major policy and governing challenges under Villaraigosa's administration. Villaraigosa's shifting political alliances during his administration suggest that his governing coalition often collided with the policy demands of his electoral coalition. The chapter shows that Los Angeles's fragmented institutional structure, the need to work with diverse constituencies, and the complex and "wicked" nature of urban problems necessitate the formation of varied, fluid political alliances to accomplish particular policy goals.

The 2005 election of Antonio Villaraigosa as mayor of Los Angeles marked an important moment in Los Angeles history, similar to the election of African American mayor Tom Bradley in 1973. Villaraigosa, a Mexican American born in Los Angeles, was the first Latino mayor elected in the city since 1872. This chapter describes the political and historical contexts in the postindustrial era that shaped the outcome of the 2005 mayoral election and examines the major policy and governing successes and challenges under Villaraigosa's administration. Although Villaraigosa was supported by a progressive labor and community movement energized by the mobilization of Latino immigrant workers in Los Angeles's postindustrial service sector, his shifting political alliances during his administration suggest, as other scholars have argued, that coalition building in contemporary urban politics may not align as closely along racial and ethnic lines as they do with practical interests dependent on the policy issue at hand and the strength of coalition leadership (Sonenshein 2003a, 2003b).

An important distinction that this chapter makes is that the types of coalitions that help mayoral candidates win may differ from those that help them govern, and Latino political influence may play a varied role in each. For example, the 2005 mayoral election in Los Angeles demonstrates that racial and ethnic political identities matter. The election signaled the strengthening political clout of Latinos in the city, buoyed not only by the growth of the city's Latino population but also by the organizing efforts of labor and community groups targeting Latino voters, as well as strong coethnic turnout that rallied around the prospect of electing the city's first Latino mayor in more than one hundred years. Latino voting participation—which grew from 10 to 25 percent of the ballots cast between the 1993 and 2005 mayoral elections—demonstrated important political gains for Latinos in the city in the past two decades.

Villaraigosa's win showed the ability of a Latino candidate to attract a multiethnic coalition of support, but it also showed that multiethnic support is not guaranteed. In the 2001 mayoral election, Villaraigosa lost to James Hahn, a white moderate liberal, in part because of the strong support of African American voters for Hahn, whose family has long-standing political ties to the African American communities of South Los Angeles. But rather than indicating the declining significance of race and ethnicity in contemporary urban politics, the 2001 mayoral election suggests that race and ethnicity, their interplay with leadership cues, and historic and contemporary contexts and relationships matter (Sonenshein and Pinkus 2002). The dramatic shift of African American support from Hahn to Villaraigosa in 2005 due to Hahn's missteps in the African American community during his administration illustrates this point.

However, in governance, racial and ethnic political identities may play a less straightforward role, given the "wicked" nature (Rittel and Webber 1973) of most urban problems, which can give rise to cleavages among and within minority groups. "Wicked problems," such as those regarding public safety, educational achievement, and individual and community health, have no easily explainable causes or solutions and are instead characterized by political contention and conflict. The growing recognition of the intersectional nature of political identities (Crenshaw 1989; Garcia Bedolla 2007)—shaped not only by race but also by class, immigrant status, gender, sexual orientation, and religion—and the emergence of complex, crosscutting issues complicate coalition building, which city mayors often must pursue to accomplish their policy goals. A diversity of interests that do not necessarily coalesce along racial and ethnic lines is expressed on urban issues ranging from economic development to education to environmental regulation. With the greater number of policy actors involved in urban politics today and the decline in the dominance of the downtown coalitions characteristic of the industrial era, coalition building in the postindustrial era in support of mayoral initiatives instead involves multiple constellations in a city around disparate policy issues. Finally, a fragmented and decentralized institutional environment, particularly exemplified in the city of Los Angeles, further exacerbates the challenges city mayors face in building coalitions and governing in metropolitan areas.

The election and administration of Los Angeles mayor Antonio Villaraigosa provide an illustration of the important differences between electoral and governing coalitions that can inform our understanding of urban politics. First, this chapter describes the changing demographic and sociopolitical landscape of Los Angeles in the past two decades. Second, it examines the election campaigns of Antonio Villaraigosa in 2001 and 2005, pointing to the growing political influence of Latinos in Los Angeles on electoral outcomes, supported not only by changing demographics but also by effective community organization and leadership. Finally, this chapter highlights several of Villaraigosa's key policy initiatives, which illustrate the complexities of urban governance in a fragmented institutional environment and the necessity of building and rebuilding diverse coalitions to accomplish policy goals.

The Changing Los Angeles Landscape

The second-largest U.S. city, Los Angeles had an estimated 2016 population of 3.98 million people extending across 470 square miles in more than one hundred distinct communities, from the Harbor area port communities twenty-five miles south of downtown to the San Fernando Valley suburbs more than twenty miles to the north. Although the immigrant boom has slowed since the mid-2000s (Stepler and Lopez, 2016), the large number of immigrants settling in the region between 1970 and 1990 largely shaped Los Angeles as we know it today. In the late twentieth century, as seen in Table 5.1, Los Angeles served as the nation's major immigrant gateway. In 2009, nearly 40 percent of the city's population had been born outside the United States.

The passage of the Hart-Celler Immigration and Nationality Act in 1965 shifted immigration toward arrivals from the Eastern Hemisphere. Los Angeles's Asian/Pacific Islander population, which rose 320 percent from approximately 105,000 in 1970 to 441,000 in 2012, demonstrated the highest rate of growth; however, the greatest migration of residents to Los Angeles came from Mexico and Central American countries, especially Guatemala and El Salvador. Beginning in the 1970s, global economic restructuring, which generated demand for low-wage labor, primarily in the service sector, contributed to the migration of Latinos from Mexico and Central America to the Los Angeles region (Rocco 1996), as did political unrest, particularly in El Salvador and Guatemala. Although Los Angeles's Latino population was significant before 1970, it grew approximately 259 percent between 1970 and 2012 with the addition of more than 1.3 million Latino residents. By 1990, Latinos constituted the largest share of the city's population, and their share of the city population in 2012 was 48.4 percent, as seen in Table 5.2.

Historically, racially restrictive property covenants and federal housing and transportation policies shaped residential patterns in Los Angeles.

TABLE 5.1   FOREIGN-BORN SHARE OF TOTAL POPULATION

	1970	1990		2009	
	Percent	Percent	Increase in share	Percent	Increase in share
City of Los Angeles	14.6	38.4	23.8	39.7	1.3
Los Angeles County	11.4	32.7	21.3	35.7	3.0
New York City	18.2	28.4	10.2	24.7	7.3
United States	4.8	7.9	3.2	12.5	4.5

Source: Adapted from Myers et al. (2010).

TABLE 5.2   CITY OF LOS ANGELES POPULATION BY RACE AND ETHNICITY

	Total population	Latino (%)	White (%)	Black (%)	Asian/Pacific Islander (%)
2012	3,857,786	48.4	28.4	9.0	11.4
2005	3,731,437	48.9	28.5	9.5	11.1
2000	3,694,820	46.5	29.7	10.9	10.0
1990	3,485,398	40.2	37.3	13.0	9.2
1980	2,966,850	27.5	48.3	17.0	6.6
1970	2,811,801	18.5	60.1	17.3	3.7

Source: U.S. Census.

Latinos settled in areas east of downtown Los Angeles, and African American residents located south of downtown and in parts of the northeastern San Fernando Valley. As immigration increased in the 1970s, these historically African American communities began transitioning into predominantly Latino communities, and African American residents moved west and south to communities outside the city, such as Inglewood, Hawthorne, Long Beach, and Carson. The city's white residents concentrated in the city's Westside and in the western portions of the San Fernando Valley. Segregation persists today, including racial segregation of local schools (Ethington, Frey, and Myers 2001; Orfield, Siegel-Hawley, and Kucsera 2011). These population dynamics have created a city with complex spatial patterns of class, race, and ethnicity.

A "New Los Angeles": The Shifting Sociopolitical Landscape

Los Angeles's immigration boom had a profound effect not only on the city's demographic composition but also on its sociopolitical landscape. In the 1990s, Los Angeles experienced a resurgence of labor and community organizing energized by the politicization of Latinos and Asians who immigrated to the region. Contrary to conventional wisdom, the emergence of this progressive movement demonstrated that immigrants and service-sector workers could be politicized and mobilized despite differences in language, culture, and citizenship status. With southern California characterized as a "harbinger of national trends" (Milkman 2006, p. 2), the region's movement turned attention to immigrant and working-class interests in the region—such as anti-immigrant policies, school funding, fair wages, local hiring, environmental justice, public transit, and affordable housing—

while also generating support for Villaraigosa's mayoral election campaigns in 2001 and 2005.

Labor leaders Maria Elena Durazo and Miguel Contreras are credited by many as the architects of progressive politics in the Los Angeles region today. Durazo, who began as leader of the Hotel Employees and Restaurant Employees (HERE) Local 11 in 1989 and later served as the executive secretary of the powerful Los Angeles County Federation of Labor from 2006 to 2014, saw the need to put unions back in touch with workers, who increasingly consisted of immigrant populations and service-sector workers. Durazo eventually joined forces with Contreras, a national HERE organizer originally brought to Los Angeles to take over the local union due to Durazo's contested election (the two later married). In 1996, Contreras—who had worked with labor leaders Cesar Chavez, Dolores Huerta, and Fred Ross in the farmworkers' movement—was elected as executive secretary of the Los Angeles County Federation of Labor.

Calling attention to a "new Los Angeles," Durazo and Contreras sought to organize immigrants and use union power to address issues of wealth inequality that the 1992 violent outbreak of civil unrest in the city made stark (Goldfarb 2006). In 1993, Durazo, Contreras, and attorney Madeline Janis also founded the policy and research organization Los Angeles Alliance for a New Economy, which served as the brains behind the progressive moment that built impressive coalitions around regional and local issues and refocused attention on the working poor and poverty. During this era, links were renewed among labor (including links with black and Jewish labor leaders), the faith community, environmental groups, local community organizations, academics, and the liberal Left and were forged with influential local media outlets (Burt 2007).

The anti-immigrant climate in California in the 1990s also helped fuel the region's burgeoning progressive movement. In 1994, in an attempt to lay blame for the state's budget problems, Republican governor Pete Wilson campaigned vigorously for Proposition 187 (known as the "Save Our State" ballot initiative), which denied undocumented immigrants access to public education, health care, and other social services. In 1996, Proposition 209 followed as an effort to end the state's affirmative-action policies. And two years later, Proposition 227 required public school instruction to be conducted in English, in effect eliminating bilingual education. Voters approved all three measures, although courts later struck down Proposition 187; however, the anti-immigrant political climate from 1994 to 1998 spurred increases in voter turnout and greater alienation from the Republican Party among Latinos in the state (Barreto and Woods 2005).

The region's progressive movement garnered several notable wins, such as a successful lawsuit against the Los Angeles County Metropolitan Transportation Authority (Metro) regarding the county's separate, unequal, and discriminatory transit systems for people of color in 1994; the adoption of a living-wage ordinance by the Los Angeles City Council in 1997; and the development of a pioneering agreement in 2001 that exacted community benefits from real estate developers redeveloping the downtown Figueroa Corridor surrounding the Staples Center (Brodkin 2007; Gottlieb et al. 2006; Milkman 2006; Nicholls and Beaumont 2004; Pastor, Benner, and Matsuoka 2009).

Thus, in addition to the growth of the Latino population in Los Angeles, the surge of community and labor organizing in the 1990s helped develop a progressive political infrastructure that filled the policy and political void created by the unraveling of Los Angeles mayor Tom Bradley's coalition in 1993 and the diminished role of the economic elite in the region in an increasingly globalizing economy. In addition to direct policy gains, the movement, facilitated in particular by Contreras, supported the election of progressive Latino candidates to office, including not only Villaraigosa but also labor leaders Gilbert Cedillo (1997) and Fabian Nunez (2002) to the California State Assembly and state senator Hilda Solis to the U.S. Congress in 2000. For Villaraigosa, "Contreras, more than anyone else, had helped construct the foundation for victory by increasing Latino voter registration and by restitching together the pieces of progressive Los Angeles that provided the basis for Villaraigosa's campaign" (Burt 2007, p. 343).

The Mayoral Election of Antonio Villaraigosa

The 2001 and 2005 mayoral campaigns involving Antonio Villaraigosa demonstrated the growing political voice of Latinos in Los Angeles and the prominent role that racial and ethnic politics continues to play in electoral coalitions. Los Angeles has long been characterized by racial and ethnic diversity; however, minority political incorporation at city hall did not occur until more recent decades. From 1938 to 1953, during the emergence of the city's redevelopment era, the city was governed by Mayor Fletcher Bowron, a white Republican reformer who won a recall election against the political machine of Mayor Frank Shaw in 1938. Bowron targeted corruption and aimed to professionalize city government; however, he also strongly supported the internment of Japanese and Japanese American residents during World War II and declined to check the Los Angeles Police

Department's racist treatment of minority communities, notably during the zoot-suit riots (Sitton 2005). These actions led minorities to believe that they were "still second-class citizens in the eyes of the Bowron administration" (Sitton 2005, p. 72).

Eventually, amid McCarthyism and fears of "creeping socialism" (Hines 1982), Bowron's support for the construction of ten thousand federal public housing units in the city—such as on the site of the Mexican American Chavez Ravine neighborhood northeast of downtown Los Angeles—put him at odds with the city's business elite and contributed to his election defeat in 1953 by Norris Poulson, a white Republican U.S. congressman handpicked to run by the city's elite (Sitton 2005). Bowron's loss set the stage for a more conservative city government in the decades to follow. For example, shortly after his election, Poulson reduced the city's plan to construct ten thousand public housing units by 57 percent (Parson 2007). He aligned closely with the city's business interests in a growth-oriented administration that focused on the redevelopment of the city's core. Poulson initiated the redevelopment of the downtown Bunker Hill neighborhood, where the construction of modern office and apartment buildings displaced the community's existing lower-income residents. Moreover, in what would become his "greatest prize" (Clark 1982), Poulson helped facilitate the move of the Brooklyn Dodgers to Los Angeles in 1958 and the construction of Dodger Stadium in Chavez Ravine, where hundreds of mostly Mexican American families originally had been displaced to make room for the failed public housing plan.

Defeating Poulson in 1961, Mayor Sam Yorty took office after running a populist campaign that critiqued the influence of the downtown elite; however, Yorty's conservatism eventually alienated minority constituents. For example, Yorty resisted federal poverty initiatives despite the greater availability of federal antipoverty funds (Sonenshein 1994). Public controversy emerged in 1964 regarding local control of federal War on Poverty funds and the establishment of the city's antipoverty agency, which delayed funding disbursal for more than a year (Sides 2003). It took the August 1965 Watts uprising to facilitate a compromise that ended the controversy (Sides 2003). Moreover, Yorty staunchly supported the Los Angeles Police Department (LAPD) despite his promise to hold the department more accountable during his mayoral campaign and growing concerns from minority communities about police brutality and racial injustice, which came to the fore in the 1965 Watts uprising.

In response to continued marginalization, political mobilization of African American residents grew in the 1960s, and a multiracial coalition emerged to support more progressive ideals in the city. After losing in the

1969 mayoral campaign to Yorty, who used race-baiting tactics, Tom Bradley, a city councilman and former LAPD officer, defeated Yorty in the 1973
mayoral election to become the city's first and only African American
mayor. With a broad coalition of support that included black, Westside Jewish, Latino, and Asian voters, Bradley's win demonstrated that multiracial
electoral coalitions could be formed and facilitated the political inclusion
of previously marginalized groups at city hall. Governing the city for twenty
years (before term limits were enacted), Bradley directed more federal
money toward social programs, increased access of minorities to city hall
through administrative appointments and affirmative-action programs,
and achieved greater civilian control over the police (Sonenshein 1994).

In the 1980s, however, Bradley's coalition began showing cracks as disparate interests emerged across the city. In a bid to elevate Los Angeles to
a "world-class city," Bradley also allied with downtown business interests
to remake the city's core while largely neglecting the conditions of dis-
tressed city neighborhoods (Sides 2003). Conflict over growth also emerged
in the city's Westside. At the same time, the region faced serious fiscal issues
because of the 1978 passage of Proposition 13, which limited property-tax
increases in the state, and a decline in manufacturing in the 1980s
brought on by economic restructuring. As middle-class jobs fell out of the
Los Angeles economy and Latino and Asian immigrants arrived in the
region to fill low-wage service jobs, the gap between the rich and the poor
widened. Moreover, the crack-cocaine epidemic, peaking in the 1980s and
marked by addiction, violence, and crime, took a toll on Los Angeles neighborhoods and families.

The 1992 outbreak of violent civil disorder sparked by the acquittal of
four white LAPD police officers charged in the beating of African American
Rodney King palpably demonstrated the anger felt by the city's marginalized communities and signaled the unraveling of Bradley's regime. Bradley declined to run for reelection in 1993. Unsettled by the unrest, city
voters elected white Republican businessman Richard Riordan, who claimed
to be "tough enough to turn L.A. around," as mayor over Asian American
city councilman Michael Woo, who political observers thought was the one
to carry on Bradley's multiethnic coalition in his bid to "make L.A. work."
During his two administrations (now subject to term limits), Riordan elevated the role of the private sector in governance, which ultimately did
little to address the issues that had brought tensions to the fore in 1992.
At the same time, the progressive movement, reinvigorated by Latino and
Asian immigrants, began to take hold, helping set the stage for a hotly contested 2001 mayoral race between white moderate Democrat James Hahn
and Villaraigosa.

Villaraigosa, a Mexican American, was born in the East Los Angeles neighborhood of Boyle Heights in 1953. A graduate of UCLA and the People's College of Law, Villaraigosa became politicized through his involvement in organizations, such as the radical Chicano organization Movimiento Estudiantil Chicana/o de Aztlan and the immigrants' rights organization Centros de Acción Social Autónomo, where he worked with Gilbert Cedillo and Maria Elena Durazo under the guidance of prominent labor leader Bert Corona. Villaraigosa later turned to the union movement as an organizer for United Teachers Los Angeles and subsequently served as president of the Los Angeles chapter of the American Civil Liberties Union and the American Federation of Government Employees.

In 1991, Los Angeles County supervisor Gloria Molina, previously the first Latina elected to the state legislature, appointed Villaraigosa to the Los Angeles Metro board. With Molina's support, Villaraigosa was elected in 1994 to the California State Assembly, where he won election as Speaker of the assembly four years later. Surprising many with his coalition-building skills, Villaraigosa as Speaker helped push through legislation that expanded funding for health insurance, school construction, and urban parks and enacted an agency fee for public-sector unions.

Subject to term limits in the California state legislature, Villaraigosa ran for Los Angeles mayor in 2001. Early polling indicated weak enthusiasm for Villaraigosa (Burt 2007); however, the Los Angeles County Federation of Labor threw its support behind Villaraigosa, who was a close friend of Contreras and Durazo. Focusing on immigrants in the city, labor and community organizers had initiated ambitious naturalization, voter-registration, and voter-turnout programs in the 1990s. For example, the weekend before the election, the federation organized 2,700 supporters to walk precincts for Villaraigosa (Frank and Wong 2004). Moreover, in an anti-immigrant climate, the prospect of electing the city's first Latino mayor since 1872 invigorated the Latino vote (Barreto, Villareal, and Woods 2005). As a result, between the 1997 and 2001 mayoral elections, the number of ballots cast by Latinos doubled to approximately 127,000, increasing the Latino share of the total vote from 15 to 22 percent, as seen in Table 5.3.

Demonstrating the powerful effect of a coethnic candidate on Latino voter turnout, for the first time, Latinos voted at the highest rate of any racial or ethnic group in the city, with a 41 percent turnout, as seen in Table 5.4 (Barreto, Villareal, and Woods 2005). Villaraigosa drew 82 percent of the Latino vote, as well as significant support from liberal white Jewish voters; however, Hahn garnered strong support from black, Asian, and conservative white voters to win the election.

TABLE 5.3   LOS ANGELES MAYORAL ELECTION RESULTS BY RACE, 1993–2005

	White	Black	Latino	Asian
1993 (June runoff)				
% of vote	72	12	10	4
% Woo	33	86	57	69
% Riordan*	67	14	43	31
1997 (April primary)				
% of vote	65	13	15	4
% Hayden	26	75	33	35
% Riordan*	71	19	60	62
2001 (June runoff)				
% of vote	52	17	22	6
% Villaraigosa	41	20	82	35
% Hahn*	59	80	18	65
2005 (May runoff)				
% of vote	50	15	25	5
% Hahn	50	52	16	56
% Villaraigosa*	50	48	84	44

Source: Los Angeles Times exit polls.

*Denotes winner; incumbent mayor Antonio Villaraigosa ran largely uncontested in 2009, winning in the primary.

The 2001 mayoral race differed markedly from the 1973 race between Bradley and Yorty in that Hahn had "modest liberal credentials" and the support of African American voters (Gottlieb et al. 2006, p. 167). The divided support of African Americans and Latinos demonstrated that alignments were not guaranteed, and that history and context matter (Sonenshein and Drayse 2006). Hahn, the four-term Los Angeles city attorney and former city controller, received support from the African American community largely because of the legacy of his father, Kenneth Hahn, a civil rights activist and Los Angeles County supervisor representing South Los Angeles for forty years. Reaching out to a newer generation of African American leadership, such as community organizers Anthony Thigpenn and Karen Bass, Villaraigosa drew some support from the black community.

However, Hahn also had greater appeal to conservative white voters from the San Fernando Valley than Villaraigosa, who was the subject of a damaging last-minute advertising campaign with racial undertones that highlighted his support for the pardon of a convicted drug dealer. Although it injured Hahn's standing with Latino voters, the campaign may have been viewed as less insidious than Yorty's 1969 race-baiting campaign against Bradley because of Hahn's moderately liberal views and strong support in the African American community. Thus Hahn's unlikely alliance of black and conservative white voters did not align as closely along ideological lines as Villaraigosa's coalition.

TABLE 5.4   RACE AND ETHNICITY IN THE 2001 LOS ANGELES
MAYORAL ELECTION

	Share of electorate (%)	Voter turnout (%)
White	52	36
Black	17	39
Latino	22	41
Asian	6	35
Citywide	100	37.7

Source: Los Angeles Times exit polls.

With no previous experience in city office, Villaraigosa ran for a Los
Angeles City Council seat in 2003 and unseated incumbent Nick Pacheco
to represent the Fourteenth District. During his time on the city council,
Villaraigosa formed a progressive voting bloc with Councilmen Eric Garcetti
and Ed Reyes. Challenging Hahn again in 2005, Villaraigosa was seen by
some as capable of rebuilding Bradley's multiethnic electoral coalition to
win the mayoral race. During his 2005 campaign, Villaraigosa drew heavily
from Latino support but strove not to alienate other racial and ethnic
groups by promising to be a mayor "for all of Los Angeles." His win against
Hahn with 58.6 percent of the ballots cast, as seen in Table 5.5, demonstrated his ability to garner support across racial and ethnic lines. The vast
majority of Latino voters (84 percent) again favored Villaraigosa, and Latino voters increased their share of the vote to 25 percent, although the
number of Latino votes declined slightly because of the lower citywide turnout in 2005 than in 2001.

However, in 2005, Villaraigosa increased his share of the white, black,
and Asian vote, as seen in Table 5.3. Although Villaraigosa's coalition-
building skills played a role, support also shifted in large part because of
actions by Hahn that African American and white San Fernando Valley
voters viewed as missteps. During his administration, Hahn hired cele-
brated New York City police commissioner William Bratton to lead the
LAPD and declined to renew the contract of black LAPD chief Bernard
Parks, which was seen as an affront to the African American community.
African American leaders such as Congresswoman Maxine Waters, Magic
Johnson, and Rev. Cecil Murray shifted their support to Villaraigosa. Further weakening Hahn's support in the black community, in 2005, Parks—
who won a seat on the city council in 2003 and placed fourth in the 2005
primary race for mayor—accused Hahn of racist campaign practices,
pointing to his 2001 advertising campaign against Villaraigosa. Moreover,
during his administration, Hahn had campaigned vigorously in opposition
to a secession movement in the San Fernando Valley, which engendered

TABLE 5.5   LOS ANGELES MAYORAL ELECTION RESULTS,
1993–2013

	Votes	Percent
1993 (June runoff)		
Woo	268,137	46.1
Riordan	314,559	53.9
1997 (April primary)		
Hayden	140,648	34.5
Riordan	250,771	61.5
2001 (June runoff)		
Villaraigosa	264,611	46.5
Hahn	304,791	53.5
2005 (May runoff)		
Hahn	203,968	41.4
Villaraigosa	289,116	58.6
2013 (May runoff)		
Greuel	187,609	45.8
Garcetti	222,300	54.2

Source: Los Angeles City Clerk.

dissatisfaction among valley voters. Endorsements from Senator John Kerry and Republican assemblyman Keith Richmond helped Villaraigosa secure votes from the San Fernando Valley.

Interestingly, in 2005, the Los Angeles County Federation of Labor, still led by Contreras, endorsed Hahn for his staunch support of labor during his administration because union leaders believed in rewarding supportive incumbents; however, individual unions lent their support and carried out organizing campaigns to turn out votes for Villaraigosa. Some observers noted that the federation did not seem to invest as much energy and resources in Hahn's 2005 campaign as in its efforts on behalf of Villaraigosa in 2001. Moreover, two weeks before the election, Contreras passed away unexpectedly, shocking the labor community and drawing attention away from Hahn's campaign. Villaraigosa had been a close friend of Contreras and served as a pallbearer at his funeral. Shortly after, Villaraigosa won 60 percent of union votes in the mayoral election (Dreier et al. 2006). In 2009, Villaraigosa faced no serious opposition and won reelection in the city primary.

Latino Politics in Los Angeles: Progress and Prospects

Latino voting participation in the city—which grew from 10 to 25 percent of the ballots cast between the 1993 and 2005 mayoral elections—

demonstrated important gains for Latinos in the past two decades. However, although Latinos are a political force in Los Angeles, the outcome of
the 2005 mayoral election does not indicate their dominance in city politics, particularly in a city with anemic election participation of less than
30 percent of registered voters since the 2009 election, as seen in Table 5.6.
For example, in the 2005 mayoral election, Latinos represented 25 percent
of the total vote, although they constituted nearly half of the city's population. The nearly 125,000 Latinos who participated in the 2005 mayoral
election represented only 6.8 percent of the city's Latino residents. In contrast, white voters contributed 50 percent of the ballots cast, while white
residents represented only 28.4 percent of the city's population. Nearly
250,000 white voters participated in the 2005 mayoral election, about
23.4 percent of the city's white population.

Moreover, in 2016, Latinos held only about one-fifth of the fifteen city
council seats, while white city councilors held about half of the seats, as
seen in Table 5.7. Latinos doubled their share of city council seats from
two out of fifteen in 1990 to four out of fifteen in 2015; however, black
city council members have consistently made up 20 percent of city council
seats despite declines in the city's black population from 13 percent in
1990 to 9 percent in 2012 and the transition of many historically African
American communities in South Los Angeles to predominantly Latino
communities.

Two important factors limit the political voice of Latinos in Los Angeles electoral politics relative to other racial and ethnic groups. First, Latinos represent younger populations in the city. In 2012, 30 percent of Latino
residents in Los Angeles were under eighteen years old, compared with
13.4 percent of the white population, as seen in Table 5.8. Second, a significant proportion of Latino residents older than eighteen are not U.S. citizens. In 2012, nearly 44 percent of Latinos over eighteen years old in Los
Angeles were not U.S. citizens and thus were ineligible to vote, compared
with only 8 percent of whites over eighteen years old. Latinos made up

TABLE 5.6   VOTER TURNOUT IN LOS ANGELES MAYORAL ELECTIONS, 1993–2013

	Registered voters	Ballots cast	Turnout (%)
2013 runoff	1,797,318	419,592	23.34
2009 primary	1,596,165	285,658	17.90
2005 runoff	1,469,296	498,729	33.94
2001 runoff	1,538,229	579,408	37.67
1997 primary	1,339,036	424,653	31.71
1993 runoff	1,331,179	598,436	44.96

Source: Los Angeles City Clerk.

TABLE 5.7   RACIAL/ETHNIC COMPOSITION OF LOS ANGELES CITY COUNCIL,
1990–2014

	Latino (%)	Black (%)	White (%)	Asian (%)
1990	13	20	60	7
1991	13	20	60	7
1992	13	20	60	7
1993	20	20	53	7
1994	20	20	60	0
1995	20	20	60	0
1996	20	20	60	0
1997	20	20	60	0
1998	20	20	60	0
1999	20	20	60	0
2000	20	20	60	0
2001*	20	20	60	0
2002*	20	20	60	0
2003*	27	20	53	0
2004*	27	20	53	0
2005*	27	20	53	0
2006*	27	20	53	0
2007*	27	20	53	0
2008*	27	20	53	0
2009*	27	20	53	0
2010*	27	20	53	0
2011*	27	20	53	0
2012*	27	20	53	0
2013	27	20	53	0
2014	27	20	53	0
2015	27	20	47	7
2016	20†	20	47	7

Source: Los Angeles City Clerk.

* Former city councilman Eric Garcetti—whose father is of Italian-Mexican descent and whose mother is of Russian-Jewish descent—is of mixed lineage.

† City Councilman Felipe Fuentes resigned in September 2016, leaving his district seat vacant. He was replaced in a May 2017 special election by Monica Rodriguez, who will begin her term in July 2017.

nearly three-quarters of the roughly 795,000 Los Angeles residents over eighteen years old who were not U.S. citizens in 2012.

In time, the city's Latino population growth likely will translate into greater political influence as Latinos come of voting age. The Pew Hispanic Center estimates that the national Latino electorate will double by 2030 (Taylor et al. 2012). Already in the 2005 mayoral election, approximately 22.8 percent of eligible Latino voters participated, a percentage not much lower than the approximately 30.5 percent of eligible white voters who participated. Unlike older generations, the city's Latino population under eighteen years old largely consists of U.S. citizens, like the city's white pop-

TABLE 5.8   CITY OF LOS ANGELES AGE AND CITIZENSHIP CHARACTERISTICS, 2000–2012

	Population	Population over 18	Population over 18 who are U.S. citizens (%)	Population under 18	Population under 18 years old (%)	Population under 18 who are U.S. citizens (%)
Total population						
2012	3,857,786	2,989,784	73.4	868,002	22.5	94.2
2005	3,731,437	2,731,412	68.6	1,000,025	26.8	91.2
2000	3,694,820	2,715,693	67.5	979,127	26.5	87.6
Latino						
2012	1,867,168	1,303,284	56.4	563,885	30.2	93.9
2005	1,824,673	1,178,739	46.3	645,934	35.4	89.9
2000	1,718,091	1,109,887	41.5	608,204	35.4	84.3
White						
2012	1,095,611	948,799	92.0	146,812	13.4	96.7
2005	1,063,460	893,306	91.6	170,154	16.0	95.0
2000	1,097,362	930,563	91.1	166,799	15.2	94.5

Source: U.S. Census.

ulation. In 2012, nearly 94 percent of Latinos under eighteen years old were U.S. citizens, compared with nearly 97 percent of whites under eighteen years old. Moreover, in 2012, Latino youth represented approximately 65 percent of the city's 868,000 residents who were under eighteen years old. Still, intensive efforts are necessary to educate and mobilize new generations of civic participants, particularly in light of growing concerns regarding the decline of civic education among American youth (National Center for Education Statistics 2011).

In the meantime, given the relatively low participation rates of Latinos in Los Angeles electoral politics, Latino voters may not fully represent the range of interests and concerns among the Latino population, which encompasses significant intraethnic diversity. As other scholars have noted, Latinos cannot be viewed as a homogeneous group. For example, Los Angeles's Latino population exhibits greater diversity in socioeconomic and immigrant status than the city's white population. In 2012, about 30 percent of Latino residents lived below the poverty line, compared with 12.2 percent of the city's white population, as seen in Table 5.9.

Moreover, approximately 47 percent of the city's Latino population was foreign born, compared with 22 percent of the city's white population in 2012. And 32 percent of the city's Latino residents are not U.S. citizens, compared with only 7 percent of the city's white residents, as seen in

TABLE 5.9   CITY OF LOS ANGELES SOCIOECONOMIC CHARACTERISTICS BY RACE
AND ETHNICITY, 2000–2012

Total population	Unemployment (%)	Below poverty (%)	Median income (2012 dollars)	Renters (%)	High-school graduate or above (%)	Bachelor's degree or above (%)
2012	12.2	23.3	46,803	63.2	75.3	31.5
2005	8.3	20.1	50,159	60.1	72.0	28.7
2000	9.3	22.1	48,915	61.4	66.6	25.5
Latino						
2012	13.3	30.3	36,909	72.5	51.6	10.2
2005	8.9	28.0	38,376	70.8	45.7	7.6
2000	10.8	29.6	38,344	73.1	35.5	6.1
White						
2012	10.4	12.2	66,546	51.3	94.8	52.3
2005	6.4	8.4	71,482	46.7	93.2	48.2
2000	6.5	10.1	68,686	48.6	90.1	42.6
Black						
2012	18.2	30.2	32,338	71.9	87.5	24.2
2005	14.4	21.3	36,332	66.9	82.1	22.5
2000	15.5	28.0	36,314	68.8	76.5	17.2
Asian						
2012	8.4	16.2	51,724	65.2	89.8	51.0
2005	6.4	15.3	52,346	63.7	88.6	48.3
2000	6.8	16.9	49,592	63.8	82.1	42.5

Source: U.S. Census.

Table 5.10. The diversity apparent among the city's Latino population warrants a finer examination of Los Angeles politics, which has revealed noteworthy variations among Latino interests along lines of class, immigrant status, and immigrant generation.

The diversity among Latinos points to the challenges of creating governing coalitions in support of mayoral initiatives, where racial and ethnic identities may play a less straightforward role given divergent interests along class, immigrant status, and other lines of cleavage. The neighborhood of Boyle Heights—Villaraigosa's birthplace—provides an illustrative case. Boyle Heights is situated just east of downtown Los Angeles across the Los Angeles River. The community began transitioning from being the center of Los Angeles's Jewish community to a predominantly Latino community in the 1920s as Jewish residents moved to the western portions of Los Angeles (Sánchez 1993). Today, Boyle Heights has a population that is about 93 percent Latino. Given the community's long-standing role as a Latino gateway, Boyle Heights exhibits diversity within its Latino population, which is a mix of multigenerational residents and newer im-

TABLE 5.10   CITY OF LOS ANGELES CITIZENSHIP STATUS BY RACE
AND ETHNICITY

Total population	Foreign born (%)	Non-U.S. citizen (%)
2012	38.6	21.9
2005	40.3	25.4
2000	40.9	27.1
Latino		
2012	47.3	32.3
2005	51.7	38.3
2000	56.2	43.3
White		
2012	22.4	7.3
2005	21.7	7.9
2000	19.9	8.4
Black		
2012	7.7	4.0
2005	6.4	3.3
2000	5.8	3.2
Asian		
2012	69.8	31.2
2005	71.8	35.6
2000	71.6	35.4

Source: U.S. Census.

migrants, homeowners and renters, and middle-class and working-class residents.

The changing nature of Boyle Heights and the extension of the Metro Gold Line subway to the community in 2012 have spurred considerable concern regarding gentrification and residential displacement, and community perspectives range from support for militant defensive strategies against development to cautious optimism (Carroll 2016; Mejia 2016). Although Boyle Heights has been a predominantly Latino community since the post–World War II era, socioeconomic stratification along class and immigrant status has led to differing perspectives on the trajectory of development activities in the community. The community's diversity contributes to competing visions of the future of Boyle Heights that play out in neighborhood cleavages and alignments.

For example, while some residents express significant concerns regarding the changing character of the neighborhood, other residents advocate for development that will provide more services and amenities for middle-income residents. Still other community members express a need for more affordable housing for working-class residents, while some oppose what they perceive as low-income housing. Controversies also have emerged regarding unauthorized street vending in Boyle Heights as conflict over public space shows the divide between lower-income residents and immigrants and middle- and upper-income residents. Many of those who oppose street vending in the community are home owners concerned with public safety, public health, and quality-of-life issues, while those in support of street vending hold the immigrant perspective of the sidewalk as a legitimate place of economic activity (Loukaitou-Sideris and Ehrenfeucht 2009) and street vending as a vital source of income for low-income families.

Policy Priorities and the
Villaraigosa Administration

In the postindustrial city, characterized by greater diversity and less consensus on the aims of urban governance, these community cleavages also play out on broader scales; thus citywide leaders in Los Angeles must delicately navigate the city's diverse constituencies to build governing coalitions, which are fragile given divergent, shifting, and often conflicting interests. With broad support from a multiethnic coalition, Villaraigosa faced particularly high expectations after his 2005 mayoral win. At his victory rally, Villaraigosa shared the stage with Jewish film director Rob Reiner, labor leader Dolores Huerta, and basketball Hall of Famer Magic Johnson. The national media touted a new era for Latino politics, although Villaraigosa repeatedly has shied away from the descriptor "Latino mayor" in favor of promoting a broader appeal. Moreover, Villaraigosa's election meant that "every progressive group in the city [had] projected its hopes onto the fifty-three-year-old Villaraigosa" (Dreier et al. 2006, p. 46). The progressive movement that helped elect Villaraigosa hoped for a "fundamental realignment of citywide political forces" (Gottleib et al. 2006, p. 165).

However, the realities of governing point to the challenges of enacting sweeping changes and the political exigencies that compel cooperation with broader constituencies. The complex, "wicked" nature of urban problems, combined with a fragmented institutional environment that diffuses political power, requires coalition building to accomplish policy goals. Because of the diversity of interests in the city, governing coalitions form and re-form depending on the issue at hand and at times lead to unlikely alliances that are difficult to predict if one uses the lens of shared racial and ethnic identity or ideology (Sonenshein 2003a, 2003b). From his early work as an organizer to his election win, Villaraigosa had been recognized as an adroit coalition builder. Capitalizing on these skills, Villaraigosa embarked on an ambitious policy agenda over his two mayoral administrations that often required bringing together a diverse array of political actors in a city with limited mayoral power. Described by one city insider as "exceedingly complex," Los Angeles's fragmented institutional structure makes coordination and decision making on citywide issues a difficult challenge.

Los Angeles has a relatively weak mayor, a fifteen-member city council, and more than 240 mayor-appointed commissioners who share governing power in the city (Box and Musso 2004). Charter reform in 1999 increased the power of the mayor relative to the city council by making it easier for the mayor to remove department general managers and commissioners; however, city council members can reinstate department general managers by a two-thirds vote, and they continue to wield significant power over their individual fiefdoms, with the mayor deferring to individual city council members on district issues.

The city's political fragmentation is amplified by the region's broader institutional context. The massive Los Angeles Unified School District (LAUSD), spread across more than 720 square miles, serves not only the city of Los Angeles but also all or parts of twenty-seven other cities and several unincorporated areas in Los Angeles County. The county government oversees public assistance, health, mental health, and other social services and shares governing power over the Metro transportation agency with Los Angeles and other regional cities. And state politics in Sacramento frequently intersects with Los Angeles politics. Despite the city's centrifugal forces, Villaraigosa coordinated support for a number of policy initiatives from an array of allies during his administrations but also drew criticism for often falling short of his policy goals and at times opposing the progressive base that supported his election, for example, in his push for school reform.

Moreover, while benefiting politically from his Latino identity and ability to mobilize Latino voters, in the business of governing, Villaraigosa quickly corrected those who called him Los Angeles's "Latino mayor." To one reporter, he said, "Almost nobody in this town describes me as the Latino mayor. . . . I love that" (Finnegan 2013); however, although several of Villaraigosa's policy priorities were not explicitly directed toward Latinos, they likely aligned with the interests of Latino constituents. For example, although Villaraigosa often used deracialized rhetoric and instead highlighted the city's diversity, he regularly made education and public safety the foci of his annual State of the City Addresses and subtly signaled his attention to minority concerns. In eight State of the City Addresses from 2006 to 2013, Villaraigosa consistently focused on the policy areas of education, public safety, and transportation and the environment, which are discussed in detail in the following sections.

Mayoral Control and Reform of Los Angeles Schools

Arguably, one of the most important initiatives to Villaraigosa's Latino supporters was his effort to institute education reform, which pitted him
against the teachers' union he had once worked for and ultimately led to
mixed success. Education consistently ranks as one of the top policy priorities of Latinos, who represent younger populations, compared with the
population as a whole. As seen in Table 5.11, in 2007, education was one of
the most common responses by Latinos to the question "What is the
most important problem facing Latinos in California?" Approximately
73.4 percent of the LAUSD's 651,000 students are Latino.

Of the policy priorities identified, education most often falls under the
purview of local government, although Los Angeles mayors have little direct influence on the local school district, which elects an independent
school governing board and provides educational services in independent
cities and communities outside the boundaries of the city of Los Angeles.
However, Villaraigosa made school reform a centerpiece of his 2005 campaign, in which he argued that the mayor should have "ultimate control and
oversight" of the school system (Fausset 2005). Thus, while focusing attention on education as a policy priority of Latino constituents, Villaraigosa
also drew ire from members of his progressive base for his bid to take over
the school system and later for his support for increasing the access of charter schools to the district. Since the 1990s, mayors of several U.S. cities,
such as Chicago and New York, have sought and won control of city school
systems, and some evidence suggests that mayoral control can lead to
increased academic achievement and improved district management
(Chambers 2006; Wong and Shen 2007). While raising questions of transparency, direct mayoral control is thought to ensure greater accountability,
insulate school boards from the influences of electoral politics, and create
more stable governing systems (Hess 2007).

Despite city-charter and California Constitution provisions that limit
mayoral involvement, Villaraigosa unveiled his plans to seek LAUSD con-

TABLE 5.11   MOST IMPORTANT PROBLEMS IDENTIFIED IN 2007 LATINO
DECISIONS POLL BY PERCENTAGE OF RESPONDENTS

	Facing California	Facing Latinos in California
Immigration reform	33	51
Education	21	20
Jobs/economy	20	16
Health care	15	10

Source: Latino Decisions (http://www.latinodecisions.com/about/).

trol in his first State of the City Address in 2006, held at a charter school in the predominantly Latino and African American community of South Los Angeles. Although he did not appeal directly to Latino or African American constituents, Villaraigosa spoke of how the problems facing the entire city—education, public safety, traffic, pollution—were magnified in South Los Angeles and asked the city to "imagine a future where it doesn't matter who you are or where you come from; whether you're African American, Latino, Caucasian or Asian; whether you're gay or straight, rich or poor; where every Angeleno has a chance to show their talent" (Villaraigosa 2006). Moreover, Villaraigosa framed education as a broad issue vital to the economic health of the city as a whole. He argued, "We can't be a great global city if we lose half of our workforce before they graduate from high school. We'll never realize the promise of our people. We won't tap our talent. L.A. won't be one city if we shrug our shoulders and adopt the path of least resistance" (Villaraigosa 2006).

To support educational achievement, Villaraigosa's school-reform plan proposed the creation of a council of mayors to represent the twenty-seven cities served by the school district. With voting power proportionate to city population, Villaraigosa would have the largest influence over the Council of Mayors and thus over appointment of the school superintendent, the district budget, collective bargaining, and school curricula (Maxwell 2006). The district's elected school board would serve largely in an advisory capacity. Facing strong opposition from United Teachers Los Angeles and the school board, Villaraigosa brokered a compromise that ultimately added to the fragmentation of school control and also drew criticism from Villaraigosa's school-reform supporters, such as wealthy philanthropist Eli Broad.

Passed by the California state legislature in 2006 through Villaraigosa's political relationships established when he was Assembly Speaker, the final plan gave Villaraigosa direct control over a cluster of three low-performing high schools and their feeder schools, established the Council of Mayors to ratify the hiring of the school superintendent, provided the superintendent with more power over budget and personnel decisions, gave school-level personnel more control over curricula, and retained the school board's final authority over the budget and system-wide education priorities (Hess 2007). Three months after Governor Arnold Schwarzenegger signed the bill into law, after a legal challenge by LAUSD and other school-district supporters, the California Supreme Court ruled that the legislation violated the state constitution and blocked its January 2007 implementation.

Determined to influence school reform, Villaraigosa shifted his strategy and backed the races of a number of LAUSD school-board candidates, in effect giving him majority control of the board. Stacked with his allies, the board allowed Villaraigosa to take over operations in 2008 of ten of the district's most underperforming schools in his Partnership for Los Angeles Schools (PLAS) initiative. The initiative aimed to "dramatically improve student achievement within partnership schools and to create a model for collaboration, school reform and community advancement that can be replicated throughout Los Angeles schools" (Mayor's Partnership for Schools 2007). Focusing on changing management strategies and fostering collaboration, the partnership later expanded to fifteen schools, raising significant private philanthropic funds to support its schools. For example, developers and philanthropists Melanie and Richard Lundquist donated $50 million to PLAS, the largest private donation ever given to Los Angeles schools. Further cementing Villaraigosa's control, the school board appointed Villaraigosa's deputy mayor of education, Ramon Cortines, school superintendent in 2008. In his 2008 State of the City Address, Villaraigosa referred to Cortines as the school district's "direct human bridge with the city."

Since its inception, however, PLAS has been criticized for its implementation strategies, and significant improvement in academic performance has yet to occur at all PLAS schools. In June 2009, eight PLAS schools gave the partnership a vote of no confidence. Moreover, while attempting to streamline school administration, according to school administrators, PLAS introduced new layers of bureaucracy because of the reliance of PLAS schools on the district for resources and support (Alvarez 2013). Over time, Villaraigosa's direct involvement in PLAS diminished; however, PLAS created the platform for district-wide reforms supported by Villaraigosa, namely, the growing use of charter schools and other organizations to manage district schools (Alvarez 2013). In August 2009, the school board passed the Public School Choice measure, which allowed outside organizations to bid for control of new and low-performing schools in the district.

Authored by Villaraigosa ally and board member Yolie Flores-Aguilar, Public School Choice allows charter schools, nonprofit organizations, and other groups to compete for control of more than one-third of the district's campuses. Again pitted against United Teachers Los Angeles, which in his own words viewed him as "Public Enemy No. 1," Villaraigosa rallied support for the initiative from Latino parents and civil rights leaders, education organizations, and the corporate elite. On the day of the school board's vote on the proposal, approximately three thousand parents, mostly Latino, rallied at the district offices in support of the proposal (Fuller 2010). However, United Teachers Los Angeles again exerted its political power in the first round of Public School Choice awards in 2010 by allying with newly formed teacher groups that won most of the district's school contracts; contrary to Villaraigosa's wishes and bending to pressure from the teachers' union, the board awarded only four district schools to charter organizations (Fuller 2010). In his 2011 State of the City Address, held at a South Los Angeles high school that participated in the first round of Public School Choice, Villaraigosa again made school reform a centerpiece, advocating for the transformation of "LAUSD into a network of independent, locally controlled campuses."

To further his agenda of expanding charter-school access to district schools, Villaraigosa continued to support like-minded candidates for school-board positions. His Coalition for School Reform—with contributions from New York mayor Michael Bloomberg, downtown developer Philip Anschutz, philanthropist Eli Broad, Netflix founder Reed Hastings, and Univision CEO Jerry Perenchio, among many others—contributed millions to school-board races in 2011 and 2013 with mixed results. However, unlikely coalitions, such as the Don't Hold Us Back Coalition with members including United Way and the Urban League, also have emerged to advocate for Villaraigosa-backed school reforms in lieu of their traditional alliances with teachers' unions (Aron 2011). In his final State of the City Address in 2013, although still without direct control over the school district, Villaraigosa cited the school district's successes during his eight years in office while continuing to advocate for school reform and censuring the 2013 mayoral candidates for devoting little attention to school issues. Initial analyses are under way to examine the implementation effects of Public School Choice on district schools (Marsh, Strunk, and Bush 2013); however, Villaraigosa's efforts demonstrate the role that the city mayor can play in influencing school reform, although this role requires considerable expense.

Expanding Public Safety Programs

A more easily measurable success of Villaraigosa's administration was his role in increasing the size of the Los Angeles Police Department to more than 10,000 officers, a plan initially proposed by LAPD chief William Bratton to augment the city's lean police force. In 2006 and 2008, Villaraigosa persuaded city council members to increase trash-collection fees to support the hiring of an additional 1,000 police officers. By the end of Villaraigosa's administration, an additional 739 officers had joined the LAPD, although 60 were transferred from the city's General Services Department, which patrols public libraries, parks, and city hall offices. Interestingly, Villaraigosa benefited from Hahn's hiring of Bratton, which had hurt Hahn in his reelection campaign, particularly among African American voters. Under Bratton, the LAPD hired more minority police officers, used more community-oriented policing strategies, and strategically analyzed crime data to target public safety problems.

In his 2012 State of the City Address—twenty years after the 1992 Los Angeles riots that reflected the rage and discontent in the city's poor African American and Latino neighborhoods—Villaraigosa lauded the city's diversity as opposed to the challenges neighborhoods continue to face: "In the two decades since those six days in April, we forged a new partnership between the LAPD based on respect. But we are a better city not just because we are a safer city. We are a better city because we also have learned to celebrate our diversity. We are proud of it. We are a better city today because we have reached beyond the lines of class and color and have come together in common purpose" (Villaraigosa 2012).

However, during his administration, Villaraigosa drew greater attention and resources to minority communities through the other cornerstone of his public safety efforts—the Gang Reduction and Youth Development (GRYD) initiative, which concentrated law-enforcement resources and social services in twelve approximately 3.5-square-mile zones that exhibit 40 percent more gang activity than other city neighborhoods. Although not explicitly described as an initiative to assist minority communities, the twelve GRYD zones—selected on the basis of an array of indicators, including high-school-dropout and unemployment rates—are located in lower-income, predominantly Latino and African American city neighborhoods. In the introduction of the initiative in his 2007 State of the City Address, Villaraigosa recounted the gang-related shooting deaths of a nine-year-old girl from Thailand in the Angelino Heights neighborhood northwest of downtown Los Angeles and a fourteen-year-old African American girl in the Harbor Gateway community in the southern part of the city along the 110 Freeway, illustrating the reach of the issue across the city. Moreover, Villaraigosa alluded to the concerns of minority constituents by referencing his personal history as one of four children raised by a single mother on the east side of Los Angeles: "If you grew up in a neighborhood like the one where many of us grew up, you know with the certainty that only experience brings that every gang member starts out like a kid just like yours and mine. You know what their moms go through. You know how families grieve. You know what a mentor can mean. You can see the vistas that open up with great public schools. And If you're observant, you can see the better angels" (Villaraigosa 2007).

Despite declines in crime in the city since the early twenty-first century and throughout Villaraigosa's administration, Los Angeles has about four hundred active gangs with more than forty thousand members according to the LAPD. In 2008, approximately 40 percent of aggravated assaults and robberies and 80 percent of homicides were gang related. Villaraigosa implemented GRYD in 2008 after discontinuing the controversial L.A. Bridges antigang program and redirecting the funds from the city's former Community Development Department to his office. Developed on the basis of recommendations from civil rights attorney Connie Rice, City Controller Laura Chick, and academics, the GRYD program funds community-based nonprofits that administer youth-development and gang-prevention and intervention programs to high-risk youth in addition to increased policing. The initiative also includes the Summer Night Lights program, which provides free activities at and extends the hours of parks and recreation centers during the summer in GRYD zones, supported in part by private donors.

Communities have welcomed GRYD's prevention and intervention programs because the city historically has relied on gang-suppression strategies through law enforcement to address gang issues. The programs instead focus more attention on the "root causes" of crime and concentrate resources in neighborhoods most affected by gangs as opposed to spreading resources more thinly citywide. To accomplish its goals, the initiative draws on a diverse array of partners, including various city entities from the Human Relations Commission to Parks and Recreation, community-based organizations, academics, philanthropic and corporate donors, and federal law-enforcement agencies, while creating a central point of coordination and accountability in the Mayor's Office of Gang Reduction and Youth Development. The city council consistently has funded GRYD since its inception. The effects of the program are not yet clear, although Villaraigosa has credited it with reducing crime and encouraging coordination among city departments.

The "Transportation Mayor"

Last, Villaraigosa—dubbed the "Transportation Mayor"—has been lauded for his transportation and environmental efforts, which have been called his most significant legacy. In his eight State of the City Addresses, Villaraigosa consistently highlighted transportation and environmental initiatives with the multiple aims of improving the quality of life for residents citywide, contributing to economic and workforce development amid the economic recession, and strengthening Los Angeles's global competitiveness. In 2008, Villaraigosa was a key figure in the successful campaign to pass Measure R, a Los Angeles County ballot initiative that approved a half-cent sales-tax increase until 2039 to finance county transportation projects. He worked in tandem with an impressive coalition of more than thirty environmental, labor, and business groups called Move LA to support Measure R, although the initiative also faced resistance from some groups, such as the Bus Riders Union, supported by immigrant workers, that opposed the regressive nature of the tax and its emphasis on funding rail and freeway projects. Moreover, to move Measure R forward, Villaraigosa helped navigate a complex political process that included working with the Metro board, Los Angeles County supervisors, and the California state legislature, which passed legislation enabling the sales tax to extend for thirty years.

After the passage of Measure R, Villaraigosa introduced his 30/10 initiative, which aimed to fast-track thirty years of transportation projects into ten years. The 30/10 initiative gained national attention when it transformed into America Fast Forward, congressional legislation passed in 2012 with bipartisan support that accelerates locally funded transportation projects through expanded low-interest federal loans. Using his role as president of the National Conference of Mayors, Villaraigosa facilitated a diverse bipartisan national coalition that included the AFL-CIO, the U.S. Chamber of Commerce, and dozens of city mayors to successfully lobby federal officials for their support. The legislation includes more than $1 billion to extend Metro's rail line to parts of South and West Los Angeles; however, it did not include enough funds for all the projects envisioned in the 30/10 initiative.

To fill the gap, Villaraigosa campaigned again for a 2012 ballot measure—Measure J—to extend the half-cent sales-tax increase for an additional thirty years to 2069; however, the measure narrowly fell short of the two-thirds vote needed with 66.11 percent of the vote. Villaraigosa laid blame for the loss in part on California's structural constraints, which require a supermajority to pass new taxes; however, opposition to Measure J was stronger, more organized, and more diverse in coalition partners than opposition to Measure R. Illustrating the fluid and at times surprising nature of coalition building in Los Angeles, not only the Bus Riders Union but also activists from historically African American communities in South Los Angeles and the wealthy white neighborhoods of Beverly Hills participated in the No on J Campaign. South Los Angeles leaders involved in the Crenshaw Subway Coalition objected to Measure J because of Metro's reluctance to incorporate a subway station in the Leimert Park Village neighborhood. Beverly Hills leaders opposed Metro's plan to construct a subway line that would pass under Beverly Hills High School.

On the environmental front, although he failed to reach his target, Villaraigosa added more than 400,000 trees to the city as part of his Million Trees Initiative. More significantly, at the end of Villaraigosa's administration, the proportion of the city's energy drawn from renewable energy sources—solar, wind, and geothermal energy—rose from 4 to 20 percent; however, the shift in the energy portfolio fell short of Villaraigosa's goal of 40 percent renewable energy by 2020 and led to two energy rate hikes supported by the city council to help cover the transition. During his administration, Villaraigosa also championed the Clean Truck Program to reduce polluting emissions at the Port of Los Angeles, which handles 44 percent of all container goods entering the United States.

Supported by a labor-environmental coalition, the Clean Truck Program required the sixteen thousand diesel trucks serving the port to meet U.S. Environmental Protection Agency (EPA) emissions standards and levied a $35 fee on each container arriving or leaving the port to help fund truck retrofitting to comply with EPA standards. However, the U.S. Supreme Court struck down parts of the Clean Truck Program, which was opposed by the American Trucking Association, in June 2013. The court ruled that the port could not impose criminal penalties for violating the program's provisions or require trucks to have off-street parking locations when they were not in service, a provision included to prevent truck parking in area neighborhoods. Finally, Villaraigosa helped add 149 miles of bicycle lanes to the city after his 2010 biking accident involving a taxi focused his attention on city bicycle transportation issues.

Legacies of Villaraigosa's Administration

After winning election in 2005, Villaraigosa entered into his role as mayor with high public approval and the weight of a city's expectations. Eight years later, views of Villaraigosa's legacy were decidedly mixed; approval rates declined from two-thirds to 47 percent of residents polled, while dissatisfaction rose to 40 percent (Mehta 2013). There are several likely reasons for the mixed views of Villaraigosa.

First, Villaraigosa's self-promotional and celebrity lifestyle often overshadowed his policy efforts. For example, Villaraigosa's staged press events were regularities in the city. His frequent trips outside Los Angeles to lobby Washington, raise funds, campaign for others, and serve as the 2011 National Conference of Mayors president and the 2012 Democratic National Convention chair drew criticism from the press and public for perceived inattention to day-to-day city management. His 2007 disclosure of his extramarital affair with a Univision news anchor, his ensuing divorce from his wife, and his subsequent relationship with another local newscaster drew public attention away from his policy priorities and damaged his image, particularly in the Latino community. Moreover, in 2011, Villaraigosa was fined nearly $42,000—the largest fine under California ethics law—after failing to report free tickets he received to more than thirty high-profile events from 2005 to 2009, including the Oscars and the Emmys, Los Angeles Lakers and Dodgers games, music concerts, and the 2009 *American Idol* finale show. The final straw for some was the surfacing of a photograph of Villaraigosa with troubled actor Charlie Sheen at a Cabo San Lucas hotel opening in 2012, which was thought to have problematized Villaraigosa's consideration for U.S. secretary of transportation (McDonald 2013).

More significantly, however, the wicked nature of urban problems, exacerbated by the structural limitations of Los Angeles's mayoral position, limited the role Villaraigosa could play in issues despite his skill at coalition building and at persuading political allies to help accomplish policy goals. In a city where the city charter limits the mayor's executive authority, Villaraigosa demonstrated his ability to muster support and cooperation not from only internal city actors and institutions but also from external players. Some observe that because of the office's limited powers compared with mayoralties in Chicago and New York, not many would seek to be Los Angeles mayor—a role for which Villaraigosa expressed enthusiasm throughout his administration.

However, Villaraigosa could not overcome all of the city's centrifugal forces. His aspirations and sweeping policy agenda required herculean efforts to come to fruition given the limited power of the mayor's office. Villaraigosa used his considerable political skills at the local, state, and federal levels and in the community and the private sector to try to deliver results, but he might have been perceived as more successful if he had been less ambitious and more targeted. His bid to control the LAUSD provides an example of his expenditure of significant resources and political capital on an effort that many predicted early on as problematic; however, Villaraigosa did focus his policy agenda on issues likely important to many Latino voters, such as education and public safety. Although he did not appeal directly to minority communities and largely used deracialized discourse, Villaraigosa drew greater attention to socially oriented policies affecting minority constituents. He also helped introduce significant policy shifts in public safety and education—such as investing in gang-prevention and intervention and youth-development activities, as opposed to only gang suppression, through his GRYD initiative and increasing the number of external

actors in the provision of public education through his school-reform efforts, although the long-term impacts of these policies are not yet known.

Moreover, with less coalescence today around the aims of city government (Purcell 2000), the need to work with diverse constituencies as mayor
to govern and accomplish policy goals meant that Villaraigosa continually
made and remade alliances despite past political relationships. He allied
with whomever he needed to advance his policy agenda, sometimes forming
unlikely coalitions and sometimes alienating past political partners.
Thus, as observed by Sonenshein (2003a, 2003b), Villaraigosa's administration also suggests that coalition building in contemporary urban cities
may not align as much along racial and ethnic or ideological lines as on
practical interests and leadership. For example, the relationship between
Villaraigosa and labor has been uneasy at times despite his roots as a labor
organizer and labor's strong support for his mayoral campaigns in 2001 and
2005. During his administration, he aligned with labor on environmental
and transportation issues but broke ranks with it on school reform. He supported a 25 percent pay raise over five years for city employees in 2007 but
later called the decision a mistake given the city's budget crises. Facing the
significant impact of the national recession on the city's budget, he negotiated with unions to increase their pension contributions in 2011 but also
cut back pensions for new employees in 2012 despite union opposition.

The moderating of Villaraigosa's positions may result from the practical realities of governing but also may be rooted in his aspirations for higher
political office. In each of his State of the City Addresses, Villaraigosa has
touted his work in Sacramento or Washington, D.C., or has called on state
and national leaders to act on transportation, environmental, and public
safety measures. After three years out of the political spotlight, Villaraigosa announced his 2018 bid for California governor just two days after the
November 2016 U.S. presidential election. Villaraigosa has stated that
his gubernatorial campaign will focus on rebuilding California's middle
class through education and repairing the state's infrastructure. Con-
trasting himself with President-Elect Donald Trump, Villaraigosa touted
his ability to unite California's diverse interests. Villaraigosa faces a competitive race with several other Democratic candidates already in the running,
most notably California lieutenant governor Gavin Newsom and California
state treasurer John Chiang; however, Villaraigosa could capitalize on the
turnout of highly motivated Latino and Democratic voters in the 2018
midterm elections, who could help elect him as the state's first Latino governor since 1875. Interestingly, Villaraigosa's political and policy ambitions
have served as a foil for his successor, Eric Garcetti, who has painted himself as the "back to the basics" mayor—more focused on the nuts and bolts

of city government than on grand political or policy plans. However, the most recent mayoral election also highlights the nature of electoral coalition politics in Los Angeles, shaped by the interaction of race and ethnicity with leadership cues and historic and contemporary contexts and relationships. With Villaraigosa subject to term limits, Los Angeles voters elected City Councilman Eric Garcetti as Villaraigosa's successor in May 2013 over City Controller Wendy Greuel. An ally of Garcetti and Greuel, who are both Democrats, Villaraigosa declined to endorse either candidate in the runoff race, which saw the lowest voter turnout in 100 years (Welsh 2013). Approximately 23.3 percent of registered voters in the city participated in the election, in which Garcetti garnered 222,300 votes to win. Garcetti and Greuel did not differ significantly on policy positions and failed to generate significant public interest in their campaigns. No defining issue appeared on the ballot to draw voters. Moreover, the political climate differed significantly from the one that had drawn Latino voters to the polls in the 2001 and 2005 mayoral elections, in the second of which communities organized to elect Villaraigosa as the first Latino leader of the city in more than one hundred years.

The great-grandson of Italian immigrants who settled in Mexico, Garcetti identifies as part Latino and part Jewish (his mother's heritage). Observers note that Garcetti did not hail from the Latino community or the Latino political establishment; however, during the campaign, Garcetti, who is fluent in Spanish, frequently invoked his mixed heritage as a means to appeal to a broad range of city voters. Garcetti effectively carried the vote from the city's Latino communities in the Eastside to the liberal white and Jewish neighborhoods in the Westside, as seen in Table 5.12, to become the city's first elected Jewish mayor. Moreover, he won the support of the city's more conservative white voters in the western San Fernando Valley largely because of what were perceived as Greuel's strong labor ties.

TABLE 5.12   LOS ANGELES MAYORAL
ELECTION RESULTS BY RACE, MAY 2013
RUNOFF

	Garcetti (%)	Greuel (%)
White	59	41
Black	31	69
Latino	60	40
Asian	55	45

Sources: Guerra and Gilbert (2013); "Los Angeles Votes 2013: Mayoral General Election Exit Poll," Thomas and Dorothy Leavey Center for the Study of Los Angeles, Loyola Marymount University, Los Angeles, California.

Greuel, who is white and once represented the San Fernando Valley on the city council, would have made history as the first female mayor of Los Angeles but surprisingly failed to garner majority support from women, winning only 49.7 percent of female voters (Guerra and Gilbert 2013). However, with ties to the African American community as a former deputy to Mayor Tom Bradley, Greuel won the vast majority of the city's African American vote. Endorsements from Latino political leaders, such as Los Angeles County supervisor Gloria Molina, labor leader Dolores Huerta, and California Assembly Speaker John Perez, also helped Greuel win 40 percent of the Latino vote. However, support from the city's Department of Water and Power union and the Los Angeles County Federation of Labor turned into a political liability as opponents painted Greuel as beholden to special interests. Greuel garnered only 39 percent of the Republican vote, 41 percent of white voters, and 51 percent of voters in the San Fernando Valley, where she had previously dominated during the primary election (Guerra and Gilbert 2013).

Thus, after the 2013 election of City Councilman Eric Garcetti as mayor, the trajectory of Latino politics in the city remains uncertain. Latino voters surely will remain a political force; however, coalitional alignments are not guaranteed in a city emblematic of the growing diversity and complex and divergent interests increasingly characteristic of U.S. urban politics. Perhaps Villaraigosa's lasting legacy will be his tireless approach to being mayor: building the coalition to meet the next challenge.

REFERENCES

Alvarez, Manuel Rene. 2013. "A California Mayor's Bid to Improve the City's Schools: A Study of the Reform He Implemented." Ph.D. diss., California State University, Los Angeles.

Aron, Hillel. 2011. "Progressives Find Religion on LAUSD Reform." *LA Weekly*, October 27.

Barreto, Matt A., Mario Villarreal, and Nathan D. Woods. 2005. "Metropolitan Latino Political Behavior: Voter Turnout and Candidate Preference in Los Angeles." *Journal of Urban Affairs* 27, no. 1:71–91.

Barreto, Matt A., and Nathan D. Woods. 2005. "Latino Voting Behavior in an Anti-Latino Political Context: The Case of Los Angeles County." In *Diversity in Democracy: Minority Representation in the United States*, edited by Gary M. Segura and Shaun Bowler, 148–169. Charlottesville: University of Virginia Press.

Box, Richard C., and Juliet Ann Musso. 2004. "Experiments with Local Federalism: Secession and the Neighborhood Council Movement in Los Angeles." *American Review of Public Administration* 34, no. 3:259–276.

Brodkin, Karen. 2007. *Making Democracy Matter: Identity and Activism in Los Angeles*. New Brunswick, NJ: Rutgers University Press.

Burt, Kenneth C. 2007. *The Search for a Civic Voice: California Latino Politics*. Claremont, CA: Regina Books.

Carroll, Rory. 2016. "'Hope Everyone Pukes on Your Artisanal Treats': Fighting Gentrification, LA-Style." *Guardian*, April 19. https://www.theguardian.com/us-news/2016/apr/19/los-angeles-la-gentrification-resistance-boyle-heights.

Chambers, Stefanie. 2006. *Mayors and Schools: Minority Voices and Democratic Tensions in Urban Education*. Philadelphia: Temple University Press.

Clark, Alfred E. 1982. "Norris Poulson, Mayor Who Lured Dodgers to Los Angeles, Dies at 87." *Los Angeles Times*, September 26.

Crenshaw, Kimberle. 1989. "Demarginalizing the Intersection of Race and Sex: A Black Feminist Critique of Antidiscrimination Doctrine, Feminist Theory, and Antiracist Politics." *University of Chicago Legal Forum* 1989, no. 1:139–167.

Dreier, Peter, Regina Freer, Robert Gottlieb, and Mark Vallianatos. 2006. "Movement Mayor: Can Antonio Villaraigosa Change Los Angeles?" *Dissent* 53, no. 3:45–52.

Ethington, Philip J., William H. Frey, and Dowell Myers. 2001. "The Racial Resegregation of Los Angeles County, 1940–2000." Race Contours 2000 Study, Public Research Report No. 2001–04, University of Southern California and University of Michigan.

Fausset, Richard. 2005. "School Reform Best in Small Steps, Mayor Finds." *Los Angeles Times*, October 4.

Finnegan, Michael. 2013. "Villaraigosa Leaves Office with His Key Goals for L.A. Accomplished." *Los Angeles Times*, June 28.

Frank, Larry, and Kent Wong. 2004. "Dynamic Political Mobilization: The Los Angeles County Federation of Labor." *Working USA: The Journal of Labor and Society* 8:155–181.

Fuller, Bruce. 2010. "Palace Revolt in Los Angeles?" *Education Next* 10, no. 3:20–28.

Garcia Bedolla, Lisa. 2007. "Intersections of Inequality: Understanding Marginalization and Privilege in the Post–Civil Rights Era." *Politics and Gender* 3, no. 2:232–248.

Goldfarb, Lyn., producer and director. 2006. *The New Los Angeles*. Motion picture. Los Angeles: Lyn Goldfarb Productions.

Gottlieb, Robert, Mark Vallianatos, Regina M. Freer, and Peter Dreier. 2006. *The Next Los Angeles: The Struggle for a Livable City*. Berkeley: University of California Press.

Guerra, Fernando J., and Brianne Gilbert. 2013. *Los Angeles Votes 2013: Mayoral General Election Exit Poll*. Los Angeles: Thomas and Dorothy Leavey Center for the Study of Los Angeles, Loyola Marymount University.

Hess, Frederick M. 2007. "Looking for Leadership: Assessing the Case for Mayoral Control of Urban School Systems." Policy Study, Show-Me Institute, St. Louis.

Hines, Thomas S. 1982. "Housing, Baseball, and Creeping Socialism: The Battle of Chavez Ravine, Los Angeles, 1949–1959." *Journal of Urban History* 8:123–143.

Loukaitou-Sideris, Anastasia, and Renia Ehrenfeucht. 2009. *Sidewalks: Conflict and Negotiation over Public Space*. Boston: MIT Press.

Marsh, Julie A., Katharine O. Strunk, and Susan Bush. 2012. "Portfolio District Reform Meets School Turnaround: Early Implementation Findings from the Los Angeles Public School Choice Initiative." *Journal of Education Administration* 51, no. 4:498–527.

Maxwell, Lesli A. 2006. "L.A. Mayor Seeks Role in District." *Education Week* 25, no. 33:1–25.

Mayor's Partnership for Schools. 2007. "The Partnership for Los Angeles Schools: Transforming Our Schools and Communities Together." Work-in-progress draft.

McDonald, Patrick Range. 2013. "Antonio Villaraigosa's Quest for Wall Street, Washington and Wealth." *LA Weekly*, May 23.

Mehta, Semma. 2013. "Poll Shows Split in Approval for Outgoing Mayor Villaraigosa." *Los Angeles Times*, June 30.

Mejia, Brittny. 2016. "Gentrification Pushes up against Boyle Heights—and Vice Versa." *Los Angeles Times*, March 3. http://www.latimes.com/local/california/la-me-las -palomas-gentrification-20160303-story.html.

Milkman, Ruth. 2006. *L.A. Story: Immigrant Workers and the Future of the U.S. Labor Movement*. New York: Russell Sage Foundation.

Myers, Dowell, Janna Goldberg, Sarah Mawhorter, and Seong Hee Min. 2010. "Immigrants and the New Maturity of Los Angeles." In *Los Angeles 2010 State of the City*, edited by Ali Modarres, 12–27. Los Angeles: Pat Brown Institute, California State University, Los Angeles.

National Center for Education Statistics. 2011. The Nation's Report Card: Civics 2010 (NCES 2011–466). Institute of Education Sciences, U.S. Department of Education, Washington, D.C

Nicholls, Walter J., and Justin R. Beaumont. 2004. "The Urbanisation of Justice Movements? Possibilities and Constraints for the City as a Space of Contentious Struggle." *Space and Polity* 8, no. 2:119–135.

Orfield, Gary, Genevieve Siegel-Hawley, and John Kucsera. 2011. *Divided We Fail: Segregation and Inequality in the Southland's Schools*. The Civil Rights Project/Proyecto Derechos Civiles. Los Angeles: University of California, Los Angeles.

Parson, Don. 2007. "The Decline of Public Housing and the Politics of the Red Scare: The Significance of the Los Angeles Public Housing War." *Journal of Urban History* 33, no. 3:400–417.

Pastor, Jr., Manuel, Chris Benner, and Martha Matsuoka. 2009. *This Could Be the Start of Something Big: How Social Movements for Regional Equity Are Reshaping Metropolitan America*. Ithaca, NY: Cornell University Press.

Purcell, Mark. 2000. "The Decline of the Political Consensus for Urban Growth: Evidence from Los Angeles." *Journal of Urban Affairs* 22, no. 1:85–100.

Rittel, Horst W.J., and Melvin M. Webber. 1973. "Dilemmas in a General Theory of Planning." *Policy Sciences* 4:155–169.

Rocco, Raymond A. 1996. "Latino Los Angeles: Reframing Boundaries/Borders." In *The City: Los Angeles and Urban Theory at the End of the Twentieth Century*, edited by A. J. Scott and E. W. Soja, 365–389. Berkeley: University of California Press.

Sánchez, George J. 1993. *Becoming Mexican American: Ethnicity, Culture, and Identity in Chicano Los Angeles, 1900–1945*. New York: Oxford University Press.

Sides, Josh. (2003). *L.A. City Limits: African American Los Angeles from the Great Depression to the Present*. Los Angeles: University of California Press.

Sitton, Tom. 2005. *Los Angeles Transformed: Fletcher Bowron's Urban Reform Revival, 1938–1953*. Albuquerque: University of New Mexico Press.

Sonenshein, Raphael J. 1994. *Politics in Black and White: Race and Power in Los Angeles*. Princeton, NJ: Princeton University Press.

———. 2003a. "Post-incorporation Politics in Los Angeles." In *Racial Politics in American Cities*, 3rd ed., edited by R. P. Browning, D. R. Marshall, and D. H. Tabb, 51–76. New York: Longman.

———. 2003b. "The Prospects for Multiracial Coalitions: Lessons from America's Three Largest Cities." In *Racial Politics in American Cities*, 3rd ed., edited by Rufus P. Browning, Dale Rogers Marshall, and David H. Tabb, 333–356. New York: Longman.

Sonenshein, Raphael J., and Mark H. Drayse. 2006. "Urban Electoral Coalitions in an Age of Immigration: Time and Place in the 2001 and 2005 Los Angeles Mayoral Primaries." *Political Geography* 25:570–595.

Sonenshein, Raphael J., and Susan H. Pinkus. 2002. "The Dynamics of Latino Political Incorporation: The 2001 Los Angeles Mayoral Election as Seen in *Los Angeles Times* Exit Polls." *PS: Political Science and Politics* 35, no. 1:67–74.

Stepler, Renee and Mark Hugo Lopez. 2016. "U.S. Latino Population Growth and Dispersion Has Slowed Since Onset of the Great Recession." Pew Research Center, September.

Taylor, Paul, Ana Gonzalez-Barrera, Jeffrey S. Passel, and Mark Hugo Lopez. 2012. *An Awakened Giant: The Hispanic Electorate Is Likely to Double by 2030.* Washington, DC: Pew Hispanic Center

Villaraigosa, Antonio. 2006. *State of the City Address.* April 18. Retrieved from https://www.youtube.com/watch?v=vz35BwaW7_c.

———. 2007. *State of the City Address.* April 18. Retrieved from https://www.youtube.com/watch?v=nV0Qp6ef16s.

———. 2012. *State of the City Address.* April 18. Retrieved from https://www.youtube.com/watch?v=zL6AnZs-yss.

Welsh, Ben. 2013. "L.A. Mayoral Runoff Another Low Mark in Voter Turnout: 23.3%." *Los Angeles Times*, June 11.

Wong, Kenneth K., and Francis X. Shen. 2007. "Mayoral Leadership Matters: Lessons Learned from Mayoral Control of Large Urban School Systems." *Peabody Journal of Education* 82, no. 4:737–768.

III Latino Mayors in the East and South

6

Two Latino Mayors in Hartford

Eddie Perez and Pedro Segarra

STEFANIE CHAMBERS AND
EMILY M. FARRIS

EDITORS' NOTE

In this chapter, Stefanie Chambers and Emily M. Farris show that Latino mayors are no longer confined to the Southwest and the West but are also found in the East. The city of Hartford, Connecticut, the state capital, has elected two Latino mayors: Eddie Perez and Pedro Segarra. Perez and Segarra, both Puerto Rican, came to power during the postindustrial era and led the city from 2001 through 2015. In Hartford, Latinos constitute a majority of the population, and a majority of the Latino residents are Puerto Rican. Eddie Perez was a community activist elected by a coalition of Latinos and blacks. Perez's election was similar to the election of other Latino mayors. It followed years of grassroots community organizing in Hartford's Puerto Rican community.

Like successful Latino mayoral candidates in Los Angeles, San Antonio, Providence, and Denver, Perez ran a campaign that did not emphasize race or ethnicity. Latino voters, however, were energized by Perez's candidacy, which generated enormous pride and high voter turnout in the Latino community. Although there had been two previous black mayors of Hartford, Perez's three successful mayoral elections demonstrated a shift in the racial/ethnic power structure and coalitional alliances among voters.

After his conviction on charges of corruption in 2010, Perez was replaced by the city council president, Pedro Segarra, the city's second Latino mayor. Segarra was later elected in his own right to the mayor's office in 2011.

Chambers and Farris examine the impact of Perez and Segarra on the political and economic status of Latinos in Hartford. Drawing on State of the City

addresses, economic indicators, and interviews with community leaders, Perez,
and Segarra, they illustrate that Perez focused more on redistributive policies,
while Segarra focused on developmental policies. Chambers and Farris observe
that during the era of the redevelopment city, Hartford was led by black mayors
(1981–1993). Mayors Perez and Segarra faced many of the same socioeconomic
challenges in the postindustrial city as their African American predecessors. A
declining tax base, state and federal reductions in aid, an abundance of nontax-
able property, and an increasingly impoverished population all contributed to the
challenges faced by these municipal leaders. Chambers and Farris conclude that
while Perez and Segarra were successful in expanding opportunities for Latinos
in the public sector, they were less successful in economic-related areas like home
ownership. Much like mayors examined in other chapters in this volume, neither
Perez nor Segarra was able to significantly elevate the position of Hartford's La-
tinos during their administrations because of external constraints. Even with
very different leadership styles and policy priorities, neither leader could tran-
scend the larger obstacles the city faced.

Hartford, Connecticut, was settled in the early seventeenth century as one of the first cities of New England. Its founder, the Reverend Thomas Hooker, proclaimed, "The foundation of authority is laid, firstly, in the free consent of the people" (Rossiter 1952, p. 477). In 2001, Hartford continued its centuries-old democratic spirit and elected the first Latino mayor in New England, Eddie Perez. At the time of Perez's election, Hartford's Latinos made up nearly 60 percent of the city's 120,000 residents. From 2001 until 2015, two Puerto Rican mayors governed Hartford: Eddie Perez and Pedro Segarra.

Eddie Perez, a Puerto Rican community activist and college adminis-trator, was first elected to the open seat of Hartford's mayor with more than 70 percent of the vote in 2001. Perez easily won reelection in 2003 to a four-year term under the new city charter, which strengthened the may-or's powers. Despite being engulfed in a state criminal corruption investiga-tion, Perez won reelection again in 2007 with 48 percent of the vote in a six-way race. Perez resigned in 2010 after his conviction on five felony counts, including bribery and extortion (Kovner 2010).[1]

Council President Pedro Segarra, a local lawyer and fellow Puerto Rican, assumed the mayor's position after Perez's resignation. Initially expected only to finish Mayor Perez's turn, Segarra decided to run again the follow-ing year. Voters elected Segarra mayor of Hartford in 2011 with more than 80 percent of the vote in an election in which only 15 percent of the city's registered voters turned out to vote for mayor. Segarra lost reelection in 2015 in the Democratic primary to Luke Bronin, a young, white, Ivy

League–educated lawyer new to electoral politics. Bronin dramatically out-spent Segarra and won the election with 55 percent of the vote to Segarra's 45 percent (Carlesso, Goode, and de la Torre 2015).

The fifteen-year period of governance of Eddie Perez and Pedro Segarra as the city's first two Latino mayors represents a new chapter in Hartford's history. Scholars of urban politics have long examined the impact of racial- and ethnic-minority city leaders on the communities they descriptively represent. Although research suggests that some benefits come with local minority representation, it also identifies the structural challenges minor-ity mayors have faced in political office (Hopkins and McCabe 2012; Nel-son 2005; Persons 1993; Rich 1989). Generations of black mayors inherited cities largely abandoned by their state leaders as middle-class residents and businesses moved to the suburbs. Black mayors faced serious obstacles in redeveloping their cities, which were crippled by a decline in the tax base needed to provide services for an increasingly poor population. Hartford's first two black mayors, Thirman Milner (1981–1987) and Carrie Saxon Perry (1987–1993), confronted similar challenges and were unable to re-verse Hartford's struggling economic condition. Moreover, both Milner and Perry served as mayor under a weak-mayor system dictated by the previous city charter. The tenure of Mayors Perez and Segarra posed the question: Would the first two Latino leaders of Hartford face the same fate? With an increase in their formal authority as mayor, Hartford's first two Latino mayors ought to have been better positioned to improve the conditions of Latinos in Hartford. However, like the Latino mayors featured in other chapters in this volume, Hartford's Latino mayors were constrained, espe-cially in elevating the socioeconomic position of poor Latinos. Perez and Segarra came to power during the postindustrial era.

In this chapter, we examine the political rise of Hartford's two Latino mayors, their policy priorities, and their subsequent impact on the politi-cal and economic position of Latinos in Hartford. Drawing on State of the City addresses, economic indicators, and interviews with community lead-ers and the mayors themselves, we examine the policy priorities of Mayors Perez and Segarra.[2] By discovering what these two mayors envisioned for their city, how community leaders evaluate the tenure of these mayors, and the relative changes in the economic situation of Hartford's Latinos, we can better understand the ways in which Hartford's Latino community has been affected by Latino mayoral leadership. The central question raised in this chapter is whether the governance of Latino mayors has affected the political and economic positions of Latinos in Hartford.

Our findings suggest that Eddie Perez and Pedro Segarra, like many of the other Latino mayors covered in this volume, were largely limited in their capacity to significantly improve the socioeconomic position of Hartford's Latino community. We begin our analysis by setting the historical context for the election of Mayor Perez, provide a biographical sketch and assessment of each mayor with assistance from interviews with the mayors, and then turn to our analysis of their State of the City speeches and economic outcomes from the years of their governance.

Hartford's Sociodemographic Evolution

Connecticut's capital city, Hartford, is the state's fourth-largest city with approximately 125,000 residents within the city's eighteen square miles. Although Connecticut is one of the wealthiest states in the nation, it is also home today to some of the poorest cities in the country, including Hartford. However, this was not always Hartford's fortune; for the first half of the city's existence, it flourished with a wealth of commercial innovation and activity.

In the nineteenth century, Hartford's economy boomed with industries such as insurance, publishing, munitions, and manufacturing. Hartford became known as the "Insurance Capital of the World," and by the late nineteenth century, it was the wealthiest city in the United States (De Avila 2012). Hartford's prosperity enticed people to the city, and from 1870 to 1920, it grew rapidly from 42,015 to 138,035 residents. Large numbers of immigrants settled there. During World War II, plentiful jobs in the nearby tobacco fields and the booming manufacturing industry attracted others, such as southern African Americans, West Indians, and Puerto Ricans, to settle in Hartford. The city's population peaked in 1950 at 177,397.

After World War II, Hartford experienced a variety of serious setbacks, economic problems, and demographic changes. Businesses, including Colt Manufacturing and Pratt and Whitney, relocated to nearby cities, moved out of state, or simply closed their doors. Many of Hartford's white residents fled to nearby suburbs (Clavel 1986). As a result of white flight, between 1950 and 1980, Hartford's population dropped by 40,000 residents (Backstrand and Schensul 1982). Meanwhile, substantial numbers of blacks and Puerto Ricans arrived at the beginning of Hartford's swift decline. From 1950 to 1970, blacks increased from 7.2 percent of the population to 27.9 percent. By 1970, about 20,000 Puerto Ricans lived in the city (Cruz 1998). In short, Hartford has experienced many of the dramatic demographic changes characteristic of many postindustrial cities.

Tensions escalated between the leaders of the city's corporate sector, known as the Bishops, and the increasing number of racial- and ethnic-minority residents of Hartford. In 1960, the city embarked on "one of the largest programs of urban redevelopment ever undertaken by an American municipality" (Weaver 1982, p. 128) and destroyed much of the central city's low-income housing. Racial change, persistent inequality, and discrimination erupted in violence in Hartford in the late 1960s, as in other cities across the United States (Spilerman 1970). In 1974, the Bishops developed a covert plan, known as the Hartford Process, to limit and concentrate Puerto Ricans in the city. After the plan was leaked to the media, Puerto Ricans mobilized a successful protest that forced the city to abandon the plan but left strains in the city (Cruz 1997).

Hartford went from being one of the nation's richest cities at the end of the nineteenth century to one of the poorest cities by 1970 and faces significant challenges today (McKee 2000). Like Providence and other capital cities in New England, Hartford's property-tax base is limited because of the large number of state-government offices, hospitals, colleges and universities, and other tax-exempt organizations. The city's tax base further eroded with the loss of a number of insurance companies, including CIGNA and Travelers Insurance, and retail and entertainment attractions in the city's downtown. By the late 1990s, schools had declined to the point that the state intervened and took them over (Burns 2002). Hartford frequently appears on lists of the most dangerous cities in the country (Burgard 2004; Goff 2014).

Despite efforts to rebrand Hartford as "New England's Rising Star" and millions of dollars spent in downtown revitalization efforts, Hartford has experienced a very limited renaissance and has largely ignored the city's poorer neighborhoods. Gentrification, a phenomenon rapidly occurring in all the other cities in this volume, is insignificant in Hartford. In 2014, the median household income for the city was $29,313, much lower than Connecticut's median household income of $69,899. In the nation's third-richest state, a third of Hartford's residents live below the poverty line. Many of Hartford's residents continue to face difficult challenges of poverty and lack of opportunities.

Latinos in Hartford

Today, amid the city's changing demographics and economic challenges, Hartford is a city with a large and diverse Latino community. As indicated in Table 6.1, Hartford is a majority-minority city. The city's Latino popula-

TABLE 6.1   POPULATION OF HARTFORD BY RACE

		Black		Hispanic		White	
Year	Total population	Count	% of total	Count	% of total	Count	% of total
1970	158,017	44,091	27.90	Data not available*		111,862	70.79
1980	136,392	46,186	33.86	27,898	20.45	68,603	50.30
1990	139,739	54,338	38.89	44,137	31.59	55,869	39.98
2000	121,578	46,264	38.05	49,260	40.52	33,705	27.72
2010	124,775	48,288	38.70	54,152	43.40	37,183	29.80

Note: Census Bureau surveys allow participants to indicate themselves as both Hispanic and of another race; therefore, the total of the individual racial populations is greater than the total population at the time. The Hispanic population has been included here without any statistical alteration and so includes participants who identify as both Hispanic and of another race.

* The 1970 census did not explicitly include the option "Hispanic," instead requiring Hispanic participants to write in their ethnicity under "Other."

TABLE 6.2   TOP FIVE LATINO NATIONAL GROUPS IN HARTFORD

National origin	Population	Percentage
All Latinos	54,185	—
Puerto Rican	41,995	77.5
Mexican	2,272	4.2
Dominican	2,191	4.0
Peruvian	2,119	3.9
Colombian	1,074	2.0

Source: Farris (2014).

tion exceeded the black and white populations in the city in 2000. Over the decades, the city's Latino population has grown, largely thanks to its Puerto Rican population, with smaller but increasing numbers of Mexican, Dominican, Peruvian, and Colombian populations settling in Hartford as well, as illustrated in Table 6.2.

Latinos in the city today are young: the median age for Hartford Latinos is twenty-eight, and 32 percent of the Latino population is under age eighteen. Hartford's Latino population is also mostly lower income. The median household income for Latinos in the city is $23,163. Forty-one percent of Latinos in the city live below the poverty line. Most of the Latinos in Hartford are native born (83 percent); this is unsurprising given that Puerto Ricans are U.S. citizens. Of the smaller foreign-born Latino population in Hartford, 38 percent are naturalized citizens. Today, of the approximately 54,000 Latinos in Hartford, only a third are estimated to be registered voters (Pazniokas 2013).

Puerto Rican Activism in Hartford

In Chapter 1 of this volume, Marion Orr and Domingo Morel explain that community organizing is often a significant variable in Latino mayoral politics. Community organizing is also an important part of the narrative in the election of Latino mayors in Hartford. As Puerto Ricans moved from tobacco plantations to manufacturing plants in the city in the mid-twentieth century, they built resources in community-based groups and agencies, like the San Juan Center (started in 1956), the Spanish Action Coalition (1967), and the Puerto Rican Parade Committee (1963). These organizations affirmed Puerto Ricans' ethnic identity, encouraged Puerto Rican activism, and developed additional advocacy organizations and programs, like La Casa de Puerto Rico, the Teacher Corps, the Connecticut Association of United Spanish Administrators, the Hispanic Health Council, and the Connecticut Puerto Rican Forum.

Puerto Ricans also organized politically through groups like the Puerto Rican Democrats of Hartford. Events during the turbulent summer of 1969 and negative backlash against the Bishops' Hartford Process plan in the early 1970s brought visibility to the collective needs of the growing number of Puerto Ricans in Hartford (Cruz 1997). During this time, Puerto Rican political groups proliferated, although infighting, personality conflicts, and scarce resources limited the effectiveness of most of them.

As Puerto Ricans focused their activities on the electoral process, individuals and groups pursued different paths. Some, like María Colón Sánchez, worked through the Democratic Party to broker with the machine boss, Nick Carbone, for Puerto Rican representation. Others, primarily younger Puerto Ricans, worked outside the party system to form leftist protest groups, such as the Puerto Rican Socialist Party, run by José La Luz and Edwin Vargas. Others, led by Eugenio Caro, formed a protest group, the Committee of 24, as a response to continued discrimination against Puerto Ricans in the 1970s.[3] Through these efforts, the partisan, organizational, and ideological differences among Puerto Ricans worked in their favor to put multiple points of pressure on Carbone to eventually fill a vacant Democratic city council seat with a Puerto Rican, Mildred Torres-Soto, in 1979.

Hartford's Racial Politics on the City Council

Hartford's city council, known as the Court of Common Council, has nine members elected in partisan elections. Unlike other New England cities, such as Providence, Rhode Island, Hartford's city council is elected at-large.

Under state statute, the city must have minority-party representation as part of its at-large representation on the city council. Two-thirds of the nine council seats are reserved for Democrats, as the majority party, and the remaining three are open for minority parties (Hassett 2010). Democrats in Hartford are organized through the Democratic Town Committee (DTC), which endorses candidates on a slate for local office.

In elections beginning in the 1980s, the Democratic Party, which has long dominated Hartford politics, developed a racially based quota system for its slate of endorsed candidates to balance the interests of whites, blacks, and Puerto Ricans in the city. For most of the 1980s and 1990s, Latinos secured at least one of Hartford's city council seats under the racial quota adopted by the DTC. Although they were successful in achieving political representation, a sign that Latino political empowerment was occurring in the postindustrial era, Puerto Rican elites frequently disagreed over their candidates, strategies, and ideologies. Efforts to unify under the Puerto Rican Political Action Committee in the mid-1980s achieved some success, but the organization later dissolved because of personal conflicts and ideological differences. In addition to their determined slots in the Democratic Party, a few Puerto Rican candidates have been elected to the city council as members of third parties. Today, Latinos continue to be elected as city councilors, and their growing numbers in the city led to the election of the first Latino mayor, Eddie Perez, in 2001. Since 2001, Hartford has had two Puerto Rican Mayors: Eddie Perez and Pedro Segarra.

The Evolution of Minority Mayors in Hartford

Hartford's pattern of ethnic/racial mayoral transition is similar to the pattern Orr and Morel discuss in Chapter 1. Hartford's two Latino mayors came to power after the city had elected black mayors. Hartford voters elected its first black mayor in 1981, during the redevelopment era. Hartford's first Latino mayor came to power during the postindustrial era.

Hartford's Black Mayors: Milner and Perry

Hartford's first black mayor, Thirman Milner (1981–1987), was elected once Hartford's population had reached a racial and ethnic balance where blacks, Latinos, and whites each constituted roughly one-third of the population (McKee 2000). As the city's black population grew, partly because of migration patterns and partly because of white flight, blacks organized politically and gained control of city hall in 1981. Under Milner, the city had a black deputy mayor and city manager, two powerful positions within Hartford city government (McKee and Bacon 2013). In 1986, after Milner decided not to seek reelection, residents elected Milner's successor, Carrie Saxon Perry, as the first black female mayor elected in the United States. Her coalition was characterized as a "true rainbow coalition" because her campaign deliberately reached out to Latinos in a way the city had never seen before.

Although Perry's electoral base was black, she was also supported heavily in Latino and liberal white neighborhoods (community interviews, February 14, 2014; February 15, 2014; and February 16, 2014). Interviews with community leaders indicated that the dedication of Mayors Milner and Perry created municipal opportunities for minority residents that had never been available in years past. As one longtime community leader put it, "Carrie not only opened doors for Blacks, but she cared about Latinos" (community interview, February 14, 2014). The municipal positions that Milner and Perry opened to blacks helped propel a new generation of black leaders into the middle class. However, over the decades, blacks' upward mobility in Hartford stalled as many of the individuals hired by Milner and Perry retired. There has been a marked decline in municipal jobs held by blacks (community interview, February 14, 2014).[4]

During Perry's three terms in office, her administration worked to transform Hartford's weak-mayor system into a stronger and more influential post. However, in the 1993 municipal elections, Perry failed to persuade the voters to approve a change in the city charter from a council-manager form of government to a strong-mayor form. The 1993 election also brought defeat to Perry. Although her endorsed slate won seats on the city council, Perry lost her primary. Local observers attributed her defeat in part to her push for charter reform (McKee 2000). Perry was defeated by Mike Peters, a veteran firefighter from a politically connected Italian family. Peters strongly opposed changing the charter to create a strong-mayor system, endorsed a bipartisan slate of city council candidates, and took a probusiness approach to leading city hall. However, the challenges of governing a postindustrial city were too great. Indeed, Peters's tenure would be remembered as the period in which the state government had to step in to take over critical municipal services, such as the school system, welfare, and economic development (McKee 2000, p. 41). Peters decided not to seek reelection in 2001, opening a door that Eddie Perez, the city's first Latino mayor, would step through.

Eddie Perez: A Community Activist Turned Mayor

Born in Puerto Rico in 1957, Eddie Perez moved to Hartford with his family at the age of twelve. Like many Puerto Rican families, Perez's family worked in the tobacco fields (Weiss 2001). As a child he moved often, living in seventeen different apartments and attending five schools, all in the same zip code (Perez interview, August 21, 2013). A gang member during his early years, Perez had a change of heart and was ultimately far more interested in community service (Weiss 2001).

Like many of the other Latino mayors featured in this volume, Eddie Perez has a background working within community-based organizations. He earned his associate's degree from Capitol Community Technical College and his bachelor's degree from Trinity College. Perez joined Trinity College as director of community relations in 1989. A decade later he served as executive director of Southside Institutions Neighborhood Alliance (SINA), a nonprofit community organization founded by Trinity College and Hartford Hospital. One of his most notable accomplishments at SINA was the $112 million neighborhood-redevelopment project known as the Learning Corridor, which transformed an abandoned bus station into a campus of four state-of-the-art public schools. In his years at Trinity and SINA, Perez forged good working relationships with Hartford business leaders.

In addition to receiving the endorsement of Mayor Peters and the support of the Democratic Party, Perez successfully created a multiracial coalition of grassroots supporters who valued his work as a community organizer. According to one black interviewee, members of the black community supported Perez because there were no viable black candidates in the race, so they viewed Perez as their only hope of having a voice in the mayor's office again (community interview, February 15, 2014).

After studying the candidacies of the city's two black mayors, Perez believed that running a racialized campaign would lead to defeat. Like successful Latino mayoral candidates in Los Angeles, San Antonio, Denver, and Providence, Perez embraced a deracialized campaign when he ran for mayor. "For black politicians, they realized that their time had come," Perez explained. "They were a significant population in the city and had very little power in the past. I realized that class and race were so divisive and realized that I wanted to run a campaign that would result in the election of a Latino mayor of a capital city—not a Latino mayor. . . . I wanted to represent everyone and make things better for the city" (Perez interview, August 21, 2013). A deracialized campaign for mayor was a wise decision. Given the general low voter turnout among Latinos in the city and the relatively young age of Hartford's Latinos, the eligible voting bloc was likely some-what diminished.[5]

Even though Perez ran a mostly deracialized campaign, his candidacy generated enormous pride in the Puerto Rican and broader Latino community. All Latino community leaders interviewed for this project agreed that Latino pride, voter turnout, and sense of political efficacy surged with the election of Eddie Perez. This finding parallels the work of Matt Barreto on the importance of "ethnic cues" for Latino voters, who often respond favorably when a Latino candidate is running for office (Barreto 2012). Although Hartford saw its first Latina on the city council in 1980, and Latinos held about 20 percent of city council seats by 2000, the election of a Latino mayor was a major event for Latinos in Hartford (Burns 2006).

Shortly after his election, Perez succeeded in persuading voters to change the city charter from a council-manager to a strong-mayor form of government. This was no small accomplishment. In Chapter 2, Carlos Cuéllar explains that the council-manager system is the most common form of city government and is most prevalent in the Southwest and the South, regions of the country with large and growing Latino populations. Under the council-manager system, the professional manager, not the mayor, is placed in charge of department heads and supervises the operation of city government. In Hartford, several previous mayoral administrations, including Mayor Perry's, had unsuccessfully tried to revise the charter to give the mayor more power. As soon as Perez was elected, he launched a high-profile campaign for charter change, claiming that without more authority, he could not lead the city. The timing of this campaign was insightful because it came on the heels of his electoral victory and allowed him to frame his future success as dependent on charter reform. His appeal was successful, and 70 percent of voters supported charter revision in 2002. Under this new governance structure, Perez became the city's official CEO, received a $75,000 salary increase, and acquired more policy authority and virtual control of large city departments, such as education, police, and fire.

Perez's electoral and charter-reform victories were eventually overshadowed by corruption issues. Like other Connecticut politicians before him, Perez was convicted on corruption charges in 2010 based on work done on his home by a city contractor and a no-bid parking-lot contract he negotiated. Although he was reelected for a third term in 2007 after these concerns emerged, he ultimately was forced out of office after his conviction in 2010.

His indictment exposed a long-simmering fault line in the Puerto Rican community. According to respondents in this study, personal politics plays a large role in the behind-the-scenes coalitions within Hartford's Puerto Rican community. Several Puerto Rican leaders, including a state legislator who represents Hartford, opposed Perez's heavy-handed leadership style (community interview, November 18, 2014). Although many stood by Perez and were deeply committed to supporting him despite his mistakes, several prominent Puerto Rican leaders pushed for a deep investigation into his illegal activities. "Eddie led with an iron fist," recalled a Puerto Rican community leader. "A lot of people resented his dominance and unwillingness to compromise. It divided a lot of Puerto Ricans, many who had their own power base and were offended by his inability to reach out and broker deals" (community interview, February 15, 2014).

Immediately after his conviction, Perez resigned as mayor. His conviction was overturned by the Connecticut Appellate Court in February 2014 but was appealed to the Connecticut State Supreme Court. That court ruled in 2016 that Perez should be retried because of procedural problems in his original corruption case (Mahony and Carlesso 2016).

Pedro Segarra: An Intellectual Turned Mayor

When Eddie Perez resigned as mayor in 2010, the city council president, Pedro Segarra, assumed the position of mayor. Like Perez, Segarra was born in Puerto Rico and moved to Hartford as a boy. Segarra arrived in Hartford as a teenager without his parents, and despite the odds against him, he excelled both academically and professionally. He earned his associate's, bachelor's, master's in social work, and law degrees within nine years. Segarra's educational journey and community work suggest a longtime commitment to assisting Hartford's Latino community. Like Eddie Perez and many of the other Latino mayors in this volume, Segarra became politicized through his involvement in Latino advocacy and community-based organizations, ranging from founding the Latino Students Association at the University of Connecticut School of Law in Hartford to being a founding member of the Hispanic Health Council in Hartford. Segarra was corporate counsel for the City of Hartford for three terms before being appointed to fill a vacancy on the city council. He won election to the council in 2007. In 2010, Segarra was selected by his fellow council members to be president of the council.

Segarra completed Eddie Perez's unfinished mayoral term in 2010 and won election to his own term as mayor in 2011. Much was made of Segarra's anticorruption crusade in the wake of the Perez scandal. In his first State of the City address, Segarra proclaimed that "we are a more transparent Hartford; a stronger Hartford; and a Hartford that is much more attractive in the eyes of others and more importantly in the hearts and souls of our people" (Segarra 2011), as well as remarking that Hartford was a "fun city" that was "open for business." It is evident that Segarra was attempting to rebuild trust, provide a sense of excitement, and restore confidence in the leadership of the city. Business leaders were particularly invested in Segarra's success in the wake of the Perez scandal. One Latino community leader noted:

> The business executives in the city wanted to restore stability in the city. Pedro was more like them—a successful lawyer with experience as the city's corporate council. He was polished, spoke their language, and they hoped he'd develop into a strong leader who could stimulate the economy. . . . I assume they also thought it was convenient that he was Puerto Rican because it was a great opportunity to have someone who could understand the business perspective, the community piece, and not be tarnished by scandal. (Community interview, August 20, 2013)

In the leadup to Segarra's 2011 election, there was one particularly strong black candidate in the race, local attorney Shawn Wooden (Green 2011). However, Wooden exited the race before the Democratic primary because Connecticut's Democratic governor, Daniel Malloy, intervened and persuaded Wooden to end his bid for the Democratic nomination and instead run for city council. This unusual move by the governor undoubtedly contributed to Mayor Segarra's victory and is assumed to have stemmed from his desire to have a popular capital-city mayor with similar ideological views. A divided electorate could have allowed a less appealing candidate to capture the mayor's office. Because Governor Malloy was electorally dependent on urban voters, having a good relationship with the city's mayor was in his interest.

Although only 16.2 percent of registered voters participated in the 2011 general election, Segarra received 81 percent of the vote. Segarra's electoral coalition was multiracial and consisted of white liberals, Latinos, and black voters (Segarra interview, September 19, 2013). Black leaders supported Segarra's candidacy (community interviews, February 14, 15, and 16, 2014). Business leaders in Hartford, many of whom live outside the city, added their financial backing to the Segarra campaign. However, among respondents in this study, there was a consensus that there was minimal excitement in the Latino community about Segarra's candidacy. Some respondents indicated that despite hope that Latino municipal jobs and leadership opportunities would expand, these opportunities have not materialized as expected (community interview, September 4, 2013). Black respondents indicated that there has been a sharp decline in job opportunities for blacks and, to a lesser extent, Latinos under Segarra's leadership.

Although Segarra is not the first Latino or Puerto Rican mayor of Hartford, he is the first openly gay mayor of the city. Connecticut is a state with progressive marriage-equality policies, and Segarra married his partner shortly after becoming mayor. Given the social conservatism among Latinos on issues like marriage equality, it is somewhat counter-intuitive that Segarra's sexual orientation was not a major issue in his election. It is possible that because of Hartford's location in New England, a region where marriage-equality laws are most common, the cultural clash with Latino conservatism on this issue was moderated. Segarra's initial ascent as the succession mayor could also have reduced the focus on his sexual orientation. Finally, it is conceivable that the threat of losing the mayor's office to a non-Latino was a greater concern than Segarra's sexual orientation. The idea that racial and ethnic minorities fear the symbolic loss of the mayor's office has been seen in cities like New Orleans, where blacks were willing to accept conservative black candidates in order to maintain symbolic control of the mayor's office (Chambers and Nelson 2014).

In Chapter 1, Orr and Morel stress that improving education and workforce development have been top policy priorities of mayors in the postindustrial era. Segarra's policy priorities overlapped with those of other postindustrial Latino mayors, including some of the mayors in this volume, like Julian Castro of San Antonio and Antonio Villaraigosa of Los Angeles. For example, Segarra supported expanded education and job-training opportunities for Hartford's youth. However, respondents in this study agreed that the excitement surrounding Segarra's election and leadership remained lukewarm, and many of his major policy initiatives were not commonly recognizable. This was particularly true for his "Opportunities Hartford" program. Based on the "Pathways to Opportunity" initiative in Providence, Rhode Island, the Hartford program was intended "to identify, enhance and expand Hartford's most promising education, jobs and income opportunities for city residents" (Hartford.gov 2013). The specific goals of the program were the following:

1. Identify the greatest opportunities that now exist in Hartford to improve the community-wide results in the areas of education, job readiness/job creation/career advancement and family sustaining income for our residents.

2. Convene and coordinate the efforts of individuals and groups who together possess the skills, abilities, knowledge, and resources to enhance existing opportunities.
3. Funnel public and private sector funds when and if available to invest in the targeted areas of opportunity. (City of Hartford n.d.)

This long-term program had several stages and included a plethora of ideas and aspirations. Some respondents were familiar with components of this initiative, but there was no consensus that the public was aware of any strategic programs launched by Mayor Segarra.

As many of the authors in this volume point out, making the city an appealing place for business investment and economic growth is an important role of mayors. For example, Mayor Segarra became a strong supporter of a proposal to construct a new baseball stadium for Hartford's minor-league baseball team. In October 2014, the city council approved a proposal for a stadium. The politics surrounding stadia is complex, and some argue that they are a losing economic endeavor for cities (Delaney and Eckstein 2007). Segarra embraced the stadium proposal because of its assumed regional appeal and because it would be built in a blighted area of the city. Business leaders and suburban residents supported the proposal from the beginning. The stadium ultimately evolved into a public-private partnership that would be paid for by a private developer; the city would lease the venue and rent it to the Hartford Yard Goats, the double-A Eastern League affiliate of the Colorado Rockies. The development is also planned to include six hundred housing units, retail space, and offices. Although many in Hartford's poor neighborhood surrounding the stadium protested the initial plan, the city council ultimately approved it after an agreement was reached on financing. Although the stadium project was temporarily suspended due to construction delays and a lawsuit between the city and the developer, it finally opened in spring 2017.

Leadership Divergence and Community Cohesion: Two Latino Mayors

In the following sections, we provide an overview of the leadership of the two Latino mayors within the context of postindustrial-era Hartford. As we will explain, although they have some similarities, Eddie Perez and Pedro Segarra developed different approaches to mayoral leadership.

Mayor Eddie Perez: Strong Leadership Approach

Mayors Perez and Segarra shared an interest in politics, Puerto Rican roots, and deracialized rhetoric, but they symbolized very different leadership styles. Perez's campaign mobilized Puerto Rican voters in Hartford in a way that had never been seen before (community interview, September 4, 2013). In addition to an increase in registration, tremendous pride surrounded his candidacy and election. One community leader recalled, "It was all about getting your grandma and extended family out to vote. People would ask whether uncle Julio could vote since he was just released from prison. There was a major campaign to get people to the polls. It was thrilling" (community interview, September 4, 2013). Another leader remembered the excitement at the Puerto Rican Pride Parade shortly after Perez's election. "I was walking beside him and people were exuberant. Seeing all the families and kids out there cheering for one of their own was an inspiration. After all the challenges we [Puerto Ricans] had faced, this was a huge victory" (community interview, August 29, 2013). It was an extraordinarily festive day in Hartford.

Beyond community pride and a surge in electoral participation, Perez claimed that his candidacy provided the opportunity to nurture a group of young Latino leaders who were subsequently offered city jobs, were elected to important city positions, or even became state legislators representing Hartford or suburbs with large Latino communities (Perez interview, August 21, 2013). All Latino community respondents in this study identified an immense sense of community pride surrounding the election of Eddie Perez. Respondents also mentioned that the initial years of his leadership represented a honeymoon. Riding high after his election, Perez mobilized enough voters to usher through charter reform. He also created a Puerto Rican caucus composed of Latinos on the city council and himself. They met regularly to discuss the policy needs of Latinos in Hartford.

However, Perez's leadership style concerned some leaders in the Puerto Rican community. Despite a high level of group consciousness among Puerto Ricans in Hartford, divisions run deep. Farris (2014) argued that Hartford's Puerto Ricans are divided because of divisive Democratic town politics and shrinking Puerto Rican and Latino historic community organizations. Along similar lines, Louise Simmons (2013) also documented the decline of Hartford's community organizations, once the central organizations that had trained Hartford's rising ethnoracial leaders. Consequently, the power center of the community has become fragmented and polarized. All respondents in this study shared perspectives in alignment with this theory.

Eddie Perez emerged as an extremely strong force. His approach to working with the city council was characterized as "dictatorial," "authoritarian," and "strong." He was also viewed in this way in regard to his relationship with the school board. Under the terms of the revised charter, Perez gained the power to appoint five of the nine school-board members. He also took the highly controversial step of appointing himself as chairman of the Hartford Board of Education. According to Perez, improving education for the children of Hartford was always a top priority (Perez interview, August 21, 2013). But the power Perez exercised reportedly increased hostility toward his leadership among some Puerto Rican leaders. His influence over the Democratic Town Committee, as well as his style of pushing his agenda, generated dissent (community interview, August 30, 2013). Although his style was not unlike that of former Hartford bosses, some saw his new powers via the revised charter and his assertive style as problematic. The fact that there was no unified Puerto Rican voice in support of Perez once the scandal emerged was a clear sign that the initial jubilation surrounding his election had subsided. Several respondents indicated that it was Puerto Rican leaders on the opposing side of the Democratic Party who pushed most for a thorough investigation of Eddie Perez's dealings as mayor.

In the context of the mayoral-politics scholarship, Perez's style resembles some of the old-school political machine-style leadership exhibited in cities like Chicago (Grimshaw 1992). His tough, no-nonsense approach to decision making was apparent to most who worked with him. One black leader commented that "Eddie had an attitude where you were either with him or against him" (community interview, February 15, 2014). In addition to his ability to penetrate the Democratic political apparatus, Perez's appeals resonated with a segment of Latinos in the city. Although his appeals were not explicitly racial, he did weave together his programmatic ideas and vision in a way that spoke to groups of Latinos. Some scholars have argued that although minority mayors are often prevented from making major changes in the lives of poor and minority residents because of factors beyond their control, the rhetorical attention to a minority mayor can be an asset for a marginalized community (Chambers and Nelson 2014). Moreover, increases in Latino city council representation, Latino city employment, and Latino small-business emergence in Hartford all accelerated during Perez's mayoralty (community interview, September 4, 2013). Perez suggested that his interest in building a base of Latino leaders spurred some of these opportunities (Perez interview, August 21, 2013).

Pedro Segarra: Working for Political Consensus

Pedro Segarra came to politics as the result of several appointments to public office—corporate council, city council, council president, and later mayor. More important, he entered the mayor's office under unusual circumstances and because of the succession order. This ascent to power provides an important backdrop to Segarra's leadership style. Unlike Perez, he entered the mayor's office trying to resurrect the image of city politicians and to increase stability. Although he generally continued the policies started by Perez, such as education reform and economic revitalization, he initiated a major blight-alleviation policy that was considered his most important accomplishment. In some ways, his decision to alleviate blight was a way to make everyone happy who lives or works in Hartford—thus a consensus move.

During the first months of Segarra's mayoral transition, he isolated himself and later spent time trying to get people to like him (community interview, August 20, 2013). As noted by Farris (2014), Segarra did not engage in significant campaign outreach in the Latino community, in contrast to the appeals made by Perez. A community leader familiar with both Perez and Segarra explained that "Eddie [Perez] had high political ambition. You can see the difference with Pedro [Segarra] who leaves you with a sense that he isn't really sure he wants the job. He doesn't even really publicize his major accomplishments" (community interview, September 2, 2013). In Chapter 1, Orr and Morel observe that fiscal stress has been a major challenge for mayors of postindustrial cities. Segarra's "Opportunities Hartford" program was a central initiative that relied on income generation, education, and employment (Segarra interview, September 19, 2013). Segarra, however, was constrained by municipal fiscal challenges. As mayor, he had to focus on keeping the city government fiscally sound. Local leaders emphasized that some of Segarra's major accomplishments included stabilization of the mill rate and the city's bond rating, as well as replenishing the city's rainy-day fund (Perez interview, September 19, 2013). Mayors do not get a lot of publicity for keeping a city's mundane fiscal house in order. As one Hartford respondent explained, Mayor Segarra "came in during a chaotic time and on the heels of a mayor who spent money irresponsibly. Pedro's been the person who has to do the clean-up work and get things back on track. I think people overlook that fact" (community interview, August 29, 2013).

Mayor Segarra's statements reflected these same sentiments. He also noted that the Perez administration benefited from stimulus funds, which made that administration more fiscally fortunate. He asserted that he had been able to reconcile deficits and bring the city to an era of surplus (Segarra interview, September 19, 2013). Under his watch, he also successfully advocated for more affordable-housing units in the city.

In retrospect, many observers believe that Segarra could never shake the perception that he was a reluctant mayor and appeared to have little passion for leading Hartford. Indeed, when Segarra automatically succeeded Perez in 2010, it was not clear that he would run to remain in the mayor's office in 2011. However, Segarra ran in 2011 and won a four-year term. In 2015, Segarra was defeated by a white challenger in the Democratic primary. Local observers noted that Segarra's 2015 reelection campaign generated little enthusiasm in Hartford's Latino community. However, many local observers also expect the possibility of the resurrection of Eddie Perez, who remains a fixture in the Latino community while he appeals his court conviction. Segarra never had the following that Perez generated. As mayor, Segarra is viewed by many as a visionless leader, more involved with Hartford's business executives than with minority communities. Latinos broadly, and Puerto Ricans more specifically, seemed unenthusiastic about Segarra. In addition, the general perception that one gains from talking with representatives of Hartford's business community is that by the end of his term, Segarra had fallen out of favor even with the city's top corporate leaders, who concluded that he lacked strong leadership skills and did not articulate a clear vision for the city's future. Interestingly, business leaders were stronger supporters of Perez because he was more assertive about his goals, was more likely to communicate, and pushed his agenda. As is evident in the two mayors' State of the City addresses, examined in the following section, Perez focused more on policies that benefited the people but was able to frame them in a way that was attractive to the corporate community. Segarra's rhetoric and his support for the new minor-league stadium, for example, reflect a leader with a greater interest in corporate or middle-class interests.

State of the City Addresses: Policy Priorities of Latino Mayors

State of the City addresses provide a snapshot of a mayor's policy priorities for the coming year. These speeches are often shaped by external variables that affect a city, such as increases in crime, national economic downturns, or changes in federal or state support of cities. The 2002 revision of the city charter specified that an annual State of the City address would be delivered each year in March beginning in 2004. Before that year, there was no formal requirement that the mayor deliver an address, and the city does not have records of earlier addresses by Mayor Perez (Hartford city clerk interview, September 24, 2013).

We categorized each new policy proposal in the State of the City speeches on the basis of Paul Peterson's conceptualization of policies as developmental, redistributive, or allocational (Peterson 1981). According to Peterson, developmental policies "enhance the economic position of the city," while redistributive policies "benefit low-income residents but at the same time negatively affect the local economy" (Peterson 1981, p. 41). Allocational policies are those that deal with public goods, such as municipal repairs, police and fire initiatives, and public health endeavors, and are "more or less neutral in their economic effects" (Peterson 1981, p. 41). Analyzing the proportion of policy proposals in each category in Perez's and Segarra's addresses provides insight into each mayor's policy focus. Figure 6.1 provides a visualization of these coded policies from the mayors' speeches.

Figure 6.1 demonstrates that Perez's addresses centered more on redistributive policies. With the exception of 2009 and 2010, when his addresses favored more developmental policies, his proposals were primarily focused on helping struggling residents in Hartford. His rhetoric did not specifically address Latino interests, but if the policies are evaluated in detail, the proposals suggest that his job-creation programs, education initiatives, and small-business-stimulation programs would help Latinos and blacks, the two largest impoverished groups in the city.

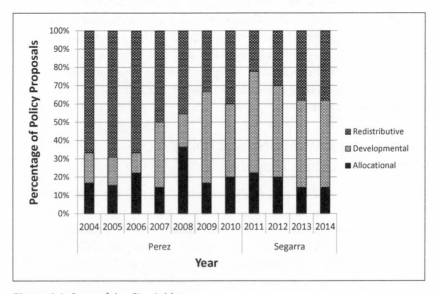

Figure 6.1 State of the City Addresses

With the exception of occasional Spanish-language pronouncements, such as "Sí se puede!" (Yes we can!), Perez's addresses were not racialized in language but demonstrated his interest in the educational, employment, and health opportunities of struggling Hartford residents. One concrete example is his 2005 address, in which he highlighted some of his programs and how they were creating a sense that Hartford was a "Rising Star":

> But, on the other side, there are residents who do not yet feel part of this new hope and opportunity. We must create opportunities for residents to become self-reliant—and move from the have not category to those who feel that if they work hard—they will have jobs, homes, and a bright economic future, for themselves and for their families. Yes, for Hartford's star to rise to its highest potential and shine its brightest light—we must become one Hartford. (Perez 2005)

This quote is interesting because it alludes to the conservative emphasis on self-reliance and individual responsibility. At the same time, it acknowledges that some people have been left behind even though there have been some improvements in the city's infrastructure. The final line suggests that meeting the needs of diverse interests, such as business and those struggling at the bottom, must happen in collaboration.

Perez's other addresses mirror this idea that developmental policies must be rooted in redistributive policies. For example, creating tax breaks for business should be reserved for those who employ Hartford residents (Perez 2006). We can see further evidence of this desire for both developmental and redistributive policies because Perez was able to successfully initiate programs aimed at renovating and building numerous schools in the city. These schools were intended to serve the city's future leaders and provided construction jobs to city residents.

Perez's last two addresses, in 2009 and 2010, were framed in the context of the nation's 2008 financial crisis and his own professional demise. As noted in Figure 6.1, these final addresses include the fewest redistributive proposals and demonstrate a shift away from redistributive policies. The 2009 address focused on the attempts of mayors in Connecticut and across the country to stabilize the city's finances in the face of overwhelming fiscal crisis at all levels of government. The 2010 address occurred as he fought for his political future in the courts. In his last address, Perez focused on what he had accomplished as mayor and appeared to be thinking of those who had helped him throughout his mayoral career.

As Figure 6.1 indicates, Segarra's State of the City addresses were more heavily developmental and placed less emphasis on the struggling residents of Hartford. Segarra's policies were primarily directed at business and arts leaders. This contrast with Perez's rhetoric is noteworthy. One example that touches on Segarra's interest in the arts is the following:

> By working with our partners at the Greater Hartford Arts Council, our jobs Grant Program has created, expanded, and retained more than 340 Hartford-based jobs, including 80 for Hartford youth. I have made a personal effort on behalf of the Mayor's Office to be an ambassador to arts organizations to help them expand their reach and impact. (Segarra 2011)

In this same address, Segarra noted:

> To create . . . job growth opportunities, we need comprehensive tax reform. As your advocate, I will fight for three main principles:
> 1. Protect our residential taxpayers against catastrophic tax increases
> 2. Provide relief and predictability for the business community
> 3. And continue to recognize the acute burden small business has to endure.

Overall, Segerra focused on developmental policy aimed at different groups than those targeted by his predecessor, Eddie Perez.

The emphasis on business interests is a noteworthy difference between Perez and Segarra. This is not meant to imply that Segarra neglected poor neighborhoods or residents of the city. Rather, his policies reflected a business perspective of stimulating business to improve employment opportunities. He also spoke to middle- and upper-class interests by discussing beautifying the city through fighting blight and increasing the visibility of the arts. Although arts initiatives are laudable goals that can benefit all in the city, they tend not to be the first and foremost policy issues for poor and minority residents. Job creation was a staple of Segarra's addresses, but not many of these programs were developmental. Education was regularly noted, but not as forcefully as in the addresses delivered by Perez. Additionally, Segarra did not mention health in any of his addresses. Although health was not an overriding theme for Perez, his 2006 address announced:

> 27,000 Hartford residents do not have healthcare. This is now changing. A few months ago, my Healthy Communities Initiative

was awarded nearly one million dollars in federal funding. As we speak, our seniors, our children, and our families are being connected to a medical home and services they need. This grant is creating a system that links hospitals and neighborhood clinics and provides bilingual assistance so we can better refer, track and monitor patients. (Perez 2006)

Taken as a whole, Perez's emphasis on community needs and redistributive policy contrasts with Segarra's focus on developmental initiatives and other programs that could improve the image of Hartford. In regard to the way in which these two approaches affected Latinos, Perez's initiatives were more explicitly connected to their upward mobility.

Assessing Outcomes

Previous sections of this chapter have largely focused on the differences between Hartford's two Latino mayors. We now turn to the overall impact of Latino mayors on the economic and political situation of Latinos in Hartford over the years when Latinos held the mayor's office. Mayors Perez and Segarra focused their policy proposals on growing inequality, one of the major concerns in the postindustrial era. In central cities like Hartford, low-wage jobs, unemployment, and housing disparities are common. Perez and Segarra attempted to address inequality by focusing on education and promoting small-business development. We look at various economic and political indicators to see the impact of Mayors Perez and Segarra in the postindustrial city.

Latino small businesses expanded under the tenure of Hartford's Latino mayors. Park Street, the city's main Latino business district, witnessed a booming economy. During Perez's term in office, assistance with small-business loans and the beautification of the street itself helped increase business success on Park Street. The majority of merchants are Latino, though not all are Puerto Rican. One respondent noted that "Peruvians and Dominicans are doing well economically on Park Street. Some of them make enough to live in the suburbs. Even if they don't, they're not all that involved in local politics because it's seen as a Puerto Rican thing" (community interview, September 4, 2013).

However, the growth of Latino small businesses does not counteract the disappointing unemployment rate among the city's Latinos. As illustrated in Table 6.3, the percentage of Latino unemployed in Hartford between 2000 and 2010 increased 6.16 percent. Although some of this jump is related to the recession, it also paints a bleak picture for the Latino residents

TABLE 6.3   NUMBER OF UNEMPLOYED HARTFORD HISPANICS, AGES 16–64, 2000
AND 2010

Year	Males	Females	Population	Unemployed (%)
2000*	1,394	1,323	32,234	8.43
2010†	2,484††	2,496§	34,140‖	14.59

* Decennial Census Summary File 3 estimates, Table C23002I.
† American Community Survey five-year estimates, Table C23002I.
†† Margin of error=±364.
§ Margin of error=±374.
‖ Margin of error=±783 (male) and±718 (female).

TABLE 6.4   LATINO POVERTY AND HOUSEHOLD INCOME
LEVELS, 2000–2011

	2000	2006–2011*
Poverty status	39.40%	39.80%
Income more than $30,000	45.50%	47.70%
Median household income	$26,609	$22,664*
Per capita income	$11,526	$11,886*

Sources: Decennial Census Summary File 3 estimates; 2007–20011 American
Community Survey 5-year estimates

* Translated into 2000 dollars.

of Hartford. Table 6.4 reflects a similar pattern in the poor economic situation of Latinos in Hartford. Adjusted for inflation, the poverty rate and income levels remained largely the same across an eleven-year period (2000–2011). During this time, the median household income for Latinos fell by approximately $4,000. As Figure 6.2 shows, Latinos lagged behind white and black Hartford residents from 2000 to 2014. With the exception of some small-business owners, Latinos in Hartford saw little, if any, economic improvement during the decade of the Perez administration.

Mayors Perez and Segarra both dedicated themselves to housing issues, another indicator of the economic and societal health of the Latino community. Under Perez, a number of housing projects were demolished and replaced with single-family homes. One of Perez's major initiatives was increasing home ownership in Hartford. This would have the dual effect of helping families build equity and increasing the city's tax base. With the collapse of the housing market and the disproportionate impact this had on people of color (Allen 2011; Barwick 2009), Hartford's Latinos suffered. Although specific data on Latino home ownership in Hartford are unavailable, Table 6.5 presents figures for housing units in Hartford that are owner occupied by whites or Hispanics. It is evident from these figures that a high proportion of Latinos do not live in residences they own. In contrast, a

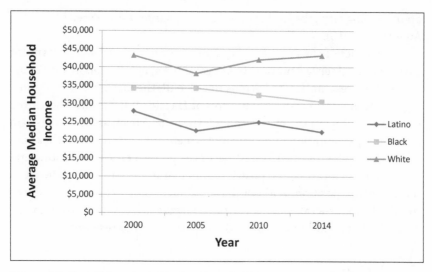

Figure 6.2 Racial Disparity in Median Household Income in Hartford, Connecticut
Source: U.S. Census.

TABLE 6.5   HISPANIC AND WHITE HOME-OWNERSHIP
LEVELS, 2000–2011

	Tenure (% of owner-occupied units)	
	2000	2007–2011
Whites	39.5	44.7
Hispanics	12.7	15.2

Sources: For 2000, Decennial Census; for 2007–2011, U.S. Census Bureau's
American Community Survey 5-year estimates.

large percentage of whites reside in owner-occupied residences. Because
the city has a large percentage of Latino residents, and because they are
relatively low income, it is safe to assume that in general, Latinos lag behind
whites in home ownership.

Overall, the economic situation of Latinos in Hartford did not significantly improve under the leadership of the city's first two Latino mayors.
However, politically, things are a bit more promising. The election of Latinos
to the city council and the school board both increased from 2002 to 2010.
Whereas both bodies had about 20 percent Latino representation in 2000,
the city council is now 33 percent Latino, and the board of education is
44 percent Latino. In addition, the percentage of Latino city employees
has also increased during this period (Hartford city clerk interview, September 24, 2013). Although this might in large part be due to the increasing numbers of Latinos in the city, Mayor Perez mentioned his emphasis

on increasing city jobs for Latinos during his interview (Perez interview, August 21, 2013).

The impact of the Perez and Segarra administrations is important for Latino political representation, but beyond the symbolic importance of descriptive representation of Latinos in city hall, the picture is less promising for the overall Latino population of Hartford. Economic indicators remain troubling in the city. Although there have been some increases in political representation and city employment for Latinos, even these appear to be moderate. Hartford is one of the poorest cities in the state and the nation. As a result, the position of mayor is constricted by the city's socioeconomic position. Without the elevation of the city or more assistance from state and federal policies, Hartford mayors will continue to have their hands tied in regard to the upward mobility of Latino residents.

Conclusion

Like the election of Barack Obama for blacks, the election of the first Latino mayor in 2001 aroused tremendous hope and optimism among Latinos in Hartford. In many respects, this hope has given way to acceptance of politics as usual. Neither Mayor Perez nor Mayor Segarra was able to significantly elevate the socioeconomic position of Hartford's Latinos. Even under a strong-mayor system, the structural limitations on Hartford's mayors made it difficult for Perez and Segarra to translate political empowerment into economic empowerment for the Latino community. Nevertheless, Perez and, to a lesser extent, Segarra expanded public-sector employment opportunities for Latinos in Hartford, although exact figures on Latino city employment are unavailable. Both ran deracialized campaigns, but they embraced very different leadership styles. Perez's machine-politics style contributed to his ultimate criminal conviction. Segarra's leadership approach was more insular, and his policy accomplishments have not been well publicized. Perez and Segarra also differed in the types of policies they promoted in their State of the City addresses. Perez focused more on redistributive policies, while Segarra focused on developmental policies. During their administrations, there was no significant improvement in the socioeconomic position of Latinos in the city. Politically, there has been an increase in the number of elected Latinos in the city, but even with more city council and school-board members, Latinos continue to struggle.

The position of Hartford's Latinos is not unlike the position of blacks in cities when black mayors came to power. In many of these cities, black mayors entered office just as cities faced federal and state retrenchment, and their constituencies were composed primarily of poor and minority residents. Mayors Perez and Segarra had the added challenge of leading a capital city with a very low tax base because of a high proportion of non-taxable property. On the heels of the Perez scandal, Segarra was further burdened with the need to reinstill hope in the region after Hartford appeared as just another corrupt city. With Segarra's loss to Bronin in the 2015 Democratic primary, it remains to be seen whether the city will soon elect another Latino mayor. Several factors will influence the likelihood of future Latino mayors in Hartford. Key among them will be the presence of Latino community organizations. The weakening of Latino organizations in Hartford not only presents challenges for developing Latino leaders and helping elect Latino mayors but also may make it increasingly difficult for the city's mayors, whether or not they are Latino, to address issues of importance to the Latino community.

In the context of what has happened elsewhere and the overall decline in many midsize cities, it comes as no surprise that Latino mayors in Hartford have been more symbolically important than substantively successful. Variables beyond their control, such as economic decline and municipal fiscal stress, make their job virtually impossible in the postindustrial city.

NOTES

1. In 2013, the Connecticut Appellate Court overturned Perez's conviction, vacated his sentence, and ordered two new trials, one on the bribery charges, the other on the extortion charges. The Connecticut Supreme Court upheld the lower-court ruling in July 2016, and the chief state's attorney announced that it was the state's intention to retry these cases.

2. The first tool used to evaluate Latino mayors in Hartford was in-depth interviews with the mayors themselves, eight Latino community leaders, and three black community leaders in the city. The eight Latino leaders interviewed for this project were high-profile leaders of important community organizations in the city, elected city officials, or individuals who were viewed as important voices in their community. The three blacks were longtime leaders from Hartford's black community. We interviewed both black and Latino local leaders in an effort to gain a better understanding of how black and Latino mayoral leadership and priorities differ. Second, we categorized each mayor's State of the City addresses by policy priorities for the upcoming year. Scholars have used this method of analysis to create a typology of mayoral priorities in other scholarship (Chambers and Schreiber-Stainthorp 2013). Furthermore, the State of the City addresses allow us to assess whether the mayor draws on racialized or deracialized rhetoric during his or her major public address of the year (Gillespie 2010, 2012; Perry 1996; Persons 1993).

3. Both the Puerto Rican Socialist Party and the Committee of 24 dissolved in Hartford by the end of the decade because of personal and ideological infighting.

4. These sentiments cannot be confirmed because city officials claim that official figures for municipal employment are unavailable, despite federal requirements to collect

such data. Both black and Latino leaders interviewed consistently expressed the view
that positions for blacks have declined or leveled out over time.

5. Beyond election outcome results, Hartford's Registrar of Voters office did not
provide detailed election data, despite repeated attempts to obtain this information.
In the fall of 2016, the office was under city council investigation for dysfunction and
infighting.

REFERENCES

Allen, Ryan. 2011. "The Relationship between Residential Foreclosures, Race, Ethnicity, and Nativity Status." *Journal of Planning Education Research* 31:125–142. doi:
10.1177/0739456X11398044.
Backstrand, Jeffrey R., and Stephen Schensul. 1982. "Co-evolution in an Outlying Ethnic Community: The Puerto Ricans of Hartford, Connecticut." *Urban Anthropology*
11, no. 1:9–37.
Barreto, Matt A. 2012. *Ethnic Cues: The Role of Shared Ethnicity in Latino Political Participation.* Ann Arbor: University of Michigan Press.
Barwick, Christine. 2009. "Patterns of Discrimination against Blacks and Hispanics in
the US Mortgage Market." *Journal of Housing and the Built Environment* 25:117–124.
Retrieved from https://link.springer.com/article/10.1007/s10901-009-9165-x.
Burgard, Matt. 2004. "City Ranked among Most Dangerous: Mayor, Police Chief Dis-
pute Survey, Say Findings Skewed." *Hartford Courant*, November 23.
Burns, Peter F. 2002. "The Intergovernmental Regime and Public Policy in Hartford,
Connecticut." *Journal of Urban Affairs* 24, no. 1:55–73.
———. 2006. *Electoral Politics Is Not Enough: Racial and Ethnic Minorities and Urban
Politics.* Albany: State University of New York Press.
Carlesso, Jenna, Steven Goode, and Vanessa. de la Torre, V. 2015. "Mayoral Challenger
Luke Bronin Wins Primary over Pedro Segarra." *Hartford Courant*, September 16.
http://www.courant.com/community/hartford/hc-hartford-mayor-primary-luke
-bronin-pedro-segarra-0917-20150916-story.html.
Chambers, Stefanie, and William E. Nelson. 2014. "Black Mayoral Leadership in New
Orleans: Minority Incorporation Revisited." *National Political Science Review* 16, no. 1:
117–137.
Chambers, Stefanie, and Will Schreiber-Stainthrop. 2013. "Michael Coleman: The Midwestern Middleman." In *21st Century Urban Race Politics: Minorities as Universal Interests*, edited by R. K. Perry, 133–162. Bingley, UK: Emerald Group.
City of Hartford. n.d. *Opportunities Hartford.* http://www.achievehartford.org/upload
/files/6%2019%2012%20Update%20Brochure%20Condensed.pdf.
Clavel, Pierre. 1986. *The Progressive City.* New Brunswick, NJ: Rutgers University Press.
Cruz, José E. 1997. "A Decade of Change: Puerto Rican Politics in Hartford, Connecticut, 1969–1979." *Journal of American Ethnic History*, Spring 16, no. 3:45–80.
———. 1998. *Identity and Power: Puerto Rican Politics and the Challenge of Ethnicity.*
Philadelphia: Temple University Press.
De Avila, Joseph. 2012. "Hartford Highlights a State's Divide." *Wall Street Journal*, Sep-
tember 30.
Delaney, Kevin J., and Rick Eckstein. 2007. "Structures and Publicly Financed Stadi-
ums." *Sociological Forum* 22, no. 3:331–353.
Farris, Emily M. 2014. "Latino Leadership in City Hall." Ph.D. diss., Brown University.

Gillespie, Andra., ed. 2010. *Whose Black Politics? Cases in Post-racial Black Leadership*. New York: Routledge.

———. 2012. *The New Black Politician: Cory Booker, Newark, and Post-racial America*. New York: New York University Press.

Goff, Chelsey D. 2014. "Crime in America, 2015." http://lawstreetmedia.com/blogs /crime/crime-america-2015/.

Green, Rick. 2011. "Shawn Wooden's Vision: Ambitious and Well-Connected, He Wants to Be Mayor of Hartford." *Hartford Courant*, February 15. http://articles.courant.com /2011-02-15/news/hc-green-wooden-0215-20110215_1_project-concern-pedro -segarra-open-choice.

Grimshaw, William J. 1992. *Bitter Fruit: Black Politics and the Chicago Machine*. Chicago: University of Chicago Press.

Hartford.gov. 2013. *What Is Opportunity Hartford?* http://www.hartford.gov/government /council/236-opportunities-hartford/263-what-is-opportunity-hartford.

Hassett, Wendy L. 2010. "Hartford: Politics Trumps Professionalism." In *More than Mayor or Manager: Campaigns to Change Form of Government in America's Large Cities*, ed. James H. Svara and Douglas J. Watson. Washington, DC: Georgetown University Press.

Hopkins, Daniel J., and Katherine T. McCabe. 2012. "After It's Too Late: Estimating the Policy Impacts of Black Mayoralties in US Cities." *American Politics Research* 40, no. 4:665–700.

Kovner, Josh. 2010. "Mayor Eddie A. Perez Found Guilty on Five of Six Charges." *Hartford Courant*, June 18. http://www.courant.com/community/hartford/eddie-perez /hc-hartford-mayor-eddie-perez-trial-verdict-story.html.

Mahony, Edmund H., and Jenna Carlesso. 2016. "Supreme Court Rules Ex–Hartford Mayor Eddie Perez Didn't Get Fair Trial; State Pledges Retrial." *Hartford Courant*, July 14. http://www.courant.com/news/connecticut/hc-supreme-court-decision-eddie -perez-0715-20160714-story.html.

McKee, Clyde 2000. "Mike Peters and the Legacy of Leadership in Hartford, Connecticut." In *Governing Middle-Sized Cities: Studies in Mayoral Leadership*, edited by James R. Bowers and Wilbur C. Rich, 27–48. Boulder, CO: Lynne Rienner.

McKee, Clyde, and Nick Bacon. 2013. "A Tragic Dialectic: Politics and the Transformation of Hartford." In *Confronting Urban Legacy: Rediscovering Hartford and New England's Forgotten Cities*, edited by Xiangming Chen and Nick Bacon, 219–235. Lanham, MD: Lexington Books.

Nelson, William E. 2005. "Black Mayoral Leadership in the Twenty-First Century: Challenges and Opportunities." In *Black and Latino/a Politics: Issues in Political Development in the United States*, edited by William E. Nelson Jr. and Jessica Lavariega Monforti, 122–142. Miami: Barnhardt and Ashe.

Pazniokas, Mark. 2013. "The Potential of Latino Political Power in Connecticut." *CT Mirror*, January 8.

Perez, Eddie. 2005. *State of the City Address*. March 14. http://www.hartfordinfo.org /issues/wsd/government/state_of_city_05.htm.

———. 2006. *State of the City Address*. March 13. http://www.hartfordinfo.org/issues /wsd/government/stateofcity06.pdf.

Perry, Huey, ed. 1996. *Race, Politics, and Governance in the United States*. Gainesville: University Press of Florida.

Persons, Georgia A., ed. 1993. *Dilemmas of Black Politics*. New York: HarperCollins.

Peterson, Paul E. 1981. *City Limits*. Chicago: University of Chicago Press.

Rich, Wilbur C. 1989. *Coleman Young and Detroit Politics*. Detroit: Wayne State University Press.

Rossiter, Clinton. 1952. "Thomas Hooker." *New England Quarterly* 25, no. 4:459–488.

Segarra, Pedro. 2011. *State of the City Address*. March 14. http://www.hartfordinfo.org/issues/wsd/Government/State_of_the_city_2011.pdf.

Simmons, Louise. 2013. "Poverty, Inequality, Politics, and Social Activism in Hartford." In *Confronting Urban Legacy: Rediscovering Hartford and New England's Forgotten Cities*, edited by Xiangming Chen and Nick Bacon, 85–109. Lanham, MD: Lexington Books.

Spilerman, Seymour. 1970. "The Causes of Racial Disturbances: A Comparison of Alternative Explanations." *American Sociological Review* 35 (August): 627–649.

Weaver, Glenn. 1982. *Hartford: An Illustrated History of Connecticut's Capital*. Woodland Hills, CA: Windsor Publications.

Weiss, Eric M. 2001. "A Political Perez Learns about Being a Politician." *Hartford Courant*, September 9. http://articles.courant.com/2001-09-09/news/0109090016_1_campaign-brochure-new-leadership-eddie-perez.

7

Carlos Giménez's Conservative Reforms in Miami-Dade County

DARIO MORENO AND MARIA ILCHEVA

EDITORS' NOTE

In this chapter, Dario Moreno and Maria Ilcheva provide a discussion of mayoral politics in Miami-Dade County, the largest U.S. county with a majority-Hispanic population. Miami has a unique two-tier structure of local government that assigns many of the functions usually reserved for municipal government to county government. Municipalities provide police and fire protection, zoning and code enforcement, and other typical city services, paid for by city taxes. The county's responsibilities are more regional, such as emergency management, airport and seaport operations, public housing, health care, transportation, and environmental services, which are funded by county taxes on all incorporated and unincorporated areas. The majority of residents in Miami-Dade County live in unincorporated areas, and the county provides their municipal services as well. Miami-Dade County is ruled by a county charter that establishes a federated form of government led by an elected executive, the mayor.

Moreno and Ilcheva show how Latino politics is different in Miami-Dade County. Cuban Americans, who are considerably more conservative and more Republican than other Latinos, play a prominent role. Since 1996, both the city of Miami and Miami-Dade County have elected Cuban American mayors. Moreno and Ilcheva pay close attention to the election and leadership of Mayor Carlos Giménez, who was elected in 2011. Miami-Dade County's previous two mayors, Alex Penelas and Carlos Alvarez, were part of growth-machine coalitions, supported by the county's major economic interests. Giménez was elected after voters overwhelmingly voted to recall Mayor Carlos Alvarez, signaling that they had grown

*tired of Miami-Dade's traditional growth-machine policies. By describing and
analyzing the effectiveness of the middle-class coalition that swept Giménez into
office, this chapter illustrates the diversity of Latino communities in the
United States. The presence of a large middle-class Latino enclave in Miami-Dade
County was essential for Giménez's election. The chapter describes Giménez's effort to construct and sustain a coalition centered on the county's home-
ownership population and small businesses.*

L atino politics in Miami-Dade County is unlike Latino politics in any
       other place. According to 2015 American Community Survey esti-
       mates, 66.8 percent of its 2.7 million residents were of Hispanic de-
scent; Miami-Dade County is thus the largest county in the United States
with a Hispanic-majority population. More than half the Hispanic population is of Cuban origin. The prominent role played by Cuban Americans,
who are considerably more conservative and more Republican than other
Latinos, gives local Miami politics some unique characteristics.

Miami's exceptionalism manifested itself in the 2011 mayoral race, in
which Carlos Giménez was elected county mayor by riding the wave of a
taxpayer revolt. Giménez created a coalition of middle-class Latinos and
whites to win on a "good-government" platform that promised to fight corruption and called for significant tax cuts and major cuts to the county
bureaucracy. Giménez's path to the mayoralty differed significantly from
those of other Latino mayors. Most Latino mayors are elected as part either
of a liberal progressive coalition or of a growth-machine coalition. In contrast to Giménez, Miami-Dade County's previous two Hispanic mayors,
Alex Penelas and Carlos Alvarez, were part of growth-machine coalitions
that promoted private-public partnerships, job growth, and big government
projects. They were backed by the county's major economic interests: developers, construction companies, banks, unions, and the major law firms.

Miami was never a major manufacturing center, in contrast to former
heavy manufacturing hubs around the Great Lakes like Pittsburgh, Detroit,
Cleveland, and Milwaukee. In the 1950s and 1960s, the Miami neighborhoods of Wynwood and Allapattah and the city of Hialeah were filled with
manufacturing warehouses that produced garments for major national
retailers. According to an article in the *New York Times* from May 25, 1969,
Greater Miami was the nation's third-largest garment-manufacturing center
("Miami Turns Out" 1969). As a result of globalization and production
outsourcing, the textile and apparel industries declined in the 1990s. Except for the garment-manufacturing sector, the city's economy has been
primarily service based since its founding in 1896, and tourism has been at
the epicenter of Miami's economic activities. Up to the 1960s, Miami's

level of economic activity was highest during the in-season months between November and April. It was common for restaurants, hotels, clubs, and businesses to close for the off-season months from May to October up to the 1970s. Miami was also a major base for service-industry airlines. The best middle-class jobs were those for Miami-based Eastern Airlines or Pan American, which had a major hub in the city. But by the 1990s, both airlines fell victim to deregulation and filed for bankruptcy.

The arrival of large numbers of Cubans and South Americans in the 1960s expanded Miami's service-based economy. Real estate development and international banking joined tourism as major employers. Meanwhile, Miami's tourist industry expanded in the 1990s to accommodate wealthy Latin Americans who came to Miami to shop and escape the Southern Hemisphere winter. Suddenly, Miami's tourist season was year-round, and the city was labeled the "gateway" to Latin America. The iconic "Closed for the Season" sign became an artifact of the past. Miami's service-based economy is largely made up of a network of local small and middle-sized businesses, most of them Hispanic owned. The existence of this network of Hispanic-owned businesses helped create the conservative middle class that was important in the election of Carlos Giménez.

The Era of Latino Mayors in Miami-Dade County

The city of Miami and Miami-Dade County operate under a two-tier system of governance in which the city provides municipal services such as police and fire, community development, and public works to city residents while the county takes on this role in areas that are not incorporated into any of the area's thirty-four municipalities. In ten of these municipalities, Latinos constituted more than two-thirds of the population in 2014. The city of Miami, the largest municipality in Miami-Dade County with over 400,000 residents, was 71 percent Hispanic. The largest concentration of Hispanics (96 percent), primarily Cuban, was in the city of Hialeah with approximately 230,000 residents (U.S. Census Bureau, 2010–2014 American Community Survey five-year estimates).

The growth of Hispanic residents and voters began in the 1960s, accelerated in the 1980s, and eventually led to their electoral success. In 1960, Dade County's population was 80 percent non-Latino whites, less than 5 percent Hispanics, and about 15 percent blacks. By 1990, Hispanics constituted almost half of the county's population, followed by non-Latino whites, who were about one-third, and blacks, who were slightly over one-fifth (Boswell 1993). The clout of Latinos in city and county government first became evident in the 1970s when Hispanics gained important positions in county and city governments. The first Latino mayor of the city of Miami was Puerto Rican–born Maurice A. Ferré, who served from 1973 to 1985. He was succeeded by the first Cuban-born mayor of Miami and current Miami-Dade County commissioner, Xavier Louis Suárez. For the past two decades, since 1996, the city of Miami has been led by Cuban American mayors. In 2001, when Cuban-born Manny Diaz won the mayor's race for city of Miami, his opponent's campaign manager, Manny Alfonso, put it bluntly: "If you're not Cuban in Miami, you don't have a chance" (Ross, Weaver, and Corral 2001).

Miami-Dade County has followed a similar pattern, with voters electing Latino mayors since 1996. In 1980, the county had 1.6 million inhabitants, of whom 36 percent were of Hispanic origin. The demographic dominance of Hispanics in the county was reflected in political statements such as one issued by then City of Miami commissioner and candidate for county mayor, Miriam Alonso, who urged Hispanic voters in 1993 to keep the mayor's post as "a Hispanic seat." A sign of the changing times was the 1993 abolition of the English-only law prohibiting the county's government from conducting business in any language, written or spoken, other than English. The only exceptions were emergencies and election ballots. The changing demographics led to the election of three consecutive Cuban-born county mayors.

The Urban-Development Perspectives

The administrations and policies of Miami-Dade County's first two Hispanic mayors, Alex Penelas and Carlos Alvarez, can be studied through the theories that emerged in the 1980s to describe the challenges facing modern American cities and to explain the motivations of actors advocating urban development. The urban regime formed by Penelas and Alvarez between 1996 and 2011 as a coalition between local government and private business interests is very close to the concept of the city as a "growth machine" (Molotch 1988). Alex Penelas, the first executive mayor of Miami-Dade County, cobbled together a governing coalition of Cuban developers, the non-Hispanic white downtown business elite, and Cuban Americans and Jewish voters. Carlos Alvarez, who succeeded Penelas, was elected with the same coalition except that non-Latin white Republican voters replaced Jewish voters. He and his county manager, George Burgess, vigorously pursued a pro-development, pro-growth policy culminating in the so-called megadeal with the City of Miami that established public finance schemes for a port tunnel and a baseball stadium, and operating funds for the newly built Performing Arts Center. These controversial projects had support from the business community but very little public support, and their unpopularity grew with the onset of the recession and the collapse of the southern Florida real estate market. Alvarez's decisions fit within the argument that "cities, regions, and states do not compete to please people; they compete to please capital—and the two activities are fundamentally different" (Molotch and Logan 1987, p. 42).

The collapse of the housing market, the recession, and questionable public investments, such as Marlins Park, called into question the wisdom of Alvarez's growth strategy. The strain of financing county services amid an economic crisis, coupled with unwise expenditure of public money, silenced most growth-machine supporters.

The revolt against politics as usual and putting the tax burden on home owners can be interpreted as an indicator of the diminishing role of the growth machine in local politics. However, voter dissatisfaction expressed through the recall of the mayor emerged in response to specific unpopular decisions and did not have the characteristics of a slow-growth movement similar to that in San Francisco, for example. The slow-growth initiative adopted in San Francisco in 1986 provided for a yearly ceiling on commercial office construction (Deleon 1992). In an interesting contrast to decision making in Miami-Dade County, in 1990 San Francisco voters rejected a ballot initiative that would have committed the city to help finance a new baseball stadium for the San Francisco Giants.

The presence of a large Hispanic community with a politically conservative middle class and a large percentage of home ownership among working-class Hispanics meant that Miami did not have the conditions to develop a middle-class progressive regime such as that in San Francisco, which pursued aims such as environmental protection, historic preservation, affordable housing through inclusionary zoning, and linkage fees on development. Miami also lacked the conditions for a progressive liberal regime that emphasized human capital and expanded access to employment and ownership because working-class Cubans and blacks were part of different political alliances (Hill, Moreno, and Cue 2001). A majority of African Americans voted against Penelas in 1996, Alvarez in 2004, and Giménez in 2011. Instead, the collapse of the growth regime gave way to a coalition between middle-class Hispanic home owners and non-Latino whites that focused on low taxes, good government, and traditional government services. The 2011 recall of Alvarez and the ensuing mayoral elections in 2011 and 2012 marked the end of Miami's growth-machine politics and the establishment of a maintenance regime committed to good government and low taxes.

Although Miami-Dade County voters had reelected a pro-growth mayor in 2008, in 2009 the City of Miami electorate placed a more conservative mayor, Tomás Regalado, at the helm. He replaced the term-limited, pro-growth Manny Diaz, who led the city between 2001 and 2009. Mayor Diaz presided over the rapid urban redevelopment of Miami and its transformation into a world-class city. After four years of development, in October 2009, only a month before the election would bring in a new mayor, the City of Miami Commission approved the Miami 21 zoning plan, which sought to encourage more mixed use and bring stricter height restrictions to residential areas. Mayor Diaz proclaimed that he was "proud that Miami is the first large U.S. city to adopt a citywide comprehensive zoning code based on the principles of Smart Growth and New Urbanism" (Cove 2009). By 2004, with Carlos Giménez as his city manager, Mayor Diaz changed Miami's bond ratings, rated at junk status as recently as 2002, to A+ thanks to a record $115 million in reserves and the launch of the city's first-ever capital improvement plan. Diaz claimed that by 2004 the city's tax base increased by 50 percent to nearly $21 billion, and many applauded him for his corporate management style, the sound reorganization of the city administration, and his consensus-building approach in his dealings with the city commission (Villano 2004).

In 2005, at the onset of Diaz's second term, Miami had seventy thousand new condo units planned or under construction. The poster child of the development boom was Shops at Midtown Miami, the largest urban infill project at the time, built on the old fifty-six-acre site of the Florida East Coast rail yard. Simply referred to "Midtown" by Miami residents, the area of warehouses, empty lots, and abandoned rail yards turned into a 645,000-square-foot retail development and mixed-use buildings just a few miles north of downtown Miami.

Diaz's progrowth approach was not without opponents. Some residents objected to the rampant development all over the city, supported by rezoning that allowed high-rises to be built in quiet middle-class neighborhoods. Some commentators suggested that the challenge for Mayor Diaz was to "really take a creative stance on things like affordable housing, zoning and the preservation of Miami's traditional neighborhoods" (Dario Moreno, quoted in Davis 2005).

In line with the mayor's goal to make Miami a world-class city for tourism, entertainment, and sports was his support for the use of public funding in the development of a baseball stadium for the Miami Marlins. He considered the construction of Marlins Park one of the great achievements of his mayoralty. In his 2012 book, he wrote, "There is no doubt that our unprecedented investments served to strengthen our neighborhoods, create jobs, increase property values, and lower taxes. It also became evident that for Miami to continue growing, investments in other large-scale projects in the urban core would be necessary" (Diaz 2012, pp. 155–156). The stadium deal saw the county pay more than $300 million, the City of Miami chip in $119 million, and the Marlins contribute more than $100 million to pay for the new facility. The stadium was estimated to cost Miami-Dade County taxpayers $2.4 billion spread over forty years to repay the debt to finance the stadium's construction.

At a February 2008 City of Miami Commission vote, Tomás Regalado was the only Miami commissioner to oppose the plan to finance the construction of the new stadium. Although he was in favor of the construction of the stadium, he opposed the use of Community Redevelopment Agency (CRA) funding to finance the stadium deal. CRAs are created for the purpose of eliminating blight and slum, as well as providing affordable housing. Commissioner Regalado contended that residents should get a chance to vote on how the CRA money should be spent (Musibay and Howell 2008).

Regalado's opposition to the "Global Agreement," as the interlocal agreement among the county, the city, and the Overtown Park West and Omni CRAs was called, propelled him to the mayoralty with relative ease. As a candidate for mayor, Regalado was seen as the anti-Diaz, while his opponent, Joe Sanchez, embodied the continuation of Diaz's growth policies and was seen as the Florida Marlins' candidate. Regalado beat fellow city commissioner Sanchez 72 percent to 28 percent. His conservative policies, obtaining concessions from unions and curbing spending to cover a deficit of over $100 million in the city budget, endeared him to voters. In 2013, Regalado won reelection easily, garnering 78 percent of the vote and facing no significant opposition. Norman Braman, who led the recall campaign against the county mayor in 2011, introduced Regalado at his December 2013 inauguration ceremony.

Demographic Composition of Miami-Dade County and the Election of Carlos Giménez

As of 2015, Miami-Dade County had a population of almost 2.7 million residents; it was the most populous county in Florida and the seventh most populous in the United States. The city of Miami proper is only the forty-fourth most populous city in the United States, with a population of about 440,000 (2015 census estimates), but its population understates its true size and importance as the administrative and financial capital of Miami-Dade County.

TABLE 7.1   MIAMI-DADE COUNTY LATINO POPULATION, 1980–2010

Year	Miami-Dade County population	Miami-Dade County Latino population	Cuban	Mexican	Nicaraguan	Puerto Rican	Colombian
2010	2,563,885	1,623,859	856,007	51,736	105,495	92,358	114,701
2000	2,253,362	1,291,737	650,601	38,095	69,257	80,327	70,066
1990	1,967,000	967,764	561,868	23,193	74,244	68,634	53,582
1980	1,626,000	581,000	407,253	13,238	7,000	44,656	19,000

Source: U.S. Census.

The 1990 census showed that about 51 percent of the population of Miami-Dade County was Hispanic, and more than half of Latinos were of Cuban origin. Although the growth of the Cuban population in Miami-Dade County has been slower than that of other Latino populations, Cubans still represent the largest Hispanic group. The 2010 U.S. Census reported that Hispanics were 65 percent of the population in the county, and more than half of them, almost 860,000, were Cuban (Table 7.1). In 2010, Latinos constituted 52 percent of the over 1.2 million registered voters.

The demographic composition of the county and the growth of the Cuban population in the past fifty years have translated into electoral success for Cuban candidates. The rapid political empowerment of the Cuban community over the past fifty years is truly impressive. The county is currently represented by one Cuban American U.S. senator and three U.S. congresspersons in Washington, D.C. The Miami-Dade County state legislative delegation is made up of nine Cuban American state house members and three Cuban American state senators. The mayors of both the city of Miami and Miami-Dade County are Cuban American, as are the majority of the county commission and the school board. The political clout of Cubans has given the city yet another nickname: the capital of "El Exilio."

Hispanic voters were crucial for the success of the recall that led to the 2011 election of Carlos Giménez as mayor of Miami-Dade County, concluding one of the most eventful years in Miami politics. Three months earlier, Miami-Dade County voters had overwhelmingly voted to recall Mayor Carlos Alvarez (88 percent to 12 percent). The recall of Alvarez was the largest municipal recall in U.S. history. Voters were furious over an increase in property-tax rates, public financing of the Marlins Baseball Park, and salary increases at county hall. The recall signaled that voters had grown tired of Miami-Dade County's traditional growth-machine policies, which not only put increased tax burdens on the county's home owners but were also viewed as corrupt. The relatively high rate of Latino home ownership in

Miami-Dade County, 58 percent according to 2010 census statistics, was one of the conditions that sparked the taxpayer revolt when Alvarez raised property taxes by 12 percent in 2010. By comparison, census figures show that nationwide Latino home ownership was 49 percent. Moreover, 62 percent of owner-occupied units in Miami-Dade County were owned by Latino households. The collapse of the housing market brought an end to the belief that growth was the economic engine of Miami-Dade County.

Giménez rode this wave of antigovernment and antitax sentiment to the mayoralty by creating a "good-government" coalition made up of middle-class white and Hispanic voters. The presence of a large middle-class Latino enclave in Miami-Dade County was essential for the success of his campaign and illustrates the diversity of Latino communities in the United States. Giménez, who had been elected to the Board of County Commissioners in 2004, led the opposition to the ballpark and the tax increase from the dais. He was one of three county commissioners to oppose the public financing of Marlins Park. His opposition to Mayor Alvarez and County Manager George Burgess's big-government approach to local government made him a natural candidate to succeed the unpopular Alvarez once he was removed by recall.

Giménez's experience in the city of Miami instilled in him an appreciation for fiscal conservatism. He was a former firefighter and a union member who rose through the ranks of the City of Miami Fire Department to become its first Latino chief in 1991. In the wake of the Elián González crisis in May 2000, Mayor Joe Carollo appointed Giménez as City of Miami manager. Giménez took over a city in a fiscal crisis. Miami's municipal bonds were rated as "junk," and the governor had appointed an oversight board to control the city's finances. Giménez's tenure as city manager was a triumph. He restored the city's bond rating to "investment grade," and through a combination of budget cuts and new fees, he was able to accumulate over $140 million in reserves. The governor dissolved the oversight board as the city quickly returned to fiscal stability. Giménez then cut the City of Miami property-tax rate to its lowest level in fifty years. Giménez continued serving as the city manager under Carollo's successor, Manny Diaz, for another two years before stepping down to run successfully for election to the county commission.

History and Reform of Miami-Dade County's Government

Miami-Dade County's unique form of government was established in the 1957 charter, which created both metropolitan government and home rule.

This metropolitan form of local government operates under a unique two-tier system. Unlike a consolidated city-county, where the city and county governments merge into a single entity, in Miami-Dade County these two entities remain separate. Instead, there are two tiers, or levels, of government: city and county. There are thirty-four municipalities in the county, the city of Miami being the largest. Cities are the lower tier of local government and provide services such as police, zoning and code enforcement, and other typical city services within their jurisdiction. These services are paid for by city taxes. The county is the upper tier and provides regional metropolitan services, such as emergency management, airport and seaport operations, public housing and health-care services, transportation, environmental services, regional parks, and solid-waste disposal. These are funded by county taxes, which are assessed on all incorporated and unincorporated areas. The county was renamed "Metropolitan Dade County" in 1957 (and also referred to as "Metro-Dade") to highlight this unique form of local government.

Of the county's almost 2.7 million total residents, approximately 52 percent live in unincorporated areas, the majority of which are heavily urbanized. For these residents, the county fills the role of both lower- and upper-tier government, and the county commission acts as their lower-tier municipal representative body. Residents within this area pay an unincorporated tax, equivalent to a city tax, which is used to provide county residents with equivalent city services, such as police, fire, zoning, and water and sewer service.

The 1957 charter and an enabling statewide constitutional amendment also established home rule in Miami-Dade County. This gave the county government special powers enjoyed only by Miami-Dade County among Florida's sixty-seven counties. The Miami-Dade Commission can incorporate, annex, or abolish municipalities, place a local referendum on the ballot, and create its own constitutional officers without the approval of the state legislature in Tallahassee. The charter also established a council-manager form of government in which a professional manager runs the county on a day-to-day basis according to policy guidelines set by an elected commission. Home rule and the 1957 charter gave almost all power to the county commission to serve as the county governing body. The commission approves the budget, sets the county tax rate, and directs the administration on policy. It also must approve all contracts negotiated by the administration.

The position of Miami-Dade County mayor originally had very limited powers. The mayor was chairman of the commission and represented the county in official ceremonies. The mayor and the other eight members of the commission were all elected at-large in countywide elections. Initially,

Miami's experiment with the metropolitan style of government was viewed by scholars and the media as very successful. Edward Soften (1963) argued that Miami could be a model for other large metropolitan areas across the country.

By the late 1980s, the metro experiment began to show strain as the county's demographics changed dramatically. The county had fewer than 50,000 Hispanic residents when the 1957 charter was adopted, but by the time of the 1990 census that number had increased almost twenty times to 935,407. Similarly, the black population nearly tripled from 137,999 in 1960 to 397,933 in 1990, while at the same time the non-Hispanic white population decreased from 747,748 to 614,066 (Miami-Dade County Department of Planning and Zoning, 2009). This dramatic shift in the county's demographics created a representation crisis in the county commission. The at-large method for electing county commissioners favored non-Latino white candidates, as was reflected in the makeup of the commission after the 1992 election, which produced only one Hispanic commissioner, one African American commissioner, and seven non-Latino white commissioners.

This disparity in representation was caused by ethnic-bloc voting. African American and Hispanic voters supported their coethnics overwhelmingly, and non-Latino white voters overwhelmingly rejected Hispanic or African American candidates. Moreover, Hispanics would vote for non-Latino white candidates over black candidates, while black voters would favor non-Latino white candidates over Latino candidates (Corbett, Stack, and Warren 1990). A group of Hispanic and black plaintiffs in 1986 sued Metropolitan-Dade County under section two of the Voting Right Acts to remedy the disparity caused by the at-large countywide elections and ethnic-bloc voting. The U.S. Court of Appeals ruled in 1993 that the "at-large voting system used by Metro-Dade County, Florida, to elect the members of its County Commission dilutes Black and Hispanic voting power in violation of section 2 of the Voting Rights Act of 1965" (*Meek v. Metropolitan Dade County*, U.S. Court of Appeals, Eleventh District, February 26, 1993). Consequently, the court ordered Metro-Dade to expand the commission from nine to thirteen members, all elected in single-member districts, and to eliminate the ceremonial mayor position.

After the *Meek* decision, the composition of the county commission changed radically to reflect the diversity of the county. Today it is composed of seven Hispanics (six Cubans and one Colombian), four African Americans (one Haitian), and two non-Latino whites. The elimination of the mayor's position and the establishment of single-member districts created a need for a strong countywide executive. Alex Penelas, the only Hispanic commissioner elected at-large, was the principal proponent of creating a strong county mayor for Miami-Dade County. He argued that just as the district commissioners were advocates for the county's diverse neighborhoods, a mayor elected in a countywide election would be the advocate for the whole county. The mayor would be a unifying figure with a mandate to serve all residents.

Voters reinstated the position of mayor in 1993 when they approved Penelas's proposal for the executive mayor's position. The executive mayor of Miami-Dade County would be elected countywide to serve a four-year term beginning in 1996. The mayor would not be a member of the county commission and would have the authority to appoint a county manager, with the approval and consent of the Board of County Commissioners, and to oversee the operations of the county departments. Indicative of the shift toward greater power of the mayor vis-à-vis the commission was the mayor's veto power over decisions made by the commission. But the county manager would still serve as chief executive officer of the county, with the power to fire and hire all department heads. The position of executive mayor was approved by voters in a countywide referendum, but it is important to note that Hispanic voters supported the referendum overwhelmingly, African Americans voters rejected it overwhelmingly, and non-Latino white voters were only slightly opposed (Hill, Moreno, and Cue 2001).

The Strong Mayor in Practice

Hispanic support for the strong-mayor position was based on the belief that their electoral strength would guarantee Hispanic control over the position. All three executive mayors in the history of Miami-Dade County have been Cuban Americans. Alex Penelas was the first executive mayor, elected in 1996. Penelas, a Cuban Democrat, enjoyed the backing of Miami's powerful development community, almost all the public services unions, and most of the business community. He ran on a progrowth platform and easily raised more campaign money than any of his four opponents. In the first round, he easily bested two other Hispanic candidates—former Miami mayors Maurice Ferré and Javier Suarez (Hill, Moreno, and Cue 2001). In the runoff, his opponent was an African American Republican, Arthur Teele. The election results demonstrated the power of ethnic politics over partisanship as Penelas won the heavily Republican Cuban vote with 90 percent while Teele won the heavily Democratic African American vote with 92 percent. Non-Latino whites voted 52 to 48 percent for Teele. Jews favored Penelas, while other non-Latino whites tended to support Teele (Hill, Moreno, and Cue 2001).

Penelas's first term was a triumph. He was able to hold the line on taxes, build a new basketball arena for the Miami Heat, and support major redevelopment efforts in downtown Miami, Midtown, and Brickell. He continued to promote change and in 1997 persuaded voters to change the name of the county from Dade to Miami-Dade to take advantage of Miami's international name recognition. Penelas's influence grew and extended beyond Miami as he became a major fund-raiser for the Clintons and other Democratic candidates. In 1999, *People* magazine named him "America's sexiest politician." He was even being mentioned as a possible Democratic vice presidential candidate.

Penelas suffered a major political reversal of fortune with the Elián González affair. The affair centered on the custody and immigration status of a young Cuban boy, Elián González, whose mother drowned while attempting to leave Cuba with her son. The U.S. Immigration and Naturalization Service initially placed González with paternal relatives in Miami, who wanted to keep him in the United States despite his father's request that González be returned to Cuba. A federal district court's ruling that only González's father, and not his extended relatives, could petition for asylum on the boy's behalf was upheld by the Eleventh Circuit Court of Appeals. After the U.S. Supreme Court declined to hear the case, federal agents seized González from his relatives and returned him to Cuba in June 2000. Penelas angered non-Cuban voters when he declared that he would do nothing to assist the Clinton administration and federal authorities in their bid to return the six-year-old boy to Cuba. Later, presumably in retaliation for the Clinton administration's handling of the Elián González matter, Penelas refused to campaign alongside Al Gore during Gore's 2000 presidential bid and made no comments during the controversy over Miami-Dade County's ballots in the aftermath of the election. Critics allege that Penelas's failure to intervene in the ballot controversy, including failing to provide adequate security at the Miami-Dade County Building during the recount, was a contributing factor to George W. Bush's ultimate victory in the 2000 presidential election.

The Elián González case brought to prominence Manny Diaz, who served as the lawyer representing the Florida-based relatives of Elián González in their unsuccessful custody battle with the U.S. government to keep the Cuban boy in the United States. A year after the unsuccessful attempt, Diaz defeated the former six-term mayor Maurice Ferré to lead the city of Miami for two terms.

The Elián González case was Penelas's downfall as his popularity tumbled, especially with Democrats. His campaign for U.S. Senate in 2004 was

made more difficult when Al Gore labeled him "the single most treacher-
ous and dishonest person I dealt with" in the 2000 election ("Al Politics Is
Loco" 2004). Gore's remarks hurt Penelas with Democratic voters, and he
lost the primary, winning a mere 10 percent of the vote. Penelas's loss of
popular support emboldened his county manager to take a more assertive
role in county government. This tested the stability of Miami-Dade's
awkward two-executive—county manager and mayor—form of government. Termed out as mayor, Penelas retired from electoral politics. He was
succeeded by Carlos Alvarez in 2004.

Alvarez who was public safety director for Miami-Dade County, analo-
gous to police chief, was an underdog going into the 2004 mayoral election. Handicapped by low name recognition, Alvarez, a Republican, was
trailing the three other major candidates, who included Commissioner
Miguel Díaz de la Portilla, Commissioner Jimmy Morales, and businessman José Cancela. However, Alvarez's anticorruption and reform message
gained traction with Hispanic voters in the county's western suburban
areas. He argued that the position of mayor needed to be strengthened for
the county to improve government services and eliminate corruption. Voters were especially upset with the county's procurement process, which
gave the Board of County Commissioners the power to approve all county
contracts. This had led to unseemly deal cutting by commissioners anxious
to reward their friends and favorite lobbyists. Alvarez argued that strengthening the position would enable the mayor to control the procurement
process, and the mayor could be held directly accountable by all Miami-
Dade County voters.

Alvarez's banner of reform was effective in bringing him victory in the
2004 election. His first term was characterized by his fight with the commission over the power of the mayor. Frustrated by the commission's lack
of support for reform, Alvarez went directly to the voters. On January 23,
2007, he obtained voter approval in a referendum for the strong-mayor
position. The proposal made the county mayor the chief executive officer
for the county and took away most of the executive power from the manager. The mayor was given the authority to hire and fire the county manager and most department heads. Finally, in 2010, voters eliminated the
county manager position altogether and gave all executive power to the
county mayor beginning in 2012.

The overwhelming support of Hispanic voters in the efforts to increase
the power of the mayor was bolstered by the fact that they had the sheer
numbers to control the mayoralty. Hispanics composed 55 percent of registered voters in Miami-Dade County, while blacks made up only 18 percent,
and non-Latino whites were 20 percent. Cuban Americans had been in

control of the position since the creation of the executive mayor in 1996. Local elections in Miami-Dade County are also dominated by Hispanic Republicans. This is surprising given that there are 557,512 Democrats and 364,509 Republicans registered in the county. Miami-Dade County has given overwhelming support for the Democratic candidate in recent presidential elections. Barack Obama carried Miami-Dade County by nearly 140,000 votes in 2008 and by over 208,000 votes in 2012. However, low turnout among non-Cuban Hispanics and African Americans in nonpresidential election years tilts local elections toward Cuban Republicans. In low-turnout local elections, Hispanics make up 60 percent of the electorate, compared with 14 percent for African Americans and 20 percent for non-Latino whites. Republicans usually outnumber Democrats 42 percent to 40 percent despite the Democrats' nearly 200,000 registration advantage over the GOP.

In contrast to the county, the city of Miami has a weak-mayor form of government that gives the city commission power to hire and especially fire major bureaucrats, including the city manager. In 2012, the city commission discussed putting a strong-mayor proposition on the November ballot, but the measure ultimately failed to get sufficient support among the commissioners.

According to section 2-37 of the city charter, the mayor can remove the city manager, but the commission has the power to override the removal by a four-fifths vote of the commissioners. Conversely, the commission can also vote to remove the manager and needs a four-fifths vote, but the mayor has the right to reappoint the same individual. In April 2016, two Miami commissioners moved to fire the city manager, Daniel Alfonso, but did not obtain the necessary four out of five votes to succeed. Mayor Regalado had threatened to appoint Alfonso again, even if all commissioners voted to remove him (Smiley 2016).

The presence of a strong mayor who has the authority to run the day-to-day affairs of the government allows voters to clearly understand the chain of command and hold the mayor directly accountable for the decisions of his or her administration. This issue of accountability was tested in 2011 with the effort to recall Miami-Dade County's mayor.

The Recall of Miami-Dade's First Strong Mayor

Despite his new powers as a strong mayor, Carlos Alvarez began his second term in a very weak position. Although he won reelection in a landslide with 66 percent of the votes, his opponent, Helen Williams, was a political unknown who raised a measly $1,000 but still obtained a third of the vote. Support for Williams was seen as a protest vote against the mayor. Alvarez's 2008 reelection took place amid the collapse of the Miami real estate market, high unemployment, and reduced county-government revenues, which had left voters in a sour mood. Despite his poor showing and the economic crisis, Alvarez led a successful effort to spend hundreds of millions of dollars of county money to build a new baseball park for the local team, the Florida Marlins. Opposition to the stadium plan, however, gained momentum very quickly. In 2008, millionaire Norman Braman filed a lawsuit to force the county and the team to put the ballpark deal before voters for approval.

Braman is a resident of Miami-Dade County, a top Republican fundraiser, and the owner of twenty-three auto dealerships in Miami and Colorado. He has been a vocal critic of Miami-Dade County and what he views as its big-government, high-tax policies throughout the years. Braman, who once owned the Philadelphia Eagles of the National Football League, in the 1980s opposed Maurice Ferré's plan to renovate the Orange Bowl for the Miami Dolphins. In 1999, he financed the campaign to oppose Mayor Penelas's proposal for a one-cent sales tax that would have generated billions of dollars to spend on mass transit. Braman won, but voters eventually approved a half-cent sales-tax increase dedicated to transit in a 2002 referendum. Given Braman's history of opposition to big government and tax increases, his opposition to the new Marlins Park and the ensuing tax hike came as no surprise.

The court ruled on Braman's suit against the county on November 21, 2008, holding that a voter referendum was not required for the 37,000-seat stadium's financing plan. The ruling allowed Alvarez and the county to finalize the deal. It took the mayor and his manager, George Burgess, another six months of negotiations to conclude the deal, and they had to go back to the commission to request increasing the interest on the bond after the original offering in Wall Street was unable to finance the project at the original rate. The final deal, supported by city of Miami mayor Manny Diaz, Miami-Dade County mayor Carlos Alvarez, and Burgess, was one of the worst ever signed by a local government with Major League Baseball. In it, the total building cost of the stadium complex rose by a few million dollars to $634 million, more than 80 percent of which would be paid with public money. Analysts of the bond sale soon publicized that with interest compounding over forty years, the total cost to the county to repay the high interest would rise to $2.4 billion. The sticker shock created a public backlash as support for the unpopular deal hit rock bottom.

The collapsing support for the Marlins stadium drove Mayor Alvarez's approval rating down to the low forties. Non-Latino whites were the most strongly opposed to the new baseball park, with over 70 percent against it. Although some grassroots activists began circulating a recall petition, public support for the recall of Alvarez was still relatively low. The mayor was apparently tone deaf to his growing unpopularity and invited a new wave of public criticism when he gave significant pay increases to his staff during the summer of 2010. His chief of staff was reported to be making well over $200,000. The straw that broke the camel's back came when the mayor proposed and secured the passage of a 12 percent increase in property-tax rates for 2011. According to U.S. Census data, in 2010, one in six families in Miami-Dade County was living in poverty. In the county, the foreclosure rate was down from 2009, but one in every fifteen properties in the county was still facing foreclosure (Miami-Dade County Office of Economic Development and International Trade 2010). Almost all support for Alvarez collapsed overnight, and his approval rating sank to the low twenties.

Braman immediately began an effort to recall the unpopular mayor. The recall effort was fueled by the Marlins deal, as well as Alvarez's tax increases, accompanied by pay raises for upper-echelon county workers. Traffic jams occurred in front of the recall offices in the Little Havana neighborhood and in the working-class Hispanic enclave of the city of Hialeah as thousands of voters rushed to sign the petition. Over one hundred thousand voters signed the recall initiative in just two weeks, more than enough to qualify it for the ballot. Public opinion polls showed support for recalling Carlos Alvarez running at over 60 percent. Meanwhile, a grassroots citizen group called Miami Voice gathered signatures to recall Commissioner Natasha Seijas. She had become the poster child of the commission's arrogance by verbally attacking voters who dared to criticize the commission. Seijas and Commissioner Bruno Barreiro had joined with the four African American commissioners and the two non-Latino white commissioners to vote for the property-tax increase. The 8–5 vote in September 2010 was the tipping point, and the campaign to oust the mayor started in earnest.

The county establishment, consisting of the public employee unions, the lobbying corps, a majority of the commissioners, and the bureaucracy, all lined up against the recall. The only commissioner to support the recall was Carlos Giménez. Despite the strong opposition from the establishment, the public anger and Braman's money were too much to overcome. Braman spent more than $1 million of his own money on the effort. Alvarez and Seijas were recalled in a special recall election on March 15, 2011. More than 88 percent of the voters (some 176,000 people) voted to recall

Alvarez. The election was the largest municipal recall vote in U.S. history and the second largest in the United States of any kind after the 2003 recall election of California governor Gray Davis.

The 2011 Mayoral Election

The campaign to replace the ousted Alvarez began two and a half months before the actual recall. Both Hialeah mayor Julio Robaina and County Commissioner Carlos Giménez announced their candidacy for Miami-Dade mayor in January 2011. If the recall was successful, they would run in 2011; if the recall failed, they would wait till 2012, when Alvarez's term expired. Both candidates promised to return integrity and stability to the county. Giménez emphasized his opposition to Alvarez's policies, especially the Marlins stadium deal and the 12 percent tax increase. He called for a rollback of the 2011 tax increase. Giménez also embraced the reform agenda being pushed by Braman and other good-government groups: term limits for commissioners, opposition to pay increases for commissioners, and stricter rules for lobbying and campaign contributions. Giménez also wanted to reduce the size of county government. Robaina's platform was similar in supporting both reforms in the county and rolling back the 2011 property-tax increase. The only major difference between the two leading candidates was that Robaina had supported the Marlins ballpark.

Robaina was the early favorite. He was supported by the city's powerful real estate industry and could easily raise more money than any other candidate. In the first quarter of 2011, he raised nearly half a million dollars, compared with $100,000 for Giménez. Eventually, Robaina's campaign coffers would surpass Giménez's by nearly two to one, $1.7 million to $900,000. However, if campaign funding raised through political action committees and other similar entities is counted, Giménez raised $2.2 million to Robaina's $5 million (Florida Secretary of State 2011; Miami-Dade Election Department 2011). Moreover, early polling showed Robaina with a commanding 42 percent to 9 percent advantage over Giménez (poll conducted by Dario Moreno Inc., March 22, 2011). The situation was so grim for Giménez by the end of March that he was giving serious consideration to dropping out of the race (interview with Juan Carlos Flores, campaign manager, May 30, 2014). However, Robaina's fortunes took a downward turn when the Center for Voter Advocacy released a poll showing that former county mayor Alex Penelas enjoyed a twenty-point lead over Robaina (37 percent to 17 percent) if he would enter the contest (Haggman and Brannigan 2011c). The poll indicated that Robaina was vulnerable, and that despite his impressive showing in raising money, the race to replace

Alvarez as county mayor was still wide open. The poll kept Giménez in the race right before the county commission set the date for the special election and the qualifying deadlines.

The wide-open mayoral race attracted a crowded field in which Robaina and Giménez were joined by state representative Marcelo Llorente, rap star Luther "Luke" Campbell, and seven other minor candidates. The crowded field was good news for the Giménez campaign since Robaina's early and commanding lead had created the possibility of a first-round victory by the Hialeah mayor. Eleven candidates made it highly unlikely that any candidate could get more than the required 50 percent in the first round. Despite the good news, the Giménez campaign still faced two important obstacles. The first challenge was that its platform was identical to Robaina's because both candidates had adopted Braman's reform and tax-cut agenda. Second, the Giménez campaign did not have enough money to get its message out through television and direct mail.

The Giménez campaign determined that Robaina's major vulnerability was his personal integrity. Robaina was a developer and had a very intimate relationship with the county's real estate development interests. Moreover, Robaina was also personally involved in some alleged shady business practices, including loan sharking, illegal gambling, and participation in a Ponzi scheme. The decision to make Robaina's personal finances a major campaign issue was coupled with the decision to use Spanish-language radio and robocalls to deliver the campaign message. Being short on funds, the campaign was forced to forgo television and direct mail in the first round and instead use cheaper Spanish-language radio to convey Giménez's message. The campaign especially targeted programs favored by the Cuban elderly, who were projected to make up half the electorate in the May 24 special election. Trailing badly in the polls, Giménez decided to fight Robaina *mano a mano* on the Spanish-language airwaves for the Cuban vote. Robocalls were used as the main outreach mechanism for non-Latino whites and English-speaking Hispanics and to supplement Spanish-language radio among elderly Cubans. The campaign decided to ignore the black vote in the first round, conceding that vote to the two most prominent African Americans in the race, Luther Campbell and Roosevelt Bradley.

The campaign's chief strategist, Alex Díaz de la Portilla, designed a robocall campaign to reinforce the negative message about Robaina on Spanish radio while at the same time providing a positive English-language message to reach non-Latino whites. The Robaina campaign invested heavily in television and direct-mail advertising and matched Giménez on Spanish radio. The volume of robocalls from Giménez's campaign increased slowly throughout April, and by the end of the month, the campaign was flooding

the county with half a million calls a day. The campaign's internal track-
ing polls found that Giménez was beginning to make dramatic gains during the robocall blitz. The Robaina campaign ignored the robocalls,
oblivious of their increasing effectiveness. In mid-May, the *Miami Herald*
published a poll showing that the county mayor race had evolved into a two-
man contest between Robaina and Giménez. Giménez, who was now at
20 percent, was only 5 points behind Robaina, who was at 25 percent (Haggman and Brannigan 2011d). Campbell was in third place at 10 percent,
while Llorente pulled only 8 percent. The Giménez campaign was elated that
its negative campaign against Robaina had led to a 16 percent shift in Robaina's support. Moreover, the poll showed that Giménez was almost assured a slot in the runoff, given Llorente's and Campbell's relatively poor
showing.

The *Miami Herald*, which, together with its Spanish-language companion, *El Nuevo Herald*, had a circulation of over two hundred thousand, endorsed Giménez on May 14, the same day it published the poll, giving the
campaign additional momentum going into the last ten days. On election
night, Robaina finished, as predicted, only 5 percent ahead of Giménez,
34 percent to 29 percent. Llorente was in third place at 15 percent, and
Campbell, plagued by very low African American turnout, finished fourth
with only 11 percent of the vote. Giménez received over half of the non-
Latino white vote and a quarter of the Hispanic vote. Robaina attracted
half of the Hispanic vote but little else. Campbell and Bradley together received over 70 percent of the African American vote. The results of the first
round changed the dynamics of the race because now, for the first time,
Carlos Giménez was viewed as the front-runner, while Robaina was fighting
for his political life. Llorente endorsed Giménez after the first round, improving Giménez's position with Hispanics, while Campbell endorsed
Robaina.

The Giménez campaign had all the momentum going into the second
round. Internal polling showed Giménez with a ten-point advantage over
Robaina. This was confirmed by a June 17 poll published in the *Miami Herald* that showed Giménez had advanced to an eleven-point lead over Robaina, 50 to 39 percent (Haggman and Brannigan 2011b). Robaina still
enjoyed a large fund-raising advantage and had a more solid and reliable
voting base among older and working-class Cuban Americans than Giménez. The candidates' margin narrowed in the final two weeks as the Robaina
campaign pounded Giménez on Spanish-language media and organized a
massive get-out-the-vote drive among his supporters. Robaina also directed
more of his resources to the black community and tried to capitalize on the
Campbell endorsement with a strong outreach to Miami's often ignored

African American neighborhoods. The lifelong Republican, who had supported Rick Scott for governor, became the second choice of Miami's black
establishment after Campbell. By comparison, the more liberal Giménez,
who had endorsed Scott's Democratic opponent, Alex Sink, could not get any
traction in Miami's black community. His call for reform in county hall was
generally greeted with skepticism. Giménez added to his woes when in the
last week of the campaign he refused to participate in any additional
debates.

Despite the resurgence in the Robaina campaign, Giménez hung on for
a narrow victory. The margin of victory was only four thousand votes out
of the two hundred thousand cast, 51 percent to 49 percent. Giménez, as
expected, overwhelmingly won the non-Latino white vote with 75 percent
and split the Hispanic vote with Robaina, 47 percent to 53 percent. Robaina
kept it close by narrowly winning the Hispanic vote and wining the black
vote decisively, 56 percent to 44 percent (Haggman and Brannigan 2011a).
The result showed deep socioeconomic cleavages between Giménez, the reformer, and Robaina, the populist. Giménez won in affluent non-Latino
white and Hispanic cities, such as Coral Gables, Miami Beach, and Aven-
tura, and the middle-class Hispanic neighborhoods Kendall and Westches-
ter, while Robaina won in the working-class Hispanic and black cities and
neighborhoods.

Giménez's First Term (2011–2012): Reform Implementation

Giménez hit the ground running with his reform program. He had articulated an ambitious program of governmental reforms during his campaign
that he was determined to carry out. However, he was immediately confronted by the county's entrenched interests. The Board of County Commissioners, the public employee unions, the large lobbying firms, and
elements of the county bureaucracy were not convinced that major reforms
were needed. They rejected the claim that the Alvarez recall election constituted a mandate for reform. Instead, they chose to interpret the election
simply as the rejection of an unpopular politician. The entrenched interests at county hall dismissed the notion that Giménez had any electoral
mandate to enact major reforms and prepared to fight each reform every
step of the way.

The new mayor was determined to reduce the public perception of waste
associated with the Alvarez mayoralty. As a first step, demonstrating his
strong commitment to change, Giménez cut the budget of the mayor's office in half and slashed his own salary from $300,000 to $150,000. He also

reduced the benefits packages for county executives, arguing that it was a time for joint sacrifice that should begin at the top. The new mayor also initiated a major restructuring of Miami-Dade government. He formally eliminated the county manager's position and replaced it with five deputy mayors who would directly oversee department directors. Four of the five deputy mayors were new to the county. The only holdover from the previous administration was Alina Hudak, who had served as interim county manager after Burgess's resignation in the wake of the recall. Some of the mayor's political advisers opposed the appointment of Hudak, who was viewed as a defender of the status quo and an opponent of meaningful reform (interview with Juan Carlos Flores, campaign manager, May 30, 2014). Giménez lowered the number of departments from forty-six to twenty-five by reducing redundancy and cutting the number of county executives. The restructuring eliminated nearly two thousand positions in county government.

The centerpiece of the mayor's reforms was the rollback of the 2010 property-tax increase, which would cut property-tax revenues by over $200 million. Cutting taxes at a time when property-tax revenues were already down because of the housing crisis required $400 million in budget cuts. The mayor's plan required obtaining $239 million in concessions from the public employee unions because the restructuring accounted for only $160 million in cuts. Bowing to public opinion, in the September 22 final budget meeting that stretched into the next day, the Board of County Commissioners accepted the new mayor's budget by a 10-2 vote, with one commissioner absent.

The public employee unions did not accept the $239 million in concessions without a fight and quickly became the focal point of opposition to the Giménez administration. Spearheaded by the police union, the unions appealed to the Board of County Commissioners to restore the benefits that Giménez had wrenched from them. Reluctant to openly oppose the popular Giménez, the commission refused to reverse the cuts. The unions were then forced to recruit the chairman of the commission, Joe Martinez, to run against Giménez in the 2012 mayoral race. Giménez began with a sizable advantage because of his victory the year before, and as the incumbent, he now controlled a well-oiled fund-raising machine that quickly raised over $2 million. Martinez's main source of support was the public employee unions.

The Martinez campaign claimed that there was enough waste in the budget to fund the tax cut without forcing public employees to make concessions. The campaign focused on Giménez's purported poor treatment of county employees. For example, it hired planes with a banner that read,

"County employees hate Giménez." After Miami-Dade County Public Schools, Miami-Dade County is the second-largest public employer in the county, with approximately twenty-five thousand employees.

Plagued by the lack of money, disorganization, and a weak message, the Martinez campaign floundered. The Giménez campaign, meanwhile, focused on the mayor's reform, specifically the tax cut, and when his new budget further reduced taxes, his reelection was all but assured. Giménez easily cruised to a first-round victory against Martinez and six other candidates with 55 percent of the vote. The mayor received over 60 percent of the Hispanic and Anglo vote but less than 40 percent of the African American vote. He had broadened his coalition to include working-class Hispanics, but African Americans were still largely unconvinced by Giménez's reform efforts and strongly opposed his small-government approach to county government.

Charter reform, specifically in regard to term limits, was also an important issue during Giménez's first year in office. The commission was far more resistant to public opinion on charter reform. Braman and many of the activists involved in the recall were demanding that the commission put retroactive eight-year term limits on the ballot. This would have disqualified ten of the thirteen commissioners from seeking reelection. Unsurprisingly, the commission refused to put the proposal to a public vote. Instead, in an attempt to placate public opinion, the commission put on the ballot a charter amendment that would limit commissioners to two consecutive terms beginning in 2012 but would also raise commissioners' salaries. A *Miami Herald/El Nuevo Herald* poll released just ten days before the election showed the voters divided, with 41 percent of likely voters saying that they planned to vote for the term-limit and salary-increase proposal, the same percentage planning to vote against it, and 18 percent undecided. This double-edged compromise pleased no one and was voted down in the January 31, 2012, special election, possibly because of the inclusion of the salary raise. In the charter authored by Harvard lawyer Dan Paul and others in 1957, the commission was designed as a part-time board of directors, while a full-time professional staff would oversee day-to-day operations. Since then, commissioners have proposed raising their salary a dozen times, and voters have rejected the idea every time. In addition to $6,000 in pay, commissioners have benefits worth over $55,000, including $2,000 a month for expenses, an $800 monthly car allowance, and a substantial budget to hire their own staff.

In the aftermath of the commission's so-called phony reforms, Braman announced that he was recruiting candidates to challenge four incumbent commissioners who had opposed term limits. This spurred the commission to accept a compromise to put eight-year term limits on the ballot for the November 2012 election. The commission also attempted to placate reformers with a highly popular amendment to require a two-thirds vote of the commission to move the Urban Development Boundary, Miami-Dade's no-build line. Both charter amendments passed overwhelmingly with over 68 percent support, but all of Braman's reform candidates lost their bids.

The property-tax cuts, the passage of term limits, and the defeat of Braman's reform candidates, coupled with Mayor Giménez reelection, created the perception that Miami-Dade was entering a new period of stability. Giménez's reelection assured that tax increases were off the table, while the defeat of the Braman slate of candidates kept in place a county commission that was pro-union and hostile to further reform. The conventional wisdom was that county government had weathered the storm.

Giménez's Second Term and Beyond (2012–Present)

County insiders articulated the view that the results of the 2012 election returned the county to its prerecall equilibrium. The defeat of all four members of the Braman slate signaled to the county establishment that the reform movement had run its course, and that voters desired stability. More important, Giménez's reelection gave the mayor a four-year break until he needed to face voters again, enough time to reach an agreement with the public employee unions and raise property taxes if necessary. The county establishment felt that public trust had been restored, and that it was time to return to business as usual.

The mayor tested the waters when he negotiated a deal with the Miami Dolphins that would provide the team with $199 million in public money to renovate Sun Life Stadium, while the team's owner, Stephen Ross, would provide the remaining balance of the $400 million required for renovation. The public money would come from both state and county sources. The state money would be from an annual $3 million rebate from sales-tax revenue generated by goods and services sold at Sun Life Stadium. The county would provide $120 million by adding another cent to the so-called bed tax paid by guests staying at Miami hotels. The mayor protected himself from public outcry by insisting that the proposal be put to a public vote through a public referendum paid for by the Dolphins. The deal collapsed when the Florida legislature did not provide the sales-tax rebate. Both public opinion polls and the count of the early and absentee ballots showed that the referendum likely would have failed.

The mayor took a bigger risk in July 2013 when he proposed a budget that would have raised the county millage rate slightly. The mayor's proposed $6.35 billion budget for fiscal year 2013–2014 was 2.8 percent higher than the year before. The hike would be different from the one that cost Alvarez his job, Giménez argued, because it would be much smaller and would not be accompanied by employee raises in the middle of an economic recession. Voters responded immediately, and Giménez's office heard from dozens of outraged home owners. A thick pile of e-mail and phone-call records compiled by his constituent services office featured messages in English and Spanish bashing the mayor for forgetting about the elderly living on fixed incomes and reneging on his small-government campaign platform. They promised consequences at the ballot box. Reading the writing on the wall, Giménez withdrew his tax-hike proposal the day before the commission's tax-rate vote. The quick flip allowed him to regain public support before the commission rejected his plan (Mazzei 2013).

The mayor told top county administrators after the debacle that he would not consider another tax increase during his tenure. He would put a tax increase on the table only if there was a countywide vote. This position upset the county establishment, especially the county's public employee unions, which were anxious to roll back the concessions that they had been forced to make in 2011. County administrators and union activists argued that voter antitax sentiment had passed. They pointed out that both the Miami-Dade School Board and Jackson Hospital had won voter approval of bonds that raised property-tax rates.

The approval of the Jackson Hospital bond gave the commissioners the opportunity to rebuff the mayor as they rolled back the concessions that the Jackson employee unions had made to the county. This opened the door for all public employee unions to demand the restoration of full benefits. In February 2014, the commission voted to restore all benefits, overriding the mayor's veto and reconfirming the commission's earlier decision to end an unpopular pay concession for county and Jackson Health System workers. Giménez had twice vetoed the commission's 8–5 vote to eliminate the 5 percent health-care contribution paid by public employees, but on the third vote, Commissioner Juan C. Zapata switched sides, giving the majority the deciding ninth vote it needed to override the mayor. The February 2014 vote was preceded by two earlier overrides of the mayor's vetoes in which two unions, representing sanitation and aviation workers, already had their pay restored. The commission's generosity created a $150 million shortfall in the 2015 budget. This budget deficit was especially troublesome because the county's revenues from property taxes rose only by 6 percent.

The deficit was addressed through cuts across various agencies, and rising property values continue to enable the Mayor to keep his promise not to increase property taxes. In November 2016, Giménez was re-elected for a second full term.

Conclusion: The Challenges Ahead

Like other conservative reformers in Los Angeles and New York, Carlos Giménez has restored public confidence in local government and cleaned up some of the waste and mismanagement of previous administrations. He has provided short-term solutions that have stabilized the government and won voter approval. The challenge for the Giménez administration is to find long-term solutions that allow Miami-Dade County to provide first-rate services in a relatively poor area without driving away middle-class residents with high taxes. Clarence Stone noted that there is "no single fulcrum of control" in any city, and that much of the time, "middle range accommodations are worked out" (Stone 1989, p. 227). His elite-driven view of urban politics cannot account for the bottom-up mobilization that has largely shaped Miami-Dade County's property-tax policies since the recall, but it seems to provide a viable forecast about the difficulty of appeasing competing interests and demands in the future. Stone argued that over the long haul, elected officials "sometimes act in apparent disregard of the contours of electoral power" because they have a natural tendency to associate with the revenue producers and organized groups, such as unions (Stone 1989, p. 34). If this observation is correct, in the long term, it should be expected that property-tax increases and developmental policies will be put on the agenda once again despite the social and economic needs of the electorate.

A significant percentage of the area's residents, 19.1 percent, have incomes below the poverty level. Median household income in Miami-Dade still has not recovered to prerecession levels, and the new construction boom only highlights the growing income inequality in the area. Bloomberg ranked Miami third in the country in income inequality behind Atlanta and New Orleans. According to a study released by the Center for Housing Policy, middle-class households in Miami spent almost three-quarters of their income on housing and transportation. The study also showed that the 44 percent increase in housing and transportation costs far outpaced the 21 percent increase in income since 2000 (Hickey et al. 2012). Rising transportation and housing costs and stagnant incomes are making any attempt to raise taxes difficult for any elected official. On the other side, the clout of established employee unions and their successful pressure to reinstitute previous benefits force public officials to seek alternative sources for financing public services to stave off potential revenue shortfalls. The administration of the county's finances will require a careful balancing act. Maintaining public opinion on his side, Giménez is better positioned than most to continue implementing his agenda of good government with small and efficient county departments providing quality services.

REFERENCES

Boswell, Thomas. "Racial and Ethnic Segregation Patterns in Metropolitan Miami, Florida, 1980–1990." *Southwestern Geographer* 33, no. 1 (May): 82–109.
Corbett, John G., John S. Stack, and Christopher Warren. 1990. "Hispanic Ascendancy and Tripartite Politics in Miami." In *Racial Politics in American* Cities, edited by Rufus P. Browning, Dale Rogers Marshall, and David H. Tabb, 155–177. White Plains, NY: Longman.
Cove, Damien. 2009. "After Years of Development, Miami Ponders Whether the Good Outweighs the Bad." *New York Times*, November 22, 2009, A22.
Davis, Phillip. 2005. "Miami Mayor Brings Building Boom, Criticism." National Public Radio, December 30. http://www.npr.org/templates/story/story.php?storyId=5076730.
Deleon, Richard Edward. 1992. *Left Coast City: Progressive Politics in San Francisco, 1975–1991.* Lawrence: University Press of Kansas.
Diaz, Manny. 2012. *Miami Transformed: Rebuilding America One Neighborhood, One City at a Time.* Philadelphia: University of Pennsylvania Press.
Florida Secretary of State. 2011. "Reports of Expenditure, Political Committees." August.
Goodnough, Abby. 2004. "Gore's Venting Stirs Up Senate Race in Florida." *Miami Herald,* June 8.
Haggman, Matthew, and Martha Brannigan. 2011a. "Giménez Drew on Broad Coalition to Get elected." *Miami Herald,* June 29.
———. 2011b. "Poll: Giménez Takes Commanding Lead in Mayor's Race; Carlos Giménez, Who Came In Second to Julio Robaina in the First Round of Voting on May 24, Has Pulled Ahead with Support from All Three Major Ethnic Groups in the County." *Miami Herald*, June 17.
———. 2011c. "Raul Martinez, Alex Penelas, Weighing Miami-Dade Mayor Bids." *Miami Herald*, April 5.
———. 2011d. "Robaina, Giménez, Lead Race for Miami-Dade Mayor." *Miami Herald*, May 14.
Hickey, Robert, Jeffrey Lubell, Peter Haas, and Stephanie Morse. 2012. "Losing Ground: The Struggle of Moderate-Income Households to Afford the Rising Costs of Housing and Transportation." Report of the Center for Housing Policy/Center for Neighborhood Technology, October 12. https://www.novoco.com/sites/default/files/atoms/files/nhc_losing_ground_101812.pdf.
Hill, Kevin, Dario Moreno, and Lourdes Cue. 2001. "Racial and Partisan Voting in a Tri-ethnic City: The 1996 Dade County Mayoral Election." *Journal of Urban Affairs* 23, nos. 3–4 (Fall): 291–307.

Mazzei, Patricia. 2013. "Miami-Dade Mayor Calls His Proposal to Raise Taxes a Political Misstep." *Miami Herald*, July 27.

Miami-Dade County Department of Planning and Zoning, Planning Research Section. 2009. "Miami-Dade County Facts." http://www.miamidade.gov/planning/library /reports/2009-miami-dade-county-facts.pdf. Accessed July 19, 2017.

Miami-Dade County Office of Economic Development and International Trade. 2010. "Recent Trends in Foreclosure Activity in Miami-Dade County and Outlook for 2011." November 2011. https://www.miamidade.gov/business/library/reports/2010 -foreclosures.pdf. Accessed July 19, 2017.

Miami-Dade Election Department. 2011. "Campaign Expenditure Report," July 2011. http://www.voterfocus.com/ws/mdccand/candidate_pr.php?c=miamidade&el =16B. Accessed July 19, 2017.

"Miami Turns Out to Have a Garment District, Too." 1969. *New York Times*, May 25, Business and Finance section, F15.

Molotch, Harvey. 1988. "Strategies and Constraints of Growth Elites." In *Business Elites and Urban Development: Case Studies and Critical Perspectives*, edited by Scott Cummings, 25–47. Albany: State University of New York Press.

Molotch, Harvey, and John Logan. 1987. *Urban Fortunes: The Political Economy of Place*. Berkeley: University of California Press.

Musibay, Oscar Pedro, and Kate Howell. 2008. "Miami-Dade Approves Marlins Stadium." *South Florida Business Journal*, February 22.

Ross, Karl, Jay Weaver, and Oscar Corral. 2001. "Cuban-American Vote Lifts Diaz to Miami Mayor's Post." *Miami Herald*, November 14.

Smiley, David. 2016. "Push to Fire Miami's Top Administrator Fizzles after Tense Morning." *Miami Herald*, April 14.

Soften, Edward. 1963. *The Miami Metropolitan Experiment*. Bloomington: Indiana University Press.

Stone, Clarence. 1989. *Regime Politics: Governing Atlanta, 1946–1988*. Lawrence: University Press of Kansas.

Villano, David. 2004. "Turnaround: Miami Mayor Manny Diaz Is Applying Private-Sector Strategies to Rebuild the Foundations of His Long-Troubled City." *Florida Trend*, August 1.

8

Managing Fiscal Stress in Providence

The Election and Governance of Mayor Angel Taveras

MARION ORR, DOMINGO MOREL, AND EMILY M. FARRIS

EDITORS' NOTE

One of the major challenges confronting mayors of postindustrial cities is municipal fiscal stress. City governments are increasingly asked to do more with fewer resources. Angel Taveras's tenure as Providence's first Latino mayor presents an important case of a postindustrial mayor attempting to manage fiscal stress. Once a declining industrial city, Providence experienced a dramatic physical restructuring in the 1980s and 1990s. The city's redeveloped downtown attracted national attention. Providence, however, suffered economically during the transition to a postindustrial city. Facing growing deficits, recent mayors have struggled to balance the city's budget.

Angel Taveras was elected in 2010. During his historic campaign, Taveras stressed public education. He advocated creating "children's zones" modeled after the neighborhood-revitalization program in Harlem, renovating school buildings, and expanding after-school programs, the kind of issues that other postindustrial-era mayors have elevated on the local agenda. However, as Marion Orr, Domingo Morel, and Emily M. Farris describe in this chapter, once in office, Mayor Taveras concentrated on closing a huge structural deficit in the city's budget that he inherited. There was speculation that the city would have to file for bankruptcy.

Taveras had to close several public schools, many of which were located in predominantly Latino neighborhoods. City agencies were directed to cut their budgets. City employee union contracts were renegotiated. And city retirees had to forgo portions of their promised pension. Orr, Morel, and Farris describe Taveras's efforts to preserve Providence's creditworthiness and to prevent it from plunging into bankruptcy.

In January 2011, on the day Angel Taveras was sworn in as the thirty-seventh mayor of Providence, Rhode Island, an elderly Latina pulled him aside. As Taveras recalled the encounter, the woman "had voted for the first time" and wanted him to know that she "had voted for me, a Latino" (Taveras 2014). Taveras is a first-generation Dominican American and Providence's first Latino mayor. Taveras's election broke the longtime Irish and Italian rule that had held political power since Providence's industrial era. Shortly after Taveras's historic 2010 election victory, a longtime observer of Rhode Island politics noted, "Many Rhode Islanders cannot remember a time when the mayor of Providence wasn't either an Italian-American or an Irish-American male" (Sorrentino 2010, p. 4). "We never imagined when we came here in the 1970s that I'd grow up to be the Mayor of Providence; never imagined it," Taveras explained (Taveras 2014). The election of Taveras signaled a new period of ethnic and racial transition in Providence's political leadership.

As in other cities, control of the mayor's office in Providence is a leading force in bringing about Latino political incorporation. As Carlos Cuéllar points out in Chapter 2 of this volume, Taveras's election followed a pattern playing out across the United States. Several other major U.S. cities, including Los Angeles, San Antonio, Miami, and Hartford, had also elected Latino mayors. The postindustrial era ushered in the rise and expansion of Latinos in Providence politics. This chapter provides an account of Taveras's election and governance in Providence. We situate Taveras's administration within the broader context of political incorporation, minority empowerment, and the mayoralty in the postindustrial city. In particular, we emphasize the fiscal and budgetary challenges that Taveras had to address throughout his term in office.

The economic well-being of Providence and many other postindustrial cities has been severely weakened by long-term trends, including deindustrialization and the exodus of jobs and middle-class residents to the suburbs. Fiscal stress, which results from failure to align revenues and expenditures, has become an increasingly common characteristic of the postindustrial city and has prompted mayors to consider significant policy changes. Facing growing deficits, mayors are reducing services, laying off municipal employees, renegotiating union contracts, rolling back benefits to retirees, and cutting back on repair and maintenance of city facilities and infrastructure. We explore how Providence's first Latino mayor addressed the city's fiscal crisis and worked to prevent Rhode Island's capital city from plunging into municipal bankruptcy.

This chapter draws on a variety of data sources, including results from a telephone survey, an interview with Mayor Taveras, interviews with Latino community leaders, election returns, and local media coverage, to address some of the significant concerns in urban and minority politics. Next, we provide a brief portrait of Providence and the city's politics. This is followed by a discussion of Taveras's historic election. Taveras, like successful Latino mayoral candidates in Denver, San Antonio, Hartford, and Los Angeles, ran a deracialized campaign, promising to work to help all Providence residents. However, we also note that Taveras did make direct appeals to the Latino community and relied heavily on the support of the Latino community to win the mayoral election. We conclude with a reflection on the lessons that can be drawn from Taveras's political leadership as the first Latino mayor of Providence and offer a brief analysis of how his election and administration may have affected the election of the city's second Latino mayor, Jorge Elorza.

Economic and Demographic Transformation in Postindustrial Providence

Providence is the capital of Rhode Island. With a population of 178,042, it is the third-largest city in New England. Founded in 1636, Providence grew around its navigation and commercial economic interests. Providence's manufacturing, textile, and jewelry industries attracted many Irish, Italian, and French Canadian immigrants, and by the end of the nineteenth century, more than 60 percent of the city was foreign born (McLoughlin 1986). Portuguese, Poles, Jews, Cape Verdeans, and African Americans also joined the city's residents; by 1920, the city had grown to over 225,000 residents, and the population peaked at 248,674 in 1950. But by 1970, Providence was considered a declining industrial city, and its population dropped to 179,116—the steepest decline in any city in the United States during the same period.

Since the 1970s, Providence's political leaders, along with the downtown business elite, have worked to revitalize the city as a "Renaissance City" and the "Creative Capital." Providence redeveloped its river walk and downtown area, leveraging federal funds to attract private business investment (Rich 2000). Over the past two decades, Providence has experienced a comeback, and the city has become known for its fine dining, large down-town mall, art galleries, and academic institutions (Orr and West 2002). Neighborhoods that were previously struggling, especially those adjacent to downtown, have undergone gentrification as more white, high-income, highly educated residents moved in.

By the 1970s, the city began experiencing a remarkable influx of Lati-nos, many from Puerto Rico and increasingly from the Dominican Repub-lic, Colombia, and Guatemala (Silver 2001). The city's overall population has increased over the past two decades as well, swelled by the large num-bers of Latino immigrants who have made Providence home (Itzigsohn 2009). The number of Latinos in Providence has expanded further over the past thirty years. According to the Pew Hispanic Center (2002), the Latino population in the Providence metro area grew by 325 percent between 1980 and 2000, making Providence one of the fastest-growing "new-destination" cities for Latino immigrants. In 2010, there were 67,835 Lati-nos in the city, up 30 percent from 2000. The Latino community in Providence is one of the most diverse Latino communities in the United States, with sizable populations of Dominicans, Puerto Ricans, Guatema-lans, Mexicans, and Salvadorans (see Table 8.1). Providence has the largest proportion of Dominicans in any city in the country (Itzigsohn 2009).

During the postindustrial era, the rapid growth of Latino residents, combined with the suburbanization of many of the city's Irish and Italian residents, made Providence an ethnically diverse city. The Latino commu-nity is the largest group (38.1 percent) in the city, followed by whites (37.6 percent), blacks (13 percent),[1] and Asians (6.3 percent). The number of Latinos in Providence continues to grow, but non-Hispanic whites con-tinue to leave the city; there was a 40 percent reduction in the number of whites from 1990 to 2010. Whites remain the second-largest group, how-ever, given the relatively small size of the black community in the city. The African American population in Providence has grown only gradually from

TABLE 8.1   TOP FIVE LATINO NATIONAL GROUPS
IN PROVIDENCE, 2010

National origin	Population	Percentage
All Latinos	67,835	
Dominican	25,267	37.2
Puerto Rican	14,847	21.8
Guatemalan	11,930	17.6
Mexican	3,188	4.7
Salvadoran	1,503	2.2

Source: U.S. Census.

3 percent of the city in 1950. Since 2000, Providence has been a majority-minority city where Latinos are the largest group and are ethnically diverse.

Providence's Latino community is located primarily on the western and southern sides of the city. The main economic artery for the Latino community in Providence is Broad Street, where there are a number of Latino-owned businesses. Latino small businesses grew from 31 in 1997 to 2,999 in 2007 (Spitzer and Carbonell 2012). Despite this positive trend, Latinos in Providence are struggling economically, particularly since the economic recession of 2008. Thirty-four percent of Latinos in Providence live below the poverty line. In 2011, Providence's metropolitan area had the highest Hispanic unemployment rate in the nation, 23.3 percent, compared with a national average of 11.5 percent (Austin 2011). The neighborhoods in Providence in which many Latinos have settled confront some of the toughest problems in the city, including a lack of access to quality health care, education, and employment.

Overall, Providence struggles with high unemployment and poverty rates, particularly since the 2008–2009 economic recession and foreclosure problems. Low-wage service-sector jobs replaced the city's old manufacturing base, and the economic recession particularly hurt Rhode Island. Unemployment rates in the state stood at 11.4 percent in 2009 and passed 14 percent by 2010. Providence's poverty levels have also increased. In 2010, the city's official poverty rate was 31.7 percent, more than twice as high as the statewide rate. Housing foreclosure rates, which skyrocketed across the country in 2008–2009, were among the highest in the Providence metropolitan region. Because property taxes constitute nearly half of local revenues, the city suffered significant revenue shortfalls. The city's financial status was hurt further by cuts in general revenue sharing from the state during the recession. Structural changes in the economy, population shifts, and the 2008 economic recession have contributed to the city's financial challenges.

Mayoral Politics in Providence

Mayoral politics in Providence has followed a trajectory similar to that of other northeastern cities. During the industrial era, Providence's economy of textiles, metalworking, and jewelry making created a class and ethnic divide between a Protestant Yankee elite and a Catholic working class (Sterne 2004). As Cornwell (1960) noted, the Yankees held power until the Irish displaced them in the mid-1920s. Since the late nineteenth century, Providence has been a machine-politics city with a system of personal rewards permeating the electoral arena. Providence mayors have not been constrained by Progressive Era reforms like city managers. In 1940, charter revisions created a strong-mayor system of government in Providence. The Irish built a strong Democratic political machine, dispensed patronage, and gained the allegiance of Italians, French Canadians, and Jews (Cornwell 1960; Daoust 1985).

The Irish hold on city hall ended in 1974 when Vincent "Buddy" Cianci, the grandson of Italian immigrants, was elected the city's first Italian American mayor (Stanton 2003). Cianci served as mayor through the redevelopment era and into the postindustrial era. His first stint as mayor ran until 1984, when he was forced to resign after pleading no contest to a charge of assaulting a man he accused of having an affair with his estranged wife. In 1990, Cianci was elected again. A significant part of the city's downtown redevelopment occurred during Cianci's tenures (Orr and West 2002).

For a long time, blacks were "better organized politically" than the city's Latino community, having arrived in Providence "during an era of strong parties and highly developed patronage systems" (Rich 2000, p. 209). Blacks first gained representation on the city council in 1969 and have held a number of top and middle-level positions in city government. Mayor Cianci courted and won the black vote and appointed African Americans to several of the city's boards. However, more recently, the city's Latino community has started to gain political strength, in many ways passing African Americans.

In Providence, Latinos represented a small share of the city's population throughout the 1970s and 1980s, and their presence in Providence politics was minimal. However, the founding of Progreso Latino, a social service agency that addressed the needs of Latinos in Central Falls, Rhode Island, in 1977 and the Center for Hispanic Policy and Advocacy in Providence in 1986 provided the organizational mechanisms that allowed the community to organize around education and employment, among other issues. Additionally, these organizations became vehicles for local Latino leaders to begin to get involved in local politics. Angel Taveras, for example, recalled that his involvement in community organizations like Progreso Latino provided an opportunity for him to "serve in the community" and try to "make a difference," especially in the Latino community (Taveras 2014). Like several of the other Latino mayors discussed in other chapters of this volume, Taveras was politicized through his involvement in Latino advocacy and community organizations.

By the late 1990s, Latinos began to flex their political muscles in Rhode Island, particularly in Providence. In 1998, to consolidate their growing numbers, Latinos formed the Rhode Island Latino Political Action Committee

TABLE 8.2   LATINO MAYORS AND CITY COUNCILORS IN PROVIDENCE

	Position	Years in office
Current		
Jorge Elorza	Mayor	2015-present
Luis Aponte	City Council, Ward 10	1999–present
Sabina Matos	City Council, Ward 15	2011–present
Carmen Castillo	City Council, Ward 9	2012–present
Previous		
Angel Taveras	Mayor	2011–2015
Miguel Luna	City Council, Ward 9	2003–2011, passed away while in office
Davian Sanchez	City Council, Ward 11	2011–2015
Leon Tejada	City Council, Ward 8	2007–2011, lost primary

Source: Compiled by authors.

(RILPAC). RILPAC launched voter-registration initiatives and endorsed candidates for offices. In 1998, Luis Aponte became the first Latino to win a seat on the Providence city council; he was joined by Miguel Luna in 2002. From the election of the first Latino in 1998 to today, there have been six Latinos on the Providence city council (see Table 8.2). In 2016, the Providence mayor, city council president, and city council president pro tempore were all Latinos. The city's Latino leadership is also reflective of the diversity within the city's Latino community. Jorge Elorza, who succeeded Angel Taveras as mayor of Providence in 2015, is of Guatemalan origin. Luis Aponte, the city council president, is of Puerto Rican origin, and Sabina Matos, the council president pro tempore, is of Dominican descent.

Under Mayor Cianci, Latinos gained recognition in the mayor's office when he created the Office of Hispanic Affairs in 2001. Cianci initially disregarded the Latino community in Providence because "Hispanics don't vote" but later reversed his position, citing the growing role of Latinos in the community (Smith 2001). Cianci appointed three Latinos to the nine-member school board, and in 1999, the school board named Diana Lam the city's first Latina school superintendent. The rapid growth of the Latino population in Providence introduced new rifts in the fragile alliance between blacks and Latinos (Orr and West 2002). As Latinos grew in numbers and political power, members of the African American community feared not only economic competition but also political marginalization (Filindra and Orr 2013).

Cianci left office in 2002 when he was convicted of racketeering conspiracy and sentenced to five years in federal prison. After his conviction, city council president John Lombardi became acting mayor. The 2002 mayoral election was unique, following a sensational FBI undercover cor-ruption operation and conviction of a sitting mayor. David Cicilline, an openly gay state legislator of Italian and Jewish descent, ran on a reform platform. As a Democratic state legislator, Cicilline represented the city's East Side, the city's mostly affluent white neighborhood and home to Brown University. Cicilline built a reputation as a liberal reform-oriented legislator.

Cicilline made a major pitch for Latino votes in the election. He estab-lished his mayoral campaign headquarters in South Providence, the heart of the Latino community, talked openly about issues of concern to Latinos and African Americans, such as police brutality, inadequate housing, and a city workforce that remained more than 90 percent white, and stressed that if he were elected, he would work to bring the Providence "renaissance" to the neighborhoods. His major opponent, former Providence mayor Jo-seph Paolino, ran a campaign that attempted to assemble the traditional white, working-class, ethnic coalition that had long dominated Providence city politics. This coalition not only had helped Paolino serve as mayor from 1984 to 1990 but also had sustained Cianci from 1991 until 2002.

In the primary, Cicilline beat Paolino and two other white contenders with 53 percent of the vote. Cicilline ran strongly in both white and minor-ity wards, and local observers emphasized his strong support in Latino neighborhoods (Bakst 2003; Milkovits 2002; Silver 2001). In an environ-ment where the incumbent mayor had been convicted and minorities felt that they were being ignored politically, Cicilline overthrew the old white, ethnic, working-class coalition and created a new coalition based on white liberals, good-government reformers, Latinos, African Americans, and Asian Americans. After serving eight years as mayor of Providence, Cicil-line decided to run for an open Congressional seat in 2010. His decision to not seek reelection provided an opening for the election of the first Latino mayor in Providence.

Political Transition in Providence:
The Election of Angel Taveras

Angel Taveras's successful campaign met many of the electoral conditions that Robert Preuhs shows in Chapter 4 are necessary for a Latino to win the mayoralty in many big cities. For example, Taveras gained the support of liberal white reformers. In the 2010 mayoral election, key political lead-ers linked to the inner-city, working-class, Latino-white liberal/reform coalition that had elected Mayor Cicilline tapped Angel Taveras as his suc-cessor (Orr and Nordlund 2013; Filandra and Orr 2013). Taveras, the son of Dominican immigrants, was born in Brooklyn, New York, and grew up on the south side of Providence, raised by his single mother. Although of humble origins, Taveras earned a degree from Harvard University and a law degree from Georgetown University Law School. During his mayoral campaign, he frequently pointed out that he went from "Head Start to Harvard" (*About Angel* 2010).

In his first campaign for public office, Taveras ran unsuccessfully for Rhode Island's U.S. House of Representatives Second District in 2000 at age twenty-nine. As a young political novice in a competitive congressional race, Taveras was polling at only 3 percent of voters before the election (Sabar 2000), but he ended up winning four times that percentage and came in third, ahead of some more established candidates. Taveras ran well in Providence, especially in the city's minority precincts. In the 2000 congressional election, he actively courted Latino voters, conducting two dozen interviews with Spanish-language media, advertising in Spanish, and campaigning during the city's Bolivian, Dominican, and Puerto Rican festivals (Farris 2014).

After losing the election, Taveras returned to his legal career but stayed active in politics during the Rhode Island General Assembly's redistricting process and campaigned for David Cicilline for mayor in 2002. Taveras had been involved as a legal adviser to RILPAC since the organization's founding in the mid-1990s, although community leaders tended to describe him as more "behind the scenes" and focused on his law career. Before being appointed to the city's housing court by Mayor Cicilline in 2007, Taveras worked for one of the city's most prestigious law firms and opened his own law firm. His education and legal career earned him a position among the city's liberal and reform-oriented white elite, while his Dominican background allowed him to maintain his political ties to the inner-city Latino community.

In the city's 2010 mayoral race, Taveras's principal opponents were two established Italian American politicians, state representative Steven Costantino and city council president John Lombardi. Costantino had been elected to the legislature in 1995, where he rose to become the chairman of the powerful House Finance Committee. During the mayoral primary, Costantino focused on the city's finances. Lombardi was a familiar political face in Providence. He was first elected to the city council in 1984 and became president of the council in 1999. In the primary, Lombardi stressed city services, including street repair, snow removal, and trash collection. Taveras stressed public education, advocating for creating "children's zones" modeled after the neighborhood-revitalization program in Harlem, renovating school buildings, and expanding after-school programs. He also developed a city environmental program he claimed would position Providence as a leader in the growing green economy. Taveras vowed to bring "the city's environmental and renewable energy activists into City Hall" (Marcelo 2010).

In Taveras's 2010 mayoral race, he continued his efforts from his 2000 election to broadly shape his appeal across the city. Taveras's deracialized campaign appeal mirrored the approach taken by other Latino mayors in this volume in Los Angeles, San Antonio, Denver, and Hartford. In his first race in 2000, Taveras had expressed his desire to "appeal to the entire district," and the *Providence Journal* had described him as "prickly about the label" as the "Latino candidate" (Sabar 2000). In the 2010 mayoral race, Taveras described his personal background in inclusive terms: "It's the story of Providence. It's the story of Rhode Island. It's the story of America" (Scharfenberg 2010). He stressed his humble roots and the role public education had in his life, having gone from "Head Start to Harvard." To further cultivate citywide appeal, Taveras relied on endorsements from others with high levels of respect among voters in different communities, such as former gubernatorial candidate Myrth York, who was popular among liberal whites in the East Side, and state senator Juan Pichardo, a leader in the Latino community (Scharfenberg 2010).

Although Taveras's campaign portrayed him as broadly appealing, it also relied heavily on the Latino community for support. One significant moment in the campaign came when Taveras had a meeting with longtime community leader Victor Capellan and state senator Juan Pichardo. All three were interested in running for mayor but understood that multiple Latino candidates would severely hurt the chances of the city electing its first Latino mayor. After that meeting, Capellan and Pichardo decided that they would not run for mayor; their decision proved to be beneficial to Taveras. Senator Pichardo's decision to support Taveras was especially significant. "We thought that I would be the stronger candidate to win and that this was an opportunity for us to make a big change here. . . . If both of us ran, neither one of us would win," Taveras recalled (Taveras 2014). When Angel Taveras announced his candidacy, Senator Pichardo was on hand to introduce him. "That was key because a lot of people were watching to see whether we both wanted to divide the vote," Taveras recalled. "That was something that really helped solidify the community in many, many ways" (Taveras 2014). While his opponents split the white-ethnic vote in Providence, Taveras was able to consolidate support from the city's Latino community.

Many Latinos were involved in Taveras's campaign as prominent volunteers and advisers. Latinos were also prominent in his campaign as advertised members of fund-raising host committees, and Taveras held

Latino-based fund-raisers in several of Providence's Latino restaurants. Taveras also received the important endorsement of RILPAC. Taveras's campaign heavily recruited and mobilized Latinos for the mayoral election, using the slogan "Todos con Angel" (Everyone with Angel), which popular Dominican singer Fernandito Villalona created as a merengue campaign tune. A group of over 150 Latinas organized as Mujeres con Angel (Women with Angel) to support his campaign (Brito 2010b). He also did interviews with local Spanish media, such as Poder 1110, Latino Public Radio, and Acontecer Latino. Dominican radio-show host Jochy Santos broadcast his popular show *El Mismo Golpe* (The same beat) live from Providence, where he interviewed and endorsed Taveras (Brito 2010a). Taveras took his deracialized message of "making this a city that everyone has the chance to succeed" to every community in Providence. His message "was very similar on the East Side and on the South Side," Taveras recalled. However, "On the South Side I probably spoke a little more Spanish than on the East Side" (Taveras 2014). Taveras, like the other successful Latino mayoral candidates in Denver, Los Angeles, San Antonio, and Hartford, garnered significant support in the Latino community despite running a largely deracialized election campaign.

On the eve of the Democratic mayoral primary, the A. Alfred Taubman Center for Public Policy at Brown University conducted a public opinion survey of 475 registered voters in Providence. The results from the poll indicated that despite being a relative newcomer to Providence electoral politics, Taveras had achieved broad support across the city. The poll showed Taveras leading with 42 percent; Councilman Lombardi had the support of 31 percent of the respondents; and state representative Costantino was supported by 22 percent of survey respondents. The poll also showed that Taveras had support across racial groups. For example, 44 percent of white voters indicated support for Taveras, 28.9 percent of whites said that they supported Lombardi, and 25 percent of whites said that they would vote for Costantino. Nearly half (48.8 percent) of the Latino respondents said that they supported Taveras. Among black voters, 43 percent said that they supported Lombardi, 37 percent supported Taveras, and 17 percent supported Costantino. The poll also revealed that Taveras was the favorite among younger voters, voters with more education, and liberal voters (Taubman Center 2010).

In the September 14, 2010, Democratic mayoral primary, the forty-year old Taveras defeated the two established Italian American politicians. Taveras won 49.1 percent of the citywide vote, John Lombardi finished second with 29 percent, and Steven Costantino garnered 20 percent of the total vote. A ward-level analysis of Taveras's electoral victory reveals some interesting findings. Taveras won eleven of the fifteen wards, indicating his electoral strength across many parts of the city. Taveras's victories included the Fifth Ward (Mount Pleasant) and the Seventh Ward (Silver Lake), once the centers of Irish and Italian political power in the city (Orr and Nordlund 2013). Faced with two prominent and experienced Italian American opponents, the Taveras campaign built an electoral coalition composed of the city's diverse minority population and liberal whites. In fact, Taveras performed best in the predominantly white wards in the city's East Side. Taveras's electoral coalition was anchored by very strong support from the city's upper-income and liberal white community. Taveras also did well in South Providence, where Providence's Latino population is concentrated. Ward-level analysis of vote returns shows that Taveras's electoral coalition was dominant in the city's affluent, white, liberal wards and wards with large populations of Latinos and African Americans (Orr and Nordlund 2013).

The Postindustrial City and Fiscal Stress: Saving Providence from Bankruptcy

After his election in 2010, Taveras was confronted immediately with the realities of the city's fiscal crisis, which he likened to a "Category 5 Hurricane" (Donnis 2011). Shortly after taking office, Mayor Taveras established a municipal finance review panel to examine the fiscal health of the city. In February 2011, just a month into his first term as the mayor of Providence, Rhode Island, Taveras learned from the review panel that he had inherited a city budget with a huge structural deficit, an imbalance between revenues and expenditures. Taveras recalled years later that his administration was constrained by city's poor fiscal capacity. "You just simply don't have the funds to do everything you want to do," he lamented (Taveras 2014).

The review panel made several findings. First, it projected a deficit of $70 million for the 2011 fiscal year and $110 million for the 2012 fiscal year in a budget of $640 million (City of Providence 2011b). Second, it found that the city's 2011 revenue projections were $17.4 million short of the budgeted amount. Third, it found that salaries, overtime, and other labor-related costs exceeded the budgeted amounts. Fourth, it noted that the city had relied too much on "one-time fixes to address ongoing expenses" (City of Providence 2011b, p. 4). Finally, it noted that the city's pension fund, which covers all city employees except teachers (who are covered under the state teachers' retirement system), was seriously underfunded and described the liability as a "significant financial challenge facing the city."

The panel stressed that in order to get Providence's fiscal house in order, the city must "aggressively pursue pension reform measures to contain the growing annual required contributions" (City of Providence 2011b, p. 3). Taveras used the municipal finance review panel's report to explain to the public why the city had to pursue significant changes to avoid a fiscal train wreck. He held a series of community meetings, called "Fiscal Honesty Forums," to explain the depth of city's fiscal stress. He plainly stated that in order to close the huge deficit, everyone in the city had to make major sacrifices. In his 2011 budget address to the city council, Taveras outlined his plan of action, calling for "shared sacrifice" that "will be painful for all, but necessary to return our city to firm financial footing" (City of Providence 2011a).

Taveras's fiscal plan to close the two-year deficit and to bring Providence municipal government to long-term financial solvency included tackling the city's huge unfunded pensions. Part of the mayor's fiscal plan involved moving retirees who were eligible to Medicare even though their contract provided city-sponsored health-care coverage. Some of the retirees sued, arguing that the city was reneging on a contractual agreement, and won in state court. The judge ruled that this move violated "constitutionally-protected contracts with the retirees." The court ruling was a major setback for Taveras and for the first time publicly raised the possibility of the city filing for Chapter 9 bankruptcy. In February 2012, Taveras delivered a speech devoted to the city's fiscal crisis and directed it at the retirees (City of Providence 2012). "Either the retirees will accept a suspension of their guaranteed yearly raises and changes in their health care . . . or have their full pensions slashed drastically in bankruptcy court," Taveras declared (City of Providence 2012, p. 2). Taveras also criticized the judge's ruling. The ruling, the mayor said, "has pushed the city to the brink of bankruptcy by a creating an additional $8 million hole in the city budget. Every advisor tells me I should never utter that word, because [municipal bond] rating agencies are listening—but the truth is that we are running out of choices and everything is on the table" (City of Providence 2012, p. 2).

Taveras began to turn up the public pressure on the unions and the retirees. In March 2012, Taveras addressed a huge crowd of retired city workers at a town-hall meeting (Schikowski 2012). Providence officials rented a large ballroom just outside the city limits to gather former firefighters, police officers, secretaries, laborers, and other city workers to discuss the city's finances. Taveras told the crowd of concerned retirees that without a meaningful negotiated agreement about pensions and cost-of-living adjustments (COLAs), the city would be forced to file for bankruptcy.

"We cannot solve our fiscal problems without permanent, meaningful and difficult structural change. It is time to suspend COLAs for all our retirees," the mayor told the retirees (Schikowski 2012). A few months later, the city announced that it had reached a negotiated agreement with the city's unions and representatives of the city's retirees.

The agreement was considered far reaching by many observers. At the heart of the city's reforms were significant reductions in COLAs. The majority of city retirees receive a 3 percent annual COLA, but increases for 775 police and firefighters who retired in the late 1980s and early 1990s— 27 percent of all retired city workers—were 5 to 6 percent each year. A pension with a compounding 5 percent annual COLA doubles in sixteen years; at 6 percent, the pension benefit doubles in twelve to thirteen years. The agreement eliminated the 5–6 percent COLAs but also suspended all COLAs for ten years and capped annual increases at 3 percent after the suspension. Another provision required retirees to enroll in Medicare once they became eligible. In all, the reforms would reduce the city's $903 million unfunded pension liability by $178 million. Mayor Taveras announced that the agreement with the retirees rescued the city from the brink of fiscal collapse.

> We have saved Providence from collapse and built a solid fiscal foundation upon which we are ready to grow our City's economy. That progress has only been possible because of the collective efforts and shared sacrifice of so many. I am grateful to Providence's retirees, police officers, firefighters and municipal employees for making difficult sacrifices to help save our City. When we come together, there is nothing we cannot accomplish. (Taveras 2013a)

Facing a $110 million budget deficit, Taveras negotiated settlements on municipal pensions, secured increased payments in lieu of taxes from some of the city's largest nonprofits, and raised taxes. Although general city financial decisions do not necessarily imply any Latino-based policy agenda, Taveras acknowledged his awareness of his ethnicity in his expectations as the city's leader. He later explained, "I didn't want the first Latino mayor of Providence to be the one who brought the city into bankruptcy" (McDaid 2013).

Taveras's speeches and press releases show that he emphasized his efforts in fiscal responsibility, along with public education, economic development, and other quality-of-life issues. Taveras's 2013 State of the City speech focused broadly on seven policy areas: economic development, education, public safety, city services, housing and infrastructure, health and sustainability, and arts and culture (Taveras 2013b). No goals articulated by Taveras in his State of the City speeches were specifically Latino based, but policies that Taveras highlighted matched the issues of the economy and education that Latino community leaders in Providence said were of top importance to Latinos.

In interviews, Providence's Latino community leaders mostly praised Taveras's leadership as effective for Latinos and well balanced for the city's needs. When asked to name Taveras's top policy initiative or program, most community leaders interviewed listed the budget crisis he inherited upon assuming office. One leader described this by saying that Taveras's "number one policy would be fiscal responsibility—making sure the city's books are in order, and we are not going into bankruptcy." One interviewee likewise noted Taveras's role in the fiscal crisis as important to the future of Latinos in politics in Providence. "He has the understanding that because he is the first Latino mayor, everyone has been focused on him. And because of the work he does, it is going to affect the possibility of electing another Latino mayor."

Although Latino community leaders widely praised Taveras in interviews and understood that he had to address a major financial crisis, he also received criticism from the city's Latino community. One of the key criticisms centered on the lack of jobs and high-level appointments for Latino residents. Latinos in Providence and other cities, like every racial and ethnic group before them, expected that the first Latino mayor would provide jobs for their community. However, the erosion of affirmative-action policies and fiscal stress in the city—both common characteristics of the postindustrial city—presented Taveras with limited opportunities to hire Latinos. Taveras was aware of the expectations the Latino community had for his mayoralty. He was also aware that historically, in Providence and elsewhere, other groups had similar expectations when their coethnics were elected mayor for the first time. However, Taveras mentioned that fiscal constraints limited his ability to provide job opportunities to Latinos and added:

> The expectations were high, and I think one of the more challenging things has been that I've had to be mayor during difficult economic times. City employment has been a source of upward mobility for minorities or ethnic groups throughout history. The Irish get in. The Italians get in. I had to reduce the workforce by about 10 percent. . . . And while we've had the most diverse class

in police history, and the two most diverse classes in fire department history . . . there's still less opportunities. When you reduce
the workforce, that's two hundred people that could have had jobs
that don't have jobs. (Taveras 2014)

Despite the limitations on the mayor's ability to hire coethnics, members of the Latino and black communities argued that the mayor could have
done more to hire people of color, particularly blacks and Latinos, on his
staff. This criticism was also extended to Taveras's successor, Jorge Elorza.
Critics argued that despite the hiring constraints, previous administrations
had been more diverse than the Taveras and Elorza administrations. Jim
Vincent, president of the Providence NAACP, said that former mayor Cicilline "hired more blacks in high ranking positions than Taveras and Elorza
combined" (Nagle 2015).

In addition to complaints about hiring practices, Taveras was also criticized for a number of decisions concerning recreation centers that angered community groups. In 2013, Taveras proposed to close several pools
in the city as a cost-saving measure. His move to close the pools led to widespread criticism, particularly from communities of color. City councilman
Davian Sanchez, who represented a ward where one of the swimming pools
was scheduled to be closed, stated that the closing of the neighborhood pool
meant that "we have a mayor that is against our kids," a claim that Taveras
rejected (Pina and Pina 2013). As a result of the political pressure, the swimming pool at the Davey Lopes Recreation Center was not closed, but the
proposed closings did create tension between Taveras and some of the city's
predominantly black and Latino neighborhoods.

Two major incidents that sparked criticism early in his administration concerned public schools. First, in February 2011, Taveras's administration sent firing notices to nearly all of Providence's almost two
thousand teachers. A Rhode Island regulation requires that teachers must
be notified by March 1 of each year if their position may be in jeopardy.
Although three-fourths were expected to be retained, teachers had to reap-
ply and be evaluated. This brought national attention and stern criticism
from teachers' unions. Next, in March 2011, Taveras announced plans to
close five public schools to save costs. Some of the schools were located in
Latino communities. However, after these incidents, Taveras's reputation on
education policy rebounded. For example, his administration was recognized for winning over $11 million for the Providence schools during his
time as mayor, which included a $5 million grant from Bloomberg Philan-
thropies for the Providence Talks program, which helps develop language
skills in low-income families with young children.

Conclusion

In 2011, when Angel Taveras took office as the first Latino mayor of Providence, he broke a long succession of Irish and Italian mayors who had controlled the office since the late nineteenth and early twentieth centuries. In April 2012, just over a year after taking office, Mayor Taveras held a ceremony in city hall celebrating the unveiling of the restored painting of former mayor Patrick J. McCarthy (1907–1909). McCarthy was born in Ireland. In 1907, he became the first foreign-born mayor of Providence. Taveras announced that McCarthy's portrait would hang prominently over the mantel in the mayor's office. The portrait ceremony allowed the new mayor to pay homage to the city's Irish American heritage. Taveras acknowledged that as the city's first Latino mayor, he found it politically expedient to provide symbolic tributes to show respect to the city's longtime Irish and Italian history. Displaying McCarthy's large portrait also allowed Taveras to correct what he said was a common misperception among Providence residents that he was born outside the United States. "I like telling people . . . I wasn't foreign born. I was born in New York" (Taveras 2014).

Taveras was elected as the city's first Latino mayor during an economic downturn. Throughout his term as mayor, he concentrated on closing a huge structural deficit in the city's budget. Hence Taveras governed during a period of municipal retrenchment. He spent a considerable amount of time explaining to the public the nature of the city's structural deficit. He faced several months of negotiating with various public-sector unions over issues related to wages, health care, and pension reform. He had to close several public schools, many of which were located in predominantly Latino neighborhoods. Voters, business leaders, state officials, and bond markets especially look to mayors to provide leadership on matters related to the city government's fiscal policy. Fuchs's (1992, p. 3) observation that "the mayor in most cities is the key fiscal decision-maker and the final arbiter of budgetary decisions" remains true. Mayor Taveras's leadership helped saved the city of Providence from bankruptcy.

Taveras's willingness to tackle the city's budget crisis earned him broad citywide approval. Indeed, throughout his term as mayor, public opinion surveys consistently showed that Taveras held the highest job-approval rating among all the state's top elected officials. Although the school closings in Providence and the pension-reform plan were controversial, Taveras emerged as the state's most popular politician. In the fall of 2013, Taveras's approval rating stood at 63.9 percent. In November 2013, he announced his candidacy for governor of Rhode Island.

Despite his positive statewide approval ratings, Taveras lost his bid for
the governorship in a three-way Democratic primary to State Treasurer
Gina Raimondo. Although there were several factors that may have contributed to Taveras's defeat, our analysis suggests that racial and ethnic
politics played a significant role in the outcome of the gubernatorial
race. Taveras's willingness to tackle the city's budget crisis earned him
high marks citywide and statewide, but his inability to meet the expectations of the Latino community on the issues of jobs and appointments,
schools, and community centers played an important role in his unsuccessful
effort to become governor of Rhode Island. In the primary, Gina Raimondo
gained more votes in Providence than Angel Taveras (41 percent to 39.8
percent). The city's eastside voters (white liberals) supported Raimondo
over Taveras.

The Latino community played a role in Gina Raimondo's victory in Providence. Several prominent leaders from Providence's Latino community,
including city councilwoman Sabina Matos, state representative Grace
Diaz, and longtime community leader Melba Depeña, supported Raimondo.
In addition, Victor Capellan, who had been an early supporter of Taveras
during his campaign for mayor, campaigned for Clay Pell, the eventual
third-place finisher. Thus the coalition of Latinos that made the Taveras
mayoralty possible faced a huge challenge in his campaign for governor.

The Taveras mayoralty helps illustrate the challenges of governance in
the postindustrial city. The Irish and Italian mayors in the machine era relied mainly on their coethnics for electoral support. In return, coethnics
benefited from city patronage. During the redevelopment period, most
black mayors relied mostly on African American voters for their electoral
success. Although patronage and employment opportunities were not as
available in the redevelopment period as in the industrial period, black
mayors were able to rely on affirmative-action policies to provide employment opportunities to black residents in their cities. In both the industrial
and redevelopment periods, a reliance on coethnics for electoral support
and the expectation that the support would translate into favored status
for the coethnic group were established features of city politics.

The political environment in the postindustrial city differs in significant ways from those of earlier periods. However, our study suggests that
despite efforts to appeal to the entire city and minimize overt connections
to the Latino community, the success of Latino mayors may depend on
a lasting feature of city politics: the ability of mayors to deliver to their
coethnic group.

Despite his defeat in the 2014 Democratic primary for the governorship,
Mayor Taveras provided a path and a model for future Latino mayors in

Providence. In 2014, Providence elected its second Latino mayor, Jorge Elorza. Elorza, of Guatemalan descent, followed a trajectory similar to that of Taveras. A Harvard-trained lawyer, Elorza was a law professor and became involved in several community organizations before running for mayor in 2014. To win the mayoralty, Elorza relied on the East Side/South Side coalition that Cicilline and Taveras had relied on for victory.

However, whereas Cicilline and Taveras relied on strong support from the heavily Latino wards in the South Side, Elorza relied on moderate support from the Latino strongholds. Although he won Ward 9, he lost in Ward 10 to his opponent, former Providence mayor Vincent "Buddy" Cianci. Thus, while the Taveras administration may have made it possible for Elorza to become mayor, Taveras's challenges in his relations with the Latino community may have also made it more difficult for Elorza to win in the city's Latino neighborhoods. Elorza's success and the success of future Latino mayors in Providence may largely depend on their ability to meet the demands of the Latino electorate in both electoral and governance stages.

Note

1. Providence's black community is small but diverse, like the Latino community. Some blacks trace their heritage back for centuries; others' families came during the Great Black Migration from the South to northern cities. The community also includes black immigrants from Cape Verde, Liberia, and Nigeria.

REFERENCES

About Angel. 2010. http://www.angelforprovidence.com/en/about-angel.html.

Austin, Algernon. 2011. "Hispanic Unemployment Highest in Northeast Metropolitan Areas." Washington, D.C.: Economic Policy Institute.

Bakst, Charles M. 2003. "Martinez to Keep Carcieri in Touch." *Providence Journal*, January 26, H-1.

Brito, Marisabel. 2010a. "'El Mismo Golpe' resaltó a dominicanos sobresalientes en programación desde Providence." *Acontecer Latino*, August 14.

———. 2010b. "'Mujeres con Ángel' gana fuerza y seguidoras en Providence." *Acontecer Latino*, August 8.

City of Providence. 2011a. "Mayor Taveras' Budget Address." Providence, RI: City of Providence. http://www.gcpvd.org/2011/05/02/mayor-taveras-budget-address/.

———. 2011b. "Report of the Municipal Finances Review Panel." Providence, RI: City of Providence.

———. 2012. "Mayor Taveras' Fiscal Address: Saving Providence, How We Got Here; Shared Sacrifice." Providence, RI: City of Providence.

Cornwell, Elmer. 1960. "Party Absorption of Ethnic Groups: The Case of Providence, RI." *Social Forces* 38:205–210.

Daoust, Norma L. 1985. "Building the Democratic Party: Black Voting in Providence in the 1930s." *Rhode Island History* 44, no. 3:81–88.

Donnis, Ian. 2011. "Rhode Island Tip Sheet: Providence's 'Category 5 Hurricane.'" *On Politics*, Rhode Island National Public Radio, March 11.

Farris, Emily. 2014. "Latino Leadership in City Hall." Ph.D. diss., Brown University.

Filindra, Alexandra, and Marion Orr. 2013. "Anxieties of a Peaceful Transition: Ethnic Competition and the Election of the First Latino Mayor in Providence, RI." *Urban Affairs Review* 49, no. 1:3–31.

Fuchs, Ester. 1992. *Mayors and Money: Fiscal Policy in New York and Chicago*. Chicago: University of Chicago Press.

Itzigsohn, José. 2009. *Encountering American Faultlines: Race, Class, and the Dominican Experience in Providence*. New York: Russell Sage Foundation.

Marcelo, Philip. 2010. "After Delay, 4 Providence Mayoral Candidates Get to the Issues." *Providence Journal*, July 21.

McDaid, John. 2013. "Northeast Young Dems Convene in Providence." RI Future.org, May 19. http://www.rifuture.org/northeast-young-democrats-convene-in -providence/.

McLoughlin, William. 1986. *Rhode Island Politics*. New York: Norton.

Milkovits, Amanda. 2002. "Latinos Give Cicilline Victory." *Providence Journal*, September 11, C1.

Nagle, Kate. 2015. "Elorza Administration's Top Staff Are All White." *GoLocalProv*, April 1.

Orr, Marion, and Carrie Nordlund. 2013. "Political Transformation in Providence: The Election of Mayor Angel Taveras." In *21st Century Urban Race Politics: Representing Minorities as Universal Interests*, edited by Ravi Perry, 1–12. Bingley, UK: Emerald Group.

Orr, Marion, and Darrell West. 2002. "Citizens' Views on Urban Revitalization: The Case of Providence, Rhode Island." *Urban Affairs Review* 37:397–419.

Pew Hispanic Center. 2002. "Latino Growth in Metropolitan America: Changing Patterns, New Locations." Washington, DC: Brookings Institution. http://pewhispanic .org/files/reports/10.pdf.

Pina, Tatiana, and Alisha Pina. 2013. "Push under Way to Reopen Davey Lopes Pool; Taveras Won't Budge on Closing." *Providence Journal*, October 21.

Rich, Wilbur C. 2000. "Vincent Cianci and Boosterism in Providence, Rhode Island." In *Governing Middle-Sized Cities: Studies in Mayoral Leadership*, edited by James. R. Bowers and Wilbur C. Rich, 197–214. Boulder, CO: Lynne Rienner.

Sabar, Ariel. 2000. "Latino Power Shows at Polls." *Providence Journal*, September 14.

Scharfenberg, David. 2010. "The First Latino Mayor?" *Providence Phoenix*, April 15.

Schikowski, Erin. 2012. "Bankrupting Providence." *The Nation*, March 28.

Silver, Hilary. 2001. "Dominicans in Providence: Transnational Intermediaries and Community Institution Building." *Focaal: European Journal of Anthropology* 38:103–123.

Smith, Gregory. 2001. "Fast-Growing Latino Population Given Better Voice in City Hall." *Providence Journal*, October 25.

Sorrentino, Mary Ann. 2010. "The Death of Irish-Italian Political Entitlement." *Providence Phoenix*, November 5.

Spitzer, Kerry, and Sol Carbonell. 2012. "The Growth of Latino Small Businesses in Providence." Boston, MA: Federal Reserve Bank of Boston.

Stanton, Mike. 2003. *The Prince of Providence: The Rise and Fall of Buddy Cianci*. New York: Random House.

Sterne, Evelyn Savidge. 2004. *Ballots and Bibles: Ethnic Politics and the Catholic Church in Providence*. Ithaca, NY: Cornell University Press.

Taubman Center for Public Policy and American Institutions. 2010. "Providence City Survey, September 2010." Providence, RI: Brown University.

Taveras, Angel 2013a. "Economic Development Report." Providence, RI: City of Providence. http://www.gcpvd.org/2013/03/27/developing-mayors-economic-report/

———. 2013b. *Mayor Taveras' 2013 State of the City Address: Providence Is Recovering*. http://www.providenceri.com/mayor/mayor-taveras-2013-state-of-the-city- address.

———. 2014. Personal Interview with the authors, December 1, Providence, Rhode Island.

IV Latino Mayors, Urban Voters, and the American City

9

Latino Mayors and the Politics of the Postindustrial City

MARION ORR AND DOMINGO MOREL

O
ne of the most dramatic political changes in American urban
politics in the past thirty-five years has been the rise of Latino
politicians in city hall, including election as mayors. The case studies in this book have examined Latino mayors in five large cities—Denver,
Hartford, Los Angeles, Providence, and San Antonio—and Miami-Dade
County. What does it mean to be a Latino mayor of a city? A central theme
of this volume is that Latino mayors have come to power during the era of
the postindustrial city. Latino mayors are exercising executive powers and
heading cities politically at a time different from that of earlier mayors and
in a different urban context of constraints and opportunities.

This chapter captures some of the contextual features greeting today's
Latino mayors. First, we examine why American cities have elected Latino
mayors and explain how community organizing has played an important
role in the nascent Latino political incorporation. We then discuss some of
the structural and economic limitations that hinder the capacity of Latino
mayors to advance economic opportunities for their Latino constituents.
Next, we examine the myriad racial and class conflicts prevalent in the
postindustrial city, which Latino mayors cannot safely ignore. We conclude
the volume with a discussion of the role of Latino mayors in national progressive politics.

Latino Population Growth and the Postindustrial City

As we discussed in Chapter 1, the Latino population is projected to grow in the future throughout much of the United States. "The demography is relentless," exclaimed Barreto and Segura. "Live births contribute more to population growth among Latinos now than immigration does, and over 93% of Latinos under age eighteen are citizens of the United States. More than 73, 000 of these young people turn eighteen and become eligible to vote every month!" (Barreto and Segura, 2014, p. 3). As the Latino population continues to grow, especially as a result of native births, the Latino proportion of the electorate in many of our nation's large cities will expand, and we should expect Latinos to play an even greater role in city politics. For example, Latinos constitute 25 percent or more of the total population in twelve of the nation's twenty largest cities. In general, elected officials share the race or ethnicity of the majority population in the jurisdiction. As the electorate has shifted to reflect the changing demography of cities, the increasing size of the Latino population has given Latino politicians an additional opportunity to exercise political influence and clout within cities.

Since 2000, Latino mayoral candidates have mounted credible candidacies in a number of major cities. For example, Latino candidates have sought the mayor's office in Houston, New York City, and San Diego. In Chicago, Jesus "Chuy" Garcia, a Mexican American, finished second in Chicago's 2015 mayoral election, forcing a head-to-head runoff vote between himself and incumbent mayor Rahm Emanuel. Garcia lost but received a respectable 44 percent of the vote against Mayor Emanuel. As the nation's demographics continue to shift, we predict that more cities will likely elect Latino mayors. For instance, local observers predict that Newark, New Jersey, a city governed for generations by black mayors, will soon elect a Latino mayor (Gillespie 2013, pp. 56–58).

Community Organizing and Latino Urban Politics

If it is true that demographics drives city politics, then why are there not more elected Latino politicians? As we observed in Chapter 1, demographic change does not automatically translate into electoral clout. Research has shown that although Latino populations are rapidly growing, Latinos are underrepresented in public offices; that is, the share of elected officials who are Latinos is smaller than the share of the population that is Latino (Hero et al. 2000). Their underrepresentation may be explained by Latinos' low rate of political participation stemming from a large population of those who are underage, first-generation citizens, or noncitizens. Another critical factor may be the lack of organized community groups in some cities. As the case studies in this volume have shown, community organizing has played an important role in providing the space and resources for Latino communities to engage in local politics (see Orr 2007; M. B. Rogers 1988; Smock 2004; Su 2012). Community organizing has played an instrumental role in opening the way for the election of Latino local officials, including Latino mayors.

Several of the Latino mayors covered in this volume were the first of their ethnic group to be elected mayor in their particular city. They won the mayoralty after community organizations addressed the lack of governmental response to the public policy and quality-of-life concerns of the Latino community. Community organizing became the kindling for igniting the electoral energies of Latino voters. Community organizing, for example, was influential in opening an electoral path for the election of Henry Cisneros in San Antonio. As Heywood Sanders describes in Chapter 3, a powerful Latino community-based organization, Communities Organized for Public Service (COPS), formed in the 1970s after Latino leaders learned that for decades, the city of San Antonio had diverted funds targeted for improving drainage and streets in Latino communities to the white and affluent Northside. This revelation and the Latino community's reaction to it became the mechanism for changing how San Antonio officials prioritized the distribution of funds to support infrastructure improvements. COPS's organizing and mobilization of Latino communities in the 1970s set the stage for the election of Henry Cisneros in 1981 as San Antonio's first Latino mayor in modern history. In Miami-Dade County, the Cuban American community was jolted into community organizing and political mobilization after the county's voters in late 1980 overwhelmingly approved an antibilingual referendum. After the adoption of the referendum, resources from Cuban American–led organizations, which had long focused on confronting Fidel Castro, were redeployed to organize Miami-Dade's Cuban community to address local politics and policy (Portes and Stepick 1993, p. 147). "The exiles naturalized en masse and lined up at the polls to vote for their own candidates" (Portes and Stepick 1993, p. 149). Today, Cuban Americans are the "dominant participants in both municipal and county politics" in Miami-Dade (Warren and Moreno 2003, p. 287). In Providence and Hartford, Latino advocacy groups and community organizations played key roles in energizing and mobilizing the Latino community. However, in Chapter 4 on Mayor Federico Peña, Robert Preuhs shows that Latino community-based organization have not been very active in Denver.

Several of the Latino mayors in this study began their political careers by participating in community-based organizations and labor unions. Ellen Shiau writes in Chapter 5 that participating in local community organizations politicized Los Angeles mayor Antonio Villaraigosa. Before becoming mayor, Villaraigosa was part of the student organization, Movimiento Estudiantil Chicana/o de Aztlan and the immigrants' rights organization, Centros de Acción Social Autónomo. He also became a union organizer for United Teachers Los Angeles and served as president of the Los Angeles chapter of the American Civil Liberties Union and the American Federation of Government Employees. Similarly, in Chapter 6 on Hartford, Stefanie Chambers and Emily Farris note that the city's first Latino mayor, Eddie Perez, was executive director of a community organization in Hartford before running for mayor. In short, community organizations were important training grounds for several of the Latino mayors covered in this volume. As we emphasize later, community organizing will continue to play an important and significant role in Latino local politics, especially in the context of the election of Latino mayors.

Latinos and the Changing Opportunity Structure in the Postindustrial City

Like the Irish, Italian, and African American communities before them, Latinos expect that Latino mayors will address issues and needs of the Latino community. Millions of immigrants from Mexico, Central America, and the Caribbean migrated to Los Angeles, Providence, Miami, Denver, Hartford, San Antonio, and many other cities expecting unrestricted economic opportunities. Despite their expectations, the less labor-intensive political economy of the postindustrial city presents a different challenge for some newcomers. Unlike the industrial city, the postindustrial city has a serious job-development problem. This was also true for the urban-redevelopment era of the 1970s and 1980s. Today's Latino mayors are in the vortex of this economic transformation. As we discuss next, compared with mayors who governed during the industrial era, Latino mayors face institutional constraints that limit their capacity to provide opportunities for their Latino constituents.

The Limits of Latino Mayoral Power

In a now-classic article, Jeffrey Pressman (1972, p. 511) argued that effective mayoral leadership required several "preconditions." One of them was that the mayor had to have "jurisdiction within the city government" over the policy areas that were significant and vital to the operation and function of the city. The issue today is the degree to which Latino communities benefit from the election of Latino mayors. Are the political structures and current economic situations of cities stacked against the types of political changes that Latino mayors' constituencies demand? We know that the situation is dramatically different from that during the period of the industrial city. Steven Erie (1988) noted that the "progressive" reforms adopted in the early twentieth century in many cities (at-large elections, direct primary elections, nonpartisan elections, city-manager systems, and expanded civil service coverage) were designed to wrest political control from the Irish machines and rid the cities of partisanship and corruption. The legacy of these reform structures, however, is that they put severe limits on the ability of groups who would control city hall decades later to translate political power into group social and economic advancement. For example, at-large electoral systems, a popular reform, made it difficult for minority groups to gain representation on city councils (Welch 1990).

As Carlos Cuéllar explains in Chapter 2, council-manager systems are prevalent in the U.S. regions where large percentages of Latinos reside. Under the city-manager system, the mayor possesses limited administrative, appointive, or budgetary powers. This is the dominant form of government in many southwestern and Sunbelt cities, including San Diego, Dallas, San Antonio, San Jose, Sacramento, Long Beach, Las Vegas, Tucson, Austin, and Forth Worth (Ross and Levine 2006). City-manager systems are also widely employed in the South, the region of the country that is presently experiencing the largest percentage Latino population growth (Fraga et al. 2010, p. 6).

In cities with a strong-mayor form of government, the Latino mayor has clear-cut administrative, appointive, and budgetary authority. Mayors in Providence and Denver have long had strong institutional powers. In Hartford and Miami-Dade, voters only recently granted more authority to the mayor. San Antonio voters adopted a city-manager system in 1951 after years of political battle between city reformers and the city's dominant political machine. Heywood Sanders argues that the mayor of San Antonio is constrained by the views and policy positions of the city manager. Voter-imposed term limits also constrain San Antonio's mayor. In Chapter 5 on Mayor Antonio Villaraigosa, Ellen Shiau maintains that the structural limitations of Los Angeles's office of the mayor (the mayor's office is statutorily weak, and municipal governance is fragmented) limited Villaraigosa's ability to make substantive changes in policy and administration. In short, the cases in this volume show that not all Latino mayors are equal structurally, and that some are clearly not first among officials in city government.

Black mayors were able to overcome some of the institutional constraints through the use of affirmative-action programs (Eisinger 1982). For example, the Progressive Era civil service reforms established a process of written and oral exams for municipal employment and a tenure and seniority system for long-term city employees. When African American mayors took office for the first time in the 1960s and 1970s, many of them implemented race-conscious affirmative-action plans to diversify the municipal government's workforce and to remedy a history of systematic racial discrimination in hiring and promotion in city-government employment. In addition, black-led urban regimes adopted and implemented minority set-aside programs, requiring that a percentage of government procurement contracts be reserved for minority businesses. However, a series of U.S. Supreme Court decisions have nearly dismantled affirmative-action programs and have made it difficult for minorities to claim group-based or institutional discrimination. For example, in 1984, in *Firefighter Local 1784 v. Stotts*, a case from Memphis, the Supreme Court ruled that under Title VII of the Civil Rights Act of 1964, a court may not order an employer to protect the jobs of recently hired black employees at the expense of whites who have more seniority. In 1989, in *J. A. Croson v. City of Richmond*, the U.S. Supreme Court declared Richmond's minority set-aside ordinance unconstitutional (Drake and Holsworth 1996). Rodney Hero (1992, p. 97) argued that judicial rulings like the one in *Croson* make clear that the Supreme Court has put Latinos "in a difficult position to make certain legal claims and arguments." The judicial rulings impose additional institutional constraints on the capacity of Latino mayors to leverage economic opportunities for Latino voters via the public sector.

Work and Economic Restructuring in the Postindustrial City

In addition to the institutional limitations of the mayor's office, economic restructuring in the nation has dramatically altered the nature of work and the structure of economic opportunity, in particular for the most recent Latino immigrants. For instance, during the industrial era, mayors worked closely with machine bosses to steer jobs and benefits to various coethnics. City dwellers could find jobs in the growing industrial plants or the many small businesses that dotted the urban landscape. Douglas Rae's (2003) look at New Haven mayor Frank Rice's (1910–1917) tenure helps us understand that mayors are advantaged or disadvantaged by the city's context. For Mayor Rice and other mayors of the industrial era, "the city's economic and social strength was an inherited fortune" (Rae 2003, p. 209). This was the era when cities occupied a privileged position in the nation's political economy. In the postindustrial city, the place of cities in the economy has changed.

First, work in the postindustrial city is increasingly service oriented. The employment structure of the postindustrial city is bifurcated into many well-paying skilled service-sector jobs for those with training and education and many more low-skilled, low-wage, dead-end jobs for those with little training or education. Second, the benefits of work—wages and fringe benefits—have diminished. During the 1970s and 1980s, business leaders were successful in changing labor laws, helping weaken labor unions (Milkman 2006). The result was a sharp drop in union density, or the percentage of unionized workers. Today, fewer than 8 percent of private-sector workers are union members. Deunionization affected autoworkers, steelworkers, associated heavy-industry employees, and a wide swath of other workers, including service workers. For example, from the 1940s until the 1970s, janitors who cleaned downtown office buildings in Los Angeles were heavily unionized (Milkman 2006, pp. 26–76). "In those days most L.A. janitors were native-born whites and African Americans. Unionization brought them middle-class wages, extensive fringe benefits, and decent working conditions for the first time. These gains were rolled back in the 1970s, however, when the city's building services industry was radically restructured and 'flexible' employment arrangements based on highly competitive subcontracting gradually replaced the old union-based regime" (Milkman 2006, pp. 6–7). After unionism was effectively killed, wages, fringe benefits, and job security for janitors declined precipitously, and native-born workers left the industry. Employers then turned to Los Angeles's growing immigrant population to fill the vacancies. By the early 1990s—near the beginning of the postindustrial era—most of Los Angeles's downtown office buildings were cleaned by immigrants from Mexico and Central America, many of them undocumented (Waldinger et al. 1998). Significantly, Milkman (2006, pp. 187–190) observed that what happened to the janitors in Los Angeles was not isolated to Southern California nor confined to the cleaning industry. These changes, she argued, "impacted cities nationally and globally (Milkman 2006, p. 7).

Finally, the move toward a service-sector economy transformed the nature of work in the postindustrial city. There has been a pronounced expansion of "casual" employment and "informal" work (Sassen 2001, pp. 289–305). Casualization of the workforce occurs whenever workers are employed in a casual, temporary, or otherwise nonpermanent and non-full-time capacity. These workers typically are subjected to lower pay, barred from the right to join a union, and denied medical and other benefits. For example, in a service-sector economy, there is considerable expansion of part-time work (Sassen 2001, p. 291). There has also been a marked increase in "informal" work (e.g., lawn-care and home-care providers and au pairs). As gentrification has increased, the renovation and alteration of old homes have helped support an informal economy in the construction trades. In many U.S. cities, immigrant workers from Mexico, Latin America, and the Caribbean are central players in the casual and informal postindustrial economy.

The millions of Latino immigrants who poured into the city arrived after globalization had restructured the economy and shifted more and more jobs to the service sector. Indeed, the huge growth in the U.S. Latino immigrant population is closely intertwined with the powerful economic forces that have helped shape the postindustrial city—rapid technological change and globalization. Manufacturing jobs with good wages and fringe benefits that had been central to the economy of the industrial city have disappeared. Innovation and human capital development are essential components driving the economy of postindustrial cities (Florida 2002). Research and development, high technology, information technology, entertainment, media, design, advertising, providing databases, and legal counsel are the kinds of good-paying jobs that dominate the postindustrial economy. People with college degrees have a far easier time finding these types of jobs. Today, the postindustrial urban dweller is not nearly as likely as his or her immigrant predecessors to find a job with decent wages and benefits. The rise of postindustrial capitalism and the increase in global competition have put a premium on educated workers.

Education in the Postindustrial City

The case studies in this volume show that Latino mayors have put public education and school reform high on their action agenda. This is a dramatic political change from the postwar redevelopment era. With no formal authority over education, most big-city mayors of the redevelopment era strategically put a distance between city hall and public schools and seldom showed interest in them. Their focus was not human capital development but physical redevelopment (Orr 1992). In Boston, St. Louis, Buffalo, Cleveland, Pittsburgh, New York, and Baltimore, so-called "messiah" mayors gained national reputations for revitalizing their city's downtown but did little to improve the schools (Teaford 1990, p. 253). Similarly, the pioneering black mayors elected in Atlanta, Detroit, Newark, Gary, Washington, D.C., Los Angeles, and other cities recognized the limits of mayoral influence on school affairs and duplicated the hands-off approach in their cities (see Rich 1996). The view of Detroit's first black mayor, Coleman A. Young, was perhaps typical of other mayors during the redevelopment period. "The mayor can't do a damn thing in education," Mayor Young explained. "I try to support it all I can. But I try to stay out of things I can't control" (quoted in Orr 1993, p. 119).

As many of the chapters in this volume show, the dynamics between mayors and school districts have changed. Latino mayors have been actively involved in education and school affairs whether or not they have had formal authority in school affairs. For example, in Los Angeles, Mayor Villaraigosa proposed a bold plan to seek mayoral control of the Los Angeles Unified School District. The plan was blocked after vigorous opposition from unions representing teachers and administrators. The California Supreme Court ruled unconstitutional a compromise plan that would have given Mayor Villaraigosa control over a cluster of three high schools. In keeping with its reform tradition, San Antonio's school system is also administratively separate from city hall. Nevertheless, Mayor Julián Castro felt obligated to use his office to promote public education. Once he was elected, Castro pushed for full-day prekindergarten classes for all of the city's four-year-olds and proposed to pay for them by increasing the city's sales tax by one-eighth of a cent. In November 2012, city voters approved the sales-tax hike by a vote of 53.6 percent.

In 2002, when Hartford voters changed the city government from a city-manager to a strong-mayor system, they also approved a charter revision that gave the mayor authority to appoint five members to the nine-member school board. In 2005, when the new provision took effect, Mayor Eddie Perez appointed himself the school board's chairman. At the time, Perez explained that he believed that the city's mayor should be accountable for the success or failure of the city's public schools. In Providence, school-board president Keith Oliveira criticized Mayor Jorge Elorza for being too involved in the school district's affairs. Oliveira eventually resigned when it became clear that that Mayor Elorza, who has the authority to appoint school-board members, was interested in moving the board's leadership in a different direction.

The case studies presented in this volume suggest that Latino mayors will likely be more involved in public education and school reform than mayors of previous eras. The changing demographics of public schools will dictate this interest. In fact, over the past fifteen or more years, a coalition of school reformers, good-government advocates, and business leaders has led a national movement devoted to changing the governance structures of local school systems to give mayors more formal authority over public schools (Henig and Rich 2004; Wong et al. 2007). The postindustrial city is a different context from earlier periods. Making the city appealing to the "creative class" and gentrification have heightened the importance of education and school reform. In addition, political pressure and community mobilization by Latino parents will likely keep education and school reform high on the action agenda of many Latino mayors. Latino mayors must develop ways to work to improve local public education. Their electoral base demands that they do so. National public opinion surveys consistently show that education is one of the top policy issues among Latino voters (Fraga et al., 2012, pp. 386–387). In focus groups, Latinos "indicated that they valued education as a means to facilitate securing gainful employment and achieving upward mobility in the United States generally" (Fraga et al., 2010, p. 64). The tragic story in the shift from the industrial era to a postindustrial economy has been the collapse in real economic opportunity for people who do not continue their education beyond high school. The clear message to workers is to acquire more education. As the American and global economies continue to shift more and more to services and a more educated workforce, education and workforce development will continue to be a major focus for Latino mayors.

Latino Mayors and Managing Group Conflict in the Postindustrial City

In his book on black mayors, Zoltan Hajnal (2007) observed that compared with African American mayors who emerged in the 1960s and 1970s, Latino mayors came to power after less racially divisive election victories. Nevertheless, the postindustrial city is a political environment replete with diverse racial and ethnic groups. Mayors of the postindustrial city must manage lines of racial/ethnic conflict that are more complex than the black-white conflicts that mayors had to manage during the postwar redevelopment period. Next, we explore some of these potential conflicts.

Fiscal Stress, Racial/Ethnic-Group Conflict, and the Postindustrial City

As we noted in Chapter 1, mayors of the redevelopment period governed cities that were often riven by conflict and division between blacks and whites (C. H. Levine 1974). By the 1990s, the relationship between blacks and Latinos in urban politics became a focus of interest (Nelson and Mon-

forti 2005). The preponderance of this research is more suggestive of conflict and competition than of cooperation (Browning, Marshall, and Tabb
1984; McClain 1993; McClain and Karnig 1990). However, the election of
Latino mayors in Denver, Hartford, and Los Angeles, all supported by a
"rainbow coalition" of African American and Latino voters, illustrates in-
stances of mutually beneficial political behavior. Has the division between
blacks and Latinos eased over time?

The answer is unclear. It is possible to argue that black and Latino politicians may understand the efficacy of coalition formation, but their respective constituencies are not there yet. For instance, Denver is a city in
which it would be easy to predict that Latinos would be successful at capturing the mayor's office. However, as Preuhs reports in Chapter 4, since
Frederico Peña's 1987 reelection as mayor of Denver, no other Latino mayoral candidate has been able to win the mayor's office. In 2010, Denver's
Latino, African American, and Asian residents constituted a much larger
percentage of the city's total population than when Federico Peña was
elected mayor in 1983. Denver has long had a sizable liberal white population that has grown larger in recent decades as gentrification has taken
place in historically Latino neighborhoods like La Alma/Lincoln Park
(Clarke 2015). Two African American mayors have been elected since Peña's tenure, but racial/ethnic-bloc voting has prevented development of a
liberal coalition behind a strong Latino candidate.

However, there is no reason to believe that black-Latino cleavage is fro-
zen in place or is the same everywhere. Racial and ethnic conflict ebbs and
flows. For example, in the 2001 mayoral election in Los Angeles, the vast
majority of black voters supported James Hahn, a white politician whose
family had deep roots in the African American community, over Antonio
Villaraigosa (Austin and Middleton 2004). Hahn won the election. However, in a 2005 rematch, "Blacks split their vote between" Mayor Hahn and
Villaraigosa (Sonenshein and Pinkus 2005, p. 717). Villaraigosa won the
election by nearly 20 percentage points. No two cities are the same. Chambers and Farris, in Chapter 6 on Mayors Perez and Segarra, suggest that
black and Latino leaders in Hartford were able to work out an accommodation of sorts. Perez and Segarra were elected by a coalition of Latinos,
white liberals, and African American voters.

Karen Kaufmann (2004) reminded us that racial/ethnic and social
diversity do not automatically lead to group conflict and racial/ethnic competition. Group conflict occurs in a context of scarce resources. Some years
ago, Ladd and Yinger (1989) observed that national economic forces had
imposed significant fiscal hardship on city governments. Cities are required
to balance their budgets. However, since the late 1980s and early 1990s,

cities have found it hard to make revenues keep pace with expenditures. The trend for city revenues has been flat. The long-term trend for assistance from the state and federal governments is down. Revenue growth generally lags behind the growth of city operating costs. Personnel costs and benefits for both current employees and retirees have continued to skyrocket. For example, mayors and other local leaders argue that the financial demands of fully funding public employee pensions threaten the ability of governments to adequately pay for other priorities, including essential public services (Munnell 2012; Orr, Morel, and Farris 2014). City governments have no choice but to do more with less. Doing more with less means that city officials are obliged to make political choices of where to spend and where not to spend the municipal government's limited funds.

What do all these competing choices means for Latino mayors? Although some cities are in better fiscal condition than others, the typical postindustrial city faces fiscal stress (Ladd and Yinger 1989). The experience of Mayor Angel Taveras of Providence illustrates the fiscal challenges many Latino mayors face. As postindustrial cities struggle with fiscal stress, Latino mayors are expected to make the tough fiscal choices. The surge in the Latino population has occurred as cities have grappled with the changing global economy. The demographic changes put pressure on localities to address issues of importance to the changing population. Local police departments, traffic courts, libraries, recreation centers, housing-assistance programs, and the array of other public service providers must prepare to serve the new and growing population. Local libraries, for instance, must begin stocking Spanish or bilingual titles. Like other ethnic/racial groups of previous eras, Latino leaders can be expected to demand that Latinos be appointed to city boards and commissions and be hired as police officers, firefighters, and other city employees. Latino mayors face intense pressure from the expectations of the Latino community. However, given the economy of the postindustrial city, Latino mayors must balance the expectations of their coethnics with the reality of municipal fiscal stress.

When cities experience fiscal stress, and when demands for increased municipal services and spending do not keep pace with city revenues, competition between and among groups for scarce resources increases (Kaufmann 2004). Because race, ethnicity, and class remain heavily embedded in the contours of American urban geography, many local policy decisions have racial/ethnic implications. For Latino mayors, these policy choices are likely to be closely scrutinized. Survey research shows that white and African American voters believed that Latino mayoral candidates would likely have city hall pay more attention to or favor Latinos over other racial/ethnic groups (see Filandra and Orr 2013; Sonenshein and Pinkus 2005).

Gentrification, Class, and the Postindustrial City

Another area of conflict that Latino mayors must manage is the growing community displacement in housing. Poor people, blacks, and Latinos living in the central city and sometimes in historical parts of the city have been displaced by white middle-class residents. Gentrification is much more widespread than it was just a few decades ago. All the mayors covered in this volume governed cities that have neighborhoods undergoing some degree of gentrification. The Boyle Heights neighborhood, a largely Latino community just east of downtown Los Angles, "is facing gentrification pressures" (Shiau, Musso, and Sellers 2015, p. 147). In Denver, the La Alma/Lincoln Park community, once a majority black and Latino neighborhood, has experienced extensive gentrification (Clarke 2015, pp. 72–75). In Miami, artists, craftsmen, graphic designers, and other members of the "creative class" are leaving the high-priced Wynwood neighborhood (once a haven for local artists) for working-class Little Haiti, once a predominantly Caribbean neighborhood in Miami that was showing signs of "impending" gentrification by 2015 (Sokol 2015). Gentrification is also occurring in smaller cities like Providence, where neighborhood associations, working closely with developers and city planners, are transforming the city's West Side, especially in the West End and Armory District neighborhoods (Donnis 2006). Hartford has experienced less gentrification. However, in 2015, the city released a master plan to redevelop land just north of downtown. The city, the University of Connecticut, St. Joseph's University, and Trinity College have all expressed interest in revitalizing the area.

Gentrification is not new. What is new is the "much more aggressive role" played by government to act "as a catalyst to encourage gentrification" (Newman and Wyly 2006, p. 26). Because gentrification often introduces "individuals from a different class and sometimes racial background, gentrification was found to spark clashes that center on differing norms and expectations" (Freeman 2006, pp. 14–15). Tensions between renters and new home owners can occur. Longtime Latino and black home owners living in gentrifying neighborhoods benefit as their home values increase. Nevertheless, many of them resent that their neighborhood is changing culturally. Balancing the needs and concerns of low-income and longtime residents in gentrifying neighborhoods with the imperative of urban economic growth is a thorny political act. We suspect that Latino mayors, because they "often" win office "emphasizing" their "connection to the Latino community," find these conflicts especially difficult (Barreto 2007, p. 427).

Consider, for example, a challenge Mayor Julián Castro faced over gentrification in San Antonio. As mayor, Castro "sought to build partnerships with the city's business leaders and Anglo power structure in order to further local economic development" (M. A. Levine 2015, p. 130). Shortly after his 2010 election, Castro announced a major downtown redevelopment initiative. The plan was designed to promote residential and commercial development in the central core of the city, largely to attract young, educated people to live in the area, as well as economic opportunities. Castro developed a reputation among many community activists as being "too cozy with business and for pushing upscale housing plans that would change the nature of the center city" (M. A. Levine 2015, p. 131). Grassroots leaders argued that Castro's downtown plan ignored the housing needs of San Antonio's poor and working-class residents.

In 2014, the issue of rezoning the Mission Trails Mobile Homes' land on the city's South Side to make way for luxury apartment units came before the San Antonio City Council. The rezoning would clear the way for the sale of the land and the involuntary relocation of nearly three hundred low-income Latino residents. In May 2014, the city council held hearings to consider the rezoning. Dozens of poor Latino residents from Mission Trails, including young children, the elderly, and representatives from advocacy groups, delivered heartfelt and oftentimes teary-eyed requests that the council vote against the rezoning proposal (Baugh 2014). The city council voted 6–4 to rezone the trailer-park land. The decision was controversial and extremely emotional. Mayor Castro, however, reversed course from his usual push for economic development and not only voted against the zoning change but also urged his fellow council members to do the same. "We move mountains to create jobs in the city, we move mountains to preserve our aquifer, we move mountains to save bats, we move mountains to save historic buildings—and we need to move mountains for people," Castro announced (Baugh 2014). Castro argued that the city needed to develop a policy for addressing the issue of displacement for the sake of development. In July 2014, before resigning to become U. S. secretary of housing and urban development, Castro established a task force on gentrification. Mayors are reluctant to support any policy that is likely to deter investment in neighborhoods. Latino mayors will have to work out some sort of political accommodation that will bring capital investment into disadvantaged neighborhoods but minimize or prevent the displacement of poor, working-class Latinos.

We add that as mayors seek to attract middle-class residents, and as more cities experience gentrification, we see a potential source of conflict centered on public schools. In an increasingly bifurcated job market, the stakes are high. However, high-quality education is a scarce commodity in most U.S. urban centers. Middle- and upper-income parents, fearing that their children may not retain their affluence, fight to put and keep their children in the limited number of high-quality public schools (Taylor 2015, 2016). Governors and other state officials are increasingly prodding city officials to improve educational outcomes for minority students or face state takeover of city schools (Morel 2018). Parents of working-class and lower-income Latino students also press for school policies that will enable their children to move up the socioeconomic ladder (Orr and Rogers 2011). For Latino constituents, improving the schools may require increasing English-language services, increasing the number of Latino teachers and administrators, investing in school-community services, and addressing the unique challenges of educating first-generation and low-income popu-lations. These concerns and the investments they require may collide with the education concerns of the middle-class residents the mayors want to lure into the cities. Gentrification will continue. A related line of research might explore how Latino mayors navigate the convergence of gentrifica-tion and public school reform politics. What happens when Latino mayors are faced with competing school demands?

Inequality in the Postindustrial City

Another dimension of the class divide that Latino mayors must manage is the growing concern about rising inequality. At the local level, the issue of inequality has played out in the politics surrounding "living-wage" ordi-nances (Luce 2004). In 1994, a coalition of community-based organizations pushed Baltimore's mayor, Kurt Schmoke, who initially opposed the idea, to adopt the first living-wage law for employees of firms with city contracts (Orr 1999, 2001). Over the next decade, more than one hundred local gov-ernments adopted similar living-wage laws that applied to companies receiving public contracts or subsidies (Dreier 2007; Luce 2004; Pastor, Ben-ner, and Matsuoka 2009). The movement was led by coalitions consisting "chiefly of unions, community-based organizations in low-income mi-nority neighborhoods, immigrants' rights groups, affordable housing advocates, environmental organizations, and networks of liberal churches, synagogues, and mosques" (Meyerson 2014). The leaders of these coalitions argued that local communities must fight the proliferation of low-wage, dead-end jobs associated with globalization and economic restructuring. By 2010, the movement shifted to support for the creation of citywide minimum wages above the federally required minimum for all workers. During 2012 and 2013, fast-food workers walked off their jobs in Boston,

New York, Atlanta, Los Angeles, Chicago, and other major U.S. cities. By 2015, several cities, including Los Angeles, San Francisco, Chicago, Seattle, Louisville, San Diego, and Washington, D.C., had approved increasing their minimum wage above the federal requirement (Medina and Scheiber 2015).

What makes these "new labor-community coalitions" significant for Latino mayors is that they are led largely by labor unions whose "members and potential members are often overwhelmingly minority and substantially immigrant" (Meyerson 2014). In many major cities, the Service Employees Union International (SEIU) and Hotel Employees and Restaurant Employees (HERE) provide key logistical and financial support for these new labor-community coalitions (Dreier 2007; Meyerson 2014; Milkman 2006; Turner and Cornfield 2007). The SEIU and HERE are powerful national unions that represent janitors, hotel housekeepers, hospital orderlies, and supermarket clerks. Many of their members are Latino immigrants. SEIU's successful "Justice for Janitors" unionization campaign in Los Angeles in the 1990s was a watershed event in that city's recent labor-movement resurgence (Waldinger et al. 1998).

Los Angeles's labor movement was built in part on the mobilization of a large Latino community and its advocacy organizations (Milkman 2006; Waldinger et al. 1998). The organizing in the 1990s, as Ellen Shiau describes in Chapter 5, "helped develop a progressive political infrastructure" that eventually formed the foundation of the electoral coalition that propelled Antonio Villaraigosa into the mayor's office. Labor scholars, however, emphasize that Los Angeles's labor movement played a central role in persuading national labor unions to focus on the rights of undocumented workers. Significantly, labor's success in Los Angeles challenged the conventional wisdom that Latino immigrant workers could not be organized (Milkman 2006, pp. 114–144). As Milkman (2006, p. 133) explained, "Not only in the workplace but also in community organizations and electoral politics, the labor movement effectively mobilized the vast and supposedly 'unorganizable' Latino immigrant population in southern California." The success of union organizing in Los Angeles encouraged SEIU, HERE, and other national service-worker unions to target other major cities on issues related to low-wage workers and urban inequality.

How might Latino mayors in the postindustrial city respond to grassroots demands for an inclusive city where all racial, ethnic, and income groups have access to living-wage jobs and safe and affordable housing? In Los Angeles, Mayor Antonio Villaraigosa came into office with strong support from labor unions, community-based organizations, and immigrants' rights groups. In city hall, Villaraigosa remained an advocate and supporter of workers and immigrants' rights. In April 2016, Providence mayor Jorge Elorza joined dozens of workers and union officials at a local branch of a national grocery-store chain to show support for higher wages and benefits for the workers. In Miami-Dade, the reputation of Cuban American Republicans, stereotyped as politically conservative, has undergone a change. They have increasingly shown support for a "progressive social justice infrastructure to support union and political organizing" (Nissen and Russo 2007, p. 159). As Nissen and Russo (2007, pp. 150–151) observed, "The Republican edge in many local political structures does not necessarily translate into hostility to unions. More than a few Cuban American Republican politicians campaign on progressive social and economic policy issues in order to mobilize their working-class bases. They may sponsor and vote for legislation defending unions as often as some Democrats, and oftentimes more effectively."

There has been a strong labor-union resurgence, especially in efforts to unionize employees in the growing service sector. Latinos constitute a growing share of the U.S. labor movement. Labor scholar Ruth Milkman (2006, p. 136) explained that "Latinos generally, and immigrants in particular, have more favorable attitudes toward unions than most other workers do." Moreover, "Organized labor is consistently one of the strongest advocates for Latino civic engagement and immigration reform" (Barreto and Segura 2014, p. 73). We suspect that in the future, Latino mayors will continue to be on the front line of disputes between largely Latino immigrant workers (led by unions like SEIU and HERE) and the city's business communities.

These are just a few of the potential conflictual issues that Latino mayors are likely to confront as they govern postindustrial cities. Managing the interests of competing groups will be an important part of the job of any mayor in the postindustrial city. Latino mayors will also have to develop leadership strategies to address the complex politics of race/ethnicity and class. We believe that the political and electoral experiences of Latino mayors may present a template for how mayors can resolve conflict by relying on a collective ethos that embraces coalition building. Our assessment is based on two observations: the electoral experience of the Latino mayors examined in this study and the racial and cultural diversity of the Latino community.

In the industrial city, Irish and Italian mayors relied primarily on their coethnics to win mayoral elections. In the redevelopment period, mayors depended on cross-racial and ethnic coalitions to a larger extent than in the industrial period. For instance, in 1973, Tom Bradley won the mayoral race in Los Angeles because he forged a multiracial coalition in the city.

Similarly, Harold Washington created a multiracial coalition that helped him become Chicago's first black mayor in 1983. However, in many cities in the redevelopment period, racial tensions and white voters' refusal to support black candidates required black mayors to be largely dependent on black voters (Hajnal 2007).

In the postindustrial city, Latino mayors have had to rely on Latino and non-Latino constituencies to get elected. In the majority of the cases in this study, Latino mayors had to cultivate cross-racial and ethnic coalitions to win their elections. Henry Cisneros, the first Latino mayor of a major U.S. city, had to build a cross-racial coalition to become San Antonio's mayor in 1981. In Denver, Hartford, Los Angeles, and Providence, Latino mayors won their elections because of their ability to create racially, ethnically, and economically diverse coalitions. In the industrial city, these types of coalitions were not necessary to win mayoral elections, but in the postindustrial city, they will be increasingly important.

We suspect that Latino mayors might be especially skilled in putting together coalitions and negotiating mutual accommodations. As the case studies in this volume confirm, Latino mayors are typically elected in campaigns that deemphasize race and ethnicity. The Latino mayors in this volume viewed themselves as the "mayor for all the people." Latino mayors tend to make broad electoral appeals. Moreover, like African American political leaders, they have had to cope with marginality, having risen through educational, professional, and political systems that are "historically, stubbornly resistant to social change and reform, but especially when such change and reform involves race" (Smith 1996, p. 277). In addition, because the Latino community in many cities is composed of varied nationality groups, Latino mayors must confront diversity from the start. Latinos are diverse in race and nation of origin. In cities like Providence, where there is no dominant Latino subgroup, Latino mayors Angel Taveras, who is of Dominican origin, and Jorge Elorza, of Guatemalan origin, had to rely on a strategy that appealed to a panethnic Latino identity. Neither candidate could have succeeded by simply relying on Dominican voters or Guatemalan voters to win the Latino vote in his city. By fostering a panethnic Latino identity, Latino mayors in Providence have developed a coalition-building strategy that can be transferred to coalition building with non-Latino groups.

Future Latino communities in U.S. cities are likely to consist of Latinos from multiple nations of origin. Cities like Boston, Chicago, Los Angeles, Miami, and New York City have increasingly diverse Latino populations. In the future, what kinds of strategies will Latino mayors have to use to build and sustain local panethnic electoral coalitions? Reuel Rogers's (2006) work on African Americans and Afro-Caribbeans reminds us that intraracial coalitions are not easy to build or sustain in a system of single-member-district elections. How might Latino panethnic strategies differ across cities? As Latino communities become increasingly diverse in cities across the United States, will the example that the Latino mayors in Providence have provided continue to be a useful model for coalition building among Latino subgroups and between Latinos and non-Latinos in the postindustrial city?

Miami-Dade provides a good example of the challenges and potential of panethnic and multiracial coalition building in the postindustrial era. Cuban Americans have been able to develop a strong political base that has dominated Miami-Dade politics since the 1980s. In Chapter 7, Moreno and Ilcheva show that Cuban political power in Miami-Dade is partly a result of the community's population growth since the 1980s. At the same time, there have been significant demographic changes in the county over the past four decades. In 1980, Cubans represented 70 percent of Miami-Dade's Latino population. As of 2010, Cuban Americans represented 53 percent of the Latino community in Miami-Dade. Immigrants from Nicaragua, Colombia, Peru, and Mexico, among other countries, have added to the diversity of the Latino population in Miami-Dade. As Miami-Dade's Latino community becomes increasingly diverse, how will the groups respond to these changes? How will non-Cuban Latinos access political power in Miami-Dade? As the most politically empowered group in the county, will the Cuban political base make efforts to incorporate members of other Latino nationalities into leadership positions? Will Cuban political power rely on strategies that exclude other groups, or will Cuban Americans embrace a panethnic Latino identity the way Latinos in Providence, for instance, have done? Latino mayors in Miami-Dade will be both the by-products of these dynamics and the leaders who will help shape these dynamics.

Latino Mayors and the Future of Progressive Politics

In 2002, John Judis and Ruy Teixeira published an important book in which they argued that America's transition from an industrial to a postindustrial economy was also producing "progressive centrist" voters who trend strongly Democratic (Judis and Teixeira 2002, p. 4). According to Judis and Teixeira, three categories of voters formed the foundation of this new progressive coalition: (1) racial and ethnic minorities, (2) educated working women, and (3) skilled professionals. Judis and Teixeira (2002) showed that these voters tend to support "a larger and stronger social safety net and

generous spending on education and worker training," "regulation of business to protect the environment," and "equality for women in the workplace and their right to have an abortion." "They envision America as a
multiethnic and multiracial democracy, and they support targeted
programs to help minorities that trail the rest of the population in education and income" (Judis and Teixeira 2002, p. 5). Judis and Teixeira (2002,
p. 4) emphasized the growth of the Latino population and its important
role in what they called a new "emerging Democratic majority." Latinos are
significantly more liberal than non-Hispanic whites "on virtually every
issue of public policy," including "issues with no implicitly racial content"
(Barreto and Segura, 2014, p. 33). Research shows that among Latinos,
"there is a general enthusiasm for an active, growing, and problem-solving
government and little enthusiasm for the alternative as described by the
right: a shrinkage of government and reliance on the free market. . . .
Latinos' underlying ideology appears to be solidly progressive" (Barreto
and Segura 2014, p. 39). Cuban Americans are somewhat of an exception.
However, there is growing evidence that the "Cuban distinctiveness appears to be eroding" (Barreto and Segura 2014, p. 23). The views of younger
Cuban Americans "most closely reflect those of other US Latinos" (Barreto
and Segura 2014, p. 24).

Using a wealth of demographic and voter-turnout data, Judis and Teixeira (2002) showed that these progressive centrist minority, women, and
skilled professional voters emanate from postindustrial cities and their surrounding metropolitan regions. They called these regions "ideopolises" to
reflect the "creative" capital that drives the economy of the postindustrial
city (2002, p. 71). Judis and Teixeira argued that because many of these cities are strategically located in important Electoral College states, their
voters will form the basis for an "emerging Democratic majority" that will
allow Democrats an advantage in presidential elections similar to the edge
that Republicans enjoyed during the 1970s and 1980s.

Latino voters from postindustrial cities have emerged as an important
part of the Democratic coalition. Moreover, Latino population growth in solidly Republican states like Arizona and Texas may have a profound effect
on the Electoral College map in the coming years. As of 2015, Latinos represented 31 percent of Arizona's population and nearly 40 percent of Texas's
population (U.S. Census). Since most of the Latino mayors in the United
States are elected in southwestern states, we anticipate that Latino mayors
will play a key role in the changing political landscape in these states.

The new labor-community coalitions mentioned earlier that have been
forming and mobilizing in major U.S. cities since the early 1990s were
crucial local components of the national progressive centrist coalition

that elected and reelected President Barack Obama. Journalist Harold Meyerson (2014) has argued that in many urban communities, Latinos are a central and growing part of these coalitions, which also include African Americans, Asian and African immigrants, white progressives, and young voters. These urban coalitions are supporting progressive mayors and other city leaders who are "raising minimum wages, requiring contractors to hire inner-city residents and to increase pay on municipal projects; back local union organizing efforts; initiating pre-K schooling; extending public transit into poor neighborhoods; and requiring police to videotape contacts with citizens."

For many decades, community organizations have provided the space and resources for disadvantaged and minority residents to engage in local politics (Orr 2007; Smock 2004). Writing about Latino political incorporation in the 1980s, Browning, Marshall, and Tabb (1984, p. 125) found that community organizing played a "distinctive" role in the process of Latino political incorporation. The case studies in this volume show that community organizations continue to encourage and facilitate naturalization, promote voter registration, educate Latinos on issues, and motivate them to participate in politics (see Anderson 2010, pp. 71–88).

The Latino mayors examined in this book were elected in the kind of postindustrial communities that, according to Judis and Teixeira (2002), formed the geographic center of the "emerging Democratic majority." Although the mayors covered in this volume are not representative of all Latino mayors, they all were chief executives of important municipalities that are key economic and cultural centers within their metropolitan regions. From a practical and policy perspective, it is the Latino mayors in large cities and urban counties like Miami-Dade who are in a position to help set the tone and direction of key policy discussions concerning urban America. This is the role that big-city African American mayors like Detroit's Coleman Young played as they rose to power and influence in national Democratic politics (Young and Wheeler 1994, pp. 222–230). We expect that Latino mayors, with their strong base of support in Latino communities, are likely to play a politically strategic role in helping shape a progressive national urban agenda.

REFERENCES

Anderson, Kristi. 2010. *New Immigrant Communities: Finding a Place in Local Politics*. Boulder, CO: Lynne Rienner.
Austin, Sharon Wright, and Richard T. Middleton IV. 2004. "The Limitations of the Deracialization Concept in the 2001 Los Angeles Mayoral Election." *Political Research Quarterly* 57, no. 2 (June): 283–293.

Barreto, Matt. 2007. "¡Si Se Puede! Latino Candidates and the Mobilization of Latino Voters." *American Political Science Review* 101, no. 3 (August): 425–441.

Barreto, Matt, and Gary M. Segura. 2014. *Latino America*. New York: Public Affairs.

Baugh, Josh. 2014. "Council Approves Controversial Zoning in Split Vote." *San Antonio Express News*, May 15, A1.

Browning, Rufus, Dale Rogers Marshall, and David Tabb. 1984. *Protest Is Not Enough: The Struggle of Blacks and Hispanics for Equality in Urban Politics*. Berkeley: University of California Press.

Clarke, Susan E. 2015. "The New Politics in a Postindustrial City: Intersecting Policies in Denver." In *Urban Neighborhoods in a New Era: Revitalization Politics in the Postindustrial City*, edited by Clarence N. Stone and Robert P. Stoker, 155–181. Chicago: University of Chicago Press.

Donnis, Ian. 2006. "Class Warfare in Olneyville." *Providence Phoenix*, May 24.

Drake, W. Avon, and Robert D. Holsworth. 1996. *Affirmative Action and the Stalled Quest for Black Progress*. Urbana: University of Illinois Press.

Dreier, Peter. 2007. "Community Organizing for What? Progressive Politics and Movement Building in America." In *Transforming the City: Community Organizing and the Challenge of Political Change*, edited by Marion Orr, 218–251. Lawrence: University Press of Kansas.

Eisinger, Peter K. 1982. "Black Employment in Municipal Jobs: The Impact of Black Political Power." *American Political Science Review* 76:380–392.

Erie, Steven P. 1988. *Rainbow's End: Irish-Americans and the Dilemmas of Urban Machine Politics, 1840–1985*. Berkeley: University of California Press.

Filandra, Alexandra, and Marion Orr. 2013. "Anxieties of an Ethnic Transition: The Election of the First Latino Mayor in Providence, Rhode Island." *Urban Affairs Review* 49 (January): 3–31.

Florida, Richard. 2002. *The Rise of the Creative Class: And How It's Transforming Work, Leisure, Community and Everyday Life*. New York: Basic Books.

Fraga, Luis Ricardo, John A. Garcia, Rodney E. Hero, Michael Jones-Correa, Valerie Martinez-Ebers, and Gary M. Segura. 2010. *Latino Lives in America: Making It Home*. Philadelphia: Temple University Press.

———. 2012. *Latinos in the New Millennium: An Almanac of Opinion, Behavior, and Policy Preferences*. New York: Cambridge University Press.

Freeman, Lance. 2006. *There Goes the 'Hood: Views of Gentrification from the Ground Up*. Philadelphia: Temple University Press.

Gillespie, Andra. 2013. "Beyond Booker: Assessing the Prospects of Black and Latino Mayoral Contenders in Newark, New Jersey." In *21st Century Urban Race Politics: Representing Minorities as Universal Interests*, edited by Ravi Perry, 33–68. Bingley, UK: Emerald Group.

Hajnal, Zoltan. 2007. *Changing White Attitudes toward Black Leadership*. New York: Cambridge University Press.

Henig, Jeffrey R., and Wilbur C. Rich, eds. 2004. *Mayors in the Middle: Politics, Race, and Mayoral Control of Urban Schools*. Princeton, NJ: Princeton University Press.

Hero, Rodney E. 1992. *Latinos and the U.S. Political System: Two-Tiered Pluralism*. Philadelphia: Temple University Press.

Hero, Rodney E., F. Chris Garcia, John Garcia, and Harry Pachon. 2000. "Latino Participation, Partisanhip, and Office Holding." *PS: Political Science and Politics* 33, no. 3 (September): 529–534.

Judis, John B., and Ruy Teixeira. 2002. *The Emerging Democratic Majority*. New York: Scribner.

Kaufmann, Karen M. 2004. *The Urban Voter: Group Conflict and Mayoral Voting Behavior in American Cities*. Ann Arbor: University of Michigan Press.

Ladd, Helen, and John Yinger. 1989. *America's Ailing Cities: Fiscal Health and the Design of Urban Policy*. Baltimore: Johns Hopkins University Press.

Levine, Charles H. 1974. *Racial Conflict and the American Mayor*. Lexington, MA: D. C. Heath.

Levine, Myron A. 2015. *Urban Politics: Cities and Suburbs in a Global Age*. New York: Routledge.

Luce, Stephanie. 2004. *Fighting for a Living Wage*. Ithaca, NY: Cornell University Press.

McClain, Paula D. 1993. "The Changing Dynamics of Urban Politics: Black and Hispanic Municipal Employment; Is There Competition?" *Journal of Politics* 55:399–414.

McClain, Paula D., and Albert K. Karnig. 1990. "Black and Hispanic Socioeconomic and Political Competition." *American Political Science Review* 84, no. 2:535–545.

Medina, Jennifer, and Noam Scheiber. 2015. "Los Angeles Lifts Its Minimum Wage to $15 per Hour." *New York Times*, May 19.

Meyerson, Harold. 2014. The Revolt of the Cities, *The American Prospect Longform*, April 22. http://prospect.org/article/revolt-cities. Accessed July 5, 2017.

Milkman, Ruth. 2006. *L.A. Story: Immigrant Workers and the Future of the U.S. Labor Movement*. New York: Russell Sage Foundation.

Morel, Domingo. 2018. *Takeover: Race, Education, and Democracy*. New York: Oxford University Press.

Munnell, Alicia H. 2012. *State and Local Pensions: What Now?* Washington, DC: Brookings Institution.

Nelson, William E., Jr., and Jessica Lavariega Monforti, eds. 2005. *Black and Latino/a Politics: Issues in Political Development in the United States*. Miami: Barnhardt and Ashe.

Newman, Kathe, and Elvin K. Wyly. 2006. "The Right to Stay Put, Revisited: Gentrification and Resistance to Displacement in New York City." *Urban Studies* 43, no. 1 (January): 23–57.

Nissen, Bruce, and Monica Russo. 2007. "Strategies for Labor Revitalization: The Case of Miami." In *Labor in the New Urban Battleground: Local Solidarity in a Global Economy*, edited by Lowell Turner and Daniel B. Cornfield, 147–162. Ithaca, NY: Cornell University Press.

Orr, Marion. 1992. "Urban Regimes and Human Capital Policies: A Study of Baltimore." *Journal of Urban Affairs* 14, no. 2:173–187.

———. 1993. "Urban Regimes and School Compacts: The Development of the Detroit Compact." *Urban Review* 25, no. 2:105–124.

———. 1999. *Black Social Capital: The Politics of School Reform in Baltimore*. Lawrence: University Press of Kansas.

———. 2001. "BUILD: Governing Nonprofits and Relational Power." *Policy Studies Review* 18, no. 4 (winter): 71–90.

———, ed. 2007. *Transforming the City: Community Organizing and the Challenge of Political Change*. Lawrence: University Press of Kansas.

Orr, Marion, Domingo Morel, and Emily Farris. 2014. "Mayors and Municipal Pension Reform." Paper presented at the Annual Meeting of the Midwest Political Science Association. Chicago, Illinois, April 5–8.

Orr, Marion, and John Rogers. 2011. "Unequal Schools, Unequal Voice: The Need for Public Engagement for Public Education." In *Public Engagement for Public Education: Joining Forces to Revitalize Democracy and Equalize Schools*, edited by Marion Orr and John Rogers, 1–24. Stanford, CA: Stanford University Press.

Pastor, Manuel, Jr., Chris Benner, and Martha Matsuoka. 2009. *This Could Be the Start of Something Big: How Social Movements for Regional Equity Are Reshaping Metropolitan America*. Ithaca, NY: Cornell University Press.

Portes, Alejandro, and Alex Stepick. 1993. *City on the Edge: The Transformation of Miami*. Berkeley: University of California Press.

Pressman, Jeffrey L. 1972. "Preconditions of Mayoral Leadership." *American Political Science Review* 66, no. 2 (June): 511–524.

Rae, Douglas W. 2003. *City: Urbanism and Its End*. New Haven, CT: Yale University Press.

Rich, Wilbur C. 1996. *Black Mayors and School Politics: The Failure of Reform in Detroit, Gary, and Newark*. New York: Garland Press.

Rogers, Mary Beth. 1988. *Cold Anger: A Story of Faith and Power Politics*. Denton: University of North Texas Press.

Rogers, Reuel R. 2006. *Afro-Caribbean Immigrants and the Politics of Incorporation*. New York: Cambridge University Press.

Ross, Bernard H., and Myron A. Levine. 2006. *Urban Politics: Power in Metropolitan America*. Belmont, CA: Thomson/Wadsworth.

Sassen, Saskia. 2001. *The Global City*. Princeton, NJ: Princeton University Press.

Shiau, Ellen, Juliet Musso, and Jeffrey M. Sellers. 2015. "City Fragmentation and Neighborhood Connections: The Political Dynamics of Community Revitalization in Los Angles." In *Urban Neighborhoods in a New Era: Revitalization Politics in the Postindustrial City*, edited by Clarence N. Stone and Robert P. Stoker, 131–154. Chicago: University of Chicago Press.

Smith, Robert C. 1996. *We Have No Leaders: African-Americans in the Post–Civil Rights Era*. Albany: State University of New York Press.

Smock, Kristina. 2004. *Democracy in Action: Community Organizing and Urban Change*. New York: Columbia University Press.

Sokol, Brett. 2015. "Miami's Art World Sets Sights on Little Haiti Neighborhood." *New York Times*, November 23.

Sonenshein, Raphael J., and Susan H. Pinkus. 2005. "Latino Incorporation Reaches the Urban Summit: How Antonio Villaraigosa Won the 2005 Los Angeles Mayor's Race." *PS: Political Science and Politics* 38, no. 4 (October): 713–721.

Su, Selina. 2012. *Streetwise for Book Smart: Grassroots Organizing and School Reform in the Bronx*. Ithaca, NY: Cornell University Press.

Taylor, Kate. 2015. "Race and Class Collide in a Plan for Two Brooklyn Schools." *New York Times*, September 22, A1.

———. 2016. "2 Brooklyn Schools in Gentrifying Area Will Get New Zones." *New York Times*, January 6, A20.

Teaford, Jon C. 1990. *The Rough Road to Renaissance: Urban Revitalization in America, 1940–1985*. Baltimore: Johns Hopkins University Press.

Turner, Lowell, and Daniel B. Cornfield, eds. 2007. *Labor in the New Urban Battleground: Local Solidarity in a Global Economy*. Ithaca, NY: Cornell University Press.

Waldinger, Roger, Chris Erickson, Ruth Milkman, Daniel J. B. Mitchell, Abel Valenzuela, Kent Wong, and Maurice Zeitlin. 1998. "Helots No More: A Case Study of the Justice for Janitors Campaign in Los Angeles." In *Organizing to Win*, edited by Kate

Bronfenbrenner, Sheldon Friedman, Richard W. Hurd, Rudolph A. Oswald, and Ronald L. Seeber, 102–119. Ithaca, NY: Cornell University Press.

Warren, Christopher L., and Dario V. Moreno. 2003. "Power without a Program: Hispanic Incorporation in Miami." In *Racial Politics in American Cities*, 3rd ed., edited by Rufus P. Browning, Dale Rogers Marshall, and David H. Tabb, 291–308. New York: Longman.

Welch, Susan. 1990. "The Impact of At-Large Elections on the Representation of Blacks and Hispanics." *Journal of Politics* 52, no. 4 (November): 1050–1076.

Wong, Kenneth K., Francis X. Shen, Dorothea Anagnostopoulos, and Stacey Rutledge. 2007. *The Education Mayor: Improving America's Schools*. Washington, DC: Georgetown University Press.

Young, Coleman, and Lonnie Wheeler. 1994. *Hard Stuff: The Autobiography of Mayor Coleman Young*. New York: Viking Press.

Contributors

Stefanie Chambers is professor of political science at Trinity College in Hartford, Connecticut. Her research and teaching interests include urban education policy, urban politics, racial and ethnic politics, and migration. She is the author of *Mayors and Schools: Minority Voices and Democratic Tensions in Urban Education* and *Somalis in the Twin Cities and Columbus: Immigrant Incorporation in New Destinations* and the coeditor of *The Politics of New Immigrant Destinations: Transatlantic Perspectives* (all with Temple University Press).

Carlos E. Cuéllar holds a Ph.D. in political science from Rice University and currently serves as the director of institutional assessment at the University of Texas Rio Grande Valley. He also has a part-time faculty appointment in the Department of Political Science, where he teaches courses on U.S. Latino politics. His area of expertise is American politics, with a particular focus on Latino politics, public policy, state and local politics, and campaigns and elections. His research examines the causes and consequences of Latino representation in municipal government. He is a recipient of the Byran Jackson Dissertation in Ethnic and Racial Politics Research Support Award presented by the Urban Politics Section of the American Political Science Association. His work is published in *Politics, Groups, and Identities* (June 2015) and *The Keys to City Hall: Local Politics and Mayoral Elections in 21st Century America* (Routledge).

Emily M. Farris is an assistant professor of political science at Texas Christian University (TCU). She also holds affiliations with Women and Gender Studies and is core faculty in Comparative Race and Ethnicity at TCU. She received her M.A. and Ph.D. in political science from Brown University and her B.A. in political science and urban studies with honors from Furman University. At TCU, she teaches courses on American government, urban politics, the black and Chicano/a civil rights movements, and survey research. Her published research focuses on the politics of urban education, the political behavior of Latino/as and African American women, and sheriffs. Her research has been supported by awards from the Fund for Latino Scholarship, and she is a recipient of the Stone Scholar Award and the Byran Jackson Dissertation in Ethnic and Racial Politics Research Support Award from the Urban Politics Section of the American Political Science Association.

Maria Ilcheva is an assistant scholar at the Metropolitan Center, Florida International University (FIU). She received her doctorate in political science from Florida International University with a dissertation on ethnic-minority politics in central and eastern Europe. In addition to her publications on nationalism and the role of ethnicity in decision making in Europe, since 2004 she has collaborated on articles and book chapters on voter turnout, Latino influence in local and national elections, and local government politics in South Florida. At the FIU Metropolitan Center, she serves as principal investigator or project manager on studies in the areas of demographic research, urban planning, program evaluation, strategic management, and policy development. She is also an instructor at the FIU School of International and Public Affairs, specializing in comparative politics, international relations, and research methods.

Domingo Morel is assistant professor of political science at Rutgers University, Newark. He is also an affiliate member of Global Urban Studies and the Center on Law, Inequality, and Metropolitan Equity at Rutgers-Newark. His research program and teaching portfolio focus on racial and ethnic politics, urban politics, education politics, and public policy. Specifically, his research explores the ways in which state policies help expand or diminish political inequality among historically marginalized populations. He is the author of *Takeover: Race, Democracy, and Education* (Oxford University Press). In addition to his scholarship, he has years of applied experience in political affairs and public policy. He is a cofounder of the Latino Policy Institute at Roger Williams University and past president of the Rhode Island Latino Political Action Committee. He received his Ph.D. in political science from Brown University in 2014.

Dario Moreno is an associate professor in the Department of Politics and International Relations at Florida International University. He completed his Ph.D. at the University of Southern California. He conducts research on Miami politics, Florida politics, and Cuban American politics. He has published over twenty scholarly articles, book chapters, and two books. He is a nationally recognized expert on Florida and Miami politics and is often quoted in both the national and local media. He has been a Pew scholar at the Kennedy School of Government at Harvard University and a Fulbright scholar in Costa Rica. He teaches a variety of classes, including Miami politics, Cuban politics, Florida politics, and a graduate seminar on urban politics.

Marion Orr is the Frederick Lippitt Professor of Public Policy and a professor of political science and urban studies at Brown University. He is the author of *Black Social Capital: The Politics of School Reform in Baltimore, 1986–1999* (University Press of Kansas); editor of *Transforming the City: Community Organizing and the Challenge of Political Change* (University Press of Kansas); and coauthor of *The Color of School Reform: Race, Politics, and the Challenge of Urban Education* (Princeton University Press), among other books.

Robert R. Preuhs is an associate professor of political science at Metropolitan State University of Denver. His research focuses on issues of representation and democracy through the lens of racial and ethnic politics, state and national political institutions, and public policy. His publications have appeared in leading peer-reviewed journals in the discipline of political science, such as the *American Journal of Political Science*, the *Journal of Politics*, and *Political Research Quarterly*. He has also coauthored (with Rodney E. Hero) *Black-Latino Relations in U.S. National Politics: Beyond Conflict or Cooperation* (Cambridge University Press), the first study of minority intergroup relations at the national level.

Heywood T. Sanders is professor of public administration at the University of Texas, San Antonio. His most recent book, *Convention Center Follies* (University of Pennsylvania Press), offers a critical view of convention centers within urban redevelopment. Sanders is a longtime observer of San Antonio politics and has written extensively on the subject. His other books include *The Politics of Urban Development* (University Press of Kansas), co-edited with Clarence N. Stone.

Ellen Shiau is assistant professor of political science at California State University, Los Angeles. She completed her Ph.D. in policy, planning, and development from the University of Southern California's Sol Price School of Public Policy. Her research focuses on three areas: urban politics and public policy, particularly around neighborhood redevelopment; diversity and cultural competency issues in public administration and policy; and the use of GIS methods to analyze relationships among fear, crime, public policy, and the built environment. She has published articles in the journal *Nonprofit and Voluntary Sector Quarterly* and the planning journal *Environment and Planning B* on GIS methodology. She is also coauthor of *Urban Neighborhoods in a New Era: Revitalization Politics in the Postindustrial City* (University of Chicago Press).

Index

Page numbers followed by *f* or *t* indicate figures or tables, respectively.